AFRICAN AMERICANS IN HIGHER EDUCATION

CRITICAL RACE ISSUES IN EDUCATION BOOK
EDITED BY THEODOREA REGINA BERRY,
SAN JOSÉ STATE UNIVERSITY, SAN JOSÉ, CA

Critical Race Issues in Education presents innovative, in-depth, and provocative inquiry and investigations, explorations, and examinations connected to educational spaces, places, and endeavors in the context of race and power. Of particular interest are essays and analyses that involve critical race theory, critical race feminism, LatCrit, QueerCrit, AsianCrit, and Critical White Studies.

African Americans in Higher Education
by James L. Conyers, Crystal L. Edwards, and Kevin B. Thompson (2020)
African-Centered Education
by Kmt G. Shockley and Kofi Lomotey (2020)

The series editor, Dr. Theodorea Regina Berry, invites individuals to submit proposals for any book-length manuscript, including but not restricted to the following:

- monographs
- textbooks
- edited collections
- primers
- readers
- anthologies
- handbooks
- conference proceedings

The series will be published by Myers Education Press. Prospectus guidelines can be found at the following link to their website: http://myersedpress.com/sites/stylus/MEP/Docs/Prospectus%20Guidelines%20MEP.pdf. If you have a project that you wish to have considered for publication, please send a proposal, one or two sample chapters, and your current CV to: Chris Myers, Publisher, Myers Education Press (c.myers@myersedpress.com).

AFRICAN AMERICANS IN HIGHER EDUCATION

A Critical Study of Social and Philosophical Foundations of Africana Culture

EDITED BY JAMES L. CONYERS, JR.
CRYSTAL L. EDWARDS AND
KEVIN B. THOMPSON

Myers Education Press

Gorham, Maine

Myers Education Press

Copyright © 2020 | Myers Education Press, LLC
Published by Myers Education Press, LLC
P.O. Box 424
Gorham, ME 04038

All rights reserved. No part of this book may be reprinted or reproduced in any form or by any electronic, mechanical, or other means, now known or hereafter invented, including photocopying, recording, and information storage and retrieval, without permission in writing from the publisher.

Myers Education Press is an academic publisher specializing in books, e-books, and digital content in the field of education. All of our books are subjected to a rigorous peer review process and produced in compliance with the standards of the Council on Library and Information Resources.

Library of Congress Cataloging-in-Publication Data available from Library of Congress.

13-digit ISBN 978-1-9755-0205-8 (paperback)
13-digit ISBN 978-1-9755-0204-1 (hard cover)
13-digit ISBN 978-1-9755-0206-5 (library networkable e-edition)
13-digit ISBN 978-1-9755-0207-2 (consumer e-edition)

Printed in the United States of America.

All first editions printed on acid-free paper that meets the American National Standards Institute Z39-48 standard.

Books published by Myers Education Press may be purchased at special quantity discount rates for groups, workshops, training organizations, and classroom usage. Please call our customer service department at 1-800-232-0223 for details.

Cover design by Sophie Appel

Visit us on the web at **www.myersedpress.com** to browse our complete list of titles.

Contents

Acknowledgments	xi
Preface	xiii
Introduction	xv

ONE Revisiting *The Brownies' Book*: (Re)Imagining Black Males' Youth   1
James Earl Davis

TWO "Me Versus Them": An African American Male Professor's Approach to Teaching Race at a Predominately White Institution   15
Reuben A. Buford May

THREE Challenges Faced by African American Adult Students: Within Higher Education   41
TaNeisha Page

FOUR Educating for Social Justice: The Potential Role of Historically Black Colleges and Universities in the 21st Century   51
Abul Pitre and Tanya Hudson

FIVE Where Am I: An Analysis of the Incongruence Between Black Men and the Teaching Profession   67
Kevin B. Thompson

SIX   Carter G. Woodson and the Association
      for the Study of African American Life
      and History: A Reflexive Analysis of the
      History of Black Education   77
      James L. Conyers, Jr.

SEVEN "You Have to Get Your Mind Right for
       This": Black Women's Graduate School
       Experiences   91
       Crystal Edwards

EIGHT No Parent Left Behind: The Narratives of
       African American Fathers in Texas on
       Their Parental Involvement   115
       Joshua D. Hughes

NINE   Toward an Afrocentric Antiracist Pedagogy
       for Brazilian Music Ensembles   145
       Cory J. LaFevers

TEN   The Need for Beloved Community: Black
       Graduate Students and the Collaborative
       Creation of Counterspaces   181
       Monique Liston

ELEVEN Counseling Psychology of African
       Americans: A Review of the Literature   203
       Selena Tate

TWELVE Anti-Black Ontological Violence in
       Undergraduate Textbooks   231
       Autumn Raynor

THIRTEEN Vertically Integrated: African American
Studies Instruction as Co-Requisite to
Education-Based Ontological Manipulation   255
Deidra Lawson

FOURTEEN Teaching Through Culture: Employing
Culturally Responsive Pedagogy to
Transform Postsecondary STEM Instruction   265
*Leah McAlister-Shields, Laveria Hutchison,
and Donna Stokes*

FIFTEEN Visionary and Social Justice Leaders:
Leading by Example in Educational
Environments   289
Detra D. Johnson

SIXTEEN The Dimensions of a Departmentalized
Literacy Classroom Infused with Culturally
Relevant/Responsive Practices: Its Impact
on African American Second-Grade
Reading Achievement   305
Katina L. Thomas

Contributors   329

Index   333

Acknowledgments

James L. Conyers, Jr., Crystal L. Edwards, and Kevin B. Thompson

Assurance of having a career in the field of higher education has provided me space to think, reflexive thought, and explore ideas. More importantly, working in the field of Africana Studies has offered me liberation, autonomy, and transcendence to examine Africana phenomena from an Afrocentric perspective. Collectively, these aspects of reflection are the foundational objectives to advance onward and upward toward concerning Black philosophy. What does this have to do with the current publication of record?

Beginning with undergraduate and graduate training in Africana Studies, I have been challenged to ask unconventional query and to stretch myself intellectually. Best phrased by the late prolific historian Dr. John Henrik Clarke, whenever he would often begin his lectures and seminar talks, he would pause for a minute, disclose his transparency, and dispense he was addressing Black people wherever they resided, as African world citizens. Fascinating to be a listener of these remarks, I follow that tradition of vetting and investigation of examining African American life and culture.

Sequestered to area topics, the initial query would center on Haki Madhubuti's pivotal interrogation, "When we make decisions, are these choices made in the best interest of African people collectively." Combining both the statement and query of Clarke and Madhubuti, I am grateful for the support network of my continued learning, which is my foundation, sounding board, and circle of spiritual sobriety. As noted, my family background of mother and father, Agnes and James L. Conyers, Sr., are the beginning models of discipline, provision, and protection of me, as a youth growing up in the urban sphere of Jersey City, New Jersey. Of course, the friendship, comradeship, and spouse of Jacqueline I. Conyers are everlasting to my continuous development. Admittedly, I am still a work in progress, being the parent of three adult Black men. These men have allowed me to observe, listen, and ruminate with appreciation of being a provider and protector: Chad Hawkins, Sekou Conyers, and Kamau Conyers. Indeed, this circle of young lions is the core of my common sense and acumen. Companionship is relative and necessary, referring to my girlfriend Kim M. Gay. She is a sounding board for humor, friendship, camaraderie, research, writing, and competitive recipes. Friends, as they exist, dwindle to transition as the years slowly fade away. But those who have passed are always remembered and their names are evoked daily, James Qawi Jamison and Bernard Robinson. Others who are still turning it up are Zane Corbin, Tony Robinson, Joe Taylor, and James Bullock.

Mentors are a resource. Mine are an aggregated group of personnel who have now retired, made transition, and some are currently in the profession of teaching. Those whom I still call, e-mail, and text are the following: Drs. Molefi Kete Asante, James Stewart, Delores Aldridge, Linda James Meyers, James Turner, and Abul Nanji. Our team in African American Studies is always a support mechanism: Jasmine Grant, Mason Carter, Van Rountree, and Angela Williams Phillips. Additionally, the administration and faculty at the University of Houston are my sounding board, which consist of: Chancellor/President Renu Khator, Provost Paula Short, Dean Antonio Tillis, Associate Dean Suresh Khator, Drs. Gerald Horne, Shayne Lee, Demetrius Pearson, Billy Hawkins, Cedric Toliver, Rheeda Walker, Donna Stokes, Phil Howard, and Robert McPherson.

Collectively, the editors of this publication would also like to acknowledge the administration and staff of Academic Affairs of the University of Houston and the following individuals: Cassandra Edwards, Antonio McGill, Timothy Edwards, Britney Rimpson, Lula Johnson, Drs. Ruth Simmons, Derek Wilson, Angela Branch-Vital, James Jones, and Kaye Norman.

Preface

Crystal Edwards

Throughout history, African Americans have fought various forms of discrimination, marginalization, and oppression. A primary struggle has been in pursuit of equity and access to quality education. Despite desegregation, as mandated in the 1954 court decision of Brown v. Board, African Americans continue to be faced with many challenges in educational spaces, K–12 and beyond.

From the founding of the first Historically Black Colleges and Universities (HBCUs)—Cheney University of Pennsylvania in 1837, the first degree granting institution Lincoln University of Pennsylvania in 1854, and Wilberforce University in 1856 touted to be "the oldest Black-controlled HBCU in the nation"—to the integration of African Americans in Primarily White Institutions (PWIs), African Americans have had to overcome countless obstacles (Brown II & Ricard, 2007, p. 119). Both in the past and contemporarily, challenges have included access to financial and material resources, lack of pre-collegiate preparation, lack of overall support and mentorship, and discrimination. In addition to shared challenges, scholars have also identified obstacles associated with particular students' intersectional identities such as gender, socioeconomic status, sexual orientation, and spirituality or religion, among others. Despite the challenges, African Americans have persevered, identifying and implementing strategies for success. While enrollment and attainment of degrees is still significantly less than that of their white counterparts, since 2000, degree attainment has increased to 23% for four-year degrees and 33% for two-year degrees (The Postsecondary National Policy Institute, 2019). Enrollment rates for graduating African American high school students has remained steady since 2000 at 56% (ibid.).

In this book, scholars explore the many factors associated with African Americans in higher education, specifically from an Africana lens. The studies presented in this text provide an interdisciplinary examination of the varied experiences of African Americans in higher education.

References

Brown II, M. C., & Ricard, R. B. (2007). The honorable past and uncertain future of the nation's HBCUs. *Thought & Action*, 117.

The Postsecondary National Policy Institute. (2019, February 21). Factsheets. Retrieved from https://pnpi.org/african-american-students/#

Introduction

James L. Conyers, Jr.

Arranging ideas to examine Africana thought and social space is engaging, enthusiastic, and energetic. Pulled together under the interdisciplinary matrix of Africana Studies, the social and philosophical foundations of analyses expressed in this study attempts to assess the educational experiences of Africana phenomena. Pressing forward, the concept of Africana Education is a relevant epistemological modality of sustained understanding. Put another way, Africana Education can be defined as the process, preparation, and position, to assess Africana phenomena from an Afrocentric perspective. Effectively is the prepositional axiom of—the use of knowledge, as an instrument of cultural and organizational emancipation.

Knowingly, the posture to establish a context for this discussion has been put in the order of 14 chapters, which represents scholars in the humanities, social sciences, professions, and professional practitioners. Articulated in the way of discussing issues and schemes of Black Male Identity, Hip Hop Culture, Adult Learners, Leadership at Historically Black Colleges and Universities, Critical Black Pedagogy, Black Women's Narratives, Black Male Single Parenting, Afro-Brazilian Music, Resistance Strategies, Ontology of Africana Rhetoric, Visionary Analysis, and Cultural Literacy are comparative points of probe to the assigned subject matter. Mutually, these chapters express various modules of Ubuntu and Africana Education in an interdisciplinary scope.

Indeed, living in a market culture, the concept of learning and education is often measured by capital and material acquisition of goods and services. Too often, the passion, perception, and propensity of learning—mastery of knowledge, is dismissed. Forsaken then becomes the urge of developing a thirst for learning, with regard to the direct and indirect correlates of arrangements of comprehension. On the other hand, we are engaged with narcissism and sound punctures of lobbed communication. Unique are the goals and objectives of this book, to coordinate an epistemic and axiological method interconnected to the global Pan Africanist experience from an Afrocentric perspective.

Transition then becomes the locus for refereeing sustainability and formation. Assembled under the interdisciplinary boundaries of Africana Studies, the social and philosophical foundations of African Americans in higher education are vexing. Explained alternatively, the posture and context for this treatment hubs around Africana cultural sovereignty and autonomy.

Asserting these ideas forward, the objective of this publication is to provide space, concerning analytical dialog of the germaneness of education to African Americans. Basic tasks include the pros and cons of school choice, disparity in distribution of funding to school districts, and the systemic impact of educational resources correlated to the direct and indirect impact of the quality of life for African American communities. Curiously, the concept of subordinate group status is relative within this market culture of capitalism in the United States. Nonetheless, the idea of education still remains one of the key components of the process of Black sovereignty and cultural autonomy. Collectively, these are salient issues, with regard to uplift, advancement, and economic mobility. Perhaps, this examination contributes or establishes a boundary for engagement relevant to the crisis of Black education.

ONE

 Revisiting *The Brownies' Book*: (Re)Imagining Black Males' Youth

James Earl Davis

NARRATIVES OF BLACK BOY JOY have captured the imagination of many who are interested in capturing aspects of Black youth that tends to be invisible. For sure, there is something compelling about these narratives, yet they exist alongside pejorative conceptions steeped in deficit and danger. This juxtaposition of joy and fear calls our attention to the complex ways of imagining Black male youth, especially in schools. Educators, researchers, policy leaders, and the media are implicated in how we make meaning of the educational lives of Black boys and young men. However, clarity in the representation of this group is challenging given the barrage of stereotypes and misinformation that hide their realities.

The current plight of Black boys in school is one that continues to captivate the interest of those concerned with issues of educational equity and outcomes. This observation does not distract attention away from the plight of Black girls in school. A fair and meaningful experience for all Black children in school is the broader social justice project in which our energies are directed. As such, the broader concern for research and scholarship is to produce knowledge and perspective aimed at increasing education opportunities for Black boys and girls. The growing expansion of social science research focusing on Black male youth brings needed attention to understand the complexities of these students. New scholarship is emerging that moves beyond stereotypical problem-based themes and toward broader conceptions and considerations of Black boys. For instance, *The Brilliance of Black Boys: Cultivating School Success in the Early Grades* (Wright & Counsell, 2018) expands our knowing of Black boys and, in turn, holds schools and educators accountable for responding to these new understandings. The increasing use of narratives questioning stale assumptions of enliven scholarship to go beyond traditional notions about schooling and social competencies of young Black male students. This is especially true when considering the role of identity in academic engagement and development.

The development of identity is complicated by the heavy dosages of messages young people get from their immediate and distance social environments. These social cues provide information about place, purpose, and possibilities. Media sources are often considered common enemies in the struggle to communicate positive images to Black youth. The frustration that parents, teachers, and other cultural workers experience in cultivating healthy learning spaces is ever-growing. To create these nurturing spaces of self-discovery and community awareness where Black boys are not deprived of imagining their greater selves (past, present, and future) becomes more critically important given the volatile family and schooling circumstances many Black male youth face. These concerns are not new or solely the product of contemporary schooling experiences of Black boys. W. E. B. Du Bois was well aware of the pressing need to expose the youth of the Black community to a history representing positive social and cultural contributions of Black people. This strategy of countering the preponderance of negative Black images in the mass media took on a radical and idealist form. In January 1920, a new monthly magazine was published by Du Bois for the expressed purpose of highlighting the history and achievements of Black people (Johnson-Feelings, 1996). *The Brownies' Book* was a vehicle to change ideas and images about Black children, the Brownies: children of the sun and the communities that nurtured them. An October 1919 issue of the *Crisis Magazine* announced the forthcoming *Brownies' Book* and stated its purpose as:

> A monthly magazine for children, designed for all children, but especially for ours. It will be a thing of Joy and Beauty, dealing in Happiness, Laughter and Emulation, and designed especially for Kiddies from Six to Sixteen. It will seek to teach Universal Love and Brotherhood, for all little folk—black and brown and yellow and white. (*The Crisis*, Vol. 18, No. 6, October 1919, p. 285.)

Contemporary concerns of images and meaning are amplified with each glance of a music video that overexposes the flesh of Black bodies to indulgences of material culture, sexual subjugation, and reckless judgment. These constructions of social identities are not only influenced by the media sources, but they are also embedded in the messages Black boys get at school from teachers and their peers. The current plight of Black boys in education offers yet another opportunity to learn from Du Bois's historical experiment about reimagining Black male youth.

This chapter considers a significant historical publication aimed at developing positive identities for Black youth. *The Brownies' Book*, conceived and developed by W. E. B. Du Bois, was an innovative vehicle of conceptual change to shift the negative stereotypes to positive self-images and identities among Black children. In particular, the chapter focuses on Du Bois's strategy for countering the preponderance of negative Black images in the mass media and has implications for contemporary work with Black boys and young men. In this light, this chapter also addresses issues of masculine identity with specific relevance to educational engagement and achievement.

Toward (Re)Imagining Black Male Youth

Research suggests that Black male youth deserve the special attention of researchers, policy analysis, and practitioners. Scholars have noted cultural messages about Black boys and men and how they are negatively portrayed in the media and negatively perceived in everyday life. These images overwhelmingly cast this population as angry, violent, intellectually disengaged, hypersexual, and threatening. These cultural messages do not stop at the school door; rather, they are ever present in schools and consistently threaten learning opportunities and teacher and peer relationships. For instance, the physical appearance and deportment of Black boys are read negatively often, are misunderstood by many teachers, and are seen as defiant, threatening, and intimidating. Therefore, that in almost every positive academic category, Black male youth are disproportionately unrepresented while they are overrepresented in negative categories is not surprising.

The experiences of Black male youth in school are often represented by image victimization. Although that is not the entire narrative of these students' experience in school, they are clearly being victimized by an explosive convergence of more severe disciplinary policies, adultification, an aggressive assessment agenda, and discretionary decisions of teachers and school personnel that are often informed by narrow perspective of who these students are and how they behave in school. Indeed, we have much to learn about images of Black male youth and ways to invert the narrative.

Clearly, the need to change the damaging narrative of Black male youth is ever present. The question remains, however, what are the new narratives? For sure, outstanding Black male youth in schools today represent the "change narrative" pushed by Du Bois because it attempts to represent a spectrum of Black male education experiences. Generally, our attention is drawn to the extremes. Interestingly, most Black male youth reside in the middle academically and socially; their experiences are not always at the margins. Yet Black male youth in the middle are often overlooked and not given the attention needed.

Like the importance of images of Black male youth reflected in the *Brownies' Books*, recently the mattering of Black people has captured the nation's attention, at least in part, of those who are genuinely concerned about the life chances of Black folk and others who are perplexed by "direct" and unapologetic messaging of the importance of Black lives—inclusive of Black male youth. This shift from deficit focus and challenges to issues reflected in counternarratives of mattering, success and contributions is showing up specifically in research on Black male students across the education pipeline (Brooms, 2017). In the main, I argue that this work is about identity and identity management. In short, this scholarship is a treatment of and reaction to identity with the objective of understanding how Black boys and young men get constructed in both the imagination of scholars and the public. The broader "maning-up" project renders Black boys as miniature men with the ingrown inclinations and expectations to embody adulthood. These pernicious effects of adultifying Black boys that Dancy (2014a) warns about still haunt us in our effort to let Black boys be. But is this a dream? As Dumas and Nelson (2016) remind us, Black boyhood is socially unimagined and unimaginable, largely due to the devalued position and limited consideration of all Black children within the broader social conception of childhood.

Our imagination of Black boys and men is constrained by the language used to described then. There is a growing concern about the power of terminology and labeling (Carey, 2017). The popular terms *Black male* or *Black males* are consistently used in the literature, and on the surface, I have no severe problems with this usage. However, in favoring terms such as *Black boys*, *Black young men*, *Black emerging adult men*, and *Black male youth*, there is an attempt to capture a development accuracy and give attention to an emerging manhood across the life course. The use of these more appropriate developmental descriptors avoids a "dumping effect" of boys and men into a composite identification as males without regard to age distinctions.

Schooling and Imagination

Education and opportunities of Black boys and young men continue to capture the imagination of those interested in the power and possibilities of schooling in the United States and beyond (Davis, 2008). For instance, the grave consequences that schooling disparities have for economic stability, family formation, community uplift, and global competitiveness may be even more acute for Black boys located in under resourced schools. During the past three decades, a corpus of journal articles, reports, social media commentaries, blogs, and scholarly and popular books have detailed the precarious position and the promise of Black boys and young men in school. Although the vast majority of this work points to these students as problems and schools in which they are located as a primary source of these problems, the full story remains untold. Most of this work generally starts with a deficit-centered conceptualization and unsurprisingly ends with implications that are limited by the same deficit thinking. By focusing on how Black boys and young men challenge schools, very little is really understood about the ways schools and the communities in which they inhabit affect their educational experiences and outcome.

Schools should be intentional spaces where Black male youth are liberated to attempt to make sense of their various identities. Identities formation for students is a collective undertaking by the whole school community. The development of social identities at school will surely be affronted by identity spaces outside of school. Indeed, these broader messages provide Black male students concrete information about their place, purpose, and peril. Schools, however, are powerful in their potential to become counterspaces where various identities are wrestled with and experienced. These students have to be supported in their negotiation of possible race/gendered identities in similar ways they are supported in academic concerns. The schooling experiences of too many Black boys represent limits and constraints rather than options and opportunities. These identity possibilities at the intersection of race and gender, however, represent an imagined hope of possible selves for Black male youth that is transformative and enduring.

Research about the ways race and gender connect to schooling outcomes and experience is compelling, although mostly not instructive. Scholarship on Black boys and schooling, although important in its aim to tell authentic narratives, wrestles with uncertainty about capturing the dynamics between structure and behavior. Namely, same-sex schools offer a way to understand these tensions, especially the study Black boys and young men in these learning spaces where race and gender are offered as explicit and hidden curricula (Fergus & Noguera, 2014). Unfortunately, there is a tension between the scholarship on Black boys in education and the politics of schooling reform and accountability (Stovall, 2013). Scholars are attempting to manage this challenge in two primary ways. First, there is the emergence of studies of Black boys and young men that focus on theorizing the unique schooling experience of Black gendered bodies or provide a critique of opportunity structures that make positive learning experiences and outcomes impossible (Dancy, 2014b; Dumas & Nelson, 2016). On the other hand, some researchers are engaged in studies attempt to capture actual indicators of success, such as academic performance measures or college enrollment. The intent is for the later research strategy to incorporate variables that hold schools accountable to the larger public (Payne, 2008). Variations in these approaches still do not clearly help reimagine Black boys in school. The overall objective of reimagining the education of Black boys and young resides in its ability to disrupt deficit and delinquent narratives and create space for the possible in schools and beyond.

Although research on Black male youth achievement, performance, and behavioral disparities serve as the core of most of the traditional education literature, Warren (2017) offers a nuanced contextual understanding that informs how schools limit as well as liberate Black boys and men. He provides an overview of the historical and contemporary knowledge base about Black boys and young men in schools. He also considers the limitations of the current knowledge base and frames directions for future work. The emerging work should be guided by careful attention to contexts of gender, racial, and class in schools in which these students develop academically and socially. This is also true for research that considers pathways to college to Black male youth. But until the lives of students inhabiting these spaces of education reform are understood beyond problem-centered narratives and numbers, efforts to increase academic and life success will be inadequate.

Long-standing concerns about how Black boys and young men are imaged and represented still linger in education and social science research. Although some of the work has kept a focus on pathways of possibility that implicate the daunting challenges of schooling Black children generally, the studying efforts and interventions to change the social construction of the children, especially Black boys, are limited. Scholarship that highlights narratives hidden by the discourse of stereotypes and deficit that instill hope and habits of possibilities is being called for. The ultimate goal is to actualize the possibilities and counter the perils of schooling for Black boys and men in our social imagination.

Du Bois and Early Education

Concerning education, most of Du Bois's writings focused on higher education. His critiques of the role and functions of historically Black colleges and universities fueled much contempt by school administrators and praise from students and progressive thinkers in collegiate education. Although his scholarship and writings were not voluminous on the specific issue of primary education, what he writes is clear from what he offers as the role of primary education. In a 1910 address to a White audience in Brookline Massachusetts and later published as the essay "College-Bred Negro Communities" (Aptheker, 1973), Du Bois situates his thinking about primary schooling and college education when he asserts:

> Primary schools are simply one means of making education possible. The chief and great method, of course, by which a people come into the great social heritage of the modern culture-world and by which they gain close and efficient knowledge of methods of the world's work is the training which come from primarily and essentially from human contact—a contact of those who know with those who are to learn. (p. 49)

Early education settings are important sites for study because they represent a generated masculine space where Black boys make meaning of who they are, what they do, and how they are perceived by other students and teachers (Davis, 2004). Black boys often engage in gender-specific stylistic behavior often embodied in detachment and disinterest that further problematizes their school experience and results in increased conflict with teachers and peers. However, little research attention has been given to the social construction Black boy images and how they capture the cultural imagination of their lives in and out of school. The *Brownies' Book* takes on this project by engaging in an explicit image campaign of Black children. The narratives of Black boys offered by Du Bois, a social construction of the masculine in relation to education is revealed. Parameters about Black masculine narratives were expanded to show a self-presentation in relation to school that unraveled common thinking about this group. Du Bois was intentional and unapologetic about his politics of respectability and representation during the two years of this publication.

Considering Historic Images of Black Male Youth

Du Bois was the editor of *The Brownies' Book*, although he is credited on the masthead as the conductor. Augustus Granville Dill had the responsibilities as business manager. He held the same position with *The Crisis* magazine. Jessie Fauset, a brilliant literature scholar and writer, served as the literary editor and then as managing editor. She was actually responsible for much of the content of the magazine (Johnson-Feelings, 1996). This experiment in centering the cultural contribution of Black folk throughout the Diaspora lasted only two years. Twenty-four issues of *The Brownies' Book* were published before the magazine was terminated due to insufficient sales. Even though short-lived, *The Brownies' Book* signified a literary social movement oriented toward the reeducation and reimagining of Black children. This experiment in racial pedagogy and representation is no less relevant today than it was in 1920. These concerns of images and meaning are amplified with each glance of the nightly news that showcases the hyper-policing and criminalization of Black boys and men. In addition, we witness social media and music videos that overexpose the flesh of Black bodies to indulgences of material culture, sexual subjugation, and reckless judgment. These constructions of social identities are not only influenced by the media sources, but they are also embedded in the messages children get at school, at home, and from their peers.

There were many lessons that Du Bois wanted to teach. He offered a radical/activist intervention that promoted positive self-portrayals and more enlightened possible selves of Black school-age children. In anticipation of the forthcoming magazine, a young Black boy from Philadelphia writes of this eagerness and excitement about the new publication (this letter was published later in an issue of *The Brownies' Book*):

Dear Mr. Editor:

My mother says you are going to have a magazine about colored boys and girls, and I am very glad. So, I am writing to ask you if you will please put in your paper some of the things which colored boys can do when they grow up. I don't want to be a doctor, or anything like that. I think I'd like to plan houses for men to build. But one day, down on Broad Street, I was watching some men building houses, and I said to a boy there, "When I grow up, I am going to draw a lot of houses like that and have men build them." The boy was a white boy, and he looked at me and laughed and said, "Colored boys don't draw houses." Why don't they, Mr. Editor? My mother says you will explain all this to me in your magazine and will tell me where to learn how to draw a house, for that is what I certainly mean to do. I hope I haven't made you tired, so no more from your friend, Franklin Lewis, Philadelphia, Pennsylvania. (*The Brownies' Book*, 1(1), 1920, p. 15)

In particular, he sought to privilege a kind of masculinity for Black boys that was closely linked to the salience of schooling and academic achievement. A masculinity that is reflected in the voice of this young man such James Alpheus Butler, Jr. from Tampa, Florida:

I am a colored boy, brown skinned and proud of it. I am 14 years old. My home is now in Tampa, but at present I am a second year student at the Florida A. & M. College.... I play four musical instruments: the violin, piano, clarinet and cello, but I like the violin best of all. I started playing the violin when I was six years old.... I agree with anyone who says music is great. I find very much pleasure in my violin. You might infer that it is my aim to be a violinist from the above statements. Perhaps it'll sound strange to you for me to say that I don't, but that's the fact of the affair. I wish to be a writer and give the work that intense feeling of altruism that is ever an anon tugging at my heart [sic]. (*The Brownie's Book*, 1(7) 1920, p. 215)

From the June issue of the publication during its first year, readers are introduced to two high school boys, Joe Washington and Harold P. Tardy, whose accomplishments and valor are being recognized:

> Joe Washington is the star player on the football team of Eramus High School in Brooklyn, NY. He plays left end and has made himself popular among this schoolmates, not only by his playing ability but because of his personality and sportsmanship. He was elected captain of the team in 1920 and has been awarded a gold medal by the Public School Athletic League. (*The Brownies' Book*, 1(6), 1920, p. 174)

In Du Bois's treatment of Mr. Tardy, there are more details provided probably because of the nature of his heroic act. This case offers both evidence and symbolism of the humanity of young Black men:

> There are big heroes, but whoever hears of the little heroes? His name is Harold P. Tardy, and his in his sophomore year at the Fifth Avenue High School at Pittsburgh, Pa. On January 23, Harold was on his way to school. When he passed the home of a white family name Bleckley, 1771 Webster Avenue, he heard screams. Thinking that he might be of some service, he ran into the house and found little Margaret Bleckley, four years old, in flames. With great presence of mind at considerable personal peril, he seized a blanket and wrapped the child in it. Then he pick her up and rushed to the office of Dr. P.W. Bushong, 1824 Webster Avenue, where first aid was administered. Then, despite the fact that the streets were a glare of ice, he carried the child to the Passavant Hospital, about the distance of nearly a half mile. She was burned so severely that she died a few days later. Now what a big hero could do more? (*The Brownies' Book*, 1(6), 1920, p. 174)

A photo for each of the boys accompanies the narrative. The notes at the bottom of photos read, "Tardy posed impeccably dressed in suit and tie" and "Joe Washington in his football uniform positioned in a defensive line stance"

(*The Brownies' Book*, 1(6), 1920, p. 174). There is a clear message from the text and images about the importance of presentation, athletic prowess, deportment, values, and courage. These masculine ideals, although complicit in the maintaining patriarchy, were purposeful in their attempt at Black community uplift. How Black male youth in the passages are presented is an image intervention during the early part of the 20th century. Given the historical context, these examples of Black boys in the *Brownies' Books* were used to create a disruptive alternative narrative. This is a narrative that can be easily described as idealized, but these images also carry with them a cultural reimagination of who Black youth were at the time and who they were possible of being.

New Directions for New Imaginations

Schools, however, are powerful in their potential to become counterspaces where various identities are wrestled with and experienced (Fergus & Noguera, 2014). Black students have to be supported in their negotiation of possible race, class, and gender identities in similar ways they are supported in academic concerns. The experiences in educational pathways (from preschool to university) of too many Black male youth represent boundaries and constraints rather than options and opportunities. The need to conceive new meanings of education trajectories and college pathways is obvious given who are students are at this historical moment and the contexts that inform the meaning of their lives. Identity possibilities at the intersection of race, class, and gender, however, can represent an imagined hope of possible selves for Black boys and young men that can be transformative and enduring.

These concerns of images and meaning are amplified with each glance of a music video that overexposes the flesh of Black bodies to indulgences of material culture, sexual subjugation, and reckless judgment. These constructions of social identities are not only influenced by the media sources, but they are also embedded in the messages Black male youth get at home, at school, and from their peers. The current plight of Black boys and young men in school is one that has captivated the interest of those concerned with issues of educational equity and outcomes.

The need to change the narrative of Black male youth, which is primarily a narrative of despair, desperation, and, dereliction, is obvious. The question remains, however, what are the new narratives? For sure, outstanding young

Black male youth today represent the "change narrative" pushed by Du Bois because it attempts to represent a spectrum of experiences. Generally, our attention is drawn to the extremes. Interestingly, most Black male youth reside in the middle academically and socially; their experiences are not always at the margins that get most of the media coverage. Yet Black male youth in the middle are often overlooked and not given the attention needed. Like the importance of images of Black youth reflected in the pages of the *Brownies' Books*, over the past few years, the mattering of Black people has captured the imagination of the public. This is due, in part, to those who are genuinely concerned about racial equity in life chances and by others who are perplexed by direct and unapologetic messaging of the importance of Black lives—inclusive of Black male youth.

Indeed, these broader messages provide Black male students concrete information about their place, purpose, and even peril. Schools, however, are powerful in their potential to become counter spaces where various identities are wrestled with and experienced. These students have to be supported in their negotiation of possible race/gendered identities in similar ways they are supported in academic concerns. In general, traditional educational pipeline experience, from preschool to university, for too many Black male youth represent limits and constraints rather than options and opportunities. New identity possibilities at the intersection of race and gender, however, represent an imagined hope of possible selves for Black male youth that can be transformative and enduring.

In some parallel ways, the education of Black boys and young men also signals what is most toxic about how schooling is actualized, how justice is established, and how we do equity is produced. Unfortunately, too many Black boys and young men experience death, both academic and physical death, at the hands of the state and systems more interested in protecting self-interests and less interest in understanding Black boys in their full complexities.

To conclude, for educational settings, including higher education, to be purposeful locations for where Black male youth to have freedom of identity and cultural expression, they must also be free in pedagogy, structure, and authority to engage image management. In doing so, identities can be created and explored like Du Bois did in the *Brownies' Books* with the help of caring communities, parents, teachers, and other educational professionals. Indeed, this effort has the possibility to move us from the peril to the possibilities of schooling and the development of social identities that build individuals and communities.

The effort here is to advance anti–deficit thinking about Black boys and asset-based approaches to research and practice. The achievement of the *Brownies' Book* is in providing a framework that helps in changing the narrative and challenging how we see Black boys, especially in discussions about education. The importance of the social experiment emerges from its audacity to assert a way to reimagine Black boys in relation to schooling and their communities. In turn, there is a recentering of a cultural authenticity of Black male youth that is inclusive of masculine identity, agency, and school experiences. This was an ambitious, but short-lived, undertaking; however, the lesson of Du Bois and his colleagues still resonates with our contemporary needs to alter the understanding of the potential and power to ignite a reimagination of the beauty and brilliance of Black youth.

References

Aptheker, H. (1973) (Ed.). *The education of Black people: Ten critiques, 1906–1960 by W. E. B. Du Bois*. Amherst: University of Massachusetts Press.

Brooms, D. R. (2017). *Being Black, being male on campus: Understanding and confronting Black male collegiate experience*. Albany, NY: SUNY Press.

Carey, R. L. (2018). "What am I gonna be losing?" School culture and the family-based college-going dilemmas of Black and Latino adolescent boys. *Urban Education and Society, 50* (3), 246–273.

Dancy, T. E. (2014a). The adultification of Black boys. In K. J. Fasching-Varner, R. E. Reynolds, K. A. Albert & L. L. Martin (Eds.), *Trayvon Martin, race, and American justice* (49–55). Rotterdam, The Netherlands: Sense Publishers.

Dancy, T. E. (2014b). (Un)doing hegemony in education: Disrupting school-to-prison pipelines for Black males. *Equity and Excellence in Education, 47*, 476–493.

Davis, J. E. (2004). Early schooling and the achievement of African American males. *Urban Education, 38*, 515–537.

Davis, J. E. (2008). Toward understanding African American males in K–12 education. In L. Tillman (Ed.), *Handbook on African American education* (399–416). Thousand Oaks, CA: Sage.

Du Bois, W. E. B. (1910). College-bread Negro Communities: Address of Prof. W. E. B. Du Bois at Brookline, Mass. *Atlanta University Leaflet*, No. 23.

Du Bois, W. E. B. (Ed.). (1920, January). *Brownies' book: A monthly magazine for the children of the sun, 1*, 1–12.

Dumas, M. J., & Nelson, J. D. (2016). Re(Imagining) Black boyhood: Toward a critical framework for education research. *Harvard Educational Review, 86* (1), 27–47.

Fergus, E., & Noguera, P. (2014). *Schooling for resilience: Improving life trajectories for Black and Latino boys.* Cambridge, MA: Harvard Education Press.

Johnson-Feelings, D. (1996). *The best of the Brownies' book.* New York: Oxford University Press.

Payne, C. (2008). *So much reform, so little change: The persistence of failure in urban schools.* Cambridge, MA: Harvard Education Press.

Stovall, D. (2013). Against the politics of desperation: Educational justice, critical race theory, and Chicago school reform. *Critical Studies in Education, 54* (1), 33–43.

Warren, C. A. (2017). *Urban preparation: Young Black men moving from Chicago's south side to success in higher education.* Cambridge, MA: Harvard Education Press.

Wright, B., & Counsell, S. L. (2018). *The brilliance of Black boys: Cultivating school success in the early grades.* New York, NY: Teachers College Press.

TWO

 "Me Versus Them": An African American Male Professor's Approach to Teaching Race at a Predominately White Institution

Reuben A. Buford May

RACISM IN AMERICA IS A fact of life. African Americans have been subjected to racial hostilities and animus at the hands of Whites since their forcible removal from the African continent and arrival on the shores of America. Although legal slavery ended more than 150 years ago, the oppression of African Americans has persisted through periods of sharecropping, convict leasing, Jim Crow segregation, and racial violence and intimidation at the hands of White supremacists. Perhaps more important, African Americans continue to endure structural inequalities and discrimination embedded within American institutions—for example, schools, banks, policing, prisons, and corporations—that help to reproduce disparate conditions for many African Americans.[1]

Within the public sphere, African Americans and other peoples of color continue to feel the debilitating effects of racism. For instance, the election of President Donald J. Trump in 2016—with his often brash, if not outright racist and sexist, comments[2]—brought a context within which many of the closeted racists were emboldened to speak forthrightly. With White supremacists such as Richard Spencer, David Duke, and Chris Cantwell enjoying mainstream media coverage, White supremacists rallies have surfaced in various places in America, including the 2017 "Unite the Right" rally in Charlottesville, Virginia (Conti, 2017). Field, Jr. was sentenced to life in prison on June 28, 2019, after pleading guilty to 29 of 30 charges, including Heyer's death. Such outward manifestations of racial and ideological hostility create tension in a public sphere too fragile to host intense debate over volatile issues, such as race, racism, inequality, conservatism, and liberalism in America.

Even American universities—often held out as public spheres wherein the free exchange of ideas is encouraged—have become fertile battlegrounds for protests and antiprotests that have turned violent. For instance, in 2017, students at the University of California, Berkeley organized a protest of the scheduled appearance of ultra-conservative right-wing Trump supporter Milo Yiannopoulous that ended in a clash of multiple groups including Antifa, anarchists, and pro-Trump supporters.[3]

More troubling than this heightened tension of protest and counterprotest at universities is the microaggressions, harassment, intimidation, and threats of personal violence against African American professors and their families, most notably at predominantly White institutions (PWIs). These kinds of experiences make for very difficult contexts within which African American professors are to teach about the very topics that spur protests and counterprotests. Given this situation, how do African American professors carry out the task of instruction?

Drawing on my more than 20 years of experience and success at teaching in two PWIs, I offer insights from my pedagogical approach. The key goal here is to present my approach from which others may borrow to craft their own approach for negotiating conversations about race and other sensitive topics in the classroom. Although I am an African American male from Chicago and my approach may have limits for Black professors with other identity characteristics (e.g., an African American woman, lesbian, gay, bisexual, transgender, queer, intersex, and asexual Lesbian, Bisexual, Gay, Transexual, Queer, Intersex, and Asexual (LBGTQIA), and others), I believe sharing this narrative of teaching in sometimes hostile environments can help others develop their own effective strategies for confronting challenges in the classroom. At minimum, this chapter sheds light on problems African American professors share across a number of teaching experiences at PWIs.

In the first part of this chapter, I briefly explore three incidents wherein African American professors from PWIs were harassed and threatened with physical violence stemming directly from their roles as professors. I use these incidents to illustrate the constant challenges African American professors face as they simply carry out the mission of exposing students and university communities to different points of view while maintaining their own rights as private citizens. One key insight is the realization that irrespective of one's strategies for teaching or exposing the university community to new ideas, African American professors can experience harassment and threats of violence instantaneously due, in part, to the racism that supports the "othering" of African Americans more broadly.[4]

In the second part of this chapter, I briefly discuss my personal teaching biography in order to contextualize the insights I share later regarding teaching at a PWI. My own training—or lack thereof—as a graduate student learning the craft of teaching and then experimentation with different approaches once in the professorate have provided me with experiences that inform my current approach to teaching.

Finally, in the third part, I outline a pedagogical approach that I refer to as the "Me Versus Them" approach. In brief, this approach is based on the idea of creating a context wherein students are drawn together to use their collective critical thinking to challenge and evaluate ideas shared in class. In doing so, there is a personalization of the learning experience that is transformative. One might think of this approach as more of an art than as a science. Although this approach may be effective in a number of teaching contexts, I have found it particularly effective when teaching racially sensitive topics at PWIs. My goal here is to offer a point of reflection for professors engaged in the task of teaching in an increasingly hostile environment.

Threats to Black Professors

Becoming a professor and teaching at a university is challenging in and of itself, but this pursuit is made more complicated for many African Americans, who have to navigate the racial terrain of graduate school. This terrain is rife with challenges that may be instigated directly by professors or insinuated within an institutional structure that views African Americans as less-than-equal peers.[5] The burden then falls on the African American graduate student to interpret not only the power dynamics typical of professor/student relations but also the implicit or explicit racial dynamics of those interactions.[6] Hence, after completion of their graduate studies, that many African American professors feel a sense of accomplishment and freedom or duty to engage in conversation on sensitive topics is little wonder. Indeed, this is what they are often hired to do.

Yet as the following three examples illustrate, African American professors continue to meet with hostility, even in cases where they are using polemics from within the academic traditions they have studied. The intensity of the hostility that professors receive is ratcheted up in the age of social media where words and actions can go viral with very little context.

For instance, in 2017, Professor Tommy Curry, a philosophy professor at Texas A&M University, received "online threats and race-based harassment" after *The American Conservative* posted excerpts from a 2012 YouTube podcast in which Curry stated, "In order to be equal, in order to be liberated, some white people might have to die" (Flaherty, 2017a, para. 1–2). Curry's statements were within a very specific context wherein he was critiquing the movie *Django Unchained* (Sher, Hudin, Savone & Tarantino, 2012) starring Jamie Fox. As Curry later pointed out, the crux of the matter is that in discussions of freedom and liberation, Whites are privileged to talk about bearing arms against threats from others—for example, African Americans and immigrants—yet African Americans are not privileged to invoke the same language about second amendment rights to bear arms against their own concerns about race-based violence (Alonzo, 2019; Curry, 2012; Kolowich, 2017).

Interestingly, Curry's comments had been made five years prior to their inclusion in *The American Conservative* (Alonzo, 2019; Dreher, 2013; Kolowich, 2017) and seem to have been intentionally sought out for quoting. Curry, like other African American professors, was being targeted in the public sphere. Curry's subsequent response affirmed his original position, and his refusal to capitulate brought pressure for Texas A&M University president, Michael K. Young, to act. Young published a statement indicating that, while the university did not approve of Curry's "disturbing" comments, he had the right of free speech (Kolowich, 2017). President Young's comments left Professor Curry feeling unsupported. Indeed, both colleagues at the university and outside the university felt that President Young had left Professor Curry open to further attacks and acts of hostility, for doing what in Curry's view was the job for which he had been hired. The threats of violence grew so intense that Professor Curry ultimately had to have a police escort to and from the university for a short stint. Professor Curry left Texas A&M University in 2019 to become Chair of Africana Philosophy and Black Male Studies at the University of Edinburgh in Scotland (Watson, 2019).

Some professors receive harassment from within the university community for simply acting supportive of African American students at PWIs. For instance, in 2017, Dr. Jessica Ayo Alabi, an instructor of sociology at Orange Coast College, had her e-mail correspondence subjected to a public records request by the Orange Coast College Republicans Club (OCC Republicans)—an on-campus student organization—after she refused to let members of the organization attend "Curl Talk," a Black History Month event that had been postponed until March.

In May 2017, the organization filed a complaint with the university alleging that Dr. Alabi discriminated against them when she refused to allow them to attend the Curl Talk. Dr. Alabi defended her actions, stating, "African American female students had and still have an expectation that this is a safe space event. If the college will not stand up to the Republican club, I have decided to stand up for myself and other students" (Beale, 2017, para. 11). Students staged a demonstration in support of Dr. Alabi, who was investigated for an entire year after the OCC Republicans launched its claims of discrimination. Although the college and district for which she worked ultimately cleared Dr. Alabi of any discrimination, her reputation had been damaged, and she and her family endured numerous racist, sexist, and vulgar threats. Dr. Alabi continues to teach at Orange Coast College.

In response to the attention generated by some African American professors for sharing controversial comments in the public sphere, some universities have placed the offending professor on administrative leave. For instance, Professor Johnny Williams, a sociology professor at Trinity College in Hartford, Connecticut, was placed on administrative leave after sharing an article on Twitter that suggested letting racial bigots die—the post included the hashtag, #LetThemFuckingDie, which referred to the title of the article that appeared in *Medium* (see Flaherty, 2017b). Professor Williams received threats, and the university shut down for half a day in light of those threats. Williams confirmed later that he left the state amid those threats.

Although Professor Williams later apologized for the post and pointed out that his only aim was to bring attention to White supremacy, the president of Trinity College, Joanne Berger-Sweeney, placed Professor Williams on administrative leave until his case could be reviewed. Ultimately, Williams was cleared of any wrongdoing and remains employed at Trinity. Still, many of his colleagues found the manner in which Professor Williams's case was handled unsettling (Flaherty, 2017c).

To be sure, the experiences of the three African American professors discussed above can be taken within a broader context of attacks on professors at colleges and universities in general.[7] Still, a large number of those threatened have been African American professors according to the American Association of University Professors (2017). Hence, that African American professors, who often are charged with teaching courses with potential for controversy, are positioned to disproportionately receive threats as they go about the business of engaging students and the university community on difficult topics while at the same time maintaining their rights as private citizens seems clear.

Certainly, a professor's pedagogical approach does not avert the potential for the kinds of threats described earlier—indeed, some threats arise from activities related to one's rights as a private citizen—but it is worth exploring pedagogy as a way of thinking through classroom dynamics because the ultimate goal is to effectively instruct students about important topics such as race.

The Context for My Approach

Teaching as a Graduate Student

Before attending the University of Chicago for my PhD in Sociology, I—like many entering graduate students—was unaware of what teaching college students would entail. Of course, I knew that I would have to lecture, test, and grade students' work, but I had no idea about how I would deliver instruction. Furthermore, I knew from attending college that there were different types of professors, but what kind of professor did I want to become? As an undergraduate student at Aurora University, a small liberal arts college 50 miles west of Chicago, I had enjoyed professors who were engaging and focused on getting the students to actively participate in the learning process. I also appreciated professors who seemed to take interest in their students' success. Yet I had no road map for achieving this. Besides, as graduate students, we were encouraged to simply focus on learning the craft of conducting top-notch research.

Fortunately for me, I was afforded the opportunity to serve as a teaching assistant for a large lecture course during my first year of graduate school. I was one of three first-year graduate students who served as teaching assistants for an undergraduate course on the scientific method. Our responsibilities included grading students' examinations and conducting breakout sessions for students. In those sessions, we would review the material that the professor had covered during the lecture and then answer questions. I found this to be a particularly challenging task for me for at least three reasons.

First, the undergraduate students intimidated me. I suspected that most had been better high school students than I had been and that they had attended far better schools.[8] In my mind, these students had attended some of the best public or private schools in the country, and my Chicago public school training was no match.[9] Sure, I had attended Kenwood Academy, one of the better public schools in the city, but like most schools, Kenwood was clearly stratified. As a neighborhood kid, I had moved to Hyde Park with my family when I was 13 years old, so Kenwood was my community school. It was also the neighborhood school for many students from the "low end"—or what we alternatively called "the hood."[10]

Kenwood was racially mixed with a majority of African American students and a sizably smaller, but academically accomplished, minority of White students.[11] Some African American students who attended Kenwood were there because their parents, who were successful Black professionals (e.g., mid-level managers in corporate offices, lawyers, doctors, dentists, and prominent entertainers) and who lived farther south, felt that Kenwood, as one of a few academies that attracted good students from all over the south side of Chicago, would provide their children with an excellent education. Indeed, Kenwood did just that for those middle-class White and Black students in the honors courses, but because of my lack of demonstrated academic ability, I was relegated to what I like to call "the general population" with students from the "low end." This meant that I was in classes with students who were sometimes disruptive, occasionally fought with one another in and out of class, and had a general disregard for teachers and school authorities (the truly delinquent simply cut class altogether).

Interestingly, one of my scarier moments at Kenwood occurred when I was a freshman. It was my first day of class, and because I had registered late for my classes, my assigned locker was located in a row of junior lockers. Between classes, I stopped at my locker to exchange books. Standing with his locker open to the right of my locker was a 5 ft 8 in., slender, brown-skinned, student. Although he was only a few inches taller than me, he appeared to be a giant. He was wearing tan slacks, tan leather loafers, and a tan button-down shirt that was untucked, long and flowing. He finished the outfit off with a matching tan cap. I had never seen anyone dressed so "sharp" to come to school. After I opened my locker, he turned to me and said, "Shorty, you look kinda young to be over here."

"I am," I said. "I'm only a freshman."

"How did you get a locker over here?" he asked. "This is for juniors."

"My mother registered me late, and this is where they put me."

"What's your name?"

"Reuben," I replied as I stacked my books in the locker.

"My name is Bernard, shorty."[12]

"What's up," I said awkwardly.

I focused on gathering my books as Bernard turned and chatted with a few girls passing his locker. After about a half-minute or so, Bernard leaned toward me and said, "You seem pretty cool, shorty. Let me know if anybody tries to mess with you."

"Okay," I said.

Bernard then leaned in and asked softly, "Hey, shorty, you ever seen one of these before?" He turned the left side of his waist clockwise toward me and slowly lifted his loose-fitting shirt. Tucked in his waistline between his brown leather belt and white T-shirt was a dark-colored small revolver.

"No," I said in a soft voice. "Is that a gun?"

"Yeah," he said.

"Is it real?"

"Yeah, but don't tell nobody I got it."

"I won't," I said softly as I grabbed my last book, shut the locker, and began walking to class.

That evening, I went home and told my mother what I had seen. The next day, she escorted me to the school's main office and spoke with the assistant principal. She explained what I had seen and then demanded that my locker be changed immediately. She added, "I don't even want my son going back up there to get his books. Send someone over there to get the books and bring them to his new locker."

Before the year was out, there was a shooting and a stabbing incident in the school parking lot during a lunch period. Rumor had it that Bernard was involved. Although no charges were ever filed against him, I learned that Bernard was the local captain of a faction of the Black P. Stone Nation, a notorious street gang in Chicago.[13] Fortunately for me, my mother had anticipated that Bernard's approach to me was a step toward recruitment and took action to move me.

With each successive step through my educational experience, I became increasingly aware of the educational and social challenges I had experienced such that by the time I was a graduate student, I was well aware that few undergraduate students at the University of Chicago were likely to have had similar challenges.

The second reason I felt that leading the breakout sessions was challenging was because I was well aware that many of my graduate student peers were Ivy League–trained and –educated and could rest on their social and cultural capital to help them manage their responsibilities as teaching assistants.[14] I, on the other hand, had to expend significant energy and time just to develop a general level of competency. To illustrate, I had been up late one night attempting to digest a text from Karl Marx for my Classical Theory graduate course. Although I had been in a liberal arts college and had read secondary texts that distilled Marx's ideas, this was my first direct exposure to Marx's writings. As I walked into the classroom the next morning, I observed one of my classmates sitting with her head down reading a book, but it was not the Marx reading. It was a brown paperback. I said to her, "What's that?"

"Oh. It's a novel by an African novelist Chinua Achebe," she replied.

"What? You have time to read a novel?"

"Yeah. I read the Marx reading a couple of days ago. I've read Marx before so I'm familiar with his ideas," she replied matter-of-factly.

"Oh. I wish I had time to read a novel," I said in frustration.

Occurrences such as this were a constant reminder of my distinct disadvantage given my own educational experiences. They also highlighted the challenges that I would have to overcome to not only successfully complete my PhD but to also provide instruction to the undergraduate students with whom I was charged.

The third reason I felt leading the breakout sessions was challenging was because I was being placed in the position of evaluating White students, many of whom I believed secretly questioned the intellectual capabilities of African Americans.[15] I felt this way, despite having shown consistently what psychologist Angela Lee Duckworth and colleagues (Duckworth, Peterson, Matthews & Kelly, 2007) call "grit"—that is, the ability to work strenuously toward challenges, maintain effort and interest over years despite failure, adversity, and plateaus in progress. I had had success, but I knew there was much more work required. All it would take was one student to make a simple snide comment questioning my ability and suddenly I would be angered.[16]

The anxiety of that potential moment kept me on edge and guarded about all of my responsibilities as a teaching assistant. This was particularly evident when, for the first time, the professor leading the course assigned each teaching assistant an instructional unit to teach to the entire class of 120 students while she observed. I was anxious about presenting, but I prepared well. Leading up to my lecture, I mastered the content and practiced what I would say.

On the day of the lecture, I stood before the class with confidence. I stepped to the board to write the first step in the process: *hypothesis*. Instead of writing the entire word out, I decided to abbreviate the word as *hypo*. I finished lecturing over the four steps in the process, answered students' questions, and received applause from the students at the command of the professor. After the class session, I went to erase the board and noticed that my abbreviation, which should have read *h-y-p-o* actually read *h-y-t-h-o*. I had misspelled the abbreviation. Frustrated for making this error, I turned to the professor and asked, "Why didn't you correct me when I spelled the abbreviation wrong?"

"It's no big deal," she replied. "Everyone knew what you meant."

"But I didn't want to make any mistakes."

"Oh come on," she said as if to reassure me. "Professors make mistakes like this all of the time."

Sure they do, I thought, *but Black professors cannot afford to make these kinds of mistakes*. In my estimation, the professor did not understand the significance of making such an error. Although she was likely aware of the inherent and implicit bias she received as a woman, she had no idea about the extent of bias and even surveillance that a Black male was subjected to for simply walking into a room. Surely, I felt, someone in the class judged my competence based on that simple error. This particular experience reiterated to me the importance of "crossing your *t*'s and dotting your *i*'s."

Serving as a teaching assistant for this class would be the only formal training that I received for teaching at the University of Chicago. If I wanted further experience teaching, I would have to prepare an application and compete with graduate students collegewide for a prestigious liberal arts teaching position, or I would have to attempt to serve as a lecturer at one of the local colleges in the area. I decided to take advantage of an opening to teach at one of the local colleges. In my second-to-last year of graduate training, one of my graduate student peers and I agreed to co-teach a course on popular culture at the Illinois Institute of Technology.

Co-teaching was an important experience in my development as an instructor. My African American graduate student peer was academically accomplished, well spoken, and possessed a wonderful sense of wit. She had been not only validated through her academic success within our department, but she also had received recognition from outside of the university for her excellence. Hence, although I was moving successfully through the program, I was much less confident in my abilities as both an instructor and an expert in the field than she was. Despite the fact that we were teaching mostly engineering students who sought simply to receive their liberal arts credit in sociology, I was often anxious about lecturing.

My co-lecturer and I decided that we would both attend all the classes but alternate turns lecturing over various topics on the syllabus. Unlike my previous success of presenting to someone else's students, I found it far more challenging to prepare lectures every other day in the way necessary to have consistent success. To make matters more difficult, my co-lecturer seemed to present with a sense of ease that drew the students into engagement. The students could easily compare our abilities, and in my judgment, my skills were lacking. My self-confidence took such a beating that I began to refuse to lecture on the days I was assigned—not an outright refusal but, rather, an act of refusal. I would go before the class with an admittedly "half-assed" lecture and muddle my way through it. My co-lecturer, wanting to do a good job, would consistently step into the breach to help fill in the assortment of holes in my lectures.

When she realized that my behavior was habitual, she confronted me. "Reuben, you have to do your part."

"I don't want to. You do a better job than me."

"Yes, but you have to do your part. I'm tired of doing all the lectures."

"You know you teach better. And the students know you teach better. They don't even want to listen to me," I said.

"So. We are both getting paid to lecture. You won't get better if you don't lecture more."

We continued to have conversations such as this throughout the semester. I am relatively certain that I only improved moderately over the semester.

Still, this experience was valuable for me. It was just the right kind of embarrassing, anxiety-producing, and difficult experience needed to help me understand just how much work I needed to do in order to have consistent success in the classroom.

Teaching as a Professor

When I took my first position at the University of Georgia, I had a thorough grasp of race and ethnic relations and urban sociology course content but still lacked confidence in my teaching. I had received little specific training in instruction, I did not know how to construct a syllabus, and I had yet to become acquainted with the nuances of classroom management on my own. These kinds of concerns, I suspect, most new professors have as they enter the instructional phase of their careers, especially if they have received limited training. Yet perhaps more anxiety-producing than the impending classroom instruction was the anticipated "culture shock" of moving to Athens, Georgia, after having lived my entire life in Chicago.

For me, Georgia was part of "The South"—a collection of states with a history of slavery and lynching, ardent racists, high levels of segregation, continuous racial hostility, conservative politics, and the overall oppression of African Americans. Indeed, I took the fact that the university itself had not been desegregated until 1961, after having been founded in 1785, as evidence of this history. The imagery of "The South" was further affirmed during my initial drive through South Milledge Avenue in Athens, Georgia, where I viewed several blocks of large antebellum fraternity homes, some of which were draped with the "Stars and Bars," the Confederate battle flag. I later learned that one of the fraternities actually had an annual gathering where they dressed in Confederate uniforms and sipped mint juleps, as was the tradition in "The Old South."

One of the first goals I set for myself upon my summer arrival was to get to know more about the students that I would be teaching. It was summer, so classes were smaller and laid-back. I walked the campus and visited cafeterias, the student union, hallways, and school bus stops. I observed students as well as casually talked with them about their experiences at the university. What became evident to me as I listened to and spoke with a number of students was that beyond the overarching culture of the South, students at the university were like other college students. They were concerned with managing their course work, day-to-day activities, and having fun. When the school year began, I was relatively certain that I could engage the students because I was well aware of the overall student culture.

Waking up for my first day of class, I sat on the edge of my bed and prayed that I would be able to teach the students. I had constructed a list of 10 points I wanted to cover for class that day, but I worried that I would not have enough material to cover, not only for that class session but also throughout the course. After I introduced myself to the mix of 45 mostly White students and a few Black students, I began the first lecture in my urban sociology course. Students took notes and freely asked questions.

Responding to the students' questions was somewhat of an out-of-body experience for me. I was impressed with the depth with which I could respond to their questions. More important, I queried the students with incisive questions in return such that by the end of class we had only covered approximately 3 of the 10 points I had outlined. I felt satisfied that the first class had been successful insomuch as I was able to deliver an effective lecture and engage students in discussion. Over the next few weeks, I learned the students' names. I had decided to address them by "Mr." or "Ms." and their last names so as to maintain an air of formality. I suspected that this would be one measure for maintaining civility as we came to challenging topics on race. My sense overall is that the students understood my expectations and that my examinations were in line with those expectations. My first-semester student evaluations seemed to reflect my observations. I was pleasantly surprised to have earned very good evaluations.

Still, not until my third semester of teaching did I experience the full weight of "The South" and the tension of teaching about race. I was teaching a course on Race and Culture—one that was focused on the ways in which institutional inequalities created the context for cultural responses. So we talked a lot about notions of "the culture of poverty," "victim blaming," and implicit and explicit racial bias. I had 45 students enrolled, and by this time many African American students on campus had heard by word of mouth that I was teaching. This meant that I had an unusually high enrollment of eight African American students.[17] It seemed as though these students had a collective awareness of their presence, and thus, they were outspoken in a way that many of the White students might not have experienced in the context of other university classrooms. My presence as an African American professor likely emboldened the students further.

Added to this mix was a White male student who was also outspoken. Not only was he comfortable making unsupported assertions about race, typically of the negative sort, but he also seemed to genuinely believe that such assertions were factual. Further heightening tensions was the fact that, as a member of a White fraternity, he frequently wore to class a T-shirt emblazoned with his fraternity's Greek letters and some visual representation of the Stars and Bars or the phrase "The Old South." His particular fraternity had a sordid reputation among African American students. As one African American student pointed out to me one day after class, "That's the fraternity that has cotton plants growing in their front yard. They're racists." Hence, for the African American students in class, this White male student was an iconic representation of the stereotypical White racist southerner who frequently drew his other White classmates into the discussion as allies.

What this meant was that during classroom discussions, the exchanges became hostile, with each group incensed by the most extreme points of view on any side of an issue. Much to my disappointment, the discussions often devolved into anecdotal shouting matches and venting sessions that were counterproductive to instruction based on facts. I certainly wanted students to engage in lively debate but found it troubling when students began to hurl personal insults at one another. My immediate response was to make a self-deprecating remark about my own teaching that would cause the students to laugh and give them a moment to "cool down." I would then indicate that we "want to be respectful" toward one another. My goal was not just respect within the context of the classroom but also respect with an understanding of racial oppression. For me, finding a way to effectively teach students while maintaining an open dialogue format in the classroom was a struggle.

The semester ended with me thinking about ways to get students focused on facts, maintaining respect during discussions, and helping them to understand the complex ways in which institutions continue to uphold racial inequality. One of the key observations that I had taken from this particular classroom experience was that, despite students being emotionally riled up, I could redirect their attention toward me as the object of attack instead of their classmates. It was as if the students were willing to collectively join together in their engagement with me. I gave this idea more thought and began to develop an overarching approach that I now call "Me Versus Them."

Me Versus Them

Some African American professors, particularly those teaching on topics of race, face the prospect of challenges to their effectiveness because of racism. Indeed, we have observed in the cases of Professors Curry, Williams, and Alabi that being an African American professor and challenging racism or social injustice can bring one quickly under attack. This is especially true in the world of social media where these attacks can be stimulated by third parties who take a professor's spoken or written words out of context, misrepresent them to others, and cast them out into cyberspace, creating a frenzy. There is little defense that will prevent such attacks.

Despite the potential for these attacks, we must remain vigilant and continue to develop creative ways to challenge students and help them to grow and understand the nature of oppression and how those who cannot speak for themselves experience it. Here I offer one such creative approach, "Me Versus Them," which I have found to be successful. Although the numerous university teaching awards that I have received might be taken as an indicator of this success, I take the students' testimonies of life-changing experience as a far better indicator of my success.[18]

Given some of my own challenges with using this approach, offering two caveats that might be intuitive but still worth mentioning is important. First, no singular approach to teaching is useful for every professor, course, or student. All of us come from different backgrounds such that the instructional tools in the hands of one person might aid in transformational learning, while those same tools in the hands of another person may prove to be an impediment to such learning. Second, the description I provide here cannot possibly reveal the dynamic flow of my approach. Oftentimes there are contingencies that arise during classroom instruction and such contingencies require a modification in approach. Hence, maintaining a degree of flexibility in their instruction is important for professors. It is worth also remembering that society is constantly in movement and our teaching should be dynamic as well.

Origins

The origins of the "Me Versus Them" approach began many years ago, perhaps not surprisingly, within the context of sport. Many African American young men are encouraged to participate in sport and, in many cases, to hang their entire dream of social mobility on their ability to master hitting, running, passing, shooting, dribbling, tackling, and catching.[19] Indeed, sport was important to my own development, but my experience was different from the typical young men who desired social mobility through sport.

As a 19-year-old sophomore at Aurora University, I decided to try out for our college basketball team despite never having played competitive high school basketball. Although the Aurora University team played in the NCAA Division III—wherein athletes do not receive scholarships to compete—many of the players had varsity high school experience and could have played for schools that offer athletic scholarships. My mother warned me not to try out because as she put it, "Son, there are so many other things you could be doing." Truthfully, I think she was worried that I might become preoccupied with basketball and continue to underperform in school. Still, I tried out.

On my first day of tryouts, I witnessed what would be a recurring process. Coach let us shoot around as he walked through the gym smiling and chatting with players. Then he would blow the whistle and we would start practice drills. He was supportive and offered words of encouragement. After 90 minutes of practice drills, Coach blew the whistle and shouted in a very different voice than the one he had used all practice, "Put the balls on the rack".

"Everyone on the baseline," Coach added. "We're running down and back."

I followed the lead of the older players who trotted to the baseline under one basket and faced the other basket. Coach put his whistle in his mouth and blew it. Everyone took off running for the opposite baseline, touched it, and sprinted back.

"On the line again," Coach barked.

He blew the whistle once more. We took off running again and then returned to the baseline. Coach kept up this process for a few minutes. After the 9th or 10th time, Coach said, "Okay this is the last one."

By this time every player was laboring to breathe and some were even crouched over grabbing their stomachs, resting with both hands on their knees, or standing with their arms folded behind their heads. I was somewhat traumatized by this experience.

"On the line again," Coach barked.

We all stumbled to the line, and Coach blew the whistle. We took off running, but just as we were about to reach the half-court line, Coach blew the whistle and shouted, "Stop. Go back! We're starting over because Robert is not running hard."

I did not know who Robert was, but I wished he would do what he was supposed to do. Meanwhile, the older players started shouting at Robert,

"C'mon man."

"Yo', Rob, you better run."

"Let's go, man."

By the time we reached the baseline, Coach had blown the whistle again. We collectively took off running with more effort, reached the opposite baseline, touched it, turned around, and started back, but before we could reach the baseline again, Coach blew the whistle and shouted, "We're gonna keep running until everyone runs hard. You can blame Dennis. He's jogging."

Finally, we finished the last few sprints, and Coach dismissed us to the locker room. In the locker room, the players who had slacked off during the sprints were cornered by various members on the team and told to run harder next time. I was surprised at how the other players confronted one another.

At the time, I did not know that, the next day, this process would be repeated. I survived it, and after a few days, I made the team. Here is where I also began noticing a change with the other players. Instead of responding to one another with hostility at the end of practice, we began to cheer for one another and provide encouragement. It was as though we knew that we had to work together to "defeat" Coach and his pressure. It was "Us Versus Him."

Not until I started teaching in the university classroom did I actually marvel at the innovative way that Coach brought us together as a unit by playing the villain. He forced us to unite in our collective efforts to defeat him. Still, I had not thought to use this approach in the classroom. Not until I experienced the second event, while teaching at the University of Georgia, would I fully recognize the utility of this approach.

Implementation

Early in my teaching career, I could effectively deliver lecture content like most professors, but I had no underling philosophy structuring my approach to teaching. This changed 13 years ago when Michael, one of my former White male students, took the time to write me a 4.5 page, single-spaced, type-written letter. The letter began with the statement "I don't really know the point of this letter."

Yet, as I read through his detailed recollections of his classroom experience with me, something interesting occurred to me. Michael had actually unknowingly identified a process that I could standardize so that I could have uniform success in my courses. Particularly, his statement that "The entire semester is the experience that counts" best captured for me my course as a process: a journey over time so to speak. I thought, if done properly, I could consistently engage students in difficult topics, focus on the student experience, and bring many to understand the complicated system of inequality experienced by Black and Brown people.

With these goals in mind, I returned to my basketball-playing experience and decided to try a "Me Versus Them" approach. Drawing on Michael's experience and that of my previous students, I began to develop steps for creating a transformative experience in the classroom. I have used this approach in some variation since Michael first shared his thoughts. Here I present these steps in an effort to stimulate thought about additional approaches.

Steps in the "Me Versus Them" Approach

Step 1: Emphasize Institutional Distance in a Bold Way. Most everyone understands that professors have different institutional positions at the university than their students do. My goal on the first day of class is to emphasize this institutional distance in an over-the-top theatrical manner. Recall that my experience as a player was such that on my first day of basketball tryouts I was traumatized by my coach's change in demeanor. I attempt to create a similar effect in the classroom by "shocking" the students with the very ideas that I believe they have about me as an African American professor—for example, viewing me as the stereotypical "angry Black male."

I begin the first lecture by reading classroom conduct rules and being short and direct with students, almost to the point of being rude. I do this based on two assumptions. First, students will understand, if properly conveyed, that my power to direct conduct within the classroom is supported by my institutional authority and hence will make it easier for me to curtail personal hostilities students might advance toward one another. Second, that if a student is unable to endure my off-putting demeanor on the first day, then he or she is unlikely to survive the more engaged talk of their classmates about racially sensitive topics. This exercise primes the students for personal and direct engagement. Thus, being informed in advance, students can choose to continue on with the course or to drop the course. In fact, I tell them emphatically, "If this is a problem, then drop the class!" Some students are intimidated by this approach—at least that is their later testimony—but by and large, they return the next day. Their return signals an implicit agreement to push the boundaries of understanding in a new and transformative way, despite not being sure what that will look like.

Beyond establishing institutional distance between the students and myself, this presentation also helps create a collective experience for the students in the course. It is a break from the traditional start of a course, and as my student Michael noted in his letter, "At first you're caught in the excitement and uniqueness of the class." This approach draws students in while at the same time emphasizing institutional distance.

Step 2: Directly Engage Students on the First Day. Some professors use "syllabus day" as a way to give students an overview of course material or to begin the lecture. I take it as an opportunity to engage students. I do this by collecting note cards on which each student has been instructed to write his or her names. I shuffle the cards and then call on students randomly and ask seemingly random questions. For instance, I might ask the question, "What's the name of your favorite band?" This question is followed by a series of questions in a Socratic-like manner to press the student for an explanation. Asking these kinds of questions has at least four functions.

First, I am able to establish a direct connection with students and learn their names. This makes for a more personalized and meaningful classroom experience. Second, I am able to get a sense of the student's demeanor and response to questions. Understanding how a student responds is useful for facilitating later discussion. Third, I am able to demonstrate a real-life example of how the students will be engaged. I believe showing students how they will be engaged is far more effective than telling them how they will be engaged. Fourth, I am able to create an interchange that becomes part of the broader social experience for the students. Such experiences become important reference points for the students as a collective "Them."

Step 3: Reduce the Social Distance Among the Students. After learning the 100 or so students' names over the next few weeks, I then make sure that they become familiar with one another. I do this by putting them in groups of about six students and then asking them to introduce themselves to one another and talk about their favorite food, movie, or hobby. I do this twice a week for about two weeks. Each time, I reconfigure the groups; I rotate individual members from one group to another group so that students have an opportunity to meet different students throughout the classroom. As students talk about their favorite item within their groups, they typically begin to share personal stories about why they like something. They also begin to make connections with one another based on shared commonalities. This exercise helps build the familiarity necessary for engaging in penetrating discussions about race and racism.

Step 4: Challenge Individual Students but Encourage Mutual Support in the Context of "Me Versus Them." After the students have had some time to become loosely familiar with one another, I begin the serious challenge. I do this by posing questions to individual students over increasingly sensitive topics in the course content—for example, slavery, White supremacy, and lynching. As the students undergo this "grilling," I begin to acknowledge students' support of one another's ideas, even if they are not in complete agreement with one another.

For instance, one student might be asked whether they think America is built on White supremacy. If so, they will be encouraged to give examples. After the student answers, I will permit another student to volunteer an answer. These answers may be seemingly contradictory or less consistent with that of the first student's. Instead of pointing out the inconsistencies between the two answers, I affirm elements of support and then begin to further extend the question. This step in the "Me Versus Them" approach is perhaps the most amorphous aspect of what I do. This step requires creativity on my part and is more of an art than as a science. Admittedly, it is based on a "feeling" that I get regarding the ways in which the students are engaging one another. Ultimately, what can be observed is that students begin to show a clear connection and respect for diverse opinions as they see how their elements of thought are consistent with or inconsistent with other students in the class. Students begin to understand for themselves, the inconsistencies, in fact, and draw on readings to support their own assertions.

After about 13 weeks of class, typically a collective transformative experience occurs. This experience is marked by the transition from the theoretical/abstract concepts that we have been exploring in class, to a student's personal recognition and application of those concepts. It is a realization, for example, that a student has benefited personally or been oppressed by the racialized system of inequality. These kinds of transformative events I find personally rewarding. They are also the kinds of events that students recall with such clarity many years later. In short, these experiences have made a mark on the student as an individual and on the students collectively.

Conclusion

African American professors, given their propensity to be trained in scholarly areas that cover controversial topics, as well as the fact that they themselves as African Americans may not be readily welcomed into the academy, are likely to be vulnerable to harassment and threats based on race. As demonstrated in this chapter, these threats can arise out of the nature of teaching itself or can be generated from third parties outside of the academy. This leaves African American professors challenged to engage in scholarship and teaching.

In this chapter, I have presented my "Me Versus Them" approach as a means of helping connect students with one another, engage in dialog about controversial topics, build students' critical thinking, and demonstrate the value of understanding facts. My hope is that I have been able to inspire a passion for thought and exploration that allows students to always use these tools for understanding. More important, I hope that students are able to put what they learn into action for change. After all, this remains our charge as intellectual leaders in society.

Notes

1. For a discussion of the various structural inequalities and discrimination, see Pager and Hana (2008), Alexander (2012), and Feagin (2016).

2. For a discussion of Trump's use of language, see Karenga (2018).

3. Antifa is short for Anti-Fascists, which originated as groups organize to confront neo-Nazi groups, particularly in Germany. For a discussion, see Stanglin, (2017). For a discussion of anarchists, those generally against the state, see Avrich (2005).

4. This is not to deny that White professors may also receive such threats. For instance, George Ciccariello-Maher, an Associate Professor of Political Science at Drexel University, resigned after receiving death threats for comments he made on Twitter. See Gray (2017).

5. For a discussion of the experiences of African Americans within the academy, see the essays in Cleveland (2004). A shining example of an African American scholar being perceived, and hence treated, as less than equal to peers is exemplified in the experience of W. E. B. Du Bois. Sociologist Aldon Morris articulates a narrative of Du Bois's contributions to the founding of sociology and the efforts by White scholars to write Du Bois out of this history. See Morris (2015). Although Du Bois's experience is highlighted as a historical example, some African Americans today note its relevance for their own lives.

6. For a discussion of some challenges that might be experienced because of race in graduate school, see Buford May (2000).

7. There are notable cases of White professors being fired or resigning after they received threats for their comments or behavior. For instance, see the case of George Ciccariello-Maher, the former Drexel University political science professor who resigned after receiving threats to his family and himself, after his Twitter comments were reposted to right-wing media outlets. See Eltagouri (2017).

8. For a discussion of my early childhood educational experiences, see Buford (2016).

9. The University of Chicago boasts a rejection rate below 10% annually, such that more than 90% of the students who apply to the university seeking admissions are denied. For instance, in 2018, only 7.2% of the students seeking admissions were admitted to this highly competitive university (Grieve, 2018).

10. Hyde Park, the home of the University of Chicago, was more than 50% African American in the 1980s, with community areas directly to the north, south, and west being predominantly poor Black communities (see "Chicago Racial Demographics," 2017). From the late 1980s to the present, the community has experienced considerable revitalization, largely due to the efforts of the University of Chicago. It remains one of the most racially diverse communities in Chicago. I attended Kenwood Academy as the community was beginning its revitalization and there were visible signs of a period of decline at the school.

11. Kenwood Academy currently draws students primarily from the Hyde Park/Kenwood area. The current Black enrollment is 84% of the school. For complete demographics, see Illinois State Board of Education (n.d.).

12. Pseudonyms are used throughout the chapter for the names of people involved in my early childhood and high school experiences.

13. The Black P. Stone Nation, at one time also known as the Black Stone Rangers, has an interesting history. It was considered by some to be a street gang, by others an activist organization, and by still others a terrorist group. Irrespective of its various iterations, it operated as a street gang within the context of Kenwood Academy High School. Since some students that attended Kenwood Academy came from other Southside neighborhoods with rival gang factions, the school was a space where conflict arose among gangs. Yet the gangs typically maintained a truce with rivals inside of the school. Their conflict was left to areas outside of the school building. For an interesting historical account of the Black P. Stone Nation, see Moore and Williams (2011).

14. For a discussion of my perceived academic distinction between myself and my graduate peers, see Buford May (2000).

15. Between the mid-1980s and mid-1990s, conservatives launched attacks against affirmative action programs on the grounds that they were simply quota systems that admitted unqualified minorities into colleges and universities. Some African Americans (after benefiting from affirmative action) questioned such programs on the grounds that they unfairly stigmatized minorities in college—some of whom were in fact actually brighter than their White classmates. For instance, see Carter (1992).

16. Although I was aware of the academic inequalities experienced between my graduate student peers, my undergraduate students, and myself, I did not feel as though I was an imposter—that is, when people feel their accolades are falsely bestowed on them. For a discussion of imposter syndrome, see Clance and Imes (1978).

17. At the time I taught at the University of Georgia, approximately 84% of the students identified as White, 5.5% as foreign nationals, 5.5% as African American, 1.5% as Latino, and 3.5% as Other. See University of Georgia 2004 Statistics (Allen, 2004) retrieved December 9, 2019). Hence, having such high Black student enrollment in my class was not typical for other classes at the university.

18. There is little doubt that there are many professors who have added life-changing value to their students' educational experiences but have never been recognized by their departments, colleges, or universities. Admittedly, I have been fortunate to have the support of my colleagues, despite some challenges in the classroom. Ultimately, this allowed me to continue to grow as an instructor and has translated into eight teaching awards over my career, totaling over $95,000 in cash, including the Presidential Professorship, the highest teaching award a professor can receive at Texas A&M University.

19. In my study of boys high school basketball, I conduct a nuanced analysis of the ways in which the coaches, the community, the media, and the playing context

provide young African American men with the impetus for pursuing their dreams of social mobility through sport. For a discussion, see Buford May (2008).

References

Alexander, M. (2012). *The new Jim Crow: Mass incarceration in the age of colorblindness*. New York, NY: The New Press.

Allen, Marsha. (2004). *The University of Georgia Fact Book 2004*. Athens, Georgia. Retrieved https://oir.uga.edu/_resources/files/factbook/UGA_Fact Book2004.pdf.

Alonzo, J. (2019). Ethnic avengers: machete, django and the uncertain futures of race and immigration in the United States. In F. L. Aldama (Ed.), *Latinx cine in the twenty first century* (226–227). Arizona: University of Arizona Press.

American Association of University of Professors. (2017, September 7). *Taking a stand against harassment, part of the broader threat to higher education* [Letter]. Retrieved from https://www.aaup.org/sites/default/files/Statement%20on%20Harassment.pdf.

Avrich, P. (2005). *Anarchist voices: An oral history of anarchism in America*. West Virginia: AK Press.

Beale, M. (2017, May 18). OCC Republicans club files second instructor complaint. *Coast Report Online*. Retrieved from http://www.coastreportonline.com/campus_news/campus/article_466302ce-3c24-11e7-b385-731902acb2d8.html.

Buford May, R. A. (2000). The Sid Cartwright incident and more: An African American male's interpretive narrative of interracial encounters at the university of Chicago. *Studies in Symbolic Interaction, 24*, 75–100.

Buford May, R. A. (2008). *Living through the hoop: High school basketball, race and the American dream*. New York, NY: New York University Press.

Buford May, R. A. (2016, September 7). *Never underestimate the power of your inspiration* [Video file]. Retrieved from https://youtu.be/70RvM94Rdj8.

Carter, S. L. (1992). *Reflections of an affirmative action baby*. New York, NY: Basic Books.

Chicago racial demographics, 1910–2000, in GIF form. (2017, December 6). *Huffington Post*. Retrieved from https://www.huffingtonpost.com/2013/01/29/chicago-racial-demographi_n_2575921.html.

Clance, P., & Imes, S. A. (1978). The imposter phenomenon in high achieving women: Dynamics and therapeutic intervention. *Psychotherapy: Theory, research, and practice, 15*, 241–247.

Cleveland, D. (Ed.). *A long way to go: Conversations about race by African American faculty and graduate students.* New York, NY: Peter Lang.

Conti, A. (2017, August 13). Inside the chaos and hate at Charlottesville. *VICE News.* Retrieved from https://www.vice.com/en_us/article/kzz8we/inside-the-chaos-and-hate-at-charlottesville.

Curry, T. (2012). Killing whites. YouTube uploaded by Rob Redding, December 27, 2012, www.youtube.com/watch?v=hzzUhknV_o.

Dreher, R. (2013). Django's revenge fantasy. *The American Conservative*, January 11. www.theamericanconservative.com/dreher/djangos-revenge-fantasy/.com.

Duckworth, A., Peterson, C., Matthews, M. D., & Kelly, D. R. (2007). Grit: Perseverance and passion for long-term goals. *Journal of Personality and Social Psychology, 92*, 1087–1101.

Eltagouri, M. (2017). Professor who tweeted, "All I want for Christmas is white genocide," resigned after year of threats. *The Washington Post.* Retrieved from https://www.washingtonpost.com/news/grade-point/wp/2017/12/29/professor-who-tweeted-all-i-want-for-christmas-is-white-genocide-resigns-after-year-of-threats/?utm_term=.30baca3a2677.

Feagin, J. (2016). *How Blacks built America: Labor, culture, freedom, and democracy.* New York, NY: Routledge.

Flaherty, C. (2017a, May 11). Furor over philosopher's comments on violence against White people. *Inside Higher Ed.* Retrieved from https://www.insidehighered.com/news/2017/05/11/furor-over-texas-am-philosophers-comments-violence-against-white-people.

Flaherty, C. (2017b, June 27). Trinity suspends targeted professor. *Inside Higher Ed.* Retrieved from https://www.insidehighered.com/news/2017/06/27/trinity-college-connecticut-puts-johnny-eric-williams-leave-over-controversial.

Flaherty, C. (2017c, July 17). Trinity clears threatened professor. *Inside Higher Ed.* Retrieved from https://www.insidehighered.com/news/2017/07/17/trinity-connecticut-clears-johnny-williams-wrongdoing-he-remains-leave-now-voluntary.

Gray, M. (2017). Drexel professor resigns amid threats over controversial tweets. *CNN*. Retrieved from https://www.cnn.com/2017/12/28/us/drexel-university-professor-resigns/index.html.

Grieve, P. (2018, May 3). Acceptance rate plummets to 7.2 percent for the class of 2022. *The Chicago Maroon*. Retrieved from https://www.chicagomaroon.com/article/2018/5/3/university-chicagos-acceptance-rate-plummets-7-2-c/.

Illinois State Board of Education. (n.d.). Illinois report card 2017–2018. Retrieved from https://www.illinoisreportcard.com/school.aspx?source=studentcharacteristics&source2=studentdemographics&Schoolid=150162990250025.

Karenga, M. (2018). Trump's mind, mouth and fecal matters: Racism's red meat and raw sewage. *Africology: The Journal of Pan African Studies, 11* (4), 4–7.

Kolowich, S. (2017, August 3). What is a Black professor in America allowed to say? *The Guardian*. Retrieved from https://www.theguardian.com/world/2017/aug/03/what-is-a-Black-professor-in-america-allowed-to-say-tommy-j-curry.

Moore, N., & Williams, L. (2011). *The almighty P. Stone Nation: The rise, fall and resurgence of an American gang*. Chicago, IL: Chicago Review Press.

Morris, A. (2015). *The scholar denied: W. E. B. Du Bois and the founding of modern sociology*. Berkeley: University of California Press.

Pager, D., & Shepherd, H. (2008). The sociology of discrimination: Racial discrimination in employment, housing, credit, and consumer markets. *Annual Review of Sociology, 34*, 181–209.

Sher, S., Hudin, R., Savone, P. (Producers) & Tarantino, Q. (Director). (2012). *Django unchained* [Motion picture]. United States: A Band Apart and Columbia Pictures.

Stanglin, D. (2017, August 23). What is Antifa and what does the movement want? *USA Today*. Retrieved from https://www.usatoday.com/story/news/2017/08/23/what-antifa-and-what-does-movement-want/593867001/.

Watson, J. (2019, March 3). Dr. Tommy J. Curry is leaving the U.S. to establish Black male studies in the UK. *Diversity Issues in Higher Education*. Retrieved from https://diverseeducation.com/article/140089/.

THREE

Challenges Faced by African American Adult Students: Within Higher Education

TaNeisha Page

EDUCATION IS SOMETHING THAT TAKES a lot of time, commitment, and support to be able to endure all the different obstacles that may arise. No matter if it is a college or university that an individual chooses, it is a decision that will change the direction of someone's life. Adults are deciding to go back to college to not only gain knowledge but to also earn a degree that will help them attain a better paying career. However, as more students are going back to school, they are finding various obstacles standing in their way. The nontraditional student population has increased and is expected to remain stable or potentially increase more during the current decade (Hussar & Bailey, 2009). Due to this increase, that these nontraditional students are set up for success is imperative. Because these students come with additional life experiences, as well as other responsibilities, that they are able to balance the student role with their other life roles is imperative. Embracing that adult learners are unique students that have different needs than a traditional student is necessary for an institution. The National Urban League (Rawlston-Wilson, Saavedra & Chauhan, 2014) reported that 65% of African American college students are identified as nontraditional students, which refers to these learners having other obligations other than school. Based on this percentage, educational environments are becoming more diverse and are experiencing conflicts that might not have been as prevalent in the past.

The types of obstacles that African Americans can face are cultural differences, being underrepresented, student/teacher communication issues, institutional issues, personal conflicts, or just feeling like outsiders. Each of these identifiable concerns is valid and could inhibit the success of African American adult students. As this chapter discusses, these issues are very real and do present challenges for African American adults as well as institutions.

African American Nontraditional Students

The term *nontraditional student* refers to students who tend to be older, employees first, and/or balancing work and family responsibilities while going to school (Rawlston-Wilsom, Saavedra & Chauhan, 2014). These students incur various challenges throughout their academic careers. In conjunction with being a nontraditional student, African American adult students also have to deal with other institutional challenges. Many strides have been made to ensure inclusion for all students; however, there is still a struggle for African Americans to feel included during their studies. It is up to the institution to create a culture of inclusion and decrease any plausible barriers that have a negative impact on their students. Understanding and acknowledging the type of climate and cultural differences that African Americans encounter in higher education settings are important. Understanding the feelings and emotions attached to being an African American adult learner might be hard, but understanding this perspective can prove insightful to others who share similar or even different experiences.

Conflicts

Adult learners have a lot of other things to think about besides getting their education. Because of this, many things stand in the way of their trying to get through school. Although each individual might not experience similar challenges, at least knowing that they could exist is important. When you have outside factors such as a job, family, and other situations that might have an impact on school, it creates a time and obligation conflict. These conflicts can be taxing on individuals and can have a tremendous impact on their ability to be successful in a program. Barriers caused by the institution can also be also hinder adult learners' success rate. These barriers include things such as not having counselors, academic affairs, office hours, and any other support systems available to accommodate the schedule of these adult learners.

Unlike traditional students, most adult learners have other significant obligations that interfere with their learning. Even though adult students do have other obligations, the fact they have chosen to enroll in a higher education program shows their commitment to education. Although having these commitments can lead to struggles for these students, they can also serve as a reason for adult learners to stay focused on their goal. However, professors have to recognize these obligations and play a part in helping these students feel empowered.

Adjusting to the System

By now, the point has been made that adult learners face situations different from traditional college students. Not every adult learner has a family that depends on them or even a job that can be considered as a conflict. Yes, the institutional barriers are not really things that a person can control, but they could be looked at as only being an issue depending on the adult's position in his or her life. Kazis et al. (2007) put together a report that discusses accessibility, affordability, and accountability for adult students. Being older is something that a lot of people associate with being confident and resourceful. However, when a person is in an environment that he or she is not accustomed to, being that same person, no matter what your age is, is hard. Accessibility is an important issue for adult students because this is a key part of helping them move in the right direction. Based on the number of outside activities that an adult learner might be involved in, when it comes to school, that things can still be attainable is important. Adult-focused teaching methods, flexible scheduling, employment focus, accelerated degree time, and course content are just a few things that Kazis et al. (2007) explained can help with accessibility for adult students. Adult students want to feel valued and enjoy the experiences they have in school. In looking at the items that are listed earlier, each deals with the ability to acknowledge the things adult students have been through, are going through now, or will go through eventually for them to get the best results. Separate administrative support, advising, registration and orientations can be tremendous additional supports to help adult learners, especially if these things took place during the hours that the adult learners would be getting to campus after work. Currently, if an adult student gets to campus after 5 p.m., he or she walks into a building with empty offices and a lack of available resources. Adjusting to students needs is what institutions need to look into to help their recruitment and retention.

Affordability is another struggle that Kazis et al. (2007) talked about as it relates to these adult students getting the funds for school. With all the things adult learners do have going on, the obvious choice would be to get some type of financial aid, whether it be loans of some sort or Pell grants. Pell grants are considered "free money," but they are limited, and they are monies that have to be deducted from an individual's taxes at the end of the year. Another issue with obtaining this aid is there are certain requirements to be able to qualify for it. Students have to be enrolled at least half-time to receive the aid. Even though this seems like a simple request, making students take more classes than maybe their lives can handle can be a constraint on them. Another issue that Kazis et al. (2007) brought up is the rules regarding satisfactory progress by the government. This time limit can end before adult students are able to get through school because of their other obligations. Being able to maintain a consistent, satisfactory progress is something that adult students receiving aid must be able to do to keep their funding coming. If students do not stay on the right track, the aid will be taken away, and students will have to pay back all the money they have received to be eligible to receive money again if they ever decide they want to go back to a higher education institution again.

Schools can also help with the financial aspect of education by allowing students to be able to bring in prior learning assessments (PLAs) in for credit. By doing this, they are acknowledging the adult learners' past experiences and giving them a head start in college by giving them class credit. With the students being able to utilize these past experiences to earn college credit, it can also save on expenses for classes that they will not have to take. Adult students who earn credit for prior learning were more likely to earn a bachelor's degree within seven years, at a rate of 43% versus 15% for non-PLA students (Ross-Gordon, 2011). Because of this higher graduation rate, allowing PLAs can help the institution as well as students.

Who should be accountable for making sure these adult students have all the information and support they need to be successful within these higher education institutions? Some people would argue that it is the students' responsibility, while others would argue is the schoolteachers' and advisors', while others might say that it is the institution's. Kazis et al. (2007) state that the students, employers, institutions, and federal and state policy makers all should share an interest in having better outcomes for adult students. Each group has a piece of accountability in making sure that adult students are successful because each one of them has something to gain. The students will gain the education they need, and employers will have well-educated people representing their organizations. Also, institutions are able to keep enrollment high and have higher success rates. Federal and state policy makers' benefit for having smarter, more well-rounded people within communities in order to help make great decisions. This is similar to a circle-of-life scenario because every level can do their part to ensure that the outcomes happen in a way that benefits everyone.

Does Ethnicity Matter?

As individuals, stepping into a new setting that might not be as familiar to us can bring up feelings we did not know existed. When it comes to African American adult students, racial identity could play a major role in the way they perceive college. Studies show that when an African American identifies themselves with being African American, they are impacted more by the color of their skin (Sellers & Shelton, 2003). This is where perceived racial discrimination comes in and begins to hinder the way that an African American can view a situation that they are in. The perception for these students is what can give them issues when it comes to new educational settings.

In a recent study, when eliminating historically Black colleges and universities from the numbers, 4% of faculty are African American in the United States (Stewart, 2012). This astonishing number leaves a lot of African American adult students with nobody they feel as though they can relate to or few people who represent their racial identity. For these students to be able to relate to their professors is still possible. However, having an African American professor can be the difference in a students' ability to feel comfortable or someone who can understand students' perspective. Being able to have someone that looks like you in the classroom can be the difference in the student fully expressing their ideas and getting the most out of a class. These professors are the ones who will be handing out feedback to the students, and if students feel like a professor does not or cannot understand their perspective or ideas, that will be another hurdle for the students.

Adult students are playing a big role in causing institutions of higher learning to rethink the focus of academic programs. Currently, adult students are the ones who have to make adjustments and put themselves in situations that will help them in the long run. The best resource for these students is a support system, whether the support system comes from family members, friends, teachers, or other students. No matter where people come from or what course they take in life, having support is something that a majority of people need.

The support of the faculty is an important step to making sure that students feel comfortable. These faculty relationships are an essential component in the success of adult learners (Love, 2008). They are able to provide support for students and because they are the facilitators of the student's education, it weighs heavily with these students. Another important support system for African American adult students is their peers. Because the number of African American students in a classroom is usually lower than other ethnicities, for these students to feel support from their professors is important. This is typically something that Anglo-American students usually do not have to deal with, and because of this, a different type of struggle is created for African American adult students. Last, the support from family members and friends can usually positively affect someone's ability to remain in school and deal with the teachers and students who might be having trouble adjusting to them being around. People always say that there is strength in numbers and that same statement can be true for African American adult students struggling to get through college. Dealing with exclusion, a lack of representation, and support is a struggle for students. However, being able to understand the internal and external challenges that have an impact on African American adult students can help create long-term solutions.

Sense of Belonging

Being in unfamiliar territory is something that makes many people feel uncomfortable. When people usually go to new places, they try to sit or talk to the group or the person they feel they have more in common with. Because of this, when adult students are already in a difficult situation, they are not considered the dominant group on campus. On top of that, African American adult students are more of a specific minority and being able to find a person they feel most comfortable with could be an issue. Stepping on a university campus can be a different experience especially for adult learners. As a teenager on a college campus, blending in and looking like everyone else is easier. Unless minority adult students are attending a predominately Black university, they are going to immediately stand out on campus. Most of this is due to these students not *looking* like they fit the mold as to what it would take to fit into the student body of a college campus. The process or, in some cases, the lack of process through which students of color are integrated into the social environment on campus plays a tremendous role in students questioning how they fit into the institution. Gaining a sense of belonging and feeling like it is somewhere that you *should* be are important. An inclusive and welcoming institutional environment and the connection of students to that environment have been linked to persistence (Carter, 2006). Socialization is a catalyst for making sure that these African American adult students do not disappear and are able to engage in the full college experience.

A Way Toward Inclusion

Everyone has a different feeling about welcoming into an institution. Historically, higher education research and social discourse include assumptions that students of color come to college with deficits and subsequently deserve blame for their low rates of success (Harris & Museus, 2010, p. 32). If this is the consensus, these adult students are going into a level playing field environment. It is up to the institution to integrate them in a way that they are seen as someone who can be helpful along the educational journey. African American adult students that are entering into these universities are already in an uncomfortable situation, so allowing for interaction across race and facilitating the feeling of these students being an asset could help the way the adult students are being seen. Thus, cultivating an institutional culture in which racial and ethnic minority college students are viewed as assets not only can help the students of color learn and adjust (Harris & Museus, 2010, p. 33). These adjustments can also influence the other students and create a cohesive feeling for all students.

Adult learners are making an effort to put everything else going on in their worlds at risk by deciding to enter into this unknown territory of college. In doing so, they should not have to feel like outsiders. Understanding their struggles and becoming an institution that offers a lending hand will help bridge the acceptance gap. For African American adult students, their path is met with a little bit more resistance. This underrepresented population is faced with different challenges that hinder their outlook on education and could very well affect the way others view them.

When school is not the only obligation that someone has, the amount of attention, time, and confidence one person can give to a situation decreases. Due to this, the student is trying to find ways to continue to give everyone a little piece of their attention while not being able to focus completely on the task at hand. Full-time traditional students who only focus on going to school would not have to worry about ways they have to balance their time with things that could potentially be detrimental to an entire family. The institution needs to take time to recognize what it can do to help these individuals. Flexibility coming from the teachers, better communication, or even allowing these students to have a counselor who can serve as a person of contact can help show that the institution is aware of students' outside life and that they matter as students to that college.

Another area for inclusion is for the school and teachers to know that race could be a factor for adult students. If they are aware of the possibility, then it can be addressed before the first day of class and after class starts. Examples would be making students work together at orientation to create a foundation of unity, pairing students of different ethnicities for class conversations or projects, and giving students assignments that encourage working with different people. If these situations are monitored in a way in which everyone has a voice and the teachers and students are on the same page to learn and grow as a class, the feeling of being isolated as an African American adult student disappears. This can help with building teacher–student relationships as well as student–student relationships. Positively impacting African American adult students will help them achieve personal satisfaction as well as build their confidence while obtaining their degree. Supporting these African American adult students and giving them the opportunity to meet and exceed expectations that are set for all students is what will help break through social perceptions. These students are in college to attain a college degree and gain valuable knowledge along the way. The inadvertent discrimination may hinder African American adult learners' progress and negatively affect their determination (Carter, 2006). A way to avoid this negative effect is accepting any differences that are noticed versus letting them become a distraction.

Higher education institutions have been around for many years and are constantly changing the ways they do things to best suit the needs of their students. However, most of the changes made do not keep up with how fast the student population can change. Further research on how African American adults reentering college can have a better experience is needed. By looking at how the world is advancing in not only technology but also various education disciplines, that more adult learners will be going back to college should be a foregone conclusion. One way this can happen is to research the academic support services that are out there and figure out areas where these services can be improved. Not only is it important to have these resources, but the staff that is there, the hours of operation, communication to the students, and the attitude that is geared within these support services are also important. What do these students need, and how can institutions provide these services just like they do with daytime traditional students? Another way to help with the challenges of African American adult students is having more research on the internal and external struggles they face. If more and more students start sharing their experiences, understanding different situations and obligations that have an impact on students would be helpful. With adult students, the likelihood of relocating for a job, of a family member going through a major event, or of anything else life can throw at them will affect them more. However, knowing that is only half the battle. Coming up with solutions to help them through these transitions is the best way to ensure these students are given every opportunity to be successful.

Summary

Helping African American adult students feel comfortable in a college environment is the first step into helping them flourish. People have unique chances to be inspiring and passionate to others who will give them the strength they need to be successful. Each person has his or her own reason as to why they decide to go and further their education. The time to change is here as we educate generations to come and embrace a multicultural society (Love, 2008). Placing judgment and being limited with anyone who decides to chase their dreams does not allow for the fluidity of education to work. Gaining knowledge in college does not start when people get into classrooms; it starts with respecting diversity and being able to grow together. As humans, we are all evolving and trying to overcome any obstacles that come our way. Lending a helping hand, ear, or shoulder could be the difference between these African American adult students walking across a stage and their walking out of a program. Institutions have to start being more accommodating to adults as a whole because, as we continue to evolve as humans, people will be drawn to returning back to school. Being flexible and staying committed are the only ways African American adult students will be able to overcome the barriers they face.

References

Carter, D. F. (2006). Key issues in the persistence of underrepresented minority students. *New Directions for Institutional Research, 2006, 130*, 33–46.

Hussar, W., & Bailey, T. M. (2009). *Projections of education statistics to 2018. Table 3: Actual and middle alternative projected numbers for college enrollment rates, by sex, attendance status, and age: Fall 2007, 2013, and 2018.* Washington, DC: National Center for Education Statistics. Retrieved from http://nces.ed.gov/programs/projections/projections2018/.

Kazis, R., Callahan, A., Davidson, C., McLeod, A., Bosworth, B., Choitz, V., & Hoops, J. (2007). *Adult learners in higher education: Barriers to success and strategies to improve results.* US Department of Labor, Employment and Training Administration, Office of Policy Development, Evaluation and Research. Washington, DC

Love, D. (2008). Revitalizing retention efforts for African-American college students at predominately White institutions. *Proceedings of the Allied Academies, 15*, 117–121.

Museus, S. D., & Harris, F. (2010). Success among college students of color: How institutional culture matters. In T. E. Dancy II (Ed.), *Managing diversity: (Re)visioning equity on college campuses* (25–44). New York, NY: Peter Lang.

Rawlston-Wilson, V., Saavedra, S., & Chauhan, S. (2014). *From access to completion: A seamless path to college graduation for African American students.* Washington, DC: National Urban League Washington Bureau.

Ross-Gordon, J. M. (2011). Research on adult learners: Supporting the needs of a student population that is no longer nontraditional. *Peer Review, 13* (1), 26–29.

Sellers, R. M., & Shelton, J. N. (2003). The role of racial identity in perceived racial discrimination. *Journal of Personality and Social Psychology, 84*, 1079–1092.

Stewart, P. (2012, January 19). After decades, revolving door remains for Black, Latino scholars in the academy. *Diverse: Issues in Higher Education.* Retrieved from http://diverseeducation.com/article/17227.

FOUR

Educating for Social Justice: The Potential Role of Historically Black Colleges and Universities in the 21st Century

Abul Pitre and Tanya Hudson

THE MAJORITY OF HISTORICALLY BLACK colleges and universities (HBCUs) came into existence after the Civil War, and to date, there are 101 HBCUs (M. Anderson, 2017). The majority of HBCUs began as Teachers Colleges designed to prepare teachers for the newly freed people. HBCUs, in their infancy, were oftentimes funded by wealthy philanthropists who were determined to control the education of Black people (J. Anderson, 1988). Watkins (2001) writes that immediately after the Civil War, a group of White philanthropists met to design 75 years of education for Blacks in the American South.

The educational plan was designed to make Blacks submissive and docile in preparation for a new form of slavery (Spivey, 2007). The debate by Booker T. Washington and W. E. B. Du Bois was born as a result of different philosophical views about the education of Black people. Booker T. Washington, the founder of Tuskegee University, has often been referred to as an accommodationist who sought to appease Whites through his argument that Blacks should be educated for agricultural and industrial roles rather than the liberal arts (Watkins, 1993). Du Bois, to the contrary, believed Blacks should be educated in the liberal arts and argued for a talented-tenth who could be the future leaders (Rabaka, 2008).

Over the years, Du Bois's faith in the Talented Tenth faded as he saw this group becoming more of a bourgeoisie elite that were not concerned with the plight of the Black masses. And while the debate between Washington and Du Bois was perhaps fueled by misinterpretations, there are elements of Black Nationalism in Washington's (1896) "Awakening of the Negro," in which he stated, "Let us go on for a few more years knitting our business and industrial relations into those of the white man, till a black man gets a mortgage on a white man's house that he can foreclose at will" (para. 15). Washington saw land as the basis for freedom! Elements such as landownership and the pooling of resources would later become major points of discussion in Elijah Muhammad's (1965) monumental book *Message to the Black Man in America*.

Contrary to the *White architects* who sought to use education to domesticate Black consciousness and remove the revolutionary thinking that caused Frederick Douglass (cited in Pitre, 2019) to say, "What to a Slave is the Fourth of July," in which he implored an Africana Critical Theory, HBCUs became the alma maters, or the *other mothers*, that produced Black social justice leaders. In the 1960s, a younger generation of Blacks was leading the fight for human and civil rights.

Today, there is widespread discourse around educating for social justice. Two examples of educating for social justice can be found in educational leadership doctoral programs and Black studies programs. In educational leadership, many of the doctoral programs have adopted the focus of preparing educational leaders for social justice. The Carnegie Project on the Educational Doctorate with its focus on social justice is one example.

In addition, embedded in graduate-degree programs in African American Studies are social justice topics that specifically look at the challenges of Black life in America and abroad. This growing trend of preparing social justice leaders has primarily been in predominantly White institutions (PWIs) whereas HBCUs appear to be nearly absent with regards to programmatically developing leaders for social justice. Particularly disheartening are the advanced degree programs at HBCUs that do not offer courses or conceptual frameworks that the address needs of Black people.

This chapter argues that despite these limitations, in the 21st century, HBCUs have a long history of producing social justice leaders. Drawing from the scholarship of Carter G. Woodson, it is argued that the liberation of Black people is something that they must do collectively. Although the rhetoric of social justice sounds good, it is a form of White paternalism. The arguments that we present in this chapter are deeply troubling for the most liberal Whites. In the sections that follow, we explore the Black traditions of social justice leadership and curriculum and argue the education of Black people in America is a *national security threat*. We draw from historical antecedents such as the Counter Intelligence Program and its efforts to destabilize and destroy Black leaders and organizations. The chapter concludes with a discussion on the potential of HBCUs to unleash Black creativity, thus, setting them free.

The Black Tradition of Social Justice Leadership

Social justice has become a major buzzword in the educational jargon. Across the United States, leadership for social justice has emerged to become a central component in preparing leaders for the 21st century. Although the discourse around leadership for social justice is growing, there are various perspectives about what social justice leadership means. For the purpose of this chapter, we draw from Dantley and Tillman's (2010) definition of leadership for social justice, wherein they write:

> Leadership for social justice investigates and poses solutions for issues that generate and reproduce inequities. Generally, social justice theories and activists focus their inquiry on how institutionalized theories, norms, and practices in schools and society lead to social, political, economic, and educational inequities. (p. 20)

This definition of leadership for social justice aligns with critical theory, which "interrogates the uses as well as abuses of power" (Dantley & Tillman, 2010, p. 20). Framed in this context, leadership for social justice has been a hallmark of Black leaders dating back to the arrival of the first Africans brought to America to be made slaves.

Although much has been written about the Frankfurt school of thought, which became the foundation for critical theory, according to Rabaka (2008), a critical Africana Theory predated the Frankfurt school. Rabaka (2008) cogently writes, "Frankfurt School of critical theory maybe Eurocentric, but critical theory, in a general sense, is not Eurocentric" (p. xviii). Likewise, Pitre (2011) contends there was a Critical Black Pedagogy in education that predated the largely European scholars in the field of critical pedagogy. According to Pitre (2019), critical Black pedagogues, such as Frederick Douglass, Sojourner Truth, Carter G. Woodson, the Honorable Marcus Garvey, the Most Honorable Elijah Muhammad, Reverend Dr. Martin Luther King Jr., Malcolm X, and others, offered a potent critique of schools and society.

In the educational context, critical Black educators have been conveniently left out of the conversation of leadership for social justice. One example of the absence of critical Black pedagogues is that of Black Nationalists, particularly the Nation of Islam and their potent critiques of society. In the 21st century, several of the emerging critical theories, such as critical race theory, have borrowed heavily from Elijah Muhammad's teachings. For example, Derek Bell's (1992) critical race theory concepts such as the permanence of race and interest convergence can be found in Elijah Muhammad's (1965) *Message to the Black Man in America*.

Scholars of critical race theory have noted Malcolm X's contributions to this theoretical framework but never mention Elijah Muhammad (Delgado & Stefancic, 2017). The knowledge that Malcolm received absent of "school" demonstrates the potential of underserved students to accomplish great feats. The leadership of Elijah Muhammad provided Malcolm with knowledge that made him conscious on multiple levels. The rhetoric of teaching all students is not a reality in American education because a person with Malcolm's history, which included a criminal record, would not have been admitted to institutions of higher learning. Elijah Muhammad saw something in the *essence* of Black people, which was rooted in education; thus, he advocated for the reeducation of the Blacks in America.

Under tutelage, Malcolm was inspired to become a social justice leader and lifelong learner. And after becoming conscious of the source of Black oppression, he took on the mantle for social justice, espousing a teaching that disclosed how the inequitable treatment of Black people was tied to their history in the *hells* of North America. Malcolm raised the consciousness of a younger generation of Americans in the 1960s with his powerful critique of the oppressor class construction of society. He asked Blacks in America, "Who gave you the name Jones?" He was causing Blacks in America to become conscious of the social constructs put in place by the oppressor class that resulted in Blacks being denied human rights. The contributions Blacks have made to the social justice discourse can also be explored by examining the origins of HBCUs many of which were developed as teachers colleges.

The Social Justice Tradition at HBCUs

The majority of HBCUs were developed after the civil war and established as teacher's colleges to prepare teachers for the newly freed slaves. Embodied in the founding of HBCUs is the philosophy of social justice because they were organized to empower a people who had been deprived of knowledge for more than three centuries. Through trial and error, these teachers colleges and normal schools have grown from their humble beginnings post–Civil War in the 1860s to become universities in the 21st century.

Throughout their existence, HBCUs have sought to educate Blacks in America to survive the hostile terrain of racism and White supremacy. HBCUs became the soil that produced civil rights and Black Power leaders despite the original intention of its "White Architects." Two noted examples of leadership for social justice in HBCUs were W. E. B. Du Bois and Carter G. Woodson. Through their scholarship, generations of persons have become conscious of the inequities that exist in schools and society. Du Bois's (1903) book *The Souls of Black Folks* continues to inform social justice educators, and likewise, Carter G. Woodson's (1933) book *The Mis-Education of the Negro* predated European critical pedagogues.

Social justice education has a long tradition in Black universities that was highlighted by the student protest movements from the 1960s to the 1970s. HBCUs were known for producing Black teachers for Black schools. During the era of segregation, there was no documentation of an achievement gap, nor was there a discussion of high suspension or expulsions of Black males. That Black educators and schools were producing social justice leaders was clear. Derek Bell's (1992) argument that race was a permanent feature of American life was not an anomaly for Black educators and students in America. Bell's (1992) articulation of critical race theory perhaps became significant because of his affiliation with Harvard University. Working at the prestigious Harvard University, the discourse on critical race theory caused White students to look at race anew. The prestige of Harvard legitimized the race discourse that had already been taking place at HBCUs and throughout Black communities.

For example, Bell's concept of interest convergence (Delgado & Stefancic, 2017) whereby those in the power position would only concede to the demands of oppressed groups when it converged with their interest was well-known among Black Nationalist leaders and can be seen in their efforts to develop institutions for Black people. The integration of schools and universities would become a prime example of interest convergence. Jenkins (2009) writes that desegregation allowed Whites in power to control the race discourse that was occurring in Black schools.

Following the same model that was used to deculture Native Americans through carefully designed education programs that would kill the Indian but save the man, Black education was placed under the direct control of Whites (Spring, 2016). Black teachers were virtually wiped out of the education profession, and new certification requirements, such as teacher certification, exams have continued to keep the teaching force majority *White* and *female* (Loewus, 2017). The new accountability mandates along with the tricknology of psychologists who design curricular and evaluation tools have caused pandemonium in schools that are majority non-White. Education has been weaponized to demoralize Black people.

Schools and colleges of education at HBCUs have experienced a decline in the number of Black students seeking and completing degrees in education. The so-called new teacher standards have virtually wiped out the presence of Black educators, and today more than 70% of the teachers in schools are predominantly White females. In educational leadership roles, White middle-age men are dominant (Spring, 2011). Carter G. Woodson's (1933) scathing critique that "the education of the Negroes, then, the most important thing in the uplift of the Negroes, is almost entirely in the hands of those who have enslaved them and now segregate them" (p. 35) remains true in the 21st century.

Colleges of education across the United States have majority-White student populations. Some of these colleges of education enroll thousands of students whereas HBCUs are struggling to get students. The new teacher certification requirements have been instrumental in eliminating Black teachers and nearly closing colleges of education at some HBCUs. Unable to past these *so-called* basic tests, students in education preparation programs at HBCUs are not allowed to advance toward degree attainment in teacher education.

In other areas of study in HBCUs, the course offerings are limited when it comes to issues of social justice. Those working outside of HBCUs assume that these universities operate from an Afrocentric perspective that allows students to explore their studies through a perspective that addresses the needs of Black people. To the contrary, several HBCUs do not programmatically develop Afrocentric curricula across disciplines.

Curriculum

At the root of education is the curriculum. The selection of knowledge says something important about who has the power in a society. Farrakhan cogently argues those who prescribe the circumference of one's knowledge controls the sphere of their activity (Pitre, 2018). Likewise, Carter G. Woodson (1933) argued that a major problem in the education of Black people was that their education was prescribed by their oppressors. Freire (2001) continued this line of reasoning, arguing the oppressor would not support or put into practice an educational plan that would liberate oppressed people.

Curriculum scholars write the selective tradition questions such as whose knowledge is being used in the curriculum and who is selecting this body of knowledge? (Apple, 1993). The selective tradition demonstrates the politics of education. Regarding social justice course offerings at HBCUs, a dearth of courses provides students with the knowledge, skills, and dispositions to eradicate social inequities. A perusal of the course offerings related to social justice reveals the absence of courses such as Black Nationalism, Martin and Malcolm, Black Theology, or Islam, to name a few.

In each of the institutions where we proposed courses that would be reflective of social justice issues related to the Black experience, we faced challenges. The majority of the challenges came from faculty who were not cognizant of new theoretical models that would prepare students to address 21st-century inequities. Stuck in a time warp, these faculty members were fearful of the term *social justice*. Some contended that this was *Black talk* that would anger "White folks in the state certification offices."

The fear of freedom so eloquently noted by Freire (2001) captured the thinking of several faculty in these programs. Harriet Tubman's words that she could have saved more slaves if they were not fearful captured the discourse of preparing social justice leaders at HBCUs. In one of our experiences, a faculty member met with the dean to subvert a vote to include critical race theory as a course in the educational leadership program. The faculty member argued that superintendents would not welcome a course on critical race theory. And on another occasion, one of the faculty members who worked on the original proposal for a doctoral program met with the upper administration to thwart a newly designed program focused on social justice leadership.

In addition, the process for changes to the curriculum had several gatekeepers that required approval from the department faculty; the College Review Committee; the Graduate Council; in some cases, the Faculty Senate; and, last, the provost. Shockingly, as we began this process in two HBCUs, we found that White faculty held leadership roles in the curriculum review process. Our first experience in making curriculum changes was to a standing-room crowd where we had to present justification for changing the curriculum. Despite the approval of changes to the curriculum, that this was a *Black university under White power* became clear. The multilayers of White power, Black fear, and limited knowledge posed challenges to preparing students for social justice at HBCUs.

The challenge of developing social justice courses and programs resembled arguments presented in Jean Anyon's (1980) article "Social Class and the Hidden Curriculum of Work." In Anyon's (1980) study of K–12 schools, she observed that schools operated under a hidden curriculum that reproduced the larger society. She identified four types of schools: working-class school, middle-class school, affluent professional school, and executive elite school. At the opposite extremes were the working-class schools, which were designed to produce workers, thus with a curriculum and pedagogy focused on rote and memorization, and the executive elite schools, which focused more heavily on critical thinking and leadership.

In the context of educational leadership, we often noticed the preparation programs were not originally designed to develop persons who could critique the practices taking place in schools but to the contrary were being trained to enforce policies and procedures. Thus, the concept of "dress right–act right," meaning that education administrators would be trained to dress and act in certain ways to distinguish themselves from the masses. The dress right–act right concept would be a central component in the preparation process of school administrators.

Anyon's (1980) social class and the hidden curriculum of work concept applied to our curriculum experiences at HBCUs, which seem to be oriented to prepare future workers, not necessarily leaders. In addition, faculty at HBCUs are often saddled with a heavy workload that requires them to be intricately involved in various tasks, such as recruitment, retention, and are required to hold extended office hours on campus, which impairs their ability to focus on scholarly pursuits. Expecting faculty members at some HBCUs to be on campus from 8:00 a.m. to 5:00 p.m. is not uncommon, despite having a course that may be held after 5:00 p.m. Additionally, they are bombarded with paperwork for accreditation purposes.

These tasks can often interfere with the faculty members' ability to maintain ongoing research and reflection due to the addition of such activities. Many predominately White universities have specific staff to oversee such activities, which provides faculty with time for scholarly research to become leaders in the field. The battle fatigue experienced by some faculty at HBCUs leave them uninspired to imagine new and creative ways for preparing social justice leaders.

Black Education: A National Security Threat

The education of Blacks in America is a national security concern. Education scholars have pointed out that for Blacks, being found learning to read was a crime. Joel Spring (2016) writes, "Literacy was a punishable crime for southern enslaved Africans. However, by the outbreak of the Civil War in 1860, it is estimated that 5 percent of slaves could read, sometimes at risk of life or limb" (p. 55). Similarly, Watkins (2001) notes the significant amount of money spent on designing an educational plan for newly freed Blacks. He goes on to point out the education developed by these "White architects" was designed to make Blacks submissive and docile.

Throughout the Black experience in America, education has been a central concern of those in dominant positions. When Carter G. Woodson began his thrust to have Black history taught to Black people, he was viewed as a threat to the dominant group. Spivey (2003) points out, "The Federal Government saw the Black History Movement as a threat because it was intended to enlighten and inspire blacks to work to transform American society" (p. 22). He goes on to point out the role of the Federal Bureau of Investigation in monitoring Woodson and his book sales, writing, "The Federal Bureau of Investigation monitored the sales of Woodson's books" (Spivey, 2003, p. 23).

Clearly, the education of Black people has been on the radar since they set foot on the shores of America. The conscious raising found in critical pedagogy and critical educational theory has always been problematic when it comes to Black education because those in the ruling positions recognized its threat to their rulership. A good example of the education Blacks being a national security threat can be found in the U.S. Counter Intelligence Program during the 1960s.

The Counter Intelligence Program of J. Edgar Hoover sought to destroy Black organizations and Black leaders for advocating for the oppressed and downtrodden. A good example of counter intelligence targeting of Black leaders is the Rev. Dr. Martin Luther King, a social justice leader who became more radical after his 1964 meeting with Elijah Muhammad. Those in rulership positions have reimaged Dr. King to make it appear that he was only a dreamer. However, a closer examination of the speeches delivered by Dr. King demonstrates his radical critique of American society.

In his "Drum Major Instinct" speech, he outlines the core values that should underscore social justice leadership (King, 2012). And he offered a compelling vision of education that was radically different from the dominant powers whose educational ideology is driven by a human capitalist ideology. Dr. King (1947) pointed out:

> The function of education, therefore, is to teach one to think intensively and to think critically. But education which stops with efficiency may prove the greatest menace to society. The most dangerous criminal may be the man gifted with reason, but with no morals. (para. 4)

For his critiques, his phones were wiretapped, he was placed under surveillance, propaganda was spewed against him, and last, at the young age of 39, he was brutally gunned down for advocating for the rights of America's oppressed peoples.

Kenneth O' Reilly and David Gallen (1994), in their edited book *Black Americans: The FBI Files*, document the extraordinary efforts used to destroy Black leadership. Hoover's fear of the rise of a Black Messiah who could unite the masses of Black people prompted him to seek and destroy Black leadership. When Hoover mentions the rise of a Black Messiah, this would imply someone with a greater knowledge from that which is imposed on the schooling process. It could be argued that in an effort to prevent the rise of a Black

Messiah, those ruling the society would reinvent educational policies to control Blacks. Doing so would cause them to weaponize education.

Weaponization of Education

The weaponization of education means that opposed to bringing out the innate qualities that human beings possess education would be designed to be domesticating and oppressive. Carter G. Woodson (1933) offers a good example of education being used as a weapon when he says, "As another has well said, to handicap a student by teaching him that his black face is a curse and that his struggle to change his condition is hopeless is the worst sort of lynching" (p. 24). The educational experiences would become *hellish* because students' every move would be monitored. Teachers would become the new overseers, and they would primarily be concerned with managing student behavior. Test scores designed by crafty psychologists have become the center of education.

A quick review of the origins of testing in the United States beginning with Alfred Binet exposes the mind of White supremacy and the flaws inherent in the current educational practices that are test centered. How could Alfred Binet design a test for intelligence when he is not the author of human intelligence? His ability to know the depth of human intelligence would be impossible considering he is not the creator of the human species. Thus, his arrogance demonstrates the power of White supremacy that continues in the modern era through high-stakes testing. Opposed to schools serving as centers to help students learn the powers that reside within themselves, they are turned off to learning.

The weaponization of education replaces the historical antecedents whereby it was a crime for Blacks to read to one where they are forced to be schooled. Once in school, they are bombarded with educational material designed to frustrate and arrest their development. The new educational policies ensure that the majority of Black children will never learn the secret, the secret of greatness that is encoded in their DNA from a long line of ancestors who were the originators of the first learning centers in the world (James, 2001).

The challenge of preparing students for social justice leadership in HBCUs is rooted in a history that sees Blacks being properly educated as a threat. Spivey (2003) cogently writes regarding the dominant power's reaction to

Black intellectuals who were social justice advocates: "The United States government clandestinely plotted against black intellectuals and consciousness raising within the African American community" (p. 23). Preparing social justice leaders at HBCUs is threatening because it could potentially create a revolution in the society and communities of nonmainstream students. Imagine a Center for Critical Black Pedagogy in Education at HBCUs that housed the speeches and writings of great Black leaders from antiquity. At this center, students would be educated beyond the technicality of schools but have a wide range of knowledge that stimulates a vision of education to improve the lives of all human beings.

The contemporary educational jargon around social justice are offshoots from the Black leadership experience in the United States, an experience written in the blood of Black leaders such as Marcus Garvey, who taught "race first" and was charged with mail fraud in an attempt to stop him from uniting the Black masses. Spivey (2003) calls those like Garvey "race warriors" because they were the forerunners to the critical race and social justice concepts that have taken center stage in educational discourse. In the 21st century, the education of Black people continues to be a national security threat—even to the degree that degree programs in the liberal arts and education at HBCUs are placed at the margins of the social justice discourse despite its origins in the Black struggle for freedom, justice, and equality in America.

Conclusion

HBCUs have an important role to play in the preparation of leaders for social justice. Despite the many challenges HBCUs face in developing programs with a social justice framework, the fear of a "White lash" or complacency to challenge the status quo HBCUs should be set aside to produce the 21st-century leaders who are committed to making society more just and equitable. The *revolutionary leaders* are walking the campuses of HBCUs. They are the grandchildren of the Reverend Dr. Martin Luther King Jr. and Malcolm X. In the 21st century, many of them are called Hip-Hoppers. They hold tremendous potential to revolutionize society; however, unlike the revolutionary Black leaders in years past who were conscious of the injustices in American society, this generation faces more covert forms of inequity that are more difficult to detect.

David Gabbard (2004), in his coedited book *Defending Public Schools: Education Under the Security State,* uses the Matrix as an analogy to explain what is occurring through the schooling process wherein he writes, "The Matrix is everywhere, it's all around us, here even in this room. . . . So, what is our Matrix? It too is a world that blinds, or attempts to blind, us from seeing the truth–the truth that we too are slaves" (p. 5). Through a more advanced education system that holds administrators and teachers accountable, we have all been made unconscious of the multiple social inequities. The threat to the Matrix lies in access to knowledge that awakens one to the immense powers in their own being. Elijah Muhammad (1965) calls this the knowledge of self a component of the "light" that makes one an actor on the world rather than an object in the world.

From our experiences, we have observed an inclination among the majority of Black students matriculating at HBCUs who are thirsting for more knowledge in the Africana tradition. Once exposed to the dynamic and diverse literature in Africana Studies, these students experience a deeply spiritual epiphany. It enlivens or activates in these students the spirit of the ancestors causing them to become inclined to eradicate the inequities in school and society.

In the 20th century, the most dynamic expression of social justice occurred on October 16, 1995, when nearly 2 million Black men attended "The Million Man March," which offered a glimmer of hope to unborn generations. With all the discussion around leadership social justice, one might argue the absence of HBCUs in the discourse will limit social justice to only a *discussion* with no real change occurring. Paulo Freire (2001) pointed out:

> No pedagogy which is truly liberating can remain distant from the oppressed by treating them as unfortunates and by presenting for their emulation models from among the oppressors. The oppressed must be their own example in the struggle for their redemption... It would be a contradiction in terms if the oppressors not only defended but actually implemented a liberating education. (p. 54)

Freire is supporting the call for a Critical Black Pedagogy. Pitre (2011) notes that "Critical Black Pedagogy" entails *Afrocentricity, multicultural education, critical pedagogy,* and *African American spirituality.* He argues that critical

Black pedagogy deals with leadership and would ask, "What would schools or universities look like if persons like Martin Luther King or Malcolm X were the superintendent of a school district or the president of a university?" We have some idea of what these would look like from the leadership of Elijah Muhammad who had a system of schools operating throughout the United States (Pitre, 2015).

Throughout history, HBCUs have played an important role in advancing social justice issues. These universities were born out of the horrendous institution of slavery and, while many were designed to keep Blacks docile and submissive (Watkins, 2001), speak to the activism in the human spirit for social justice. Over the years, HBCUs have produced dynamic leaders who have dismantled oppressive structures. The revolutionary spirit of yesteryears can be awakened to bring us one step closer to the realization of the true practice of freedom, justice, and equality for the whole of humanity.

References

Anderson, J. (1988). *The education of Blacks in the South, 1860–1935*. Chapel Hill: The University of North Carolina Press.

Anderson, M. (2017). *A look at historically Black colleges and universities as Howard turns 150*. Retrieved from https://www.pewresearch.org/fact-tank/2017/02/28/a-look-at-historically-Black-colleges-and-universities-as-howard-turns-150/.

Anyon, J. (1980). Social class and the hidden curriculum of work. *Journal of Education, 162*, 67–92.

Apple, M. (1993). The politics of official knowledge: Does a national curriculum make sense? *Teachers College Record, 95*, 222–241.

Banks, J. (2019). *An introduction to multicultural education* (6th ed.). New York, NY: Pearson.

Bell, D. (1992). *Faces at the bottom of the well: The permanence of racism*. New York, NY: Basic Books.

Dantley, M., & Tillman, L. (2010). Social justice and moral transformative leadership. In C. Marshall & M. Oliva (Eds.), *Leadership for social justice: Making revolutions in education* (19–33). Boston, MA: Pearson.

Delgado, R., & Stefancic, J. (Eds.). (2013). *Critical race theory: The cutting edge*. Philadelphia, PA: Temple University Press.

Delgado, R., & Stefancic, J. (2017). *Critical race theory: An introduction* (3rd ed.). New York, NY: New York University Press.

Du Bois, W. E. B. (1903). *The souls of Black folks: Essays and sketches*. Chicago, IL: McClurg.

Freire, P. (2001). *Pedagogy of the oppressed* (30th ed.). New York, NY: Continuum.

Gabbard, D. (2004). Welcome to the desert of the real: A brief history of what makes school compulsory. In D. Gabbard & E. W. Ross (Eds.), *Defending public schools: Education under the security state* (3–14). New York, NY: Teachers College Press.

James, G. (2001). *Stolen legacy*. Chicago, IL: African American Images.

Jenkins, R. (2009). A historical analysis of Black education: The impact of desegregation on African Americans. In A. Pitre, L. Ray, E. Pitre, & T. Pitre (Eds.), *Educating African American students: Foundations, curriculum, and experiences* (3–18). Lanham, MD: Rowman & Littlefield.

King, M. L. (1947, January 1–February 28). The purpose of education. *The Maroon Tiger*. Retrieved from https://projects.seattletimes.com/mlk/words-education.html.

King, M. L. (2012). *A gift of love: Sermons from strength to love and other preachings*. Boston, MA: Beacon Press.

Loewus, L. (2017, August 15). The nation's teaching force is still mostly White and female. *Education Week*. Retrieved from https://www.edweek.org/ew/articles/2017/08/15/the-nations-teaching-force-is-still-mostly.html.

Muhammad, E. (1965). *Message to the Black man in America*. Chicago, IL: Final Call.

O'Reilly, K., & Gallen, D. (Eds.). (1994). *Black Americans: The FBI files*. New York, NY: Carroll & Graf.

Pitre, A. (2011). *Freedom fighters: The struggle for Black history in K–12 education*. San Diego, CA: Cognella.

Pitre, A. (2015). *The educational philosophy of Elijah Muhammad: Education for a new world* (3rd ed.). Lanham, MD: University Press of America.

Pitre, A. (2018). *Farrakhan and education (2nd ed.)*. San Diego, CA: Cognella.

Pitre, A. (Ed.). (2019). *A critical Black pedagogy reader: The brothers speak*. Lanham, MD: Rowman and Littlefield.

Rabaka, R. (2008). *Du Bois's dialectics: Black radical politics and the reconstruction of critical social theory*. Lanham, MD: Lexington Books.

Spivey, D. (2003). *Fire from the soul: A history of the African-American struggle*. Durham, NC: Carolina Academic Press.

Spivey, D. (2007). *Schooling for the new slavery: Black industrial education 1868–1915*. Trenton, NJ: Africa World Press.

Spring, J. (2011). *The politics of American education*. New York, NY: Routledge.

Spring, J. (2016). *Deculturalization and the struggle for equality: A brief history of the education of dominated cultures in United States* (8th ed.). New York, NY: Routledge.

Washington, B. T. (1896). *The awakening of the Negro*. Retrieved from https://www.theatlantic.com/magazine/archive/1896/09/the-awakening-of-the-negro/305449/

Watkins, W. (1993). Black curriculum orientations: A preliminary inquiry. *Harvard Educational Review, 63*, 331–338.

Watkins, W. (2001). *The White architects of Black education: Ideology and power in America 1865–1954*. New York, NY: Teachers College Press.

Woodson, C. G. (1933). *The mis-education of the Negro*. New York, NY: Tribeca Books.

FIVE

Where Am I: An Analysis of the Incongruence Between Black Men and the Teaching Profession

Kevin B. Thompson

THE IMPETUS FOR THIS CHAPTER surrounds the perceived enmity between Black men and the American classroom. There are countless articles, book chapters, and editorials highlighting the dearth of Black male teachers within American classrooms and the American educational system's apparent inability to connect with and educate Black males. Subsequently, these issues all but substantiate the American educational system's failure to recruit and retain Black male teachers. Although scholars have used critical race theory and other tools of analysis to evaluate the phenomenon, research combining the frameworks with theories from occupational psychology is limited. It is here that I depart from typical investigations of the phenomenon and introduce Donald Super's self-concept theory of career development into the conversation as a viable tool of analysis within inquiries regarding Black male disinterest in teaching as an occupation.

Given the fact that Black men account for fewer than 2% of the American teacher workforce (Goldring, Taie & Riddles, 2014), it behooves academicians (especially Black academicians) interested in this topic to utilize additional theoretical frameworks and methodologies within their investigations. Although race is a moderating variable within occupational choice (specifically within the occupational selection process of Black men), I contend that to understand the phenomenon in question, we must investigate the impact of individual self-concept (along with race) within the occupational selection process. For this reason, I elected to employ Donald Super's (1957; 1963) self-concept theory of career development as a tool of analysis. Contextually, Super's (1963) theory centers on a notion (the *self*) often considered an integral part of scholarly investigation. However, within most critical analyses of the shortage, investigators overlook the influence the concept has on the occupational selection process. Therefore, including Super's (1957; 1963) self-concept theory within discussions concerning the perceived rift between Black males and the American classroom provides academicians with an additional lens to analyze the phenomenon. This encourages innovative research opportunities across multiple disciplines, especially within the disciplines of Africology, education, and occupational psychology.

Within the title of the chapter is the term *critical analysis*. The term connotes a subjective interpretation of topical materials and research associated with certain subjects. Although Super's (1957; 1963) self-concept theory is the primary lens of interpretation, a *critical analysis* of his work, my work, and the work of others affords me the luxury of interpretive flexibility. Academia has long touted objectivity as the standard of intellectual rigor and quality. However, although objectivity is admirable, the more reasonable aim is to achieve *intersubjectivity*—a philosophical term loosely referring to an unofficial agreement on the definition of terms, explanation of methodologies, and interpretation of theories, among others, between the one communicating a message and the one receiving it. Last, before providing a treatment of my research methodology, I must articulate that I am not seeking to validate claims asserting that Black men do not belong in the classroom or that Black men are not interested in teaching as a profession. Conversely, my intention is to articulate counterarguments against those accusations. Findings from my research on the topic hold that Black men are interested in teaching. However, there are specific reasons why they are *disinterested* in the profession as prescribed.

Tools of Analysis

Super's Self-Concept Theory of Career Development

"Self," "occupation," and "congruence" are ideas used within Super's (1957; 1963) self-concept theory. As stated previously, intersubjectivity occurs after messenger and receiver agree on the usage of terms, definitions, interpretations, and so on. As the principal messenger within this intellectual exchange, my responsibility is to provide the reader with as much contextual information as possible. The definitions used for the terms (*self, occupation*, and *incongruence*) can be found in the *Merriam-Webster Dictionary*. These explanations were selected because they embody the essence of Super's (1957; 1963) thought.

- *Self*—the union of elements (such as body, emotions, thoughts, and sensations that constitute the individuality and identity of a person ("Self," n.d.).
- *Occupation*—the principal business of one's life ("Occupation," n.d.).
- *Incongruous*—not corresponding: disagreeing; made up of diverse or discordant elements; unsuited to the surroundings or setting ("Incongruous," n.d.).

Because *incongruence* is listed as a derivative of *incongruous*, its (the word *incongruous*) definition is listed and used within my interpretation of Super's (1957; 1963) theory.

Within his essay titled "Self Concepts in Vocational Development," Donald E. Super (1963) expresses the following sentiment:

> [A] person puts into occupational terminology his idea of the kind of person he is; that in entering an occupation, he seeks to implement a concept of himself; that in getting established in an occupation he achieves self[-]actualization. The occupation thus makes possible the playing of a role appropriate to the self[-]concept.

Super's self-concept theory of career development contends that vocational selection occurs after the establishment of *congruence* (interpreted as a harmonic relationship between the self and the occupation; Super 1957, 1963). According to the scholar, identification, experience, and awareness are three variables instrumental in achieving congruence. *Identification*—as explained by Kidd (1984)—is the "global assumption [acceptance] of a vocational self-concept" that, if compatible with one's self-concept within a particular occupational role, leads to "a desire to play that occupational role" (p. 25). Kidd (1984) defines *experience* as coincidental exposure to occupational activity (or activities) that potentially encourages "a more gradual discovery of occupational outlets for aspects of the self" (p. 25). Last, she (Kidd, 1984) describes *awareness* as an internal assessment of one's ability to perform within an occupation.

Given the combination of Super's (1957; 1963) terminology and Kidd's (1984) interpretation, the Black male teacher shortage phenomenon is explained as the possession of an incompatible vocational self-concept, undergirded by limited occupational contact with Black male teachers and corroborated with limited belief in their capacity to perform within the role. Furthermore, the framework implies that literal (physical) exposure to an occupation has the capacity to the influence occupational selection, which is especially powerful if the person acting within the occupation looks like you.

This notion resembles Woelfel and Haller's (1971) theory on the *significant other*, which they define as "those persons who exercise major influence over the attitudes of individuals" (p. 75). As cited in Woelfel and Haller (1971, p. 75), "Attitudes are relationships between a person and an object or set of objects" (Green, 1954; DeFluer & Westie, 1963), whereas the occupational *attitude* is mediated by the experiential relationship to the occupation or with the individual serving in the role. Subsequently, the Black male attitude toward the profession is dictated by (a) personal and societal attitudes toward the profession and (b) their educational experiences with (or lack thereof) Black male teachers. If a Black male has had negative experiences with teachers or has never had a Black male teacher within his educational experience, he is less likely to consider teaching as an occupation. Kidd (1984, p. 30) supports the notion with a list of ways *significant others* influence occupational choice:

a. As sources of information about the self;
b. As sources of information about occupational and educational opportunities;
c. As communicators of the suitability of occupations;
d. As models;
e. As agents in the acquisition of work experience;
f. And as facilitators in decision-making

Super's (1957; 1963) theory suggests the presence of Black male teachers within the Black male educational experience is significant within the formation of the Black male's vocational self-concept. Accordingly the self and the occupation must complement each other. Unfortunately, for the American educational system, the Black male and the teaching profession (within the American educational context) have not synchronized.

Thompson's Four Phases of the Black Male Educational Experience

As an African-American scholar, I am obligated to investigate phenomena intellectually *and culturally*. Accordingly, as a Black male who struggled mightily with the notion of becoming a teacher, I must include the thoughts and opinions of those (like me) struggling with the decision. For this reason, I am including personal research into the discussion surrounding Black male disinterest in teaching as an occupation. In 2017, I developed and employed a survey asking Black men between the ages of 18 and 30 on a large, metropolitan college campus about their educational experiences and their reasons for eliminating education (i.e., the teaching profession) as an occupational choice. Survey results indicated that *educational experience* was the leading variable within their decision (Thompson, 2017). Afterward, I conducted a focus group with six Black males (none of which attended classes on the college campus) within the prescribed age range and asked them about their educational experiences. Although some had experiences with Black male teachers, others were never exposed to Black male teachers within their primary and secondary educational experiences. While coding the focus group transcript, I discovered four *phases* within the Black male education experience—personal appraisal, observation, reflection, and mentorship. The first phase, *personal appraisal*, is defined as "an evaluation of one's actions, thoughts, and feelings within particular educational experience(s) . . . used to critically analyze one's ability to function within certain capacities" (Thompson, 2017, p. 56). In the following excerpt is an example of personal appraisal:

> I think two things kept me from . . . from ever having a desire to become a teacher. One of them was their evaluations. I can't stand this stuff. Like I'm a habitual rule breaker when it comes to like have a teacher . . . or breakdown coursework . . . anything like that . . . I'm creative and I'm animated and I'm expressive . . . a textbook or curriculum that doesn't work for me . . . like I have to break it down in a way that I can explain it to them where it will pique their interest in wanting to learn. (p. 57)

The second phase within the Black male educational experience is *observation*, which concerns "the utilization of memory within decision-making" (Thompson, 2017, p. 62). One participant observed that he "had all female teachers" and "all" the Black men within his educational experience were either "principals or coaches" (Thompson, 2017, p. 63). The third phase, *reflection*, describes "a simultaneous introduction of logic and emotion . . . paired with a critical examination of one's personal appraisal, observation, and experience," resulting in the emergence of belief (Thompson, 2017, p. 69). The following excerpt illustrates the impact of gender and physical stature within occupational choice:

> Who all got kids? Alright. If you don't got kids, think about . . . a lil' brother . . . [or] a lil' sister, but for y'all who got kids . . . let's say they are one [1-year-old] . . . you need to find a daycare. I come to you and I'm like . . . I run a daycare service, are you gonna let me watch your kid? [The group laughs] Hell no . . . you ain't about to let me watch yo' kid . . . it don't matter who she is . . . how she looked . . . but if some other chick come up and say . . . I run a daycare service too . . . she can charge more than I do . . . y'all gon' be like [gaining approval from other participants] . . . am I right . . . or am I wrong? (Thompson, 2017, p. 70)

Other members of the group contend that teachers (more specifically, male teachers within primary educational settings) are typically seen as "pedophiles" (Thompson, 2017).

Although examples of the proceeding phases appear negative, the final phase offers hope to those investigating the phenomenon in question. *Mentorship*, the final phase of the Black male educational experience, is the place where trauma meets healing. Applicable only to participants who encountered a Black male teacher within their educational experience, mentorship is the use of personal time by Black male teachers to guide and counsel, closely resembling a relationship between a father and son (Thompson, 2017). The following excerpt highlights how one participant's attitude about school and teachers changed after a Black male teacher assumed the role of mentor:

> He took me under his wing outside of school. . . . He took me up to Central State . . . show[ed] me that . . . the college campus . . . all that stuff and expanded my horizons . . . sat through a couple of college courses with him . . . took me to a couple of parties . . . I mean just really expanded my horizons . . . I'd switched up everything man . . . he was

bringing me to his church ... all kinds of stuff ... and it was ... it was all positive .... (Thompson, 2017, p. 77)

While analyzing the data, I discovered four reasons why mentorship was impactful. First, mentors willingly offered guidance "inside of and outside of the classroom" (Thompson, 2017). Thompson (2017) states that compassion shown within this exchange elicits an increased level of respect for the teacher. Next, experiencing individual attention "allowed for the formation of a loose father-son dynamic" (Thompson, 2017, p. 76). The third reason concerns a very interesting notion. Participants illustrated the utmost admiration for those who put their jobs on the proverbial line to correct behavior. Examples of such behavior include horseplay, physical restraint during student altercations, and other physical expressions of dominance. "This behavior illustrated a certain level of loyalty and convinced the participants to make necessary changes in response to their (the mentors') risk" (Thompson, 2017, p. 77).

Last, mentors were physical manifestations of who they aspired to be—mentors (Thompson, 2017). Participants spoke at length about making a positive impact within the lives of other Black males. However, they doubted their ability to effect change as a teacher.

Comparative Analysis

There are several comparisons between Super's (1957; 1963) self-concept theory and Thompson's (2017) four phases of the Black male educational experience. Contextually, both theoretical frameworks regard the self as influential within occupational selection and acknowledge the impact of the relationship on occupational attitude formation. Although both theories contend that experience (actual physical exposure to the occupation or others serving in the role) is pivotal, they depart at the juncture of coincidence. Super's (1957; 1963) theory holds that one could develop an interest in a profession after exposure to occupational activity. I contend that it takes more than a happenstance encounter to inspire Black men to assume the role of teacher within the American educational context. It has to be intentional. Black male teachers must be willing to assume multiple roles within the classroom—teacher, mentor, father, uncle, and confidant, among others. Moreover, it will take a concerted effort between society and the American educational system to change the Black male's perception of teaching as prescribed to increase the number of Black males willing to teach on primary and secondary levels. Furthermore, both frameworks riff off Woelfel and Haller's (1971) theory of the *significant other*, constituting the importance of others within occupational selection. Conversely, the frameworks in question part ways regarding the notion of race. While Super (1957; 1963) bases occupational interest on physical proximity, Thompson (2017) includes race within the discussion. Thompson recognizes the significance of having a Black male teacher modeling behavior(s) within the Black male's educational experience. Finally, both frameworks consider Bandura's notion of self-efficacy pivotal within occupational selection. As expressed previously, participants within Thompson's study were apprehensive about their capacity to influence other Black males while teaching, indirectly alluding to administrative restrictions placed on teachers within the classroom.

Conclusion

The dearth of Black male teachers within the American educational system and the much-needed infusion of occupational psychology's tools of analysis within discussions surrounding the phenomenon served as intellectual signposts for this chapter. Primarily, researchers have utilized critical race theory as the primary framework for investigations concerning Black male disinterest in teaching. Although influential, race is not the only factor considered within the occupational selection process. I attribute the overemphasis of race to Eurocentric research practices taught primarily within most American colleges and universities. In turn, researchers culturally misemploy research methodologies (e.g., Eurocentric methodologies used to investigate Afrocentric phenomena). In the name of "stretching the field," researchers revise culturally inappropriate methodologies expecting different outcomes.

To counter results from warmed-over research, the researcher's duty is to view research problems from as many angles as possible, meaning that, as opposed to utilizing a singular research approach to answer a query, we must create new tools of analysis or synthesize old methodologies with new or other technology to arrive at different conclusions. For years, researcher after researcher has attributed race and exposure as reasons why Black men are seemingly averse to teaching. Repeatedly, the American educational system has used regurgitated information to create "innovative" teacher recruitment programs for Black men.

Excluding the notion of *self* from this conversation could be the reason why the educational system has failed to connect with Black men. Subsequently, this very reason is why Super's (1957; 1963) theory seemed applicable. Nonetheless, his theory did not consider race and culture but occupational exposure. Hence, introducing a research methodology inclusive of race, culture, and the self was a necessary maneuver. Correspondingly, the merger of theoretical frameworks offered a differing perspective on a contemporary dilemma. Although this study was more inclusive of race and culture, the results are limited because they are not indicative of the Black male experience, which is a typical limitation of research. In conclusion, we need more Black male teachers if we want more Black men to teach. To do this, we need academicians to be more creative in their investigative approach. Our children are depending on it.

References

Bandura, A. (1977). Self-efficacy: Toward a unifying theory of behavioral change. Psychological Review, 84(2), 191–215. https://doi.org/10.1037/0033-295X.84.2.191

Defleur, M., & Westie, F. (1963). Attitude as a scientific concept. Social Forces, 42(1), 17–30. Retrieved from http://search.proquest.com/docview/38009822/.

Goldring, R., Taie, S., & Riddles, M. (2014). *Teacher attrition and mobility: Results from the 2012 13 Teacher Follow-Up Survey* (NCES 2014-077). Washington, DC: National Center for Education Statistics, U.S. Department of Education. Retrieved from http://nces.ed.gov/pubsearch.

Green, B. F. (1954). *Attitude measurement*. In Gardner Lindsey (ed.), Handbook of Social Psychology, Vol. 1. Cambridge, Massachusetts: Addison-Wesley.

Incongruous. (n.d.). In *Merriam-Webster's*. Retrieved May 29, 2019, from https://www.merriam-webster.com/dictionary/incongruous

Kidd, J. M. (1984). Young people's perceptions of their occupational decision-making. *British Journal of Guidance and Counselling, 12*, 25–38. doi: 10.1080/03069888408253764.

Occupation. (n.d.). In *Merriam-Webster's*. Retrieved May 29, 2019, from https://www.merriam-webster.com/dictionary/occupation

Self. (n.d.). In *Merriam-Webster's*. Retrieved May 29, 2019, from https://www.merriam-webster.com/dictionary/self

Super, D. (1957). *The psychology of careers; an introduction to vocational development.* ([First edition].). New York: Harper.

Super, D. (1963). *Career development: Self-concept theory essays in vocational development* (Research monograph [College Entrance Examination Board], No. 4). New York, NY: College Entrance Examination Board.

Thompson, K. B. (2017). *Black Male Disinterest in Teaching as a Profession.* Unpublished doctoral dissertation, University of Houston, Texas.

Woelfel, J., & Haller, A. O. (1971). Significant others, the self-reflexive act and the attitude formation process. *American Sociological Review: ASR: Official Journal of the American Sociological Association, 36,* 74–87.

SIX

 Carter G. Woodson and the Association for the Study of African American Life and History: A Reflexive Analysis of the History of Black Education

James L. Conyers, Jr.

CONSCIOUSNESS IS THE STATE OF alertness, sanity, and sustainability of a person's mindset of adjustment. Applying this ethos to African Americans is an ongoing process of development. Meaningfully, education has been one of the few outlets for African people to initiate space in a life of occupation and institutional racism. Conyers notes ideas threaded to the relevance of cultural grounding, noting:

> Written and oral communication illustrates the humanity and centering of a group's systematized method to convey or express ideas and feelings. Symbols are aesthetics used to affirm and represent the historical and cultural experiences of that particular group. Consequently, the black experience in America illustrates xenocentricism. Labeled as a subculture or counter-culture, African Americans have been removed from their culture, history, and linguistics. Therefore, I contend, culture is the ontology to begin with concept of formation in space, place and time. (Conyers, 1997, p. 199)

Yearly, each February, the United States recognizes African American history month. Transitionally, this celebration moved from a: day, week, then monthly epic commemorations of Black history and culture. Initiated by Dr. Carter Godwin Woodson, Americana history and letters were situated in a period of African Americans' advancement of civil rights, the Harlem Renaissance, and the New Negro Movement. Sometimes unappreciated, Woodson is one of the most important but largely overlooked figures in

American history. He challenged conventional wisdom while simultaneously querying disparity, inequality, hegemony, and racial discrimination. Phrased another way, he made "America Great Again." Carter G. Woodson laments about the mis-orientation and miseducation of African Americans, stating:

> As another has well said, to handicap a student by teaching him that his black face is a curse and that his struggle to change his condition is hopeless is the worst sort of lynching. It kills one's aspirations and dooms him to vagabondage and crime. It is strange, then, that the friends of truth and the promoters of freedom have not risen up against the present propaganda in the schools and crushed it. (Woodson, 1990, p. 3)

Equally important, Woodson is one of the most important but largely overlooked figures in American history. He challenged conventional wisdom, questioned authority, and sought equity. He recognized that the preservation, recovery, and writing of historical Black documents would advance the movement to focus on the African experience. As a result of Woodson's scholarly contributions and activism, Negro History Week was established in 1926 and, 50 years later, became the monthlong commemoration we observe today.

Woodson's scholarship induced the development of African American studies, in which some scholars acknowledge was the intellectual arm of the post-1950s' civil rights, Black Power, and Black arts movements. His Woodson's scholarship went beyond the boundaries of conventional historical research and writing. He not only sought to examine primary documents but also addressed the influence of culture, interpreting data and sources. His pursuit of examining African culture addressed the retention of history, mythology, ethos, and motif.

Making the attempt to discuss the ideas and analysis of the late Carter G. Woodson is a monumental task. To many, this ardent task would be difficult within the boundaries of both an intellectual or literary biographical study. Still within a reflexive analysis, the goal is to understand the common sense approach of Woodson to the study of African American history and the theoretical framework centered around an interpretative analysis of the African past.

Retaining research, writing, and discovery, Woodson collected a body of inquiry, which voiced what was referenced as Black history. From this activism and scholarly pursuit, Negro History Week was established in 1926 and, over four decades later, became the monthlong tribute we observe today. It was designated as Black History Month, today referred to as African American History month, but despite that, in the spring of 1969, Black students at Kent State University stimulated the intonation of February being nominated as Black History Month.

Woodson's scholarship prompted the development of African American studies departments and was the precursor to the modern civil rights crusade and the Black Power and Black arts movements. His scholarship went beyond the boundaries of conservative historical research and writing. Woodson not only pursued to examine primary and secondary documents but also addressed the influence of culture as the way of interpreting sources. He understood and shed light on the importance of collaborating and building professional networks in the academy and community through the establishment of the *Journal of Negro History* (1916) and the *Negro History Bulletin* (1937).

Woodson understood and shed light on the importance of collaborating and building connections. Through establishing the *Journal of Negro History* (1916) and the *Negro History Bulletin* (1937), Woodson became involved in coordinating a group of scholars trained in the academy of higher learning who expressed a commitment to the field and function of African American history.

In contemporary times, the name of the journal has been changed to the *Journal of African American History* (the name changed from the *Journal of Negro History* in 2001) and has faced the transition and office movement from Washington, DC, to Atlanta, Georgia, to its current office in New Orleans, Louisiana, at Dillard University. Still, Woodson's approach to the study of African American history and his analysis of the African past was critical. We must keep in mind the era in which he pursued his career. His scholarship was limited by several factors: Jim Crow laws, segregation, availability of funding opportunities, and even the use of manual typewriters to prepare manuscripts and documents. Yet he published more than 100 scholarly book reviews. Mentioned as the first African American of direct enslaved parentage to earn a doctorate in the United States (Goggin, 2014), Woodson became the second African American to be awarded a doctorate in history from Harvard University.

His efforts were impressive and exhibited his commitment to the field and function of African American history and prioritization of undergraduate education. Nowadays, we are afforded the amenities of freedom, technology, and information systems. Woodson's contributions should encourage us to further prepare, recover, and produce documents for the upcoming generations to advance African American history. Through his works and scholarship, he has provided a solid base for studying the educational, social, political, and economic conditions of African people throughout the diaspora.

Even so, Woodson's approach to the study of African American history and his analysis of the African past was critical. We must keep in mind the era in which he pursued his career. Cited as the first African American of direct enslaved parentage to earn a doctorate in the United States, Woodson became the second African American to be awarded a doctorate in history from Harvard University (Goggin, 1950).

Charles Harris Wesley, noted and prolific African American, ruminated on addressing the use of documents and reflexive analysis of Carter G. Woodson on the relevance of Black education, asserting in the segment:

On May 22, 1929, near the end of the year, Woodson wrote to Dr. Jesse E. Moorland, YMCA Secretary and a member of the Board of Trustees at Howard University:

"You have the weakness for good-for-nothing white people because of your broken-down theory that in the Negro schools the best of two races may be united. This has never been true and will never be until the Negroes have made such progress as to be recognized as the equals of whites. Immediately after the Civil War teachers of the missionary spirit went South to elevate the Negro and their work was noble and glorious. These teachers, however, were not the best of the white race but having the task of merely laying the foundation most of them did well. This same group of teachers, fall now far below the standard for the reason that they cannot carry the Negroes forward into the broader realms of reconstructed education . . . for they are teachers of yesterday unknown to the work of scientifically trained instructors in charge of white schools. It is all but criminal, therefore, for educational authorities to impose such medieval misfits on Negro institutions when these positions can be admirably filled by scientifically trained Negroes. As it now stands, you are largely responsible for subjecting the superior to the inferior" (Wesley, 1998, p. 146). In this connection, it is of interest to observe Woodson's philosophy of education. "When the Negro finished his course in one of our schools, he knows what others have done, but he has not been inspired to do much for himself. If he makes a success in life, it comes largely by accident" and again he said, "The time has come for all Negro schools to be turned over to Negroes" (Wesley, 1998, p. 3).

Paradoxically, the use of the terms *education* and *consciousness* are not mutually exclusive terms of reference. Whereas *education* is the structural aspect of retaining intelligence. Yolanda Sealy-Ruiz and Chance W. Lewis suspend a compelling analysis, stating:

> The field of education has been and will continue to be essential to the survival and sustainability of the Black community. Unfortunately, over the past five decades, two major trends have become clearly evident in the Black community: (a) the decline of the academic achievement levels of Black students and (b) the disappearance of Black teachers, particularly Black males. (Lewis, 2011, p. 187)

Figure 6.1 illustrates a concentric analysis of Afrocentric awareness as it relates to thought and consciousness, with the breakdown shifting to breakthrough tables: the creation of subordinate group status; identity and awareness and the Afrocentric perspective. Each sphere, which is correlated to the golden stool, draws an inference for locating African Americans with a spiritual and cultural base of development. Possibly, this initiates a context to describe and evaluate the alternative aspects of the Black perspective in a global framework.

On the other hand, consciousness is the acquisition, process, and analysis of information. In the previous, respondents begin to cultivate queries regarding the direct and indirect correlations of information. Kmt Shockley and Rona Frederick provide an assessment of Afrocentric perspective, with regard to education, writing the following:

> Hilliard's (1991) provocative question is surely one of the most important ones that has ever been asked to educationists. If "will"

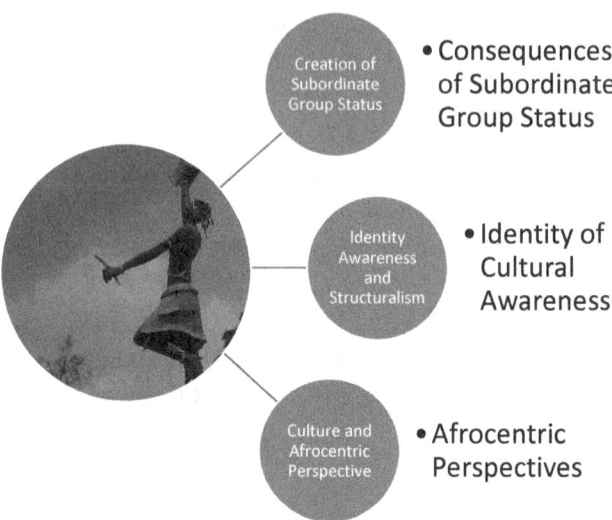

Figure 6.1 Afrocentric Awareness

includes the process of asserting one's choice to do something, the education community must ask itself whether or not it has the will to teach all children. More specifically, in this instance we must ask if educators, researchers, and policy makers actually have the will to effectively teach Black children. From an Afrocentric perspective, historical and cultural studies of Blacks require deep engagements with African history and culture because Blacks' roots are in Africa. (Shockley & Frederick, 2010, p. 1212)

A review of the literature outlines the intellectual history of this thesis can be located in selected seminal work. First, Carter G. Woodson (1933), the prolific African American historian and founder-creator of Black History Month, initiated the idea in his classic work *The Mis-Education of the Negro*. Molefi Kete Asante proposes a gloss of this source, writing:

Many of the principles that govern the development of the Afrocentric idea in education were first established by Carter G. Woodson in The Mis-education of the Negro (1933). Indeed, Woodson's classic reveals the fundamental problems pertaining to the education of the African person in America. As Woodson contends, African Americans have been educated away from their own culture and traditions and attached to the fringes of European culture; thus dislocated from themselves, Woodson asserts that African Americans often valorize European culture to the detriment of their own heritage (p. 7). Although Woodson does not advocate rejection of American citizenship or nationality, he believed that assuming African Americans hold the same position as European Americans vis-a-vis the realities of America would lead to the psychological and cultural death of the African American population. (Asante, 1991, p. 170)

Ongoing, Harold Cruse (1969), in the *Crisis of the Negro Intellectual*, ponders thought and ideas regarding the regulation of structural aspects of Black Radical Consciousness. Brilliantly organized is James Anderson's (1988) *History of Black Education*, which is an insightful and critical analysis of African American's quest to retain education.

The focus of this chapter is to examine three aspects of African consciousness, advancing an Afrocentric perspective. Using tools from both social science and humanistic disciplines, the configuration of data is interdisciplinary. Combining triangulation and meta-theoretical approaches to research, our base query is examining the epistemological and ontological parameters of Africana thought and praxis. Figure 6.2 is a triangulation configured on the contextual base analysis of consciousness. With regard to the recovery, retention, and reformation of Africana phenomena, recovery is the state of processing information. Retention, then, centers on memory and ethos.

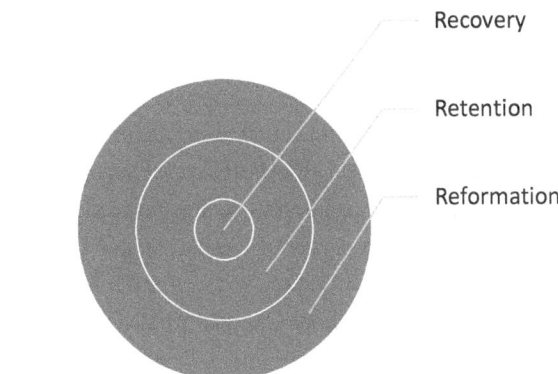

Figure 6.2 Contextual Base of Consciousness

Last, reformation is the last stage of reclaiming the two prior steps in placing in action the process of advancing toward a point of critical analysis.

Conclusion

Charles G. Woodson is one of the most prolific figures in the research and writing of African American history in the 20th century. Woodson went beyond the concepts of recognizing Black History Month or seeking his personal genealogy. He was interested in the quest for African history and culture. He carried out his pursuits by completing his own formal education and preparing documents for the teaching and application of African American history.

Woodson focused on building an institutional foundation centered around the African experience. That foundation still inspires many African American studies programs to provide corrections to old history, showing an educational balance and allowing our students to develop their own ideas and opinions about our history's truth.

In the context of his place and time, Woodson emerged as a ripened artisan who took on the challenge of entering the professorate. Although this reader is limited to the essays in this book, the body of Woodson's work extends far beyond the bounds of this primer, although this collection does organize Woodson scholarship thematically according to research areas of discovery, such as economic history, historiography, biography, and educational history.

Finally, this chapter contributes a reference, anthology, and foundational essay in the discipline of Africana Studies. In no way am I presenting Carter G. Woodson as a faultless person. Like other Americans, he had both weaknesses and strengths. Nevertheless, his overall aim was to promote research and writing on the African American experience. Reflective of the number of Black historians who have labored in the field of historiography to chronicle and discuss the Black experience, the tradition of Woodson intercedes as a predecessor for the acquisition, liberation, and restoration of Africana American history and culture. Accordingly, this chapter provides readers and researchers with a compilation of secondary sources and bibliography to examine the works of Woodson and, more important, a chronicle to conceptualize the history, occurrence, condition, and systematic subordination of African Americans.

Appendix A

Biographical Profile of Carter G. Woodson

Year	Event
1875	Woodson is born on December 19 in New Canton, Virginia, in Buckingham County, to the parents of Anne Eliza (Riddle) and James Henry Woodson. His parents were enslaved. It is reported that Woodson is the first African American of enslaved parentage to earn a PhD in history. (Goggin, 2014).
1892	Woodson is drawn by the need for employment to work in the coal mines; he moves to Huntington, West Virginia, to live with his brother, Robert Henry. Eventually, Woodson earned his living as a miner in Fayette County coalfields.
1895	Woodson enrolls in Douglass High School and completes four years of course work in two years.
1897	He receives his high school diploma from Douglass High School in Huntington, West Virginia (Douglass High School is segregated).
1896–97	Woodson is admitted to attend study at Berea College, in Berea, Kentucky.
1897	Woodson attends Lincoln University, in Philadelphia, Pennsylvania, for one year of undergraduate study.
1898–1900	Woodson begins teaching in Winona, West Virginia, and two years later, he becomes the principal at Douglass High School.
1912	Woodson is notified by Dean Louis B. Moore at Howard University that Woodson was chosen to fill a teaching position in the college of education. Woodson turns down the offer.
1914	Woodson seeks membership into the Harvard Club in Washington, DC. When it is learned that he is an African American, the membership is canceled.
1914	Woodson takes a loan out from Penn, Mutual Insurance Company to pay for the publication of the *Education of the Negro Prior to 1861*.
1915	Woodson organizes the Association for the Study of Negro Life and History (ASNLH) at Wabash Avenue YMCA in Chicago on September 9. Woodson meets with Alexander L. Jackson, executive secretary of the new Negro YMCA branch; in addition to Woodson and Jackson, three other gentlemen were present: George C. Hall, W. B. Hargrove, and J. E. Stamps. They formed the ASNLH and appointed Dr. Woodson executive director, which he held until his death.
1915	Woodson accepts an invitation from Booker T. Washington to speak at Tuskegee Institute.
1915	Woodson is engaged in research and writing at the University of Chicago.
1915	Woodson (1919) publishes *The Education of the Negro Prior to 1861*.
1916	Woodson establishes the *Journal of Negro History* (*JNH*). January 1 was the date of the first volume; in April, the second issue of JNH was published.
1916	Woodson attends America Conference.
1916	Woodson delivers a paper at the University of Chicago on the *Varying Attitudes of the White Man toward the Negro in the United States*. No copy of this paper exists.
1918	ASNLH begins its publishing program.

1918	Woodson (1918) publishes *A Century of Negro Migration*.
1918	Roscoe Bruce appoints Woodson to be principal and teacher at Armstrong Manual Training High School in Washington, DC.
1918–1919	Woodson serves as an instructor in Miner Normal School (institutional name changed later to District of Columbia Teachers College).
1918	Woodson and Du Bois meet to discuss the National Association for the Advancement of Colored People (NAACP) plan to publish a series of volumes on Black participation in the war.
1918	Woodson organizes a local club in Washington DC, which focuses on a group of five or more individuals who had interest in studying African history and culture.
1919	Red Summer Riots; there is rioting in Washington DC.
1919	Woodson is offered the presidency at West Virginia Collegiate Institute (WVCI). He declines the offer. (The institutional name was later changed to West Virginia State College.) He recommends John E. Davis for the position, and he becomes the president of WVCI.
1919	The *Journal of Negro History* becomes self-supporting.
1919	Woodson develops a graduate program in the history department at Howard University.
1920	In the spring, Woodson engages in critique and disagreements with Howard University President J. Stanley Durkee. In July, Woodson's employment is terminated at Howard University.
1920	In June, Woodson is writing correspondence to Wilberforce University, expressing his regards and interest in serving as a superintendent of the combined normal and instructional school.
1920–1922	Woodson serves as the dean of the College of Arts and Sciences at WVCI.
1920	In October, Arnette Lindsay is the first student to complete the MA in the graduate program in history at Howard University. Woodson is the thesis advisor.
1920s	During the early 1920s, Woodson spends a good deal of his time marketing and soliciting funds for the ASNLH.
1921	Woodson establishes and organizes Associated Publishers, Inc in Washington, DC.
1921	Carnegie Corporation appropriated $25,000 to ASNLH; Laura Spelman Rockefeller Memorial awards Woodson $25,000 for research and writing on the African American experience.
1921	Woodson publishes *Early Negro Education in West Virginia* and *The History of the Negro Church*.
1922	In the summer of this year, A. A. Taylor joins Woodson's research staff.
1922	Woodson receives a grant from the Social Science Research Council.
1922	Woodson participated in the NAACP marches against lynching (Goggin, 1993, p. 153).
1922	Woodson publishes *The Negro in Our History*.
1922	Woodson begins a series of spring conferences for the ASNLH.
1923	Woodson invites W. E. B. Du Bois to address the ASNLH.
1923	Langston Hughes comes to work for the ASNLH.

1925	Woodson publishes *Black Orators and Their Orations*.
1926	Woodson establishes Negro History Week in Washington, DC, to celebrate African American history and culture. In 1976, the celebration is extended to a month.
1926	Mordecai W. Johnson becomes the first African American president of Howard University.
1926	W. E. B. Du Bois nominates Woodson for the Moorland Spingarn Award; Woodson is awarded the Moorland Spingarn Award from the NAACP.
1927	Woodson establishes an alternate division of the ASNLH, called the Home Study Group.
1927	In the summer, he serves on an advisory committee for the Social Science Research Council.
1927	ASALH meets in St. Louis at the Central Baptist Church.
1927	Woodson hires Lorenzo Greene as a research assistant for the ASNLH.
1928	Woodson hires Charles H. Wesley as a researcher and writer to work on a comparative study of the Black Church.
1928	Woodson condenses his study *The Negro in Our History* into *Negro Makers of History* for junior high school students.
1930	Woodson coauthors a book with Lorenzo Green, *The Negro Wage Earner*.
1930s	During the early 1930s, Woodson assembles a cohort cluster of historians who are committed to the teaching, research, and writing of Black history. It is believed by some that this may have been the evolutionary stages for Black history to emerge as a cognitive field of study within the discipline of history (Meier & Rudwick, 1986; Thorpe, 1971).
1930	On October 27, Woodson gives an inspirational lecture on African American history and culture at the ASNLH Convention at Cleveland College.
1930	Woodson publishes *The Rural Negro*.
1930s	Woodson begins writing weekly opinion editorials for the *Negro World* (Goggin, 1993, p. 152).
1931–32	Woodson begins to write press releases voicing his criticism and views about the shortcomings of historically Black colleges' and universities' approach to teaching the liberal arts and social sciences.
1933	Woodson publishes *The Miseducation of the Negro*.
1934	John Hope, president of Atlanta University (AU), offers Woodson a teaching position at AU and also offers to partially fund the *Journal of Negro History*. Woodson turns the offer down.
1934	Woodson publishes *The Negro Professional Man*.
1935	By this year, a reported 350 articles and series monographs had been published in the *Journal of Negro History*. Of the 350 articles, more than 200 focused on the research and writing of the African American experience.

Appendix B

Primary and Secondary Sources

Microfilm
   THE CARTER G. WOODSON COLLECTION OF NEGRO PAPERS AND RELATED DOCUMENTS, 1803-1936, Washington, DC, Library of Congress
   10 reels, 35mm microfilm. Correspondence, diaries, addresses, legal documents, newspaper clippings, and other papers relating to Negro history, the *Journal of Negro History*, race relations, slavery, discrimination, Washington, DC, employment opportunities, the African Methodist Episcopal Church, State and local politics, and business. The papers of Benjamin T. Banner, Whitefield McKinlay, and John T. Clark are included in this collection.

Documents
   Moorland Spingarn Collection, Howard University, Washington, DC
   Author: Woodson, Carter Godwin, 1875-1950
   Title: Papers, 1922-1941
   Description: .5 linear ft
   Notes: Educator, historian, and founder of the Association for the Study of Negro Life and History. Chiefly correspondence between Woodson and his sister, Bessie W. Yancey, and with business correspondents, concerning the purchase and upkeep of a house in Huntington, W. Va.; together with statements, clippings, and other papers, relating to Black life and history.

References

Anderson, J. D. (1988). *The education of Blacks in the south, 1865-1935*. Chapel Hill, North Carolina: The University of North Carolina Press.

Asante, M. K. (1991). The Afrocentric idea in education. *Journal of Negro Education, 60*(2), pp. 170-180.

Conyers, J. L. (1997). Culture, Language, and Symbols in Africana Studies: An Etymological Study. In J. L. Conyers, Jr. (Ed.), *Africana studies: A disciplinary quest for both theory and method*. Jefferson, North Carolina: McFarland Publishers.

Conyers, J. L. (2000). *Carter G. Woodson: A historical reader*. New York, NY: Garland.

Cruse, H. (1969). *The crisis of the Negro intellectual*, London: W.H. Allen.

Dagbovie, P. G. (1999). *The function and responsibility of the black intellectual as personified and dictated by Carter G. Woodson and Lorenzo Greene: A comprehensive historiographical and critical assessment*. Unpublished PhD Dissertation, Michigan State University.

Goggin, J. (1993). *Carter G. Woodson: A life in Black history*. Baton Rouge: Louisiana State University Press.

Goggin, J. (2014). Carter G. Woodson (1875–1950). *Encyclopedia Virginia*. Virginia Humanities, 27 May.

Meier, A. & Rudwick, E. M. (1986). *Black history and the historical profession, 1915–80*. University of Illinois Press.

Romero, P. W. (1971). *Carter G. Woodson: A biography*. Unpublished PhD dissertation, The Ohio State University.

Sealy-Ruiz, Y. & Lewis, C. W. (2011). Guest editorial: Transforming the field of education to serve the needs of the Black community: Implications for critical stakeholder. *The Journal of Negro Education, 80*(3), 187–190.

Shockley, K. G. & Frederick, R. (2010). Constructs and dimensions of Afrocentric education. *Journal of Black Studies, 40*(6), 1212–1233

Thorpe, E. E. (1971). *Black historians: A critique*. Morrow.

Wesley, C. H. (1998). Recollections of Carter G. Woodson. *The Journal of Negro History, 83*(2), 143–149.

Williams, A. L. (1994). *Carter G. Woodson: Scientific historian of African American history and education*. Unpublished PhD dissertation, Loyola University of Chicago, IL.

Woodson, C. G. (1918). *A century of Negro migration*. Washington, DC: The Association for the Study of Negro Life and History.

Woodson, C. G. (1919). *The education of the Negro prior to 1861*. Washington, DC: The Associated Publishers, Inc.

Woodson, C. G. (1921). *Early Negro education in West Virginia Institute*. West Virginia: West Virginia Collegiate Institute.

Woodson, C. G. (1922). *The Negro in our history*. Washington, DC: The Associated Publishers, Inc.

Woodson, C. G. (1925). *Black orators and their orations*. Washington, DC: The Associated Publishers, Inc.

Woodson, C. G. (1928). *Negro makers of history*. Washington, DC: The Associated Publishers, Inc.

Woodson, C. G. (1930). *The Negro professional man*. Washington, DC: The Association for the Study of Negro Life and History.

Woodson, C. G. (1930). *The Negro wage earner*. Washington, DC: The Association for the Study of Negro Life and History.

Woodson, C. G. (1930). *The rural Negro*. Washington, DC: The Association for the Study of Negro Life and History.

Woodson, C. G. (1933). *The Mis-education of the Negro*. Washington, DC: Associated Publishers, 1933

Woodson, C. G. (2003). *The Miseducation of the Negro*, San Diego, California: The Book Tree, reprint of 1933 edition, p. 3.

Young, A. (1977). *The educational philosophies of Booker T. Washington and Carter G. Woodson: A liberating praxis*. Unpublished PhD dissertation, Syracuse University, Syracuse, NY.

SEVEN

"You Have to Get Your Mind Right for This": Black Women's Graduate School Experiences

Crystal Edwards

SCHOLARS HAVE NOTED THAT THROUGHOUT the last several decades, there have been significant shifts in the overall landscape of higher education (Anderson, 2003; Eckel, Green & Hill, 1997; Kuh, 1990; Orfield, Marin & Horn, 2005; Woodard, Love & Komives, 2000; Zamani, 2003). Zamani (2003) asserts that:

> One particularly visible change is in the composition of the college-going population: postsecondary institutions enroll increasing numbers of individuals from groups historically excluded from higher education because of their racial or ethnic background, socioeconomic class, or sex. (p. 5)

In line with this observation, the Digest of Education Statistics (2017a, 2017b) reports that between 2015 and 2016, Black Women accounted for 70,595 of the master's and doctoral degrees conferred by postsecondary institutions, almost five times the number of postsecondary degrees conferred to Black women between 1976 and 1977. Accounting for double the number of graduate degrees conferred for Black males and constituting the second-largest group among women of color, Black women represent a significant population of students enrolled in graduate programs.

Despite the increasing presence of Black women on college campuses and their enrollment in postsecondary programs, many challenges impede the progress and success of Black women graduate students. I posit that their intersectional identities account for an explanation as to why their experiences remain relatively invisible in higher education research.

Black Feminist scholar Kimberlé Crenshaw (1991) defines *intersectionality* as "the various ways in which race and gender interact to shape the multiple dimensions of Black women's [experiences]" (1993, p. 1244). Intersectionality seeks to make visible the ways in which the experiences of Black women cannot be understood within narrow frameworks that do not recognize the "multidimensionality of Black women's experiences" by expanding the traditional boundaries of analysis that isolate either race or gender (Crenshaw, 1989, p. 139; 1991). In this vein, this study seeks to explore the ways in which current and former Black women graduate students' intersectional identities have an impact on their experience in the academy. Additionally, the chapter addresses the following questions:

> What are some of the primary factors that have impacted your success in your program?
>
> What factors have been beneficial in overcoming and resisting obstacles during your academic life?

Utilizing an open-ended-question survey with current and former Black women graduate students, this chapter seeks to provide a narrative experience of Black women in graduate programs. Additionally, the chapter highlights the unique obstacles and challenges faced by Black women graduate students. Furthermore, this chapter adds to the discussion of ways in which Black women continue to resist marginalization.

Theoretical Framework: Decolonial Black Feminist Epistemology

For this study, I employ a framework I refer to as Decolonial Black Feminist Epistemology. With this framework, I engage two theoretical traditions: Black Feminist Epistemology of the Black Feminist Thought framework introduced by scholar Patricia Hill Collins (2009) and decolonial theory. In my reframing of the two theories, my position is not that Black Feminist Epistemology is not decolonial or that decolonial theory does not include components of Black Feminist Epistemology; rather, the goal of this approach is to place these frameworks in direct conversation with one another. More specifically, this approach utilizes the components of Black Feminist Epistemology to prioritize the narrative experience of Black women graduate students (i.e., the micro level) while simultaneously providing a context of the university that has historical served the function of maintaining and perpetuating oppressive conditions and existing power structures (Mignolo, 2011a; 2011b; Nyoni, 2013).

Decolonial Theory

Differing qualitatively from postcolonial theory, decolonial theory provides a critique of Eurocentrism that centers the perspective of groups that have historically been marginalized and oppressed. Specifically, decolonial theory situates and privileges subaltern thinkers, or groups that: (1) "operate within the power structures of a dominant culture"; (2) experience cultural exclusion and devaluation; and (3) are forced—either through consent or coercion—to "[accept] the concepts and values of the dominant culture including the social and evaluative place assigned" to them (Ketchum, 1980, p. 152). Decolonial theory posits three fundamental principles: (1) the coloniality of power, (2) the coloniality of knowledge, and (3) the coloniality of Being.

Coloniality of power addresses the existing global hierarchies of power associated with multiple entanglements, such as race/ethnicity, gender, politics, spirituality, epistemology, economic status, and linguistics (Grosfoguel, 2007). Ultimately, this principle asserts that oppression operates on multiple levels simultaneously. The *coloniality of knowledge* refers to the hierarchical organization of epistemologies or ways of knowing. Historically, Western knowledge has been classified as superior and the knowledge of colonized subjects has been deemed inferior or, in many cases, invisible (Grosfoguel, 2007; Maldonado-Torres, 2007; Ndlovu-Gatsheni, 2013). Particularly significant in discussions of the modern university, coloniality of knowledge functions as a critique of "traditional" educational spaces. Decolonial theory is particularly critical of the university asserting that this space has historically been a key mechanism in the perpetuation of Western hegemony. Last, the *coloniality of Being* highlights the ways in which those deemed "other" are dehumanized and made invisible. Additionally, decolonial scholar Maldonado-Torres (2007) draws the connection between the coloniality of Being and knowledge, arguing that due to the reality that people of the subaltern have been excluded ontologically, the logic of coloniality asserts an inherent irrationality and an inferior "way of thinking" (p. 258) of subaltern knowledge.

Black Feminist Epistemology

Black Feminist Thought is a theoretical framework that centers on the history and experiences of Black women in America from the diverse and unique perspective of Black women across space and time. Patricia Hill-Collins (2009) notes that Black feminist thought "reflects the interest and standpoint of its creators... emphasizing the importance of intersecting oppressions in shaping the U.S. matrix of domination" (p. 269). A key paradigm of Black Feminist Thought is Black Feminist Epistemology, which is founded on five principles: (1) lived experience as a criterion of meaning, (2) the use of dialogue in assessing knowledge claims, (3) the ethics of caring, (4) the ethic of personal accountability, and (5) Black women as agents of knowledge. Although all five principles are relevant to the understanding of Black women's experience, three principles in particular inform my research: lived experience as a criterion of meaning, the use of dialogue in assessing knowledge claims, and Black women as agents of knowledge.

The principle "lived experience as a criterion meaning" asserts that there are two types of knowing, knowledge and wisdom. Black Feminist Epistemology asserts that knowledge is learned through teaching, while wisdom is gained through experience. This principle asserts the relevance of knowledge but highlights the significance of wisdom as being "essential to the survival of subordinate [marginalized cultures]" (Hill-Collins, 2009, p. 276). The "use of dialogue in assessing knowledge claims" principle posits that mutual conversation aids in asserting humanity, "resist[ing] domination," and encourages the development of "new knowledge claims" (Hill-Collins, 2009, p. 279). Hill-Collins (2009) states, "Ethics of caring suggests that personal expressiveness, emotions, and empathy are central to the knowledge validation process... [and] individual uniqueness" is emphasized (p. 281). The principle "ethics of personal accountability" primarily addresses scholars and others who produce work on the history and experiences of Black women. This principle not only assesses an "individual's knowledge claims," but simultaneously, the principle also evaluates the "individual's character, values, and ethics" (Hill-Collins, 2009, p. 284). Last, the "Black women as agents of knowledge" principle affirms Black women's agency in their efforts to create work about Black women's history.

Decolonial Black Feminist Epistemology

As indicated earlier, to provide a cohesive discussion of the experience of Black women in graduate programs, I utilize the theory which I refer to as "Decolonial Black Feminist Epistemology," although decolonial theory provides a historical account of the interconnected oppression Black women experience in the university. Furthermore, decolonial theory centers the experiences within the global conditions that led to the historical marginalization and dehumanization of African-descended people. Finally, decolonial theory's principle of coloniality of knowledge provides crucial insight regarding the Eurocentric logic that undergirds institutions of formal education, particularly universities.

While decolonial theory offers much to the analysis of Black women's experience, decolonial theory has often been geographically centered in Latin American. Additionally, many of the founding scholars of this theoretical framework are male and self-identify as Latin American; as such, there are limited U.S.-based analyses that properly make visible the unique operations of structures of power and how defined structures perpetuate various forms of oppression in the U.S. context. Further, the voices and experiences of Black women and girls are relatively absent—although often assumed to be implicit—in the decolonial project. It is in this vein that Black Feminist Epistemology situates Black women's experience and provides an imperative shift in focus and narrative. Black Feminist Epistemology offers a lens through which the experiences of Black women graduate students experience their reality. As expressed by Hill-Collins (1990), "Placing Black women's experiences at the center of analysis offers fresh insights on the prevailing concepts, paradigms, and epistemologies of the world view" (p. 221). Although Black Feminist Thought inherently allows for the in-depth discussion of the experiences of Black girls within the existing "European/capitalist/military/Christian/patriarchal/White/heterosexual/male" matrix of domination, my position is that in discussions of the educational context, including the discussion of sociohistorical factors that have created the reality of oppressive and detrimental conditions in academic institutions is necessary (Grosfoguel, 2008, p. 8).

Placing the two theoretical approaches—Black Feminist Epistemology and decolonial theory—in direct conversation not only provides a narrative description of the experience of Black women in graduate school (i.e., the micro level) but also provides a context (i.e., the macro level) of the historical foundations of the university and the ways the institution has been established to maintain and perpetuate the oppressive conditions for Black women. Although this realization would likely be overlooked when utilizing traditional frameworks that merely seek to interpret or make deductions from the perspective of the researcher—with their own subjectivities—Decolonial Black Feminist Epistemology ensures that the perspective of Black women is expressed in its authenticity. As such, terminology remains in the original form, acknowledging that traditional frameworks tend to marginalize the knowledge of those who do not uphold the Eurocentric standards of communication and speech. Through the lens of Decolonial Black Feminist Epistemology, I provide insight on what the participants identify as not only the most pressing obstacles and challenges but also, more important, the strategies they have developed to cope, overcome, and persevere.

Methodology and Research Design

Methodology

The theoretical approach utilized in this study is Decolonial Black Feminist Epistemology. This theoretical approach has been utilized to emphasize three key points: First, formal educational spaces and academic institutions have historically been organized to establish, reinforce, and maintain ideologies and epistemologies oppressive and detrimental to those considered "other" or do not occupy the identity of "European/capitalist/military/Christian/patriarchal/white/heterosexual/male" (Grosfoguel, 2008, p. 8). Thus, that negative messages and experiences are inevitable is to be expected. Second, considering Black women occupy a unique intersectional identity, their experiences will provide a particular—and inevitably invaluable—narrative of the obstacles and challenges plaguing academic institutions, generally, and graduate programs, particularly. Third, any analysis seeking to discuss the experiences of Black women must necessarily center their experiences and allow for them to explain and describe the world and their experiences from their perspective and logic—on their terms and in their words. Recognizing the key points of my chosen theoretical framework, the method I chose for the study, as well as the way I have implemented the method, fit within this approach.

Methodologically, open-ended surveys ensure that participants can discuss their reality, in their own words, with a level of self-prioritization. This promotes the inherent goal of safeguarding that participants are exercising agency—the "capacity for autonomous social action ... [or] the ability of actors to operate independently of the determining constraints of social structure" (Calhoun, as quoted in Biesta & Tedder, 2006, p. 5; Hull & Smith, 2001). Because the primary aim of my theoretical framework—Decolonial Black Feminist Epistemology—is to privilege the perspectives and experiences of those who are often ignored and made invisible in contemporary narratives, the open-ended surveys allow for the participants to prioritize events and experiences they deem to be the most significant or relevant, inevitably "highlight[ing] issues important to the participant" (Kenten, 2010; Kitzinger, 1995). Unlike researcher observations, surveys are inherently from the perspective/lens of the individual experiencing the reality and based on self-reporting (Asante, 1988). Open-ended surveys provide the "ability to explore meanings and, in particular, meanings ascribed to events and circumstances by actors rather than observers" (Sofaer, 1999, p. 1108). In line with the study goal, open-ended surveys give the participants control and agency over the narrative that is meant to represent them.

Research Design

Methods. For this study, I utilize open-ended surveys as the sole means of data collection. Open-ended surveys are a qualitative research method that is commonly used "to learn about beliefs, attitudes, reported behaviors, or experiences prevalent in a population" (J. Carey, Morgan & Oxtoby, 1996, p. 1). Utilizing structured questions, surveys can either seek close-ended responses or open-ended responses, as is the case in this study. Additionally, open-ended surveys are utilized to "explore complex issues that do not have a finite or predetermined set of responses" (J. Carey et al., 1996, p. 1). The study survey was composed of 15 questions: 5 close-ended screening and consent questions and 10 open-ended questions. The survey was administered digitally via a confidential online form.

Participants. This study includes a sample size of 18 participants who identify as Black women and are current or former graduate students. The graduate degree pursued or earned varied, with 10 participants indicating they earned or were pursuing graduate degrees, 4 indicating doctoral degrees, and 4 participants who did not specify. Programs varied vastly, including social work, human development and family sciences, media design, East Asian studies, library and information science, education (with various focus and concentrations), biotechnology, health sciences, family nurse practitioner, public health, sociology, accounting, public administration, and operations management. An added benefit of the online survey was that recruitment of participants from across the nation was possible. The regional breakdown is as follows:

Midwest	5
Southwest	6
Southeast	2
Northeast	1
Online	4

In the same vein, nine participants identified attending a predominately White institution (PWI), two attended historically Black colleges or universities (HBCUs), and seven participants did not specify.

Inclusion/Exclusion criteria. Participants included in the study met the following criteria: racially identify as Black, have a gendered identification as women, be a graduate of or be currently enrolled in master's and/or doctoral programs, and be 18 and older at the time of consent. A series of close-ended questions were utilized at the beginning of the survey to confirm these criteria. Conversely, potential participants were excluded if they in any way did not meet the aforementioned inclusion criteria. Additionally, due to the digital nature of the survey and the limited capacity for assistance from the administrator, participants incapable of completing the digital survey were also excluded. Last, the survey was only offered in English, so non-English speakers were excluded.

Recruitment. Participants for this study were recruited through snowball recruitment and word of mouth. Recruitment was done digitally and via online mediums. E-mail invitations were sent to professional and social networks. Recognizing the growing popularity of social media sites such as Facebook, Twitter, and Instagram, scholars have begun to recognize the efficiency of utilizing the forums to aid in the recruitment of participants (Khatri et al., 2015). As such, social media sites were also utilized to solicit participants.

Data collection and analysis. Data were collected via the online survey program Qualtrics. This program was chosen for because it is user-friendly and easily accessible from a PC, laptop, or mobile device. All surveys were anonymous; identifying or contact information was not collected. In the recruitment e-mail and online postings, potential participants were provided with the survey link. The first five questions of the survey were aimed at acquiring consent and screening to ensure participants meet inclusion criteria. The 10 open-ended questions were designed to understand the participants' graduate institutions and programs, prominent identities, overall graduate experience, challenges, and solutions. Surveys were accepted for a six-week period.

Once all the surveys were collected, preliminary review and coding began. The survey software includes computer-assisted data analysis capabilities. Barry (1998) posits, computer-assisted data-analysis software:

> Help[s] automate and thus speed up and liven up the coding process; provide[s] a more complex way of looking at the relationships in the data; provide[s] a formal structure for writing and storing memos to develop the analysis; and, aid[s] more conceptual and theoretical thinking about the data. (para 2.1)

In line with this argument, the software provided a secure and convenient way to organize and analyze the data. Data were analyzed inductively, with responses coded thematically question by question. To ensure that I was remaining open to uncovering new themes and codes, I avoided merely searching for the existing codes as I analyzed the individual questions; instead, I opted to create new codes. After the analysis was completed for each question, I went through the final themes, consolidating and merging similar codes.

Practical concerns and limitations. The primary limitations associated with the study are linked to the open-ended survey method and the overall generalizability of the study. Although open-ended surveys provide a forum for participants to express a more elaborate response to the questions than close-ended responses, the lack of participant/researcher interaction impedes the ability to ask follow-up, probing, or clarifying questions. As such, unlike other qualitative methods, such as interviews or focus groups, open-ended surveys require a greater degree researcher interpretation during analysis, which, depending on researchers' familiarity and understanding of the participant population, can make misinterpretations more likely. To limit the impact of this concern, questions were intentionally framed explicitly to limit misinterpretation by the participant. Additionally, there were no limits to the participant response; this was done to encourage participants to provide responses that were as detailed as possible, with the aim of limiting researcher misinterpretation.

Another limitation of the study is associated with this study is overall generalizability. Due to the sample size and the recruitment methods utilized, this study is not intended be generalizable or to claim a monolithic representation of the experience of all Black women graduate students. However, the similarities and themes revealed by the participant responses provide a basis for a claim of some shared experience. Furthermore, the study is primarily concerned with providing a narrative of lived experience, calling "attention to the social context [i.e. academic institutions] in which events occur and have meaning," emphasizing "understanding the social world from the point of view of the participants," and providing a foundation for further exploration and solution formulation (Labuschagne, 2003, p. 103).

Findings

The following discussion includes the themes derived from the participants' responses. For ease of discussion, I first provide a brief overview of the most prominent identities as outlined by the participants. I then discuss the primary challenges the participants revealed, specifically faculty, campus environment, and individual challenges. Last, I discuss the major themes associated with solutions or pragmatic strategies the participants implemented to overcome the obstacles, such as the development of community, identifying supplemental resources, and self-care.

Identity

As the focus of this study is to understand the relationship between the intersectional identities of former and current Black women graduate students, one of the survey questions was aimed at self-identification and prioritization of most prominent identities. Although there were minor fluctuations, the most prominent identities were revealed to be (listed in order according to responses):

Race
Gender
Sexual Orientation (specific identities revealed to be Queer and Lesbian)
Religion (specific identities revealed to be Christian and Agnostic)
Age
Familial Status (i.e., married, parent, etc.)

Participants were also asked if they perceive any, all, or none of their prominent identities to have or had an impact on their graduate school experience. Although several participants noted that they did not believe their identity had a significant impact on their graduate school experience, many participants identified their race and gender to be the identities that most greatly affected their experience. Rayven reports that she "felt like people did not feel comfortable with my assertion of self as Black and woman in an intellectual space" (participants have been assigned pseudonyms for reference). Similarly, Jennifer revealed, "My Blackness and womanhood very much impacted my experience. None of the other students in my program who were not of color experienced anything close to the trauma I sustained."

Lanecia, Tiffany, and Ameia noted that their race and gender had an impact on levels of support and perceptions regarding preparedness or intellectual capacity. Three participants identified their race alone as having the most substantial effect. Erica asserted, "It was really race that impacted . . . how I was perceived and received." None of the participants identified their gender alone as a factor. Although far fewer participants explicitly identified age or sexual orientation—as expressed in Kayla's declaration that her "my sexual orientation may have been involved in a few obstacles faced"—to have had the greatest impact on their graduate experience; it is relevant to acknowledge that one participant each emphasized these aspects of their identity.

Challenges

In addition to highlighting participants' perceptions regarding their intersectional identities and the potential ways in which those identities had an impact on their graduate school experience, the survey was also designed to provide narratives of challenges and obstacles faced by the women. Participants were asked to first describe their experience, then they were asked to discuss, if any, the factors that impacted or impeded their success. Based on the participant responses, the obstacles most salient in their success fell into the following categories: faculty, campus environment, and individual challenges.

Faculty

Department faculty was one of the most discussed factors that participants perceived to have an impact on their graduate school experience. The primary grievances were (a) a lack of support and disinterest; (b) discord with committee chairs and advisors; and (c) discrimination.

Lack of support and disinterest. Several of the participants expressed that one of their greatest obstacles in graduate school was associated with the lack of support from department faculty and their overall disinterest. When asked about her experience, Erica proclaimed, "There was just an overall lack of support." She went on to assert that "faculty were allowed to dismiss your presence in the program and regularly call into question your competence." In a similar vein, Christian highlighted that when experiencing challenges in her program, her attempts to reach out to faculty were often fruitless. She asserts that when e-mailing a professor, a timely response was not guaranteed and that most times, she had to "pray that he or she answers."

Participants also communicate a lack of support specifically with regards to their academic endeavors and research interests. Rayven revealed, "I felt like I did not have an advisor or faculty advocate." To this discussion, Tiffany added that not only did she not feel supported by the faculty in her program but that she also experienced an overall disinterest. She expressed that "certain professors were visibly and vocally opposed" to her research interests.

Similarly, Ameia asserted, "I am in Year 2 of my studies and it has been abysmal. I have been discouraged by professors ... [and] I have been misadvised."

Unfortunately, Tiffany highlighted the limited recourse in mediating disinterest and a lack of support, asserting, "Despite maintaining a 3.9 GPA in the program there were never any offerings of support services, financial or otherwise during my time in the program."

Discord with committee chair and advisors. In the same vein as the lack of overall support and general disinterest of faculty, conflict with committee chairs and advisors also proved to be an obstacle. Although only mentioned by two participants explicitly, considering the vital role committee chairs and advisors play in program matriculation and degree attainment, the impact discord has on Black women's graduate school experience is relevant to note. Kayla identified "having a chair that you could not connect with caused major issues and time wasted." When asked to describe her overall graduate experience, she expressed friction and disagreement with her former committee chair was one of her greatest hurdles. Similarly, Britney elaborated on this point, revealing:

> A particular dissertation committee member created challenges for me that slowed down the progress of my dissertation due to his inability to understand bias and discrimination in education. While he was just supposed to advise me on my methodology, he truly felt that there was no systemic racism with education, and made me write additional chapters and redo statistical models to a point where I spent an additional semester writing.

As expressed by both Kayla and Britney, discord with the committee chair and members caused significant obstacles, ultimately leading to prolonging the academic process.

Discrimination. As briefly mentioned in the discussion regarding identities, racial and gendered identities, specifically, played a role in the experience of the multiple participants. Several of them explicitly noted interactions with faculty that they perceived to be blatantly racist and/or sexist. Ameia asserted that the daily challenges she and her peers faced in the program were directly connected to racism on the part of faculty. Erica highlighted this point:

With the men professors, two of them were blatantly racist. So much so, that it made you want to drop from the program. Their verbal push was used to intimidate and make you [want to] drop. So, we elected not to go to them.

Jennifer noted witnessing "highly racist and gender discriminatory behaviors of the faculty." She elaborated:

One faculty member who had hired me as an associate instructor refused to look at me when I spoke, and instead spoke through me to my White male counterpart. He was quite verbally abusive, and many other students had come forward with complaints about him, yet nothing was done because of the tenure system. Another faculty told me to my face that Black students just under-perform, and that Black males in particular were scary. Another faculty member stated that all Asian women looked the same and that we needed to not worry so much about mental health.

Jennifer concludes that despite her efforts, the faculty members received no penalty for their behavior, leaving one to surmise that the behavior likely persisted.

Campus Environment

Like the experience of discrimination in respective programs, participants expressed an overall volatile and isolating campus environment. Recognizing that the majority of participants revealed that they attended PWIs, that racial diversity posed a challenge is to be expected. Several participants note obstacles associated with the lack of diversity among the student demographic. Two participants note that due to the lack of diversity, they are routinely mistaken for another Black woman. Ameia expressed feeling like she was treated as an "other." In addition to feeling like an "other," Jennifer revealed that the lack of diversity on the campus forced her to deal with "White supremacist groups on campus" and that during her experience on campus, she was faced with the "worst discrimination and racist attitudes" she had ever experienced. This lack of diversity was not only visible regarding students, but participants also expressed challenges associated with the lack of Black faculty. Tiffany expressed that one of the things she found challenging was being the "only Black woman in all of my classes with no Black faculty." She concluded that she "would have liked to see more Black faculty within her program." Similarly, when asked about events that stand out during her graduate experience, Lanecia called attention to "the lack of presence of other African Americans teaching."

Related to the limited visibility and diversity of perspective campuses, participants point out, in several instances, feeling isolated and lacking spaces where they could build community. Aiesha communicated this challenge, stating, "I think the biggest thing that I feel has made it difficult to be here is feeling as if I am on an island." She added, "It made me, honestly, have a permanent distress." Tiffany expressed that she "often felt isolated and urged to find community outside of [her] department." Christian shared a similar feeling of isolation resulting from limited communication with her classmates.

Individual challenges. In addition to obstacles associated with faculty and overall campus environment, multiple participants disclosed individual challenges. Three participants identified familial responsibilities and finances as being individual challenges. Kayla revealed that during her program, she became pregnant and suffered major complications; as such, she asserted that it hindered her progress. Cassandra expressed that familial responsibilities associated with ill parents in a different state had an impact on her experience, particularly when she was forced to travel for emergencies. Additionally, Cassandra noted that her financial responsibilities and full-time employment prevented her from being able to take advantage of conference opportunities and that she was unable to "dedicate as much time as [she] would have liked to on campus. Similarly, Breonna revealed that she "struggled significantly when it came to finances." According to her, not only did her lack of financial awareness have an impact on her emotionally, but the lack of available family financial assistance had implications for her completing her program, an obstacle that she was able to overcome with faculty assistance.

Individual challenges were not limited to family and financial challenges. Several participants expressed challenges associated with their perceptions of self-efficacy—"an individual's belief in his or her capacity to execute behaviors necessary to produce specific performance attainments"—and their academic performance (M. Carey & Forsyth, 2019, para. 1). Hazel expressed her challenges with self-efficacy, stating she felt "intimidated" and "unprepared." She added:

> Graduate school was very tough. Starting off, I already felt behind. . . . I felt that my [prior] education and degree were of much less caliber. There was so much that I did not know or understand.

Janel shared a similar experience with feeling overwhelmed by the demands associated with the transition from undergrad to her graduate program. She revealed that "reading, writing, and application" proved to be a challenge and a significant source of stress, so much so that it interfered with her ability to maintain her "personal life responsibilities."

Three participants discussed the challenges they faced regarding academic performance. Breonna revealed that one of the major challenges she faced was associated with her performance in her comprehensive exams. She admitted, "I had no idea what I was doing or how it was supposed to be structured." Breonna added that failing her exam the first time was a "major blow." Similarly, Shantel asserted that one of her greatest "challenges faced were academic probation at one point." Lanecia expressed that her overall lack of experience hindered her productivity and academic performance.

Solutions

Black Feminist Thought inherently recognizes that although Black women have historically experienced many challenges and marginalization, they have focused energy and efforts on praxis and identifying solutions to both individual and communal problems. In this vein, I present the solutions that the participants implemented to overcome the challenges listed earlier, particularly (a) building community, (b) identify supplemental academic resources (including faculty mentors elsewhere), and (c) self-care.

Building community. Presented in the earlier discussion, one of the obstacles faced by the participants was associated with a feeling of isolation or lacking community. As such, participants discussed the ways they combated this by building community. Tiffany reveals that she sought community with students in another department as a means to combat the isolation she experienced in her program. Similarly, Rayven developed community by connecting to "Black graduate students in other programs and in neighboring campuses." Britney mentioned that she was able to formulate a "tribe" by developing community with other Black women in her program.

For the participants, part of community building included involvement in professional and social organizations and peer mentoring—meaning informal mentoring among colleagues that share similarities in regard to academic level/status. Hazel asserted that her involvement in "Black support groups and programs on campus who contained students with like interests" was a primary way of overcoming her obstacles. Similarly, Aiesha shared that through her active involvement in organizations such as Black Graduate Student Association and the Black Faculty and Staff Association, she was able to find an "outlet" to "talk about similar situations and be [herself]." Tiffany shared that her active involvement in her field's campus-based student organization was beneficial. In the same vein, Breonna posited:

> My overall graduate school experience is heavily influenced by my connection with and participation in the graduate student organization for minority students, which was primarily Black students. From day one, I was connected with this group and that made a major impact on how I experienced my doctoral journey.

In addition to student organizations, Noel expressed the significance of peer relationships and mentoring noting that a key way that she overcame her challenges was by "building relationships" with her classmates. Both Charlene and Hazel revealed that they benefited from the aid of classmates and peers to assist in the absorption of challenging concepts and theories. Erica discusses the peer mentoring she received from other Black women graduate students.

Identify supplemental academic resources. Several participants sought external supplemental academic resources as a means to overcome their challenges. Charlene and Hazel discussed doing additional "research" outside of the classroom. Hazel went on: "I taught myself as much as I could. . . . I found resources such as self-help guides, YouTube videos, Facebook groups, reached out to past instructors, etc. in order to strengthen [her] educational foundation." As touched on by Hazel, supplemental resources also included some participants seeking assistance and mentorship from faculty members who were outside of their program. Tiffany "continued to build relationships with faculty members ... who unfortunately had taken different roles at other institutions ... but continue to support in meaningful ways."

Self-care. The final solution that was identified by several participants was the implementation of self-care practices, which fundamentally refers to taking initiatives or measures to ensure overall health and well-being. When asked about initiatives taken to overcome the challenges she faced during grad school, Cassandra responded that she implemented "self-care" by "refocusing" on her goals. Britney, Jennifer, and Cassandra all communicated that assistance of mental health services provided relief and assistance with addressing the obstacles faced during their graduate school experience.

For two participants, self-care also manifested in the form of self-advocacy to promote success and combat inequity. Erica asserted that being vocal and addressing "issues of racism and sexism early on" helped her address her marginalization and overcome obstacles. Ameia advised that she believed that self-advocacy, in the form of taking her concerns to college deans, had a greater power to directly affect the "policies and systems in place that are negatively impacting students of color" and aided her in overcoming her challenges.

Summary and Conclusion

The experiences revealed by the participants uncover unique experiences and the impact of their intersectional identities. As communicated, many of the participants were in volatile academic conditions where their capabilities and intellect were called into question by faculty members who displayed a blatant bias. In understanding the academic institution that is the university and the hegemonic ideas that undergird the logic of the university, in many cases, that Black women's identity leads to a general devaluation of their intellect is clear.

In a similar vein, in many regards, the Black women participants sought to pursue research interests that directly challenged the generally accepted frameworks and areas of concentration to prioritize voices and experiences made invisible in traditional disciplines. I argue the women sought to move in the direction of "epistemological decolonialization," meaning the rejection of imperialist hegemony. Mignolo (2011b) speaks of epistemic disobedience that de-links individuals from ideas that are associated with modernity/

coloniality and exclusively Western thought. Unfortunately, as is the case commonly, they were met with dissonance, discouragement, and, in some cases, repugnance.

Another significant point highlighted from the participants' revelations was the internal challenges Black women face regarding their feeling of "not fitting in" with some of their peers. Particularly, Jennifer referred to her struggles with "imposter syndrome." Patterson-Stephens, Lane, and Vital (2017) identify imposter phenomenon as "represent[ing] characteristics and behaviors of individuals who do not attribute their success to their own intellectual abilities and prowess," and the scholars continue, asserting that this is "problematic because it can be debilitating and cause psychological harm" (p. 5). Interestingly, the scholars point out that "this phenomenon disproportionately affects women of color" (Patterson-Stephens et al., 2017, p. 5). Acknowledging that, like some of the study participants, many Black women graduate students are first-generation graduate students and, in some instances, first-generation college students, the participant responses highlight the juxtaposition of having worked hard to achieve monumental feats yet, and still, feeling like one does not belong.

Although the analysis of participant responses reveals a daunting reality for many Black women graduate students, the participants highlight a myriad of solutions that can be implemented to combat unique challenges. In addition to the solutions revealed in the previous section, other things to consider include the following:

- Thoroughly research the institution and program. Be sure to pay a great deal of attention to selecting a graduate program that includes faculty members with interest that are similar—or align—with intended research goals.
- Being prepared mentally to adjust time management routines and overall planning.
- Be prepared for the possible adversity that will likely be faced.
- Constantly be on the lookout for research, funding, and mentorship opportunities, as they will be invaluable to overall success.

The final question posed to the participants was

> What recommendations or lasting comments would you give to Black women currently enrolled or considering enrolling in a graduate program?

The participants responded as follows:

> "Do not dim your light to make others comfortable. Do not be ashamed if you are expected to know something that you do not—ask for help. It is okay to need it. Whether you crawl, walk, or run, we're all rooting for you!"

> "Be yourself, go to the top. Run the race and keep pushing even further. Go for exactly what you want and know the reason behind it—make sure it's passionate. The reminder of that is what will get you through the tough parts no matter what they are."

> "You are going to get down, you are going to want to give up. You have to keep in contact with your support systems to keep you up."

> "I would tell Black women to know what they want to study, identify faculty that is relatable to them and to not back down. They deserve to be there and to learn. Their research interest are valid and important."

> "Always go with your first mind. Do what you love no matter what."

> "Remember you are just as valuable as any and everyone else in the room. Fear is just a way of our most inner insecurities to have you second guess yourself. Do not give into the ideology—remain confident, ask questions and seek understanding. It will assist you not only in the classroom but also outside."

Ultimately, this study sought to uncover the ways in which Black women not only face challenges but also devise solutions to navigate graduate programs. In addition to providing a narrative experience, an ultimate goal of the work is to serve as a resource to the Black women graduate students of the future.

The study seeks to offer praxis as well as words of encouragement to current and future Black women graduate students.

References

Anderson, E. L. (2003). Changing US demographics and American higher education. *New Directions for Higher Education, 2003*(121), 3–12.

Asante, M. K. (1988). *Afrocentricity*. Trenton, NJ: Africa World Press.

Barry, C. A. (1998). Choosing qualitative data analysis software: Atlas/ti and nudist compared. *Sociological Research Online 3*(3). https://journals.sagepub.com/doi/pdf/10.5153/sro.178.

Biesta, G., & Tedder, M. (2006). How is agency possible? Towards an ecological understanding of agency-as-achievement. Learning lives: Learning, identity, and agency in the life course. https://www.researchgate.net/profile/Michael_Tedder/publication/228644383_How_is_agency_possible_Towards_an_ecological_understanding_of_agency-as-achievement/links/00b4952cadd9bd2b6a000000.pdf.

Carey, J. W., Morgan, M., & Oxtoby, M. J. (1996). Intercoder agreement in analysis of responses to open-ended interview questions: Examples from tuberculosis research. *CAM Journal, 8*(3), 1–5. https://doi.org/10.1177/1525822X960080030101.

Carey, M. P., & Forsyth, A. D. (2019). Teaching tip Sheet: Self-efficacy. Retrieved from https://www.apa.org/pi/aids/resources/education/self-efficacy.

Collins, P. H. (1990). Black feminist thought: Knowledge, consciousness, and the politics of empowerment. New York: Routledge.

Collins, P. H. (2009). Black feminist thought: Knowledge, consciousness, and the politics of empowerment. New York: Routledge Classics.

Crenshaw, K. (1989). Demarginalizing the intersection of race and sex: A Black feminist critique of antidiscrimination doctrine, feminist theory and antiracist politics. *University of Chicago Legal Forum, 1989*(1), 139–167.

Crenshaw, K. (1991). Mapping the margins: Intersectionality, identity politics, and violence against women of color. *Stanford Law Review, 43*, 1241–1299.

Digest of Education Statistics. (2017a, August). Table 323.20. Master's degrees conferred by postsecondary institutions, by race/ethnicity and sex of student: Selected years, 1976–77 through 2015–16. Retrieved from https://nces.ed.gov/programs/digest/d17/tables/dt17_323.20.asp.

Digest of Education Statistics. (2017b, August). Table 324.20. Doctor's degrees conferred by postsecondary institutions, by race/ethnicity and sex of student: Selected years, 1976–77 through 2015–2016. Retrieved from https://nces.ed.gov/programs/digest/d17/tables/dt17_324.20.asp.

Eckel, P., Green, M., & Hill, B. (1997). *Transformational change: Defining a journey.* Washington, DC: American Council on Education.

Grosfoguel, R. (2007). The epistemic de-colonial turn: beyond political-economy paradigms. *Cultural Studies, 21,* 211–223.

Grosfoguel, R. (2008). Decolonizing political-economy and post-colonial studies: Transmodernity, border thinking, and global coloniality. *Transmodernity: Journal of Peripheral Cultural Production of the Luso-Hispanic World 1*(1), 1–38. Retrieved from www.dialogoglobal.com/granada/documents/Grosfoguel-Decolonizing-Pol-Econ-and-Postcolonial.pdf.

Hill-Collins, P. (2009). *Black feminist thought: Knowledge, consciousness, and the politics of empowerment.* New York, NY: Routledge.

Hull, G. T., & Smith, B. (2001). The politics of Black women's studies. In N. Norment (Ed.), *The African American studies reader* (pp. 144–156). Durham, NC: Carolina Academic Press.

Kenten, C. (2010). Narrating oneself: Reflections on the use of solicited diaries with diary interviews. *Forum: Qualitative Social Research 11*(2). Retrieved from http://nbn-resolving.de/urn:nbn:de:0114- Fqs1002160.

Ketchum, S. A. (1980). Female culture, woman culture and conceptual change: Toward a philosophy of women's studies. *Social Theory and Practice, 6*(2), 151–162.

Khatri, C., Chapman, S. J., Glasbey, J., Kelly, M., Nepogodiev, D., Bhangu, A., & Fitzgerald, J. (2015). Social media and internet driven study recruitment: evaluating a new model for promoting collaborator engagement and participation. *PloS ONE, 10*(3), e0118899.

Kitzinger, J. (1995). Qualitative research: Introducing focus groups. *BMJ, 311,* 299–302.

Kuh, G. D. (1990). The demographic juggernaut. In M. J. Barr & M. L. Upcraft (Eds.), *New futures for student affairs: Building a vision for professional leadership and practice* (pp. 71–97). San Francisco, CA: Jossey-Bass.

Labuschagne, A. (2003). Qualitative research-airy fairy or fundamental? *The Qualitative Report, 8*(1), 100–103.

Maldonado-Torres, N. (2007). On the coloniality of being. *Cultural Studies, 21*, 240–270. doi:10.1080/09502380601162548

Mignolo, W. (2011a). Epistemic disobedience and the decolonial option: A manifesto. *TRANSMODERNITY: Journal of Peripheral Cultural Production of the Luso-Hispanic World 1*(2), 44–66. Retrieved from http://escholarship.org/uc/item/62j3w283

Mignolo, W. (2011b). I am where I think: Remapping the order of knowing. In F. Lionnet & S. Shi (Eds.), *The creolization of theory* (pp. 159–192). Durham, NC: Duke University Press.

Ndlovu-Gatsheni, S. J. (2013). Why decoloniality in the 21st century. *The Thinker: For Thought Leaders, 48*, 10–15. Retrieved from http://www.sabelondlovugatsheni.com/downloads/ndlovu-gatsheni-why-decoloniality-in-the-21st-century.pdf.

Nyoni, J. (2013). Decolonial multicultural education in post-apartheid South Africa: The dichotomy of pluriversality in curricula craft context. *International Journal for Innovation Education and Research, 1*(3), 83–92. Retrieved from http://www.ijier.net/assets/1-3-(10).pdf.

Orfield, G., Marin, P., & Horn, C. L. (2005). *Higher education and the color line: College access, racial equity, and social change*. Cambridge, MA: Harvard Education Press.

Patterson-Stephens, S. M., & Vital, L. M. (2017). Black doctoral women: Exploring barriers and facilitators of success in graduate education. Academic Perspectives in Higher Education, 3(1), 5–35.

Sofaer, S. (1999). Qualitative methods: what are they and why use them? *Health Services Research, 34*(5, Pt. 2), 1101–1118.

Woodard Jr., D. B., Love, P., & Komives, S. R. (2000). Students of the new millennium. *New Directions for Student Services, 2000*(92), 35–47.

Zamani, E. M. (2003). African American women in higher education. *New Directions for Student Services, 2003*(104), 5–18.

EIGHT

No Parent Left Behind: The Narratives of African American Fathers in Texas on Their Parental Involvement

Joshua D. Hughes

Literature Review

WITH REFERENCE TO EDUCATION, WHAT is parental involvement? What is its purpose, and how does one gauge its value in educating children? Many studies have been conducted by talented researchers in education, but the findings are broad-based, the participants range widely in characteristics, and the results have produced a mass of raw information in need of interpretation (Epstein, Coates, Sanders & Simon, 1980). The purpose of this literature review is to define and describe the narratives of African American fathers in the academic success of their children.

Parental involvement is documented in the literature reviewed herein throughout American history. The data reflect that parental involvement to increase academic performance by students has many variables. Nevertheless, its study is paramount to understand how parents can positively affect the academic lives of their children (Henderson & Mapp, 2002; Hong & Ho, 2005; Jeynes, 2005; Steinberg, Lamborn, Dornusch & Darling, 1992).

Understanding how to engage parental involvement positively is the premise for this study. The review of literature identified gaps in the study of this topic. Although incomplete, these variables provided the basis for many studies that are necessary to develop a richer context of the topic. The purpose of this literature review was to look at the following topics relevant to the study of African American fathers and their engagement in their children's attendance in urban elementary schools.

This literature review is organized both chronologically and topically. The topics addressed were parental involvement in education, parental involvement by social class, parental involvement in urban elementary schools, and parental involvement in African American fathers' engagement in the academic success of their children. The study incorporates a conceptual framework in understanding the meaning of the topic based on the theoretical approach.

Many studies have provided various levels of conceptualization of the importance of parental involvement from a broad perspective. Policies implemented by the U.S. Department of Education have demonstrated differences in defining parental involvement. However, these scholars have collectively defined *parental involvement* in the literature as a self-motivated, collaborating practice in which parents use multiple forms of assistance and capital to describe their collaborations through schools and among school practitioners (Lacour & Tissington, 2011). The conceptualization of the meaning of the variable *parental involvement* has developed through a process of building the whole child to encourage students through a support system while building a community for the well-being of all students (Mattingly, Prislin, McKenzie, Rodriguez & Kayzar, 2002).

Parental involvement has a steep history in American education, beginning with President Thomas Jefferson in the 19th century (Tocqueville, 1975). One of Jefferson's many visions as president was to implement a universal public education system that provided equal education systematically to give American children the opportunity to attend school and become productive citizens. His vision established the foundation and the development of American support for public education in the 19th and 20th centuries.

This development began to spread throughout the states. Recognition came from scholars, which added to the success of education in the mid-1800s. In addition, during the 1900s, scholars Horace Mann and Henry Bernard saw the importance of this development over time and emphasized the need to ensure that all states were provided with an education system that would support ongoing success in educating every child (Cremin, 1957). This served as the foundation of the parent–teacher associations, organizations controlled by middle- and upper-class mothers who wanted to get involved in education by volunteering and working with teachers on Saturdays. The association's focus was to become informed about the academic development of their children and to become active in the schools. The association is a strong supporter of the educational system.

Parental Involvement in Education

For centuries, the influence of parental involvement in education has been studied by many scholars, most of whom reported that parental involvement plays a vital part in the schooling of students. Studies of parental involvement in education have reported positive outcomes in the academic success of students throughout history (Henderson & Barla, 1994). In the 1970s and 1980s, Epstein (1987) discussed parental involvement in education from a different perspective. Many perspectives involved six steps in a theoretical approach for improving involvement in the academic success of children. Epstein created a framework consisting of six types of parental involvement: parenting, communicating, volunteering, learning at home, decision-making, and collaborating with the community (Epstein & Sanders, 2002). Epstein defined *parental involvement* as assisting families with required parenting skills and information to enhance student learning, establish proper communication with the family, involve the family in the learning process as volunteers and audiences, allow learning at home through items such as homework, and include families in decision-making in schools and collaborating with the community in school activities (Epstein & Sanders, 2002). However, the definition can vary depending on the socio-economic status (SES) of the family.

Epstein's framework for the six steps of involvement was categorized with an emphasis on looking at parenting, communication, volunteering, learning at home, and collaborating with the community. Parental involvement steps were different from those of Hawley and Rosenholtz (2002) because these authors focused on four major factors to improve students' academic achievement. The evidence from these studies placed high relevance on information to support involvement in which parents, teachers, and the community could identify key indicators of academic success.

Lareau (1996) looked at parental involvement in African American sixth-grade students; reading test scores were higher in children whose parents were involved. The involved parents were aware of the important elements in their involvement in their children's education. Lareau pointed out differences in the parents' perspectives; parents who were not involved gave explanations such as limited time in supporting their students at home, high demands from their careers, and other involvement.

Cooper (2010) reported that some parents were not able to help their children because they lacked the necessary knowledge and skills to do so. Other researchers presented other perspectives, finding that involvement by parents did not always have positive outcomes. However, other benefits emerged, such as lower absence rates and increased completion of homework (Dougherty & Dougherty, 1977). These concepts were different from those of other authors because a new idea emerged to look at the SES of all parents heavily involved in their children's education at home and at school.

Some authors saw the importance of examining ethnic groups, narrowing their focus to African American families (Crane, 2016). They also saw a different focus in parental involvement at all SES levels. For example, some noted children whose mothers were present produced higher grades in contrast to children whose mothers were limited in their involvement posted lower grades.

Huntsinger and Jose (2009) had a different perspective from that of Stevenson and Baker (1987). Huntsinger and Jose (2009) reported that low-SES students who suffered from a lack of parental involvement had parents who lacked communication and educational skills to help the child academically. Other studies of parental involvement in education explained how numerous variables are linked to positive outcomes in the success of students (Jeynes, 2012a, 2012b). The researched linked success between children and parents spending time at home with educational activities and reinforcement of doing homework with the child every day with higher levels of academic achievement in the classroom.

Parental Involvement and Low SES

Parental participation has led to a progressive effect on learners' educational outcomes (Abrams & Gibbs, 2002). Parental involvement encourages and supports students to develop positive attitudes toward learning. Abrams and Gibbs (2002) found that students who achieved high performance in school received assistance from their parents at home. Consistent with Abrams and Gibbs (2002), the findings of Huntsinger and Jose (2009) and Jeynes (2012b) empirically support the contention that parental involvement, regardless of SES, can be crucial toward a child's success.

Illustrative of this point are studies that demonstrate parents' low SES played a significant and positive role in a child's education (Czarniawska,

2004). According to Hill and Taylor (2004), parents with low SES are less likely to be involved in schooling as a result of work schedules, lack of resources, stress, and their own low levels of education. Therefore, school administrators and teachers should encourage parents to support their children at home to achieve high performance in school.

Wang and Sheikh-Khalil (2014) argued that parents with low SES find it difficult to concentrate on their children's education affairs. The authors reported that parents with low SES lacked adequate materials and equipment to facilitate study. For example, those parents lacked the ability to buy appropriate reading desks for their children. Abrams and Gibbs (2002) also noted that poor parents lacked resources to satisfy family needs. In fact, the authors claimed that parents with low SES engaged in other activities such as work, apart from assisting their children because they wanted to offer basic requirements such as nourishment and clothing to their children.

A lack of parental contribution has social and emotional impacts on student achievement in school. Wang and Sheikh-Khalil (2014) agreed that children from low-income households often perform poorly compared to children from high-income households. Children from high-income households receive more material assistance and attitudinal benefits than children from poor families. Therefore, children from low SES are at high risk of academic failure due to a lack of support from parents. Although school administrators encourage parents with low income to participate in enhancing their children's performance, Weiss (1992) affirmed that approximately 40% of the parents with low income in that study assisted their children with homework and followed their children's performance in school.

According to Wang and Sheikh-Khalil (2014), school personnel request that parents be involved in their children's academic welfare, irrespective of SES. This is supplemented by policies at the local district level to ensure that parents with low SES improve their children's performance. The policies assume the needs of a particular group in society because children from high-income households and those from low-income households need to succeed in life. Bornstein and Bradley (2014) and Wang and Sheikh-Khalil (2014) have agreed that parental involvement should focus on shaping the behavior of the child and his/her performance, regardless of the financial background.

Parental involvement has been studied by leading experts for years to measure the engagement of parents in supporting their children and the involvement of that support at different levels based on parenting styles (Huntsinger & Jose, 2009). Researchers have discovered that most families care about their children and want them to succeed in their academic and daily lives. Parents and teachers share similarities and differences in defining *parental involvement* (Jeynes, 2012a). Several of the findings deserve attention here.

First, according to Billman, Geddes, and Hedges (2005), their approach used four steps in analyzing parental involvement in parents of low social class: internal, competitive, functional, and generic. Those benchmarks were studied in students who were successful due to parental involvement. Their academic skills were correlated with the home environment, where literacy environments positively affect a child's pre-academic skills (Lareau, 1996).

In tandem with Billman, Geddes, and Hedges (2005), Anderson, Henriksen, and Spjelkavik (2008) looked at the relationships of parents in low social classes and found that families of lower classes did not show parental involvement as much as those in the middle and higher social classes, but they showed parental involvement at home, which suggested that the parents did not value education as much as those in other social classes. The finding that parents were simply helping the children at home was different from findings in other studies.

Reynolds (2010) examined parental involvement from another perspective. He studied income and parental involvement, examining the two variables to determine whether there was a significant family correlation. A significant correlation was found between income and parental involvement. Both variables were also correlated with the academic success of the students. In a study in India (Vellymalay, 2012), findings revealed that families of high social class had a greater impact on parental involvement than families of middle or low social class. That study had a different perspective involving parental involvement from lower social classes in urban schools, correlating benchmark tests with students' success.

Finally, in a study by Bornstein (2014), some schools reported involvement by parents of low social class in layering a different approach. Home and school were the two areas of focus for this research, revealing that parents of low social class participated in other ways in the success of their children. The findings indicated new ideas about home involvement; parents of low social class who could not make the time commitment to attend school engaged in other helpful practices.

Authors have examined multiple dimensions of parental involvement from the home; these dimensions correlated with accomplishments by students whose parents were of a low social class status. Dumont (2014) reported that parental involvement was slightly different from year to year; many parents had little to no education and could not help their children with homework. Authors have revealed inadequate education and increased dropout rates with parents did not affect children's academic achievement, perpetuating the low-SES statue of the community (Hill & Taylor, 2004).

Sirin (2005) studied three lower class subgroups: African Americans, Hispanics, and Pacific Islanders. All subgroups agreed that the school should be responsible to educate children and provided them with academic support, while parents should provide moral support at home. According to these authors, many urban elementary schools have shown increased success with students by improving the school system and early intervention programs that helped to reduce these risk factors and thus increased research on the correlation between SES and education (Cochran & Dean, 1991).

Turney and Kao (2009) reported that parental involvement of lower class parents related to providing character education in the home, teaching cultural values, and communicating with children. These practices did not align with those reported by other authors in the literature review. Research indicates that school conditions contribute more to SES differences in learning rates than do family characteristics (Aikens & Barbarin, 2008).

Crane (2016) looked at the relationships in subgroups and their children's achievements. All subgroups were consistent in high involvement. However, the same study looked at children who were receiving free or reduced-price lunches, and those results showed lower parental support than other subgroups.

Lacour and Tissington (2011) focused on working-class and poor parents regarding their involvement with their children. Many of those parents placed more importance on their involvement at home with love, food, and safety for the child. Those children were involved in few organized activities and had more freedom at home when parents were working. Many parents in this study did not have a high school diploma but still saw the importance of a good education, leaving the involvement at school to the educator and the involvement at home with emphasis on the developmental stages of their children and natural growth to them (Cochran & Dean, 1991).

According to Lareau (1996), lower class parents who were involved did not show the same level of engagement as the middle and high social class parents. Their involvement was stronger at home, giving moral support to their children. They often did not assume involvement at levels of other social classes.

Parental Involvement in Middle Socio-economic Status

The percentage of students whose families reported involvement in school activities in the United States increased significantly between 2000 and 2012 (Altschul, 2012). This is based on the fact that middle SES is increasing across the world (Altschul, 2012). Altschul (2012) reported that, across several measures, parents contributed significantly toward the success of students.

Park and Holloway (2013) noted that more than 50% of the world's population is composed of middle-income earners. According to Abrams and Gibbs (2002), the more people arrive in this bracket, the more children are expected to perform in school. Students with parents in middle SES receive more attention and display fewer behavioral problems. In fact, the majority of children complete school because parents are greatly engaged in their learning process.

On the other hand, Lareau (2003) stated that middle-SES parents develop a close relationship between family and school life, believing that schooling is a shared responsibility; they are concerned with the performance of teachers. Altschul (2012) argued that findings reported by Park and Holloway (2013) were inadequate because the authors focused on the benefits that children receive from parents without providing recommendations on how parents could improve their socioeconomic condition.

In the context of Frew, Zhou, Duran, Kwok, and Benz (2013) found that middle-SES parents had diverse ideas about education. Middle-SES parents assisted their children with purposeful intentions in mind. That is, some parents chose careers for their children while the children were young. Frew et al. (2013) asserted that the parents wanted to associate their children with professionals such as medical practitioners, engineers, architects, and research scientists because such jobs pay well.

Altschul (2012) argued that little attention is paid to whether middle-SES parents are doing enough to help their children achieve their dreams. There is limited research showing how middle-SES parents are helping their children to discover and nurture their talent. They pressure the children to approach learning as they were required or according to the parents' interest.

According to Park and Holloway (2013), influencing a child to perform in accordance with the parents' interest leads to negative behavior in school as children release stress through negative behavior such as bullying. Research-based studies have revealed that middle-SES parents are still doing little to ensure the child's educational success. This may be due to commitment to work and sometimes forgetting to assist their children with homework. Middle-SES parents allocate time to work as many are still making their careers. That is, they work hard to ensure promotion and salary increases. Thus, a large percentage of time is left with the housekeepers to assist the child. A survey conducted by Altschul (2012) indicated that parents' SES contributed to 70% of the children's failure or success in school. Some of the variables considered in the study were occupational status, educational levels, and income levels. Middle-SES parents can afford tutors at home, and their children receive assistance from them.

Parental involvement has played a significant role in the success of these students in urban public, charter, and private schools, according to McBride (2005). Because of previous studies on the effect of social class in education, scholars are able to conduct further research with themes that may bring research closer to providing meaningful programs to get parents to feel welcome in schools. According to Robinson and Harris (2015), middle-SES parents who are involved challenge teachers as advocates for their children by asking questions concerning grades, making telephone calls to teachers to resolve issues, and exercising parental rights. At that level, education becomes more complex, and educators spend time in getting parents involved; parents at that level should not focus on the involvement of their children (Catterall, 1998).

Hango (2007) offered the same perspective with middle-SES parents in the engagement in their children's schooling. Involvement showed inconsistent results with homework and achievement by students; enriching activities showed success in improving academics (Altschul, 2012). Students of that class were not able to achieve success consistent with the status of others in their school.

Parental Involvement in High Socio-economic Status

Jeynes (2012b) stated that parents living a high standard of life influence the success of their children significantly. Jeynes (2012b) asserted that parents with high SES inspire their children to succeed like them. Frew et al. (2013) studied sixth-grade students; they reported that parents' high SES predicted that their children would perform well. Parents with high SES also had a high level of academic achievement and assisted their children with homework. Berger (1991) described high-SES parents as individuals who are involved in the learning of their children and have high expectations.

A study by Jeynes (2012a) indicated that well-educated mothers with high levels of income had more knowledge of their children's schooling than did other parents. They were involved in the daily performance by the child and other external factors affecting the child. In most instances, high-SES parents take greater efforts to ensure that the child's academic progress is given the first priority. Similar results were reported by Park and Holloway (2013), revealing that parents who were highly learned and received high levels of income interacted and communicated with their children, leading the children to be high achievers at school.

Wang and Sheikh-Khalil (2014) took a different perspective to examine the relationship between high achievers in school and parent's income level. Hill and Taylor (2004) found that parents with high SES tended to take their children to urban schools, compared to low-SES parents who took their children to rural and government schools. A reason cited for this was that teachers in urban areas had higher occupational status and higher income. They spend quality time attending to the child and ensuring that the child attains higher performance in school. Wang and Sheikh-Khalil (2014) provided a good example in which students in the eighth grade from high-SES families scored well in mathematics and sciences, as well as in reading. This success was attributed to effective parental involvement and encouragement by parents to provide their children with many resources to help their children succeed (Crane, 2016). A similar study was conducted in Thailand by Dumont (2014) on eighth-grade students; the findings showed that highly educated parents assisted their children to perform well in mathematics because they wanted their children to succeed in life. On the contrary, Jeynes (2012a, 2012b) argued that high-SES parents spend their money on trips and business deals, leaving their children in the hands of tutors. This arrangement may lead to changes in behavior as the child may copy bad or good behaviors from a person with whom he or she spends time. This can be detrimental to the school's unity as such children bully others.

Many studies have shown that decisions vary when parents are actively participating in the academic process of their children. A great deal of parent involvement in children's academic success has various factors that contribute to those decisions. One of the factors that contributes to the level of parental involvement is the SES of parents and their awareness of the importance of parental involvement (Revicki, 1981). Many parents have moved beyond challenges and barriers to become involved in their children's academic success. These factors have been studied using various approaches, theories, and methods, leading to emerging themes to conceptualize meaning.

Frew et al. (2013) saw a different perspective in parental involvement from elementary school to middle school with parents of high social class. There were programs in school to engage those parents to participate in engagement activities. This study paid attention to each program and the correlation of relationships between the success of their children and the amount of time spent at school. When children went to middle school, high social class parents did not receive guidance on how to be involved in the lives of their children (Frew et al., 2013).

In this research, subgroups were categorized by their culture, establishing positive parental involvement in social classes of high status and revealing success leading to parents taking the efforts to be involved. However, this study did not include African American parents, so the elements in this study as it relates to the African American parents were not present (McClelland, 1958). Sirin (2005) and Nunes (1999) reported results of parental involvement in high social class status. Sirin (2005) reported higher levels of knowledge in comprehensive skills, thinking skills, and summarizing. Nunes (1999) reported similar results. Parents of high social class whose children were successful in the engaging programs were effective in the role of being supportive. The relationship between the parents and the teachers gave parents the success that they needed with their children simply by parents and teacher sharing information to ensure success for the children (Hines & Holcomb-McCoy, 2013).

Parental Involvement in Urban Schools

Middle- and high-SES parents tend to take their children to urban schools for better educational opportunities. Wilder (2014) noted that households receiving a high income take their children to private schools in urban centers. Park and Holloway (2013) found that parents rarely participated in school activities and children's progress in urban centers, based on the parents' assumption that teachers have the responsibility to ensure that the children perform well in classwork and in behavior.

Ironically, Wilder (2014) found that some urban students performed poorly compared to students in rural areas. He explained that parent involvement in school activity does not benefit either the school or students. In other words, some parents may increase inequalities in school as they express their social status in school. Such inequalities affect children indirectly because of possible competition among parents and children.

Jeynes (2012b), in a study of urban schools, reported that the children performed well depending on the teachers' involvement. Parents pay well for the school and expect high returns for their money. Resources that parents contributed to the school included books, modes of transportation, and high school fees. Wilder (2014) observed that, in some cases, parents in urban schools' report head teachers to the board of directors when school does not perform as required. The parents measure their resource input in relation to students' performance. Therefore, teachers strive to produce good results by enhancing teacher–student relationship.

Parent involvement in urban schools is limited (Wilder, 2014). That is, middle-level income parents use the opportunity to demonstrate that they are better off than low-SES parents. The efforts made by other parents are futile because the schools act as a place for status quo supremacy. According to Frew et al. (2013), parents forget schooling objectives and ruin performance levels. To improve parents' involvement and participation in education, urban schools have adopted policies to restrain parents. Dumont (2014) asserted that common policies include noninterference with school programs and fulfilling parental obligations, with the accountability of parents to guarantee that they assist children in completing their homework and paying school fees on time. Parents are also required to report to school often to monitor the progress of their children. This enables teachers to inform parents about what to do to improve the child's performance. Wilder (2014) observed that some urban schools pick parents to serve on school committees that make decisions on the day-to-day operation of the school. This allows them to understand the challenges and successes of the school. In response to the trend in the achievement gap, poor urban schools have tried to increase parental involvement (Dearing et al., 2006). Studies have defined urban schools as serving African Americans, Hispanic Americans, underprivileged students, or refugees with altered outlooks for students and relatives in an inner-city environment.

The lack of parental involvement in urban schools has been a primary focus for a while (Dearing et al., 2006). Programs have been established to help in educating parents regarding professional development to increase their involvement (Berger, 1991). A good percentage of parents have not exercised parental rights due to urban schools making working-class parents feel unwelcomed (Auerbach, 2007). Urban schools with a large percentage of middle-SES parents tend to focus solely on parental involvement consisting of giving children a support system, engaging in their learning environment, working behind the scenes with parent–teacher groups, or just the hands-on method in the classroom (Auerbach, 2007).

Jacobs and Kritsonsi (2007) provided a brief description of urban and suburban schools and how others contrast the two, stating that the urban school without parental involvement has shown high-poverty populations or just those students who consistently score lower than their White counterparts. Reynolds (2010) stated that students who attend urban schools are often challenged by obstacles during their transition to academic accomplishment. In urban charter schools, many teachers are not certified, resources are limited, and the turnover rate is high. Studies that have examined parents who engaged in the children's lives have reported a greater accountability with significant gains in children's schooling. Parents who are involved, regardless of SES, have been positive role models in influencing their children (Yanghee, 2009). The role that parents have implemented in their lives has made an impact on the success of their children in urban schools. That educators listen to the voices of actively involved parents to allow others to understand the importance of parental involvement is imperative.

Parental Involvement by African American Fathers

African American fathers constitute 7% of the U.S. population (Roopnarine & Hossain, 2013). They contribute significantly to their children's well-being in school and at home. Nevertheless, some African American fathers engage in immoral acts such as drug addiction and drug sales (Roopnarine & Hossain, 2013). This is detrimental to the family and children. Hines and Holcomb-McCoy (2013) found that the immediate environment affects a child's behavior. The child adapts to the environment and at the same time reacts positively or negatively to the environment, depending on the impact.

Roopnarine and Hossain (2013) administered a questionnaire to 110 African American fathers. Results revealed that these fathers influenced their children's attitudes and behaviors. That is, responsible parents earning a higher income influence the child's attitude positively, unlike parents who are rarely seen at home. Knowledgeable African American males promoted home–school communication whereby they received information from teachers on their child's behavior. Hines and Holcomb-McCoy (2013) affirmed that better communication between parents and African American females enhanced learning as the parents understood the weaknesses of each child. On the contrary, irresponsible parents found it difficult to communicate with teachers and their children developed behaviors such as bullying.

According to Wang and Sheikh-Khalil (2014), a father's life context plays a pivotal role in the child's development. That is, some African Americans involve their children in decision-making. This helps the child to develop analytical skills and positive behavior such as being responsible in life. On the other hand, Roopnarine and Hossain (2013) found that fewer than 40% of African American males were concerned about their child's education. However, this research was limited in the sense that it did not indicate reasons for limited assistance.

Hines and Holcomb-McCoy (2013) surveyed African Americans to learn why they were reluctant to participate in education and found that they were busy with improving their SES. Children who miss direction and support from the fathers develop negative attitudes toward education and life. Jeynes (2012b) recommended home-based involvement to improve child performance in school. This enables parents to interact with their children during homework.

Only a small percentage of African American fathers are concerned with the education of their children (Jones, 2001, as cited in Pattnaik & Sriram, 2010). Pattnaik (2013) suggested that involvement by the father is low as a result of the family structure that demands involvement by mothers. Gurian (2009) asserted that African American fathers have a tendency to resist participation in their children's learning. A lack of support by fathers may result from the belief that they are of little help to young children (Dempsey, 1997), as cited in Hornby (2011). The aforementioned conclusions tend to indicate that fathers are less concerned with their children's education.

Studies (e.g., Corley & Fowler, 1996) have indicated that many fathers are not involved in their children's academic lives, whereas other studies recognized the impact of parental involvement in children's success in schools. Bloom (1981) conducted an international study on fathers and their involvement with education at home with their children. His study revealed that fathers who remained engaged in the success of their children's education at home were a powerful indicator in determining the success of their children at school. Swap (1991) examined parental involvement from the perspective of broad family dynamics. Corley and Fowler (1996) focused on the workload of mothers and fathers from inside and outside the homes.

Studies have looked at mothers who stayed home with their children while the father worked. Mothers during the time of the study had time to go to the schools to participate in their child's life (Baker & Stevenson, 1986). Bakari (2003) looked at nonresidential fathers and found that those fathers who moved to a new setting, remarried, or developed another intimate relationship tried to improve their skills and education through parental involvement.

Lengua, Kohl, and McMahon (2000) reported that fathers cohabitating with the mother of their children were more involved in their lives than were fathers who were considered nonresidential fathers. Robinson and Harris (2015) observed that fathers who divorced within a year did not continue to be involved in their children's academic success for about one year. Fan and Chen (2001) examined various variables and reported that fathers who separated from their relationship became absent in their involvement for a year, as well. These findings mentioned subgroup differences. Every race that was unmarried moved out of proximity of their children, while African American fathers stayed close to their children.

Bempechat (1992) focused on the percentages of fathers who never or barely spent time with their children. Those percentages were 12% for African Americans, 30% for Hispanics, and 37% for Whites. Noltemeyer and Bush (2013) revealed that 4 of 10 children slept without the presence of a residential father. Hango (2007) stated that much of the research has focused on residential fathers. Park and Holloway (2013) reported noncustodial parents revealed other forms of parental involvement such as fathers being able to be prepared emotionally with financial support; these authors did not mention parental involvement as spending time with children. However, the same authors discovered four themes that correlated with father involvement; these themes were derived focused on custodial fathers, excluding nonresidential fathers.

Bronfenbrenner (1979) explained African American fathers as underrepresented; she focused on barriers to overcome. Desimone (1999) conducted studies on the positive effects of parental involvement in all social classes as being engaged at home and throughout children's academic lives. Studies have shown various levels of involvement from working-class, middle-SES, and high-SES parents who believed in developing the whole child to be successful. Without a doubt, more research should explore the role of African American fathers and the accomplishments of their children (Roopnarine & Hossain, 2013). These roles are vital in engagement by all parents, especially African American fathers, to improve the relationships among parents, teachers, and students.

Conceptual Frameworks

The conceptual frameworks examined for the study were based on exploring the narratives of African American fathers regarding parental involvement in urban elementary schools. Three conceptual frameworks were used to ground the research and provide layering for the study: critical race theory, social capital theory, and cultural capital theory. All were valuable guides in the development of African American fathers' narratives. They allowed the researcher to introduce each framework under its specific component in the study.

Critical race theory. Critical race theory is an interpretive mode that helps to examine the face of race and racism across all cultural modes of expression that are dominant (Ladson-Billings, 2005). To adopt this approach, various scholars have attempted to understand how various victims of systemic racism are likely to be affected by cultural perceptions concerning race and how they position themselves to encounter prejudice successfully.

Critical race theory is defined as a framework, among other social sciences, that focuses particularly on applying the critical theory and critically examining society and its culture to the intersection of power, law, and race (Crichlow, 2015). It draws on both the priorities set and the perceptions of conventional civil rights scholarship and critical legal studies. It is a commitment to a vision that concerns the liberation of people from racism.

According to the results of research, critical race theory developed merely out of a legal scholarship. It functioned to analyze racism and race critically from a legal perspective. It has spread to numerous disciplines because it has fundamental tenets that function to guide its entire framework. The tenets are interdisciplinary in nature and can be approached from various points of view in the learning process (Cole, 2016).

Critical race theory has acknowledged that racism is deeply rooted in American society (Delgado & Stefancic, 2012). The analytical strategy to monitor the existing structures of power illustrates that power structures were formed based on White supremacy (Ladson-Billings, 2005). This has perpetuated the marginalization of the people who are "of color." The theory has also rejected all the traditions of meritocracy and liberalism because the legal discourse of the theory highlights that the law should be neutral and not associated with color. However, this theory has challenged this highlighted legal truth by carrying out an examination of the aspects of meritocracy and liberalism acting as vehicles for privilege, power, and self-interest. In addition, it recognizes meritocracy and liberalism of stories being told from those who are privileged, wealthy, and powerful. This has been achieved because an incorrect picture concerning meritocracy has been developed; that is, anyone can attain wealth, privileges, and power through hard work, irrespective of any form of the systemic inequalities that have been developed concerning institutional racism (Singer, Weems & Garner, 2017).

In relation to race, gender, national origin, class, sexual orientation, and the combination of these various aspects as they play in various life settings, the aspect of intersectionality has been brought up, which has recognized that race alone cannot be used to account for disempowerment and has pointed out the multidimensionality of oppression. This is important because it has helped to point out that the theory has been useful, especially concerning the oppression of "people of color." This means that it has not allowed a single-dimensional approach to tackle the complexities of the world.

Narratives and counterstories have contributed a great deal to the experiences that the people of color have faced. These stories have challenged the aspect of White supremacy and have continually given a voice of hope to those who have suffered oppression because of the aspect of White supremacy. The counterstories have based their arguments on more superior cultural traditions related to oral histories, parables, and family histories. This has been very important because it has helped in the preservation of the history of marginalized groups of people who have never had opportunities to be deemed as legitimate within the main narrative. It has challenged the ideology of meritocracy and liberalism as value-neutral and has exposed racism as the main factor that has enhanced the American foundation. Finally, critical race theory has been committed to lay emphasis on the aspect of social justice, where various scholars are working hard to ensure that racial oppression is eliminated completely. This has become the main goal of critical race theory that most scholars are pursuing tirelessly (Capper, 2015).

Critical race theory was useful in this study because adopting this approach to literature among other identified modes of expressing culture has proven to be more than just identifying racism, race, and other racialized characters. It helped put emphasis on the importance of examination and an attempt to understand all forces related to the sociocultural aspects of these fathers' lives, how they are perceived and experienced, and how they help in the response to racism. It has also helped treat literature, any legal documents, or related cultural works as enough evidence concerning the collective values and beliefs of the American culture.

Cultural capital theory. Cultural capital theory offers critiques and changes to society as a whole. Cultural capital theory is not like traditional theory in that traditional theory is oriented toward offering understanding and explanation of the society. Cultural capital theory intends to dig beneath the surface of society or a social trait to bring out assumptions that enable people to have a full stature of how society works. The theory was developed by five Frankfurt school theoreticians: Herbert Marcuse, Theodor Adorno, Max Horkheimer, Walter Benjamin, and Erich From, at the University of Frankfurt in 1930 (Lee & Bowen, 2006). It enables sociologists to have a varied understanding of the elements of society and how these elements connect and bring out a systematic operation that facilitates growth and development.

The key elements of the cultural capital theory are instrumental in understanding the operational systems of society. The cultural capital theory offers a chance for one to understand the social problems that exist and offers practical solutions on how to make responses to these problems. Social problems are instrumental in bringing change to any society. Cultural capital theory centers on the common ways of engagement. The theory reflects on the individual elements within a society and how they interact in understanding the factors of production within a social setting. The society is made of many elements, such as human factors and environmental factors (Buchanan, 2010).

One thing that is instrumental in understanding the society is its traditional and historical maneuvers. Cultural capital theory considers everything within a society, including the activities, objectives, and strategies that must have a grounded historical foundation. These foundations make way for the realization of the most important aspects of life that are instrumental in the functioning of society. Apart from highlighting the functions within a society, cultural capital theory offers what each element engages as a way of making for the functioning of the system (Focus on Blacks, 2011).

When problems are detected in a social setting, cultural capital theory plays the role of providing the remedy to make way for what is important to the human and nonhuman factors. Change must be ignited in a bid to have control measures toward realizing what is important and in some way offer solutions to current challenges. The theory offers ways by which people can respond to changes and challenges to navigate a better way of living at any given time.

Social capital theory. Three concepts of social capital are used as tools for promoting school achievements: norms and social control, information channels, and obligations and expectations in social relations. Parent engagement with teachers and students in an education system helps advance information, skills, and children's access to resources of social control (Coleman, 1988). This is achieved through assisting children with their homework and school–home pacts on behavioral standards and expectations, among other agreements. The preceding activities promote a child's educational success in one way or another.

Bourdieu (1986) broadly defined his model that enhances the concept of social capital by emphasizing that inequality is also subject to the amount of money an individual possesses or is able to acquire (Lee & Bowen, 2006). Furthermore, inequality is a question of a personal and cultural fit with the culture of the larger society or the society's institutions. For example, habitus stands for a system of dispositions resultant from past encounters and social teaching (Lee & Bowen, 2006). Field, on the other hand, represents a structured system of traditional communal relations both at the micro and macro levels. When students' habitus agrees with the fields, they are regarded to have a social advantage.

In an elaborate manner, social capital with parental educational involvement involves the following: (a) parents' attitudes gained from life encounters; (b) a connection to learning resources such as textbooks, laptops, and revision materials; and (c) parents' relationships to learning affiliated institutions such as libraries, universities, and other high learning institutions. The following factors have been found to improve the quality of schools in low-SES neighborhoods.

Social capital is a function of the school system (field) and a child's habitus (family) in which they operate. Parental adult mentors who share information and other resources are clearly seen as a crucial part of the social capital that facilitates student success (Erickson, McDonald & Elder, 2009; Stanton-Salazar & Spina, 2003). The higher the cultural capital, the greater the chances of obtaining additional resources to benefit the family. Consequently, students from families with less cultural capital experience difficulties in accessing institutional resources. Practically, social capital is the capacity to promote educational achievement by students.

Social capital theory examines problems within the social setting of these fathers' narratives. The theory offers ways by which people can respond to changes and challenges. Social theory is explored in this study because everything within a society, including the activities, objectives, and strategies, must have a grounded historical foundation. These foundations make way for the realization of the most important aspects of life that are instrumental in the functioning of the society as a whole. Apart from highlighting the functions within a society, social theory offers what each element engages as a way of the functioning of the system (Focus on Blacks, 2011).

Researcher's Positionality

The researcher is an African American father with two elementary-age daughters who attend an urban school. He considers the job of co-parenting one of his most important responsibilities and, as a result, was keenly interested in the experiences of other African American fathers who played active roles in their children's education. The conventional wisdom that African American parents are far less involved in the academic lives of their children was in direct contrast with what the researcher experienced at his daughters' school. The desire to gain a deeper understanding of other fathers' parental involvement undergirded the researcher's interests in this topic and thus influenced the selection of the theoretical frameworks and the research questions. The researcher remained sensitive to areas susceptible to bias and worked diligently through the adoption of accepted research practices to mitigate those biases.

For instance, even though the researcher shared similar experiences with the fathers in this study, to the degree it was possible, the researcher maintained an outsider's perspective that was discussed in-depth. In addition, nothing in the narratives were eliminated that could have influenced the researcher's positionality. The researcher's position in this research focused primarily on being dedicated to the narratives from the participants.

Discussion and Conclusions

This study presents a discussion of the results from the analysis of interviews with implications for research and practice for educational leaders, practitioners, policy makers, other researchers, and African American fathers. This research was designed to examine African American fathers' engagement in their children's academic and social lives in urban schools. The narratives focused on the father's descriptions and insights into their involvement. The data herein increases awareness for all concerned with parental participation. This research inquiry was guided by three research questions: (1) What are the narratives of African Americans on their parental involvement? (2) What are the roles of African American fathers on their parental involvement? and (3) How do African American fathers participate in the academic experiences of their elementary school children?

Conclusions

Several conclusions were drawn from the analysis of the data in this qualitative study. First, the fathers described African American parental involvement in extended time spent in classrooms and on campuses, as well as significant time spent on academic activities at home. They defined their role as one committed to building relationships with teachers, administrators, and other school personnel. The 15 fathers stressed their beliefs that their increased presence in the lives of their children would redound greater life benefits throughout their educational careers.

Second, nearly all the fathers positioned their roles as integral to the mental well-being, emotional well-being, and physical well-being of their children. Concrete expressions of their beliefs were evident in their sharing of how they set their own level of expectations, reinforcing expectations from the classroom at home, transmitting moral values through their religious beliefs, and participating in extracurricular activities both in school and outside of school. The fathers assisted with homework assignments; some even engaged private tutorial services. They excitedly volunteered at school, offered the campus additional resources, championed their children's involvement in extracurricular activities, and embraced and initiated being role models to other children.

Finally, many commonalities in their active roles were clear from their narratives. The narratives of fathers who had sons were slightly different from those of the fathers who had girls. Many fathers spoke about the reality of life in the United States that often dehumanizes African Americans. The fathers of sons emphasized the necessity of imbuing them with self-love, respect, and dignity. Fathers of daughters accentuated building positive relationships with them through conversations about morals and values in life. In terms of similarities, all fathers talked about the significance of partnering with teachers to reinforce at home what is taught at school. The one lone exception was the father who did not support building relationships with teachers, as he stated this was against his religion. Instead, he focused on relationship building at home by devoting two to three hours of homework assistance.

References

Abrams, S., & Gibbs, T. (2002). Disrupting the logic of home-school relations: Parent involvement strategies and practices of inclusion and exclusion. *Urban Education, 37*, 384–407.

Aikens, N., & Barbarin, O. (2008). Socioeconomic differences in reading trajectories: The contribution of family, neighborhood, and school contexts. *Journal of Educational Psychology, 100*, 235–251. 10.1037/0022-0663.100.2.235.

Altschul, I. (2012). Linking socioeconomic status to the academic achievement of Mexican American youth through parent involvement in education. *Journal of the Society for Social Work and Research, 3*(1), 13–30.

Anderson, B., Henriksen, B., & Spjelkavik, I. (2008). Benchmarking applications in public sector principal-agent relationships. *Benchmarking: An International Journal, 15*, 723–741.

Auerbach, S. (2007). From moral supporters to struggling advocates: Reconceptualizing parents roles in education through the experience of working-class families of color. *Urban Educator, 42*, 250–283.

Bakari, R. (2003). Preservice teachers' attitudes toward teaching African American students: Contemporary research. *Urban Education, 38*, 640–653.

Baker, D. P., & Stevenson, D. L. (1986). Mothers' strategies for school achievement: Managing the transition to high school. *Sociology of Education, 59*, 156–167.

Bempechat, J. (1992). The role of parent involvement in children's academic achievement. *School Community Journal, 2*(2), 31–41.

Berger, E. H. (1991). Parental involvement: Yesterday and today. *Elementary School Journal, 91*, 209–219.

Billman, N., Geddes, C., & Hedges, H. (2005). Teacher-parent partnerships: Sharing understandings and making changes. *Australian Journal of Early Childhood, 30*(1), 44–48.

Bloom, B. S. (1981). *All our children learning: A primer for parents, teachers and other educators*. New York, NY: McGraw-Hill.

Bornstein, M. H. (2014). *Socioeconomic status, parenting, and child development*. New York, NY: Routledge.

Bourdieu, P. (1986). The production of belief: Contribution to an economy of symbolic goods. In R. Collins, J. Curran, N. Gamham, P. Scannell, P.

Schlesinger, & C. Sparks (Eds.), *Media, culture, and society: A critical reader* (pp. 131–163). London, UK: Sage.

Bronfenbrenner, U. (1979). *The ecology of human development: Experiments by nature and design.* Cambridge, MA: Harvard University Press.

Buchanan, I. (2010). *A dictionary of critical theory.* Oxford, UK: Oxford University Press.

Burgess, A. (2009). *Fathers and parenting interventions: What works?* London, UK: Fatherhood Institute.

Capper, C. A. (2015). The 20th-year anniversary of critical race theory in education: Implications for leading to eliminate racism. *Educational Administration Quarterly, 51,* 791–833.

Catterall, J.S. (1998). Involvement in the arts and success in secondary school. *Americans for the Arts Monographs, 1*(9), 1–10

Cochran, M., & Dean, C. (1991). Home-school relations and the empowerment process. *Elementary School Journal, 94,* 262–269.

Cole, M. (2016). Critical race theory: A Marxist critique. In *Encyclopedia of educational philosophy and theory.* Singapore: Springer.

Cole, R. L. (2009). Black single custodial fathers: Influencing the decision to parent. *Families in Society, 24,* 247–258.

Coleman, J. S. (1988). Social capital in the creation of human capital. *American Journal of Sociology, 94,* 95–120.

Cooper, C. E. (2010). Family poverty, school-based parental involvement, and policy-focused protective factors in kindergarten. *Early Childhood Research Quarterly, 25,* 480–492.

Corley, K., & Fowler, C. (1996). Linking families, building community. *Journal of Educational Leadership, 53,* 7–24.

Crane, J. (2016). Effects of home environment, SES, and maternal test scores on mathematics achievement. *Journal of Educational Research, 89,* 305–314.

Cremin, L. A. (1957). *The republic and the school: Horace Mann on the education of free men.* New York, NY: Teachers College, Columbia University.

Crichlow, W. (2015, May). *Critical race theory: A strategy for framing discussions around social justice and democratic education.* Paper presented at the Higher Education in Transformation Conference, Dublin, Ireland.

Czarniawska, B. (2004). *Narratives in social science research.* London, UK: Sage.

Dearing, E., Kreider, H., Simpkins, S., & Weiss, H. B. (2006). Family involvement in school and low-income children's literacy: Longitudinal associations between and within families. *Journal of Educational Psychology, 98,* 653–659.

Delgado, R., & Stefancic J. (Eds.). (2012). *Critical race theory: The cutting edge* (3rd ed., Article 71). Philadelphia, PA: Temple University Press.

Desimone, L. (1999). Linking parent involvement with student achievement: Do race and income matter? *Journal of Educational Research, 93*(1), 11–30.

Dougherty, A., & Dougherty, E. (1977). *Home-based reinforcement of school behavior: A review and analysis.* Berkeley, CA: American Educational Research Association.

Dumont, H. T. (2014). Quality of parental homework involvement: Predictors and reciprocal relations with academic functioning in the reading domain. *Journal of Educational Psychology, 106*(1), 144–152.

Epstein, J. L. (1987). *Effects on student achievement of teachers' practices of parental involvement.* Greenwich CT: JAI Press.

Epstein, J. L., Coates, C., Sanders, M., & Simon, B. (1980). *School, family, and community partnership: Your handbook for action.* Thousand Oaks, CA: Crown Press.

Epstein, J. L., & Sanders, M. G. (2002). Family, school, and community partnerships. In M. Bornstein (Ed.), *Handbook of parenting, Volume 5: Practical issues in parenting* (2nd ed., pp. 407–438). Mahwah, NJ: Erlbaum.

Erickson, L. D., McDonald, S., & Elder, G. H. (2009). Informal mentors and education: Complementary or compensatory resources? *Sociology of Education, 82,* 344–367.

Fan, X., & Chen, M. (2001). Parental involvement and students' academic achievement: A meta-analysis. *Educational Psychology Review, 13*(1), 1–20.

Frew, L. A., Zhou, Q., Duran, J., Kwok, O. M., & Benz, M. R. (2013). Effect of school-initiated parent outreach activities on parent involvement in school events. *Journal of Disability Policy Studies, 24*(1), 27–35.

Focus on Blacks. (2011). *Race against time: Educating Black boys.* Retrieved from http://www.nea.org/assets/docs/educatingblackboys11rev.pdf

Frew, L. A., Zhou, Q., Duran, J., Kwok, O. M., & Benz, M. R. (2013). Effect of school-initiated parent outreach activities on parent involvement in school events. *Journal of Disability Policy Studies, 24*(1), 27–35.

Gurian, M. (2009). *The purpose of boys: Helping our sons find meaning and significance and direction in their lives.* San Francisco, CA: Jossey-Bass.

Hango, D. (2007). Parental investment in childhood and educational qualifications: Can greater parental involvement mediate the effects of socioeconomic disadvantage? *Social Science Research, 36,* 1371–1390. 10.1016/j.ssresearch.2007.01.005.

Hawley, W., & Rosenholtz, S. (2002). *Educational strategies that increase student academic achievement.* Washington DC: U.S. Department of Education.

Henderson, A. T., & Barla, N. (1994). *A new generation of evidence: The family is critical to student achievement.* Washington, DC: National Committee for Citizens in Education, Center for Law and Education.

Henderson, A. T., & Mapp, K. L. (2002). *A new wave of evidence: The impact of school, family, and community connections on student achievement.* Austin TX: Southwest Educational Development Laboratory, National Center for Family & Community Connections With Schools.

Hill, N. E., & Taylor, L. C. (2004). Parental school involvement and children's academic achievement pragmatics and issues. *Current Directions in PsychologicalScience, 13*(4),161–164.doi:10.1111/j.0963-7214.2004.00298.x

Hines, E. M., & Holcomb-McCoy, C. (2013). Parental characteristics, ecological factors, and the academic achievement of African American males. *Journal of Counseling & Development, 91*(1), 68–77.

Hong, S., & Ho, H. (2005). Direct and indirect longitudinal effects of parental involvement on student achievement: Second-order latent growth modeling across ethnic groups. *Journal of Educational Psychology, 97*(1), 32–42.

Hornby, G. (2011). *Parental involvement in childhood education: Building effective school-family partnerships.* New York, NY: Springer.

Huntsinger, C. S., & Jose, P. (2009). Parental involvement in children's schooling: Different meanings in different cultures. *Early Childhood Research Quarterly, 24,* 398–410.

Jacobs, K., & Kritsonsi, W. A. (2007). *Utilizing culture to improve communication and school involvement with parents from diverse background as a means to improve student achievement levels in the United States: A national focus.* Retrieved from http://files.eric.ed.gov/fulltext/ED499648.pdf

Jeynes, W. H. (2005). A meta-analysis of the relation of parental involvement to urban elementary school student academic achievement. *Urban Education, 40,* 237–269.

Jeynes, W. H. (2012a). A meta-analysis of the efficacy of different types of parental involvement programs for urban students. *Urban Education, 47,* 706–742.

Jeynes, W. H. (2012b). The relationship between parental involvement and urban secondary school students academic achievement: A meta-analysis. *Urban Education, 42*(1), 82–110.

Lacour, M., & Tissington, D. (2011). The effects of poverty on academic achievement. *Educational Research and Reviews, 6,* 522–527.

Ladson-Billings, G., & Tate, W. F. (1995). Toward a critical race theory of education. *Teachers College Record, 97*(1), 47–68.

Lareau, A. (1996). Assessing parental involvement in schooling: A critical analysis. In A. Booth & J. Dunn (Eds.), *Family-school links: How do they affect educational outcomes?* (pp. 57–64). Hillsdale, NJ: Erlbaum.

Lareau, A. (2003). *Unequal childhoods: Class, race, and family life.* Los Angeles: University of California Press.

Lee, J., & Bowen, N. (2006). Parent involvement, cultural capital, and the achievement gap among elementary school children. *American Educational Research Journal, 43,* 193–218.

Lengua, L., Kohl, G. O., & McMahon, R. J. (2000). Parent involvement in school conceptualizing multiple dimensions and their relations with family and demographic risk factors. *Journal of School Psychology, 38,* 501–512.

Mattingly, D. J., Prislin, R., McKenzie, T. L., Rodriguez, J. L., & Kayzar, B. (2002). Evaluating evaluations: The case of parent involvement programs. *Review of Educational Research, 72,* 549–576.

Mcbride, B., & Brown, G., & Bost, K., & Shin, N., & Vaughn, B., & Korth, B. (2005). Paternal identity, maternal gatekeeping, and father involvement. *Family Relations, 54,* 360–372. 10.1111/j.1741-3729.2005.00323.x.

McClelland, D. C. (1958). *Talent and society: New perspectives in the identification of talent.* Princeton, NJ: Van Nostrand.

Noltemeyer, A., & Bush, K. (2013). Adversity and resilience: A synthesis of international research. *School Psychology International, 34,* 474–487.

Nunes, T. (1999). *Learning to read: An integrated view from research and practice.* Dordrecht, The Netherlands: Kluwer.

Park, S., & Holloway, S. D. (2013). No parent left behind: Predicting parental involvement in adolescents' education within a sociodemographically diverse population. *Journal of Educational Research, 106*(2), 105–119.

Pattnaik, J., & Sriram, R. (2013). Father/male involvement in the care and education of children: History, trends, research, policies, and programs around the world. *Childhood Education, 86*, 354–359.

Revicki, D. A. (1981). *The relationship among socioeconomic status, home environment, parent involvement, child self-concept, and child achievement.* Retrieved from https://eric.ed.gov/?id=ED206645

Reynolds, R. (2010). "They think you're lazy," and other messages Black parents send their Black sons: An exploration of critical race theory in the examination of educational outcomes for Black males. *Journal of African American Males in Education, 1*(2), 1–19.

Robinson, K., & Harris, A. L. (2015). *The broken compass: Parental involvement with children's education.* Cambridge, MA: Harvard University Press.

Roopnarine, J. L., & Hossain, Z. (2013). African American and African Caribbean fathers. In C. Tamis-LeMonda & N. Cabrera (Eds.), *Handbook of father involvement* (pp. 223–243). New York, NY: Routledge.

Singer, J. N., Weems, A. J., & Garner, J. R. (2017). Fraternal twins: Critical race theory and systemic racism theory as analytic and activist tools of college sport reform. In B. J. Hawkins, A. R. Carter-Francique, & J. N. Cooper (Eds.), *Critical race theory: Black athletic sporting experiences in the United States* (pp. 11–55). New York, NY: Palgrave-Macmillan.

Sirin, S. R. (2005). Socio-economic status and academic achievement: A meta analytic review of research. *Review of Educational Research, 75*, 417–453.

Stanton-Salazar, R. D., & Spina, S. U. (2003). Informal mentors and role models in the lives of urban Mexican-origin adolescents. *Anthropology & Education Quarterly, 34*, 231–254.

Steinberg, L., Lamborn, S. D., Dornbusch, S. M., & Darling, N. (1992). Impact of parenting practices on adolescent achievement: Authoritative parenting, school involvement, and encouragement to succeed. *Child Development, 63*, 1266–1281.

Stevenson, D. L., & Baker, D. P. (1987). The family-school relation and the child's school performance. *Child Development, 58*, 1348–1357.

Swap, S. M. (1991, April). *Can parent involvement lead to increased student achievement in urban schools?* Paper presented at the Annual Meeting of the American Educational Research Association, Chicago, IL.

Tocqueville, A. (1975). *Democracy in America*. London, UK: Oxford University Press.

Turney, K., & Kao, G. (2009). Barriers to school involvement: Are immigrant parents disadvantaged? *Journal of Educational Research, 102,* 257–271. 10.3200/JOER.102.4.257–271.

Vellymalay, S. N. (2012). Parental involvement at home: Analyzing the influence of parents' socioeconomic status. *Studies in Sociology of Science, 3*(1), 1–6.

Wang, M., & Sheikh-Khalil, S. (2014). Does parental involvement matter for student achievement and mental health in high school? *Child Development, 85,* 610–625.

Weiss, H. B. (2006). *Family involvement in early childhood education: Family involvement makes a difference.* Cambridge, MA: Harvard Family Research Project.

Wilder, S. (2014). Effects of parental involvement on academic achievement: A meta-synthesis. *Educational Review, 66,* 377–397. doi:10,1080/0013191 1.2013.780009

Yanghee, K. (2009). Minority parental involvement and school barriers: Moving the focus away from deficiencies of parents. *Eduational Research Review, 4*(2), 80–102.

NINE

 Toward an Afrocentric Antiracist Pedagogy for Brazilian Music Ensembles

Cory J. LaFevers

The Afrocentric idea must be the stepping-stone from which the multicultural idea is launched.

—Molefi Kete Asante (2003, p. 37)

Historically, ethnomusicologists have championed music's ability to mediate cross-cultural understanding, a theme readily supported by the rise of multiculturalism in U.S. education discourse since the 1970s. Our work, which includes teaching "world music" survey courses, leading "world music" ensembles, and often working as advocates for the communities we research, necessitates that we critically engage with notions of cultural pluralism and social justice. I agree with Sonia Seeman (2017), who asserts that "since our field demands that we address the question of why and how music matters," ethnomusicologists have a great deal to contribute to music education broadly." And yet as a discipline, she notes we "have been slow to recognize the implications of our research for pedagogy" (Seeman, 2017, p. 201). In a moment of increased scholarly attention to activism and applied ethnomusicology, that ethnomusicologists continue to refine best practices and work toward developing more effective antiracist teaching methods is crucial.

This chapter presents the need for Afrocentric pedagogical approaches to world music, especially in situations where the predominantly White participants and audience members are learning and performing Afro-diasporic music. Drawing from critical Whiteness studies, Mathew Hughey's (2007) criticism of antiracist education and writings on Afrocentric education, I argue that antiracist education alone is an insufficient critique and corrective of multicultural practices of White-embodied consumption of African musical performances. Such an approach to multicultural musical encounter continues to relegate African agency to the margins, resulting instead in the reification of Whiteness that continues to treat the musical expressions of Africans as objects of study—or perhaps more accurately in the context of music ensembles, as sites of embodied racial play. Reflecting on participant-observation as a musician in the Brazilian music scene in Austin, Texas, from 2011 to 2018, I suggest that Afrocentric pedagogy for Brazilian ensembles will not only address the prevalence of racial stereotypes that tend to accompany exoticized performances of African music but also specifically reduce the reification of Whiteness found within both multicultural and antiracist educational initiatives, thus bolstering the potential of the music ensemble as a space of cross-cultural understanding, critical self-reflection, and antiracism advocacy.

Afro-Brazilian Music in Austin

Recently, scholars have investigated the rapid proliferation of Brazilian music ensembles around the world, producing studies on *samba*, *capoeira*, and *tambor de crioula* in such cities as Toronto, Montreal, New York, New Orleans, as well as in Wales and New Zealand (Courteau, 2007; Eisentraut, 2001; Gibson, 2012; Mercier, 2013; Pravaz, 2010, 2013; Robitaille, 2014; Stanyek, 2004, 2011). Home to at least 15 active Brazilian music and dance ensembles, Austin is clearly part of this global trend. However, it remains absent from the scholarship, a significant oversight given Austin's branding as the "Live Music Capital of the World."

Austin offers unique aspects for studying Brazilian music performance outside of Brazil. First, unlike New Orleans (Gibson, 2012), Austin doesn't have a large Brazilian population. Brazilian music in Austin is mostly performed by and for non-Brazilians. Furthermore, unlike Toronto and Montreal, where Pravaz (2010, 2013) and Mercier (2013) indicate the majority of performers of Brazilian repertoire are recent non-Brazilian immigrants to Canada, the majority of participants in Austin's Brazilian music scene are White Americans.[1]

Any Brazilian musical performance outside of Brazil raises questions regarding (re)presentations of national identity, the articulation of Brazilianness or Latinness, and the perpetuation of stereotypes through spectacle, as well as issues of cultural appropriation, exoticization, and cosmopolitan desire for the Other. These issues are further complicated when the music performed is also almost entirely derived from—and, in many cases, still closely associated with—Black Brazilian musical practices.[2] From this point on, I use the term *Afro-Brazilian music* to more accurately describe the music performed by these groups, although it should be noted that participants refer to the music as "Brazilian." Austin, where the majority of the participants are neither Brazilians nor individuals that are marginalized in society (as suggested by Pravaz, 2010, 2013, and Mercier, 2013) but representative of White, middle-class America, highlights these issues further.

Another unique aspect of Austin's Afro-Brazilian music scene is that it is considerably larger than those of other cities. For example, Natasha Pravaz indicates that Toronto's Samba School includes around 40 drummers (Pravaz 2010, p. 211). In contrast, Austin's Samba School has nearly 200 members, including dancers who make up the fastest growing segment of the ensemble. Austin also boasts a dizzying variety of other groups playing Afro-Brazilian music. In addition to the samba school, over the course of the research period, there are three smaller ensembles, Trem do Samba, Samba Bamba, and The Sambagators that play pagode-style samba. Artists/bands such as Paula Maya, Gabriel Santiago, Morena Soul, and Os Alquimistas perform fusions drawing from samba, bossa nova, MPB (*música popular brasileiro*, Brazilian Popular Music, and jazz. Austin is also home to the Brazilian rock and fusion bands Fusca XR3 and Tio Chico, as well as the funk band Macaxeira Funk and three independent capoeira academies. Additionally, Austin supports a surprising number of ensembles performing and teaching musical styles from the northeast of Brazil, including as many as three *forró* bands; Maracatu Texas, a percussion ensemble specializing in *maracatu*, *coco*, and *afoxé*;[3] and finally Trio Massa that performs forró-funk-jazz fusion. In this chapter, I focus on examples from participants of Austin Samba School and Maracatu Texas.

Briefly consider the broader context of race relations and racism in Austin to evaluate the significance of the dissertation project is important. Austin is the only one of the top 10 fastest growing U.S. cities with a declining Black population, apparently the result of a combination of factors, including segregation, gentrification, disparities in public education and employment opportunities, a history of discrimination and abuse by the Austin Police Department, and other forms of racism.[4] The situation is especially alarming and puzzling given "Austin's reputation as a 'tolerant' city, one celebrated for its progressivism, *cultural dynamism* [emphasis added], and emphasis on sustainability" (Tang & Ren, 2014, p. 6). Black Austinite Virginia Cumberbatch argues that young Black professionals and graduates are leaving because "they realize there's this liberalism that people [keep] talking about, and this music scene that's supposed to be so awesome [but it is] apparently is only reserved for a certain [kind] of people. 'I don't feel a part of that social network. I don't feel like there's a cultural space for me.' . . . That's when you start seeing people leave" (cited in Spearman, 2016, "Gone Before You Know It," para. 2).

Indeed, that the Afro-Brazilian music scene in Austin is experiencing a sharp rise in the number, variety, and popularity of bands at exactly the same time that Austin's Black population is in a sharp decline is striking. In what ways, if any, this scene contributes to Austin's "cultural dynamism" that masks racial inequalities. In other words, how might explicitly nonracist spaces of multicultural encounter work to unintentionally perpetuate racial divisions or tensions? The Afro-Brazilian music scene is uniquely situated within the broader context of world music performance in Austin. Depending on the group, genre, venue, or event, local performers tend to present Afro-Brazilian music as a distinct and unique category while simultaneously drawing on associations with Latin dance music (some liken samba and forró to salsa and cumbia) or with Afro-diasporic music (some connect maracatu, afoxé, and coco with notions of "African drumming") in order to promote their music to a largely non-Brazilian audience.

I argue that Afro-Brazilian musical performances contribute to the construction of a White identity that views itself as alternative and progressive. For audience members, as well as performers, this is consistent with the branding of Austin as a utopian space of hip cultural diversity, sounding out a liberal cosmopolitanism that ultimately masks Austin's racial inequalities via the exotic and erotic spectacle of race. Because the pedagogy of the groups does not directly engage topics such as race, racism, and gender, and because such performances tend to represent what Eric Lott (2013, p. 53) might call sites where racial/sexual "freedom and play meet," these spaces tend to reinforce rather than expose and critique White privilege and racial stereotypes. As a result, they unintentionally perpetuate certain aspects of racial bias and exclusion while simultaneously attempting to create moments of cross-cultural encounter and understanding. We must therefore reevaluate recent scholarship that stresses the potential of Afro-Brazilian music ensembles in global cities to challenge racial stereotypes and momentarily disrupt social power structures (Pravaz, 2010, 2013; Robitaille, 2014). As Molefi Asante (2007, p. 17) reminds us, "One can practice African customs and mores and not be Afrocentric because Afrocentricity is conscientization related to the agency of African people. One cannot be Afrocentric without being a conscious human being."

Critiques of Multiculturalism

World music ensembles frequently serve as a means of presenting the work of ethnomusicologists to a wider audience; they represent an interface of public exposure and a means of developing sustained interactions outside of academia. As such, ensembles offer considerable potential for raising awareness of a "diverse" array of social-cultural issues. Both Robitaille (2014) and Pravaz (2010, 2013) argue that, in addition to "sharing" aspects of the music and culture, Afro-Brazilian ensembles in Canada can disrupt and challenge racial stereotypes and social hierarchies, even if only momentarily. Although I do not disagree, I argue that for performers and audience members alike, participating in Afro-Brazilian music and dance performance by itself is not a guarantee that individuals will embark on discussions about race, racism, and, in particular, self-reflection about concepts such as White privilege. Indeed, various authors have long made similar critiques of multicultural music education (Bradley, 2006; Volk, 1998), and their writings support the conclusions of my own research. Katrin Sieg (2002) expresses similar concerns. Likening the history of farcical impersonations of Jews in German theater to U.S. blackface minstrelsy and, in particular, the combination of desire and fear that motivated them, Sieg (2002) argues that "the self-criticism, even self-contempt, that sometimes inspires ethnic masquerades does not necessarily translate to changing one's own behavior, or engaging in collective political action" (pp. 21–22). Placing Sieg's point within the context of Afro-Brazilian ensembles in Austin, we can understand the processes of embodying Afro-Brazilianness as a potential antidote to the perceived negative qualities of Whiteness. This is in part because Brazilianness (any race) is read in Austin as hip and cool, just as Mercier (2013, p. 94) describes in Canada. When combined with the long-standing White hipster construction of Blackness as the epitome of non-White cool (Monson, 1995), Afro-Brazilian music ensembles perform and reinforce Austin's brand of weird liberal exceptionalism and color-blind hipster cosmopolitanism. Because Afrocentricity is absent from how the groups teach their members and present this music to the public, African agency is erased, resulting in the White hipster embodiment of Black cultural expressions. In agreement with Ingrid Monson (1995), Tricia Rose (1994), and Debora Wong (2000), Brian McCann (2016) stresses that although "Black Americans historically rely on various expressions of Blackness for cultural and corporeal survival amid centuries of racist violence . . . Whites adopt Blackness in ways that ultimately affirm the supremacy of Whiteness" (p. 365).

One can see the disconnect between an involvement in Afro-Brazilian music and a lack of sensitivity to racial dynamics play out in the following incident in which one ensemble member committed a microaggression against another. Racial microaggressions are verbal or nonverbal expressions that, with or without intending to, are read as demeaning and racially "Othering" the recipient. They are perceived as communicating hostility, insensitivity, disregard, and/or disrespect. Racial micro-aggressions often appear "nonracial but they contain an underlying message that has a detrimental impact on its unfortunate recipient" (Olds, 2011, p. 101). Julie, for example, is an American (White, non-Latina) student at the University of Texas at Auston who speaks Spanish, is learning Portuguese, has traveled to Brazil and other Latin American cultures, and performs in several Latin (including Brazilian) music ensembles. During the rehearsal of a Latin music ensemble in Austin, students were congratulating another student who was recently admitted to a graduate school. Malu, a Black Brazilian woman performing in the group, also shared that she was just accepted into a PhD program. Julie congratulated Malu and asked, "Are you the first in your family to go to college?"

Whatever Julie's intent, Malu perceived the utterance as a racial microaggression that insinuated Black inferiority while policing access to formerly White-only spaces, as if to say "you don't belong." Soon thereafter, Malu left the ensemble. It is important to stress that the point here is not to interrogate Julie's intent or to label particular actions and utterances as racist. It is, however, important to acknowledge that exposure to Latin American and Brazilian music and culture in and of itself did not make Julie more aware or sensitive to racial interactions and White privilege, nor did the ensemble radically alter social hierarchies of race in the Austin area.

Other examples from the Samba School indicate that racial essentialism may be reinforced rather than challenged through participation in ensembles. We can see the extent to which race and authenticity intersect for Austinites in the following example from Cristina, a self-identified Black women (*negra*) who relocated to Austin to work for a major tech company and one of the very few Brazilians to currently perform with Austin Samba. She and I are talking about racism in Austin broadly. I tell Cristina that over the course of my research, I have heard (anonymous) stories of microaggressions from samba dancers, and I ask if she ever experienced something like that. She explains that she never felt racial discrimination: '*But*, [since I am] the only Brazilian [drummer in Austin Samba], I sometimes feel the opposite. They idolize me so much because I am Brazilian. 'Oh, you should know about this." Cristina then suggests that, although she does not interpret these interactions as racism, race is nevertheless a factor in how Americans view her as an authentic source on all things samba: "I don't feel [racial] prejudice but I feel the inverse, but isn't it true that [Austin Samba members idolize me] because I am Black?"[5]

Similarly, stereotypes about Black's supposed ability to dance—and drum— inform racial discourse in Brazilian ensembles in Austin. In our conversation, I ask Rachel, an African American dancer in Austin Samba, if she experienced any racial stereotypes in the samba school. She responds:

> Of course microaggressions happen, but I don't think anyone ever told me directly, "Oh Rachel, you're Black [so] you should be able to do this or this comes easier to you." I have had someone say . . . , "Oh, well Rachel, you'll get this because you just automatically have natural rhythm, or you just have good rhythm." Yeah, so they never said like, "Because the color of your skin," but they will say that. Yes.

I should mention that Rachel stressed to me that such incidents were rare, she can "count the number of times on [her] fingers," and that she explained to me that as part of her strategy to navigate racism in Austin, she surrounds herself with open-minded people who are "willing to have those difficult conversations" (referring to discussing race). The point I want to make here is that racial stereotypes about Blacks' ability to dance, and, conversely, the inability of Whites to master samba, are circulating at least with some members of Austin Samba. The extent to which these essentialisms are present indicates that exposure to Afro-Brazilian samba music as taught and performed in Austin Samba, and Austin more broadly, reifies Whiteness's construction of itself.

A final example merits further analysis because it shows how a lack of Afrocentricity in pedagogies does little to address the intersectionality of biases and power dynamics that frame social interactions in world music ensembles, in addition to illustrating both their limitations and potential as vehicles for challenging racialized and gendered power dynamics and as forums for social justice. Vanessa, who identifies as biracial, is from Recife, where maracatu music is from, and drums with Maracatu Texas. She shares with me conversations she had with some of the members of Maracatu Texas about her discomfort with the proposal to add dancers to the group. What is especially interesting about their discussion is the importance of authenticity and the boundaries of respectful engagement with another's culture. Embedded within the debate are colonialist desires for the Other, manifestations of White privilege as related to the consumption of Blackness (viewing the dancing Black body), Blackness as a cultural commodity, and resistance to anti-Black violence.

Vanessa explains:

Amanda wanted to have a dance group with Maracatu [Texas]. And I didn't like that idea. It bothered me very, very much. And she said, "Why does it bother you so much?" It bothers João also. And I said "Because, have you seen a maracatu group? Maracatu groups don't have dancers."

[Amanda replied] "But I saw on YouTube that it has dancers."

And I said, "It had dancers because that's a performance group ... not a real maracatu group."

To fully appreciate the nuance of Vanessa's point, it is necessary to briefly describe the history of maracatu, including the difference between a "real" maracatus-nação and percussion groups. The distinction is important and addresses a history of racism, cultural appropriation, and spatio-racial formations in Recife that reverberate in Austin. Maracatu-nação (maracatu nation), also known as *maracatu de baque virado* (flipped-beat maracatu), is an Afro-Brazilian cultural form from Recife and surrounding municipalities. Likely related to the King and Queen of Kongo coronation ceremonies of colonial-era Catholic lay brotherhoods, Maracatu-nação emerged as a distinct form of parading in Recife's carnival of the 19th century.[6] The ensemble consists of a royal court whose procession is accompanied by a drum battery, traditionally composed of *alfaias* (bass drum), *tarol* (a shallow snare drum), *gonguê* (single bells), and *ganzá* or *mineiro* (cylindrical shakers).[7] Historically, White elites in Recife viewed maracatu with distain, linking it with anti-Black stereotypes, including criminality, poverty, "noise," and "witchcraft" (in reference to Afro-matrix religions). Between 1930 and 1945, officials undertook an intense campaign against Afro-religious practices in Recife that impacted maracatus as well (Guillen, 2007). During the 1960s and 1970s, scholars and folklorists worried the cultural manifestation was in decline, attempted to "save" maracatu from extinction (Lima, 2012, p. 22).

However, due to the international success of the "mangue beat" music in the 1990s and, in particular, groups such as Chico Science and Nação Zumbi, maracatu gained renewed attention. White, middle-class residents of Recife, who had long scorned maracatu, suddenly began to celebrate it, ultimately adopting it a symbol of Pernambucan identity (Avelar, 2011; Galinsky, 2002). In the wake of this renewed attention, Whites in Recife started to perform maracatu, often forming their own ensembles known as *grupos percussivos* (percussion groups). Tensions emerged between such percussion groups and the long-standing Afro-descendant maracatus-nação in Recife, with activists and maracatuzeiros as critiquing middle-class interest in and performance of maracatu as cultural appropriation, a critique substantiated by the privileged position of the new percussion groups in the Brazilian media (Carvalho, 2007; Esteves, 2008).

The debates between maracatus-nação and the middle-class percussion groups highlight the role of musical practices in defining spatio-racial formations in Recife. Lima (2013) describes maracatus-nação as a community-based cultural form headquartered in the neighborhoods in which most of the (overwhelmingly Black) members live. Traditional maracatus-nação have strong ties with Orixás and Afro-matrix religions of their community (Candomblé, *Jurema, Umbanda*). The calunga, the *eguns*, or ancestral Orixás embodied in a doll that accompanies maracatu processions, is just one example of such a tie (Lima, 2013, p. 52). In contrast, newer percussion groups are composed of mostly White or light-skinned middle-class youth who live across the Recife metropolitan area; they meet up, usually on the weekends and in iconic neighborhoods (Recife Antigo), to rehearse and perform (Esteves, 2013, p. 77; Lima, 2013, p. 54). As such, the community-based aspects of traditional maracatu-nação, and its religious significance, are not perpetuated in such percussion groups; they typically reduce maracatu-nação to its distinct aesthetic elements—"dance, music, lyrics, and performance" (Carvalho, 2007, p. 17).[8]

Returning to Vanessa, she explains that both Amanda (a White woman of Brazilian heritage raised in the United States) and Ryan (a White man from the United States) respond, "Oh, we're not a real maracatu group," implying that it would be okay, then, for Maracatu Texas to add dancers. In her reply, Vanessa suggests that the existence of Maracatu Texas as an Austin ensemble playing maracatu and other Afro-Brazilian rhythms from the Brazilian northeast is walking a fine line between cultural engagement and disrespectful appropriation: "I said 'I understand, but we're already so far [removed from grassroots practice] because we're not a maracatu group. We're so far from the original, let's not make it worse.'"

As she elaborates, Vanessa expresses frustration that, despite joining the ensemble to learn about Brazilian music and performing these rhythms, she perceives members' lack of understanding of the deep cultural (and racial) significance of maracatu-nação:

> I don't think they understand. Amanda doesn't understand because she not from Brazil. Her parents [are] from Belém, [but] she didn't grow up with the culture of maracatu, so I think it's hard to understand this idea of identity and ownership of something. Like, you look at it on YouTube and [she says], "I see dancers." But that's not what maracatu *is*. We know that we are not a Candomblé-based maracatu. But let's not make it worse. Let's not [take] it further away from its origins.... It's very important to me that we don't [turn maracatu] into just like, "*confetti festinha*" [a little confetti party]: ... No, this is not a party.

There is "a certain line" regarding performing maracatu outside of its original context that she "doesn't want to cross," and for Vanessa, adding dancers crosses it. She recognizes that she "[doesn't] belong" to maracatu. This means that she did not grow up in a neighborhood with a maracatu-nação, she has not performed in a maracatu since she was little, she does not practice Candomblé, and therefore, she is not part of the Black communities that perform the music traditionally. "But at the same time," she tells me, "I know where [maracatu] comes from. I know because, although I was not part [of it], I was closer [than other members of Maracatu Texas]." She explains to me that she did not perform with a maracatu-nação when she lived in Recife because, when she was growing up, "maracatu was considered very low class. It was considered a big 'no'" by her family. She lived in a poor neighborhood but not as poor as the adjacent one that housed a maracatu-nação. She remembers that on Sundays, her family could hear the ensemble rehearsing. Because it was so hot, her dad would watch TV from the front doorway to cool off with the breeze from the terrace. She recalls:

> When Maracatu Bairro X[9] . . . would play, [my dad] would say to my mom, "Beta! maracatu começou!" (Beta! [the] maracatu just started!). It bothered him because he couldn't hear the TV. I remember sometimes I would sit down outside with my dog just to listen to it [and wonder], "What is that? What are they doing there? What . . . is so mysterious [about maracatu]?" . . . I enjoyed listening to it. While my parents [complained] because it was loud and they couldn't watch TV, [saying] . . . "Oh, maracatu começou!" [in an aggravated tone] . . . for me it was like [in curious but hushed tone of voice, because she is not supposed to be interested]: Oh, maracatu começou. [Laughs.]

Vanessa thus has a history of proximity to maracatu, both physical (and audible) closeness. She also grew up witnessing discrimination against maracatuzeiros prior to the post-1990s transformation of maracatu into an iconic sonic marker of Pernambucan identity. For these reasons, she has a greater appreciation for what maracatu-nação means to Black communities in Recife.[10] Vanessa is concerned that ensemble members' engagement with maracatu is limited to videos seen on YouTube and that the cultural significance of the performance is not fully grasped by them. Instead, Vanessa fears, maracatu is reduced to a commodity for their entertainment.

Vanessa continues and tells me about the reaction she received from her bandmates about her stance on adding dancers:

Me: You said all that to Amanda?

Vanessa: Yeah, I did say that to Amanda, but it's hard for her to understand [She said] *"Mas que besteira Vanessa, mas que besteira"* (What nonsense, Vanessa, what nonsense).

Of particular importance is Ryan's reaction because, to use Vanessa's expression, he "knows," meaning he should have a better understanding of the issues at play because he has traveled to Recife and has some experience playing maracatu there. However, Ryan's engagement with the repertoire in Brazil has not necessarily translated into a greater sensitivity to the racial implications of performing it:

It's hard to explain, and even Ryan knowing [about where the music comes from did not seem to help] . . . For example, when I was talking to Ryan, he was saying, "But maracatu has dancers!" And I [said] "No, they don't have dancers." And he said: "Yes they do. I played in Maracatu Caxangá."[11] And I said [that was] "Maracatu Caxangá, not a real maracatu, Ryan. It's a [staged] performance of a maracatu." [Ryan]: "Yes, but even when they have the parade, [the dancers] perform" and I said "Oh whoa, whoa, whoa, my dear. You're not talking about dancers. You're talking about the Queen and the King. And you're talking about people carrying an *agbê*[12] and moving to it. Nobody tells them "1 2 3 4 5 6 7 8, turn turn turn." Nobody. "Legs up! Kick!" *Nobody* does that. There's no such [thing], I have never seen anything like that in a real maracatu group in Brazil. So do not call the Queen and the King dancers. They are *not* dancers; they are there for a very different reason. So don't call them dancers because that's disrespectful."

As George Dei (1994) explains, "Euramerican education continues to distort, misappropriate, and misinterpret many African peoples' lives and experiences" (p. 3). Vanessa continues:

We had a whole conversation about this. And he was like, "but [Maracatu Texas] is not a traditional maracatu group" [and therefore having dancers would not be inappropriate].

And I was like, "I understand, Ryan, but it's my culture, and ... if you take that away ... "

And he's like, "But culture is [ir]relevant, this thing that [we call] culture doesn't really exist, blah, blah, blah." And I was like, "Are you trying to take away my identity? That's my freaking identity. I come from Recife. I saw these things. I heard these things. I couldn't experience [the procession and the drumming] in my own skin because I knew that I didn't belong there, my parents' didn't allow me to. When it became popular [in the 1990s] I had a little taste of it. I have so much respect [for maracatu] because I went to Candomblé houses, I went to Casa de Xambá,[13] I learned about Casa de Xambá, and I have so much respect for it. Don't try to take away from me saying that culture is [irrelevant]. I was like "Fucking Bullshit, man! Are you trying to take my identity away!?" [laughs]. It was like a very heated conversation ... but then at the end of the day we're like, ok, I respect you and I don't judge you.

My aim in citing this lengthy interaction is to underscore once again my argument that learning to perform Afro-Brazilian rhythms—exposing yourself to the culture of the Other—does not in and of itself result in antiracist praxis. More than challenging social hierarchies and racial stereotypes, engagement with Black Brazilian musical forms often reinforces the social power and dominance of Whiteness—and White men as well—over circumscribed frames of Blackness. Exposure to Black Brazilian cultural forms, in this case, did not prompt Amanda and Ryan to question their White privilege, their desire for the Other, or their right to engage with and reinterpret Afro-descendant musical practices. What is needed is an Afrocentric perspective that highlights maracatu as an African story, highlighting African agency as well as fostering critical self-reflection for white participation.

Vanessa's exchanges with her fellow percussionists suggest that such ensembles could be transformed into forums for addressing social justice issues. Despite the heated argument and Vanessa's accusations that the group did not sufficiently valorize the meanings and history of such heritage, she values her friendship with other band members and their willingness to engage in difficult discussions. In other words, the powerful community bonds forged in these ensembles create an opportunity for members to work together toward antiracist and social justice education, including uncomfortable self-reflection. To better harness this potential, examining potential correctives to multicultural music education, including antiracism and its critiques, as well as the need for Afrocentric music pedagogical methods, is necessary.

The Pitfalls of Antiracist Music Education

Deborah Bradley (2006) argues that liberal multiculturalism "works with the notion of our basic humanness and downplays inequities of difference by accentuating shared commonalities" (p. 13). In contrast, she argues for an antiracist approach that "seeks to identify, challenge, and change the values, structures, and behaviors that perpetuate systemic racism and other forms of societal oppressions (Bradley 2006, p. 13–14). However, there are at least two problems with Bradley's model. First, it is not exactly clear how her approach differs from that of other ethnomusicologists. For example, David Locke, Michelle Kisliuk, and Kelly Gross all describe world music ensembles' abilities to challenge racial essentialisms and expectations through performance (Solís, 2004). Locke (2004, pp. 182) states that an "African ensemble is a rare setting in which nonblack participants may seem racially out of place," a challenge to their own racialized experience as well as a potential source of discomfort to audience expectations. Similarly, Kisliuk and Gross (2004, pp. 249, 257–260) argue that a nearly all-White BaAka ensemble "is a fundamental challenge to racial and ethnic essentialisms" that also emphasizes dynamic, continual cultural flows and interpretation over cultural fixity, tradition, and representation. David Harnish (2004, p. 136) argues that musical performance can guard against orientalism in that it breaks down distinctions between the Self and Other. Both Pravaz (2010, 2013) and Robitaille (2014) claim Brazilian ensembles in Toronto achieve similar results. Other than advocating for conversations about race, racism, and White privilege, therefore, it is unclear how Bradley's (2006) model differs in practice.

Second, whether antiracism is effective at addressing the shortcomings of multiculturalism is unclear. As Mathew Hughey explains, proponents of antiracist activism are heavily influenced by Eduardo Bonilla-Silva's (2014) argument that contemporary racism is perpetuated via color-blind mechanisms that mask anti-blackness without appearing to be "racist." Bonilla-Silva's (2014) solution is for Whites to stop claiming to be nonracists. He believes that they should educate themselves about institutional racism and White privilege and only then engage in antiracism practices. However, Hughey's (2007) research suggests this approach is untenable. In his ethnographic study of an antiracist activist organization, Hughey (2007) notes that despite being "hyper-aware" of racism and White privilege, White antiracist members of the organization continued to "[reproduce] racist ideology in at least three specific valences: (1) belief in racial essentialism, (2) expectations that Whites should be at the center and the subject of racial discourse, and (3) contradictory viewpoints regarding racial segregation and the freedom of association"[14] (pp. 73-74). Hughey's (2007) assessment corroborates the argument (Rasmussen, Klinenberg, Nexica & Wray, 2001, p. 13) that "antiracist practice is often undermined by the desire of White people to remain comfortable" or, to use George Yancy's terminology, to remain "sutured" (Yancy, 2017, p. 13). In her analysis of antiracism in British social work education, Mekada Graham (2000) further explains the shortcomings of antiracism from an Afrocentric perspective, noting that "the existing parameters of antiracism in social work reflect a Eurocentric project that fails to understand, recognize or respond to black autonomy" (p. 424).

Where, then, does this leave Brazilian music ensembles? Given the desire of participants to shed "normalcy" by donning the trappings of non-Whiteness, Brazilian music ensembles are particularly apt to be used as a method of non-White association that appears "trendy, cool, and cutting-edge" (Hughey, 2007, p. 79). As I argue earlier, Austinites engage with Brazilian music and dance at least in part to articulate a hip Whiteness that correlates with Austin's urban branding and liberal reputation. It seems that antiracist tactics such as discussing the social construction of Whiteness, unmasking Whiteness as an unmarked norm, drawing attention to White privilege and how it shapes White experience, can function to reify Whiteness rather than decenter it. Antiracism, then, runs to risk of reproducing the pitfalls of multiculturalism, producing "racism that is activated in the form non-white 'others' as spectacles who only have voice when interpellating the white subject, or when serving as entertaining exoticism while teaching whites about things previously unknown" (Hughey, 2007, p. 97).

Strengthening Antiracism With Afrocentricity

Rather than abandon antiracist pedagogy in light of its potential pitfalls, I suggest that antiracism and critical Whiteness still offer considerable potential for mitigating against reinforcing race and gender stereotypes, provided they are reinforced with Afrocentricity. I read Hughey's (2017) conclusions as evidence of what George Yancy calls "the ambiguous reality of white racism" (p. 223). Yancey (2017) stresses that "dismantling whiteness is a *continuous* project," and that we must "continue to undo white racism even as it repositions [antiracist Whites] as privileged" (p. 223). Afrocentricity's focus on centering African agency allows for a critical analysis of Whiteness while maintaining the agency of Africans as subjects in the creation and performance of Afro-Brazilian music. Continuing to interrogate the hegemony of Whiteness from an Afrocentric perspective is necessary for addressing the deep-seated conventional wisdom or embodied "knowledge" of racial formations. Yancy (2017) refers to this quality as the insidiousness (etymologically linked to ambush) of Whiteness: the ability of racist actions to surface despite one's active attempts to dismantle White privilege. Yancy (2017) asserts that Whiteness "is a master of concealment; it is insidiously embedded within responses, reactions, good intentions, postural gestures, denials, and structural and material orders" (p. 219).

Ann Berlak (2008) explains that, despite her best efforts and her perception that students made considerable strides in disrupting the hegemony of White racism, she witnessed during supervised student teaching a "gap between students' espoused beliefs and values" (p. 48) and their actions in the classroom. She cites as an example supervising one of her student teachers who put the names of three misbehaving Black boys on the board, ignoring the identical behavior of White boys. She conceptualizes the same phenomenon through psychologist Timothy Wilson's theory of the adaptive unconscious. Berlak (2008) explains that according to Wilson, attitudes "toward concepts such as race or gender . . . operate at two levels—at a conscious level our stated values direct our behavior deliberately, and at an unconscious level we respond in terms of immediate but quite complex automatic associations that tumble out before we have even had time to think" (p. 51). She continues:

The adaptive unconscious is far more sophisticated, efficient, and adult-like than the unconscious portrayed by psychoanalytic theory. It can set goals, interpret and evaluate evidence, and influence judgments, conscious feelings, and behavior. People can think in quite sophisticated ways and yet be thinking "non-consciously." In fact, the mind relegates a good deal of high-level thinking to the adaptive unconscious. (Berlak, 2008, p. 51)

Note the similarity with Yancy's conceptualization of Whiteness as ambush.

Yancy (2017) argues that "the moment a white person claims to have arrived [as an antiracist], he/she often undergoes a surprise attack, a form of attack that points to how Whiteness ensnares even as one strives to fight against racism" (p. 219). Berlak (2008) states, "Individuals can honestly claim they are aware of the diverse set of racist practices that hold in place the hegemony of Whiteness and yet be completely unaware of them at an implicit automatic level" (p. 51). Both Berlak's (2008) adaptive unconscious and Yancy's (2017) insidious Whiteness betray the inadvertent behaviors of anti-racist Whites. This theory helps to explain Hughey's observations, how antiracist Whites can consciously engage in discussions about racism and White privilege and unwittingly reproduce the same racist behaviors they are attempting to correct. White racism insidiously creeps back in, through racial microaggressions, unconscious bias, and repositioning itself at the center of racial discourse, reifying power over Black bodies.

For this reason, we need to continue to pursue antiracist and critical Whiteness in our pedagogies while refusing to romanticize antiracism as a state to be achieved. As mentioned, the struggle against antiracism is continual. Conceptualizing antiracism as a place of "arrival" functions to keep Whiteness intact, or "sutured," and thus prevents Whites from "lingering with the profound and intricate layers of white supremacy" (Yancy, 2017, p. 13). Yancy (2017) suggests that "lingering" with Whiteness is "the necessary deeper critical work required to unearth the various ways in which one is actually complicit in terms of racist behavior" (Yancy, 2017, p. 222). He stresses that embedded within the idea of an "actualized" ("woke" or arrived) antiracist White person is a sense of "self-glorification," of self-understanding that "obstructs" this deeper critical work (Yancy, 2017, p. 222). To begin to reshape the adaptive unconscious, Yancy (2017) argues we have must "[nurture] a disposition to be un-sutured ... to crack, re-crack, and crack again the calcified operations of the white gaze" (pp. 13–14). In situations of Afro-Brazilian ensembles, Afrocentricity offers a means to continually un-suture Whiteness's centered position. But this does not mean that Afrocentricity is anti-White. As Asante (2007) explains:

> Afrocentric education represents a new interpretation of productive transmission of values and attitudes. Students are made to see with new eyes and to hear with new ears. African American children learn to interpret phenomena from themselves as centered; *whites learn to see that their own centers are not threatened by the space taken by African Americans or others* [emphasis added]. (p. 83)

Additionally, Afrocentricity helps address Hughey's (2007) argument that "[antiracism] must focus less on the conceptual make-up of what whiteness essentially is. One of the largest problems with the white antiracist praxis I encountered was their reification of racial identity" (p. 97). Smith (2016) and Muñoz (2006) also stress the need for zeroing in instead on what racism/Whiteness *does*.

In an education context where White participants are learning and performing African and Afro-Brazilian music, what racism/Whiteness *does* is place Whiteness at the center, treating Africans and their culture as objects for study/consumption and relegating their agency to the margins. Asante (2007) elaborates:

> Afrocentricity is about location precisely because African people have been operating from the fringes of the Eurocentric experience. Much of what we have studies in African history and culture, or literature and linguistics, or politics and economics, has been orchestrated from the standpoint of Europe's interests. Whether it is a matter of economics, history, politics, geographical concepts, or art, Africans have been seen as peripheral to the "real" activity. *This off-centeredness has impacted Africans as well as whites in the United States. Thus, to speak of Afrocentricity as a radical redefinition means that we seek to re-orientation of Africans to a centered position* [emphasis added]. (pp. 31–32)

If the investigation of White racial formation and our implicit racial bias is not coupled with an Afrocentric perspective that breaks with the entire pedagogical history of Whites, who have always been centered in our education systems,[15] then we will continue to pursue antiracism as mainstream history classes on slavery—from the sole subjective position of Whites. Such an approach allows us to deconstruct unintentional racist thinking embedded in Whiteness without maintaining Whiteness at the center of experiencing Afro-Brazilian music.

Multiculturalism and Music as Aesthetic Object

Music education presents unique challenges related to performing as well as how music is treated vis-à-vis culture. Deborah Bradley (2017) acknowledges that "the traditional [Western music education] focus on music as aesthetic object occludes the social issues embedded in music," (p. 209) and as a result, even multicultural music education functions within a wider ideology of Whiteness. Rather than working as an agent of social change, multicultural music education—the approach most commonly informing performance in Brazilian ensembles in Austin—"reifies whiteness and otherness" by removing racial politics from the music (Bradley 2017, p. 208).

A desire to separate Brazilian music from racial or political issues repeatedly surfaced in my interactions with ensemble members and leaders. Jessica tells me, "I like to keep my music free of politics, frankly," and "just appreciate the art for art's sake." She elaborates, "So, when I'm playing music with the Austin Samba bateria, I'm just enjoying the rhythm. I am not trying to think of the broader political message we might be sending, and I don't think I want to. You know what I mean?" Bradley's (2006) point about focusing solely on the musical object aligns with Arnold's comment about the Austin Samba School: "We're more focused on creating, making this music happen in a much more visceral [way]: a 'here's how it sounds and here's how you get there' kind of a thing."

One might counter these statements by suggesting that the music in Brazil, like all musical practice, is embedded in webs of sociopolitical significance and must be understood in that way. In addition, separating the musical product from its sociopolitical origins reduces the humanity of the people who produced it and becomes a potential mechanism with which to maintain

Whiteness and the myth of Brazilian racial democracy. Jessica, who during our interview (discussed earlier) told me very clearly that she does not like to mix music and politics, also explained in a separate e-mail communication that she was admonished for bringing up race and politics at rehearsals. As a result, she "learned her lesson" and chose to "just dance." Thus, the avoidance of politics reflects a traditional approach to music making in the West and the tendency to consider it only as an aesthetic object. At the same time, it demonstrates the way ideologies of Whiteness work can support "forms of social amnesia" in that they obfuscate our complicity "in maintaining systems of privilege and oppression (Bradley 2017, p. 208).

In response to my inquiries about the relationship of music to social issues in Brazil, performers frequently commented on the structural limitations of time in rehearsal contexts and the paramount goal of learning the repertoire well enough to perform. Rachel explains, "As an Austin Samba school community, [when] we get together, we're just there to dance. There's not a lot of speaking about current global issues or things that are happening in Brazil." Sarah recalls, "We [are] so busy learning steps and learning music and practice, practice, practice that we kind of [forget why we started dancing (i.e., fun, community) in the first place].... It kind of [becomes] show business, I guess... because we're just pumping: gigs and choreography and sweat and tears." As Arnold explains it, the primary goal is "to have a performance ensemble that sounds awesome. There's not always time to go into the historical aspects of it." The importance of perfecting performance, at least in the samba school, is perhaps one of the reasons why members are usually only interested in discussing samba music as it relates to their community in Austin, rather than its original meanings for Black Brazilians. Sociocultural issues may be of some interest, yet the mechanics of the music/dance as aesthetic object again emerge as the primary focus.

Even so, some performers express desire for more cultural engagement, suggesting that centrality of the performance needs to be revisited. Sarah reflected, "Maybe that's one of the reasons why I loved Brazil Camp because, you know, we weren't performing, we were learning." Similarly, David explains that one of the reasons he prefers to perform with Maracatu Texas is that he gets more discussion about the cultural aspects of the music. He attended a few Austin Samba rehearsals and notes that "they just play the whole time, they don't talk much about culture or religion." By contrast, David asserts that the leadership of Marcatu Texas "[makes] a point of trying to, talk to us about boundaries, things that we need to do to be respectful [of], and I never heard anybody in the samba school even talk about that." Rachel expresses a desire for more conversations about the politics involved in Austin Samba's performance, noting that she learned a lot from the few members who traveled to Brazil and "brought back information about what it is like to be a person of color there, and how that translates to [the context] here." "But," Sarah reflects, "I think collectively as a group, and especially [given] the Whiteness that we see in the samba school . . . it's necessary to have these very public and open conversations. And I don't think, . . . [up until now], the model of the samba school [has been] a platform for that at all."

Cristina and Vanessa believe that an overemphasis on performance prevents ensemble members from gaining a deeper understanding of the music they play. Referring to Austin Samba, Cristina argues that:

> [Performers] understand [samba] is . . . a Brazilian dance, a way of dancing, but they don't understand the reality of it . . . [b]ecause there is a lack of, not culture, but a lack of information. I think that if right now we did a workshop in the Samba School to explain how it was that samba came to be, then perhaps they would be more interested in [the broader sociopolitical issues].[16]

Cristina actually links the lack of cultural and historical knowledge to the often-touted authenticity of Austin Samba:

> I think that if [Austin Samba] really [wants] to be a samba school, it's going to have to have this more theoretical information: What is samba? Why is samba played? Samba as resistance; the issue of [racial/religious] prejudice in Brazil. Who plays samba? Well, poor people, right? All of this [discussion] would be interesting to have.[17]

For Cristina, regardless of how well the group performs or how strong their community is, without a deeper understanding of samba's history and sociopolitical implications in Brazil, Austin Samba will fall short as an institution.

Although David feels that Maracatu Texas addresses the cultural aspects of the music more effectively than Austin Samba, Vanessa feels Maracatu members need to do more as well. She explains that she is very happy people in Austin are interested in and learning to perform maracatu: "I love that people are doing that." However, she wishes the leadership "took more time to explain to people what it means." I clarify: "When you say that, are you talking about explaining to the people in the group? Or in the audiences at shows? or both?" Vanessa responds, "In the group. I wish he would take the time [to educate them].... He was like 'Yeah, there are some videos they can watch,' but the videos are in Portuguese. They can't [watch them for that reason]." Vanessa describes the limitations of the current pedagogical approach in Austin ensembles by comparing it to learning a language. She recalls one rehearsal:

> But he teaches, "'Oi,' that's how you respond." So [he is able to create a] call and response, and that's how you respond. And in my mind I was like, "Dude, when you [learn] how to speak English you cannot just repeat something that someone says to you: Repeat this. No, you need to read." Give them the opportunity to ... *understand* what the lyrics are saying. Give them the opportunity to understand the context in which these lyrics were written. What they really mean. You know? That's what is missing. (emphasis in original)

I ask Vanessa if she has talked with the leader of Maracatu Texas about her concerns, and she explains, "Yeah, I have told him, and we've tried to set up days in which we could have a gathering for people to watch a documentary and then we can talk about it, but [it] just never happened."

Afrocentricicity Pedagogy, Ethnomusicology, and Community Engagement

Afrocentricity is an effective tool for reinserting music as an aesthetic object within its proper sociocultural context that centers African agency and history. According to Maulana Karenga (1995), "The Afrocentric critique is concerned with the distortion and deficiency of what is present in the curriculum and larger social discourse and about the abundance and emancipatory possibilities of that which is absent" (p. 49). By recentering the social and historical conditions that produced and continue to shape Afro-Brazilian music, an Afrocentric pedagogy will underscore the significance of music beyond White enjoyment, seeking instead to "to rescue and reconstruct black history and culture in order to define more correctly black humanity" (Karenga 1995, p. 49).

Presenting Afro-Brazilian music from an African-centered position rather than exoticism for white embodied entertainment maintains the ability of music to act as a powerful tool for breaking down the self and the Other, what ethnomusicologist Sonia Seeman (2017) frames as a "near-far juxtaposition" (p. 193). Seeman (2017) elaborates: "To effectively transform students' perception of the world around them, we must constantly de-exoticize that which seems far and hold at a new distance that which seemed near" (p. 201). As explained by Asante (2007) earlier, Afrocentricity enables all students to "hear with new ears." Afrocentricity enables world music ensembles to achieve a "second level of teaching that is necessary for the students' experience of far-near juxtaposition in such a way that they engage with a higher level of understanding ... what music is and what music does" (Seeman, 2017, p. 193). Similarly, ensembles can use music, a cultural product embedded in racial formations and one that can be experienced through embodiment, as a means to uncover what race/Whiteness does. This is especially true of ensembles in university settings, where the performers are students rather than community members who join of their own interest. Ensemble members in the university setting are perhaps more open to exploring and critiquing the broader sociocultural issues involved in performing the Other's music, because many of them do so in academic classes.

Seeman (2017) asserts that educators can use musical case studies to encourage students to "move between their taken-for-granted notions of selves" (p. 194). I argue that when combined with Afrocentricity and critical antiracism, an embodied pedagogical approach will enable ethnomusicologists and students to effectively interrogate their consumption of (or participation in) Brazilian musical performance, for example, the appropriation/embodiment of foreign signs into familiar assemblages of racist meaning.[18]

Similarly, Seeman's (2017) embodied pedagogical approach aligns with Afrocentricity's emphasis on transforming token multicultural encounters with difference into social justice activism by better preparing students to participate in "social issues outside of the classroom" (p. 202). Hughey (2007, p. 99) similarly warns against the proliferation of "racial sensitivity" workshops and "diversity training" instead of political struggle. Instead, "Antiracist 'activism' should be constituted by both study and action" (Hughey, 2007, p. 99). World music ensembles could use an Afrocentric pedagogical approach to cross-cultural musical encounters as springboards for community activism. For example, instead of highlighting samba as an *alegria*-inducing rhythm, groups could emphasize samba as an Afro-diasporic political project and seek to dialogue and collaborate with Black communities in Austin and beyond. For world music ensembles, this means forging relationships not only with foreign or immigrant musical communities that first created the music being performed but also with local communities to explore how our performance of the music reverberates at home.

Brazilian ensembles in Austin tend to overly rely on just a few authoritative voices for information about Brazil and the musical styles groups perform. A plurality of perspectives is needed for performers to explore the complex and frequently contradictory meanings of Brazilian music, both in Brazil and abroad. Multiple voices are also critical for students or community members to more completely interrogate their privilege, power, and sense of entitlement as it pertains to their relationship with the Other. The uncritical acceptance of, and overreliance on, a limited number of authoritative voices surrounding Afro-Brazilian music performance is present in the following exchanges with members of Marcatu Texas.[19] I talk with Allison, David, and George about issues of cultural appropriation, and I challenge their collective understanding that their performance of maracatu rhythms is appropriate by asking, "What if someone else from a different maracatu disapproved of the way you represent their tradition, have you ever thought about that?" David responds first, claiming that he trusts the group's leader, João, and discounting the idea that another *maracatuzeiro/a* would disapprove:

> I guess I'm questioning whether that would happen, because I feel like, again, the way that João has presented this music . . . to us, he doesn't seem to be stepping outside of his authority. From what I can tell and the messages that Dudu [the Afro-Brazilian band leader from Recife who gave lessons to Maracatu Texas] seems to be sending to João and to us, [he believes] this is cool, [that] what [we] are doing is [acceptable].

George interrupts David, "But that doesn't mean that somebody else with authority maybe [wouldn't] see it that way." [David: Yeah, that's true]

George elaborates:

> My answer to that question is that I would listen to that person, and really listen, for as long as they wanted to talk about it. But I can't say without knowing what they have to say is, how I would feel at the end of that conversation. I'm prepared to say that I'm [willing to hear] that person out, but [I also recognize that] other people with authority are saying [different] things.

An example of a more critical view of Maracatu Texas's performance is found in Malu's commentary. I ask Malu, a Black women from Recife, what bothers her about Maracatu Texas. In an e-mail, she identifies a number of issues that center around White privilege and entitlement that enables forms of cultural appropriation that erases Blackness, rendering the musical expressions as simply Brazilian, or "Black culture without Black bodies." Echoing Vanessa's concerns cited earlier, Malu explains:

> As an Afro-Brazilian woman who is connected with Candomblé and understands [its importance] for Black people in Brazil, the mere fact that they call themselves a "maracatu" is already upsetting. They are not maracatu; they could be at the most a percussion group.

However, Malu further critiques the group for performing *afoxé* music, which she views as a desecration of Black religious music. Afoxé music is a secular form of Afro-religious music, also known as "*candomblé da rua*" (Candomblé for the [public] streets). Although it is viewed as acceptable for nonpractitioners of Candomblé to attend afoxé performances, the bands themselves are often connected to specific terreiros and comprised of Candomblé followers. Malu asserts, "They should not play afoxé. As simple as that. There is no afoxé without a terreiro. There is no afoxé without Orixás." For Malu, White Americans with no connection whatsoever to Afro-Brazilian religion have no business, no right, to perform afoxé, especially when there "is no quid pro quo," meaning that the group is not engaged or partnered with Black Brazilian communities working toward social justice. Instead, she suggests that:

They do it because they can. Because of their [White] privilege. Because it's cool . . . Afoxé is not a "feel-good" kind of music, [which is] how they approach it: "I play it and people immediately feel good," I have heard [members of Maracatu Texas] say this multiple times. It is absolutely wrong. Unacceptable.

Malu provides a counterexample to illustrate the absurdity of Maracatu Texas performing afoxé:

If they were doing something Holocaust-related, it would not even be a question [i.e., they would not be comfortable appropriating and performing Jewish religious music]. But, [we Black people] always have to define our boundaries and our humanity. Where in the world is it ok for people who don't belong to a religion to play religious songs at a club where people go to get high and get laid?

When confronted with Malu's criticisms, whether George would alter his stance on the performance of maracatu and (especially) afoxé is unclear. However, here we see the potential that dialog with multiple viewpoints could have in altering performers' worldviews, particularly when coupled with antiracist- and social justice-oriented pedagogies. Certainly, such engagement would help George, David, and Melissa crack (or unsuture) the "egocentric hegemony of Whiteness" (Lea & Lea, 2008), calling attention to their sense of entitlement in performing Black cultural forms. Thus, multiple points of engagement with community partners, with a variety of perspectives, is an essential component of the embodied near–far juxtaposition as described by Seeman (2017) and vital for effective world music pedagogy. My analysis here indicates the importance of presenting multiple viewpoints for performers of voluntary, community-based world music ensembles, but my larger argument is that varied perspectives and community connections are also essential for university-based music ensembles. This is especially true given our positions as professors in universities, where students tend to bestow in us an incredible amount of definitive authenticity. Afrocentricity is necessary not only to localize African voices but also to pursue the plurality of those voices so often silenced. This is a fundamental aspect of an Afrocentric pedagogical stance, what Karenga (1995) refers to as the practice of critique and corrective, "that suppressed and marginalized voices of various cultures will bring an enriched and enlarged agenda to the educational table . . . will challenge and change Eurocentric hegemony" (p. 51).

Conclusion

In this chapter, I have argued for an Afrocentric pedagogical approach for ethnomusicologists and world music ensembles. Specifically, in performance groups in which the ensemble members and audiences are predominately of European descent and the music being performed is of African descent, Afrocentricity provides the necessary perspective to resist the reification of Whiteness and racial stereotypes. Asante (2007) argues that "Afrocentricity provides the necessary instruments to transform the condition of the colonized, the victimized, the wretched, and the nihilistic" (p. 31). But it also can transform the oppressor and the colonizer. By centering our perspective, study, and engagement with Afro-Brazilian cultural expressions from an Afrocentric perspective, we begin to decenter the objectification of Africans as culture bearers, and we instead interact with them as subjects with agency in the creation of their own story. We interrogate the language and myths that have romanticized the history of the culture and restricted it to national-building narratives that uphold and control over the narrative. The re-centering of African agency is essential as Whites perform Afro-diasporic music because it decenters Whiteness as universal expression, opening up the interrogation of perspectives, assumptions, and entitlements regarding White consumption and enjoyment of Black musical expressions. That is, Afrocentricity forces Whites to engage with the music as a manifestation of Afro-Brazilians themselves, directly related to their history and agency, rather than a hot rhythm only for our enjoyment and consumption. Such a position fundamentally alters how Whites engage with the music, the culture, and African peoples.

Only through such critical antiracist assessments informed by Afrocentricity can we begin to explore the implications of the following observation by bell hooks (1992): "Exploring how desire for the Other is expressed, manipulated, and transformed by encounters with difference and the different is a critical terrain that can indicate whether these potentially revolutionary longings are ever fulfilled" (p. 22). Afrocentricity allows for both the (re)examining of

White desire while simultaneously removing Whiteness from the center of engagement with non-White cultural expressions, and it can therefore help guard against exploiting world music as mere trappings of non-Whiteness to articulate and perform a hip Whiteness.

Notes

1. As such, it draws a strong resemblance to the Balkan music and dance scene in the US. Mirjana Laušević (2007) documents a surprising absence of participants (performers and dancers) from the Balkans, just 2%.

2. Examples of the Afro-Brazilian musical forms frequently heard by Austinites include *maracatu*, *coco*, and *afoxé*, as well as more nationalized forms such as samba or capoeira music/dance.

3. Previously, there were two separate ensembles Maracatu Austin and Batuque Raíz that merged to form Maracatu Texas. A third group, Origens, was active from 2011 until 2015, when it also merged with Maracatu Texas.

4. Between 2000 and 2010, Austin experienced a general population growth of 20.4%. The African American population declined 5.4%, whereas Whites, Latinos, and Asian Americans grew in population (Tang & Ren, 2014). Also see Sweets (2015), Spearman (2016), and Buchele (2016).

5. "Em relação ao racismo, nunca senti na samba school racismo, *mas*, por ser a única brasileira, eu sinto que as vezes as pessoas, é o contrário. Eles me idolar tanto porque eu sou brasileira. Ai tu, tu deve sabre isso, Tu fazia isso, tu tu, né? Então eu não sinto preconceito mas eu sinto o inverso, que as vezes não é verdade também porque eu sou negra."

6. The first record of a coronation of an African ethnic royalty (the king and queen of Angola) in Brazil is from Recife's Nossa Senhora do Rosário dos Pretos (Our Lady of the Rosary of the Blacks) Church in 1666. However, the ritual dates back to at least 1642 in Portugal (Metz, 2008, p. 67). In fact, African royalty coronation ceremonies connected with Catholic brotherhoods occurred throughout colonial Latin America and the Iberian Peninsula (Andrews, 2004, pp. 69–72; Crook, 2009, pp. 147–148; Fryer, 2008, p. 61; Metz, 2008, p. 67). Ivaldo Marciano da França Lima is highly critical of the predominant view in maracatu historiography that the maracatu represents a continuation of the King of Kongo rituals in Africa, "as if maracatus were a mere survival, sometimes understood as totemic, of old/ancient (*antigos*) African customs brought by the slaves and perpetuated/maintained (*perpetuados*) by their descendants that did not even know what they were doing" (Lima, 2012, pp. 67–69). For more on this, including the influence of Herskovitsian retentionist theories on maracatu scholarship, see LaFevers (2014).

7. Ivaldo Marciano da França Lima reminds us that "the Black king and queen are accompanied by a royal in which each element has its own function and symbolic significance" (Lima, 2012, p. 48).

8. Maracatu-nação as a community practice falls into what Turino terms the "cultural formation" of Black Recifenses, whereas grupos percussivos might be described as "cultural cohorts" (Turino, 2008, pp. 159–161).

9. A pseudonym.

10. I describe the implications of maracatu-nação and percussion groups in the wake of Chico Science in greater detail in LaFevers (2018).

11. A pseudonym.

12. A gourd shaker, also known as a *chequerê*.

13. Vanessa is referring to *Ilê Axé Oyá Meguê* or Terreiro Santa Bárbara, commonly known as the terreiro Xambá or casa Xambá. Feeling religious discrimination in the neighboring state of Alagoas, *babalorixá* Artur Rosendo Pereira moved to Recife and founded the terreiro in 1930. After violent repression forced the terreiro to close in 1939, it was reopened in 1950 and moved to its present location in Olinda in 1951. See Oliveira and Campos (2010) and www.xamba.com.br.

14. Here, Hughey (2007) is referring to the way in which members of the antiracist group he studied, when discussing the need to address racism through contact with racial others, "[frame] non-White 'others' as more than the victims of discrimination, but as the partial cause of racism through 'self-segregation.'" (p. 90).

15. "For students of European heritage in America, this goes without saying because almost all of the experiences discussed in classes are from the standpoint of European history" (Assante, 2007, p. 79).

16. "Elas entendem que [samba] é uma parte de uma dança brasileira, é uma maneira de dançar e . . . mas elas não entendem a realidade da coisa. Elas não entendem, Porque falta cu—cultura não, mas falta a informação. Vamos lá, eu penso assim, se agora se a gente faz um workshop na samba school pra explicar como é que nasceu o samba, aí, talvez elas vão dar mais importância pra isso."

17. "Acho que se o samba school quisesse realmente ficar uma escola de samba, teria que ter essa informação mais teórica do que que é o samba? Porque que se toca samba? [a] resistência do samba; a questão de preconceito no Brasil que tem— quem toca um bom samba é pobre, né. Então tudo isso seria interessante na samba school."

18. Examples of such foreign signs and meanings include the masculine power perceived in drumming, the notion of Black rhythm as irresistible contagion, and the interpretation of dance movement as evidence of natural rhythm or Black sexuality.

19. Additionally, when reflecting on the role of clinicians who come to give workshops to Austin Samba and Maracatu Texas, they uncritically repeat similar viewpoints. It is important that we recall Hordge-Freeman's point that many Black Brazilians "who are left with few options make a living by performing stereotypi-

cal ideas about blackness" (2016, p. 45). At the very least, it is against the interests of musicians who earn a living by teaching to suggest that Americans should not perform certain styles.

References

Andrews, G. R. (2004). *Afro-Latin America: 1800–2000*. Oxford, England: Oxford University Press.

Asante, M. K. (2003). The Afrocentric idea in education. In J. L. Conyers, Jr. (Ed.), *Afrocentricity and the academy: Essays on theory and practice* (pp. 37–49). Jefferson, NC, and London, England: McFarland.

Asante, M. K. (2007). *An Afrocentric manifesto: Toward an African renaissance*. Cambridge, England: Polity.

Avelar, I. (2011). Mangue beat music and the coding of citizenship in sound. In C. Dunn & I. Avelar (Eds.), *Brazilian popular music and citizenship* (pp. 313–329). Durham, NC: Duke University Press.

Berlak, A. (2008). Challenging the hegemony of whiteness by addressing the adaptive unconscious. In V. Lea & E. J. Sims (Eds.), *Undoing whiteness in the classroom: critical educultural teaching approaches for social justice activism* (pp. 47–66). New York, NY: Peter Lang.

Bonilla-Silva, E. (2014). *Racism without racists: Color-blind racism and the persistence of racial inequality in America* (4th ed.). Lanham, MD: Rowman & Littlefield.

Bradley, D. (2006). Music education, multiculturalism, and anti-racism: "Can we talk?" *Action, Criticism, and Theory for Music Education 5*(2). Retrieved from http://act.maydaygroup.org/articles/Bradley5_2.pdf.

Bradley, D. (2017). Standing in the Shadows of Mozart: Music Education, World Music, and Curricular Change. In R. Moore, (Ed.) *College Music Curricula for a New Century* (pp. 205–222). New York and Oxford, England: Oxford Univeristy Press.

Buchele, M. (2016). Austin's population is booming. Why is its African American population shrinking? *KUT*. Retrieved from http://kut.org/post/austins-population-booming-why-its-african-american-population-shrinking

Carvalho, E. I. de. (2007). Diálogo de negros, monólogo de brancos: transformações e apropriações musicais no maracatu de baque virado [Black

Dialogue, White Monologue: Musical Transformation and Appropriations in Maracatu de baque virado] (Master's thesis). Universidade Federal de Pernambuco.

Courteau, M.-L. (2007). Music and dance performance, longing, and the construction of Brazil in Auckland, New Zealand (Master's thesis). University of Auckland, Australia.

Crook, L. (2009). *Focus: Music of northeast Brazil* (2nd ed.). New York, NY, and London, England: Routledge.

Dei, G. J. S. (1994). Afrocentricity: A cornerstone of pedagogy. *Anthropology & Education Quarterly 25*(1), 3–28.

Eisentraut, J. (2001). Samba in Wales: Making sense of adopted music. *British Journal of Ethnomusicology 10*, 85–105.

Esteves, L. L. (2008). "Viradas" e "Marcações": A participação de pessoas de classe media nos grupos de maracatu de baque-virado do Recife-PE ["Turn-arounds" and "Marcations": The Participation of Middle-Class People in maracatu de baque-virado groups in Recife, Pernambuco] (Master's thesis). Universidade Federal de Pernambuco, Recife, Brasil.

Esteves, L. L. (2013). Grupos percussivos: Práticas, interesses, e tenões de 'ser ou não ser' um maracatu [Percussive groups: Practices, Interesses, and Tensions of 'to be or not to be" a maracatu]. In I. C. Martins Guillen (Ed.), *Inventário Cultural dos Maracatus Nação* (pp. 73–91). Recife, Brazil: Editora UFPE.

Fryer, P. (2000). *Rhythms of resistance: African musical heritage in Brazil.* Hanover: Wesleyan University Press.

Galinsky, P. (2002). *"Maracatu Atomico": Tradition, modernity, and postmodernity in the mangue movement of Recife, Brazil.* New York, NY: Routledge.

Gibson, A. M. (2012). *Post-Katrina brazucas: Brazilian immigrants in New Orleans.* New Orleans, LA: University of New Orleans Press.

Graham, M. (2000). Honouring social work principles—exploring the connections between anti-racist social work and African-centered worldviews. *Social Work Education, 19*, 423–436.

Guillen, I. C. M. (2007). Catimbó: saberes e práticas em circulação no Nordeste dos anos 1930–1940 [Catimbo: knowledge and practices in circulation in the Brazilian Northeast 1930–1940]. In I. M. de F. Lima & I. C. M. Guillen (Eds.), *Cultura Afro-descendente no recife: Maracatus, valentes e catimbós* (pp. 203–230). Recife, Brazil: Edições Bagaço.

Harnish, D. (2004). "No, not 'bali hai'!": Challenges of adaptation and orientalism in performing and teaching Balinese gamelan. In T. Solís (Ed.) *Performing ethnomusicology: Teaching and representation in world music ensembles* (pp. 168–188). Berkeley and London, England: University of California Press.

hooks, b. (1992). *Black looks: Race and representation.* Boston, MA: South End Press.

Hordge-Freeman E. (2016) Brokering Black Brazil or Fostering Global Citizenship? Global Engagement that Empowers Black Brazilian Communities. In: Mitchell-Walthour G.L., Hordge-Freeman E. (eds) *Race and the Politics of Knowledge Production.* Palgrave Macmillan, New York.

Hughey, M. W. (2007). Racism with antiracists: Color-conscious racism and the unintentional persistence of inequality. *Social Thought & Research, 28,* 67–108.

Karenga, M. (1995). Afrocentricity and multicultural education concept, challenge, and contribution. In B. P. Bowser, T. Jones, & G. A. Young (Eds.), *Toward the multicultural university* (pp. 41–61). Westport, CT, and London, England: Praeger.

Kisliuk, M. & Gross. K. (2004). That's the "it" that we learn to perform: Teaching BaAka music and dance. In T. Solís (Ed.), *Performing ethnomusicology: Teaching and representation in world music ensembles* (pp. 249–260). Berkeley and London, England: University of California Press.

LaFevers, C. (2014). Revisitando estudos de retenção: construindo sobrevivências puras de uma África imaginada e o impacto nas políticas culturais Negras [Revisiting Retention Studies: Constructing Pure Survivals of an Imagined Africa and its impact on Cultural Politics]. *Revista África(s) 1,* 101–141.

LaFevers, C. (2018). *Embodying Brazilianness: Performing Race and Place in Austin, Texas.* PhD Dissertation, University of Texas.

Laušević, M. (2007). *Balkan Fascination: Creating an Alternative Music Culture in America.* Oxford, England: Oxford University Press.

Lea, B. & Lea, V. (2008). Polyrhythms as a metaphor for culture. In V. Lea & E. J. Sims (Eds.), *Undoing Whiteness in the classroom: Critical educultural teaching approaches for social justice activism* (pp. 97–100). New York, NY: Peter Lang.

Lima, I. M. de F. (2012). *Maracatus do recife: Novas considerações sob o olhar dos tempos* [Recife's Maracatus: New Considerations on the Lens of Time]. Recife, Brazil: Edições Bagaço.

Lima, I. M. de F. (2013). Maracatu-nação e grupos percussivos: diferenças, conceitos e histórias. [Maracatu-nação and Percussion Groups: Differences, Concepts and Histories] In I. C. M. Guillen (Ed.), *Inventário cultural dos maracatus nação* (pp. 49–72). Recife, Brazil: Editora UFPE.

Locke, D. (2004). The African ensemble in America: Contradictions and possibilities. In T. Solís (Ed.), *Performing ethnomusicology: Teaching and representation in world Music ensembles* (pp. 168–188). Berkeley and London, England: University of California Press.

Lott, E. (2013). *Love and theft: Blackface minstrelsy and the American working class*. Oxford, England: Oxford University Press.

McCann, B. (2016). Proletarian blackface: Appropriation and class struggle. In M. Judge's *Office space. Communication, Culture & Critique 9*, 362–378.

Mercier, C. G. (2013). *Interpreting Brazilianness: Reception and representation in the Brazilian music scenes of Toronto and Montreal*. PhD Dissertation, University of Toronto, Canada.

Metz, J. D. (2008). Cultural geographies of Afro-Brazilian symbolic practice: Tradition and change in Maracatu de Nação (Recife, Pernambuco, Brazil)." *Latin American Music Review, 29*(1), 64–95.

Monson, I. (1995). The problem with White hipness: Race, gender, and cultural conceptions in jazz historical discourse. *Journal of the American Musicological Society, 48*, 396–422.

Muñoz, J. E. (2006). "Feeling Brown, Feeling Down: Latina Affect, the Performativity of Race, and the Depressive Position." *Signs 31*(3), 675–688.

Olds, T. (2011). Marginalizing the president: The concerted effort to 'other' Obama. *Race, Gender & Class 18*(3–4), 100–109.

Oliveira, J. S. de L. & Campos, Z. D. P. (2010, November). *Tradição e resistência no terreiro Xambá: O resgate de uma herança* [Tradition and Resistance in the Xambá terreiro: The Rescue of a Heritage]. Paper presented at IV Colóquio de História, , Universidade Catolica de Pernambuco (Unicap), Recife, Pernambuco, Brazil.

Pravaz, N. (2010). The well of Samba: On playing percussion and feeling good in Toronto. *Canadian Ethnic Studies, 41*, 207–232.

Pravaz, N. (2013). Tambor de Crioula in strange places: The travels of an Afro-Brazilian play form. *Anthropological Quarterly 86*, 825–850.

Rasmussen, B. B., Klinenberg, E., Nexica, I. J., & Wray, M. (2001). *The making and unmaking of whiteness*. Durham, NC, and London, England: Duke University Press.

Robitaille, L. (2014). Promoting *Capoeira*, branding Brazil: A focus on the semantic body. *Black Music Research Journal 34*, 229–254.

Rose, T. (1994). *Black noise: Rap music and Black culture in contemporary America*. Hanover, NH: Wesleyan University Press.

Seeman, S. T. (2017). Embodied pedagogy: Techniques for exploring why and how music matters. In R. Moore (Ed.), *College music curricula for a new century* (pp. 191–203). Oxford and New York: Oxford University Press.

Sieg, K. (2002). *Ethnic drag: Performing race, nation, sexuality in West Germany*. Ann Arbor: The University of Michigan Press.

Smith, C, (2016). *Afro-Paradise: Blackness, Violence, and Performance in Brazil*. Urbana, Chicago, and Springfield: University of Illinois Press.

Solís, T. (2004). *Performing ethnomusicology: Teaching and representation in World Music Ensembles*. Berkeley and London, England: University of California Press.

Spearman, K. (2016, January 8). We're still here: Assessing the continuing Black Austin experience. *The Austin Chronicle*. Retrieved from www.austinchronicle.com/news/2016-01-08/we-re-still-here.

Stanyek, J. (2004). Diasporic improvisation and the articulation of intercultural music. PhD dissertation, University of California San Diego.

Stanyek, J. (2011). *Choro do Norte:* Improvising the trans*regional* roda in the United States. *Luso-Brazilian Review 48*(1), 100–129.

Sweets, E. (2015, December 22). Farewell, Austin. *TribTalk.org, of the Texas Tribune*. Retrieved from http://www.tribtalk.org/2015/12/22/farewell-austin.

Tang, E. & Ren, C. (2014). *Outlier: The case of Austin's declining African-American population* (Issue Brief). Austin, TX: The Institute for Urban Policy Research and Analysis. Retrieved from http://www.utexas.edu/cola/iupra/_files/pdf/Austin%20AA%20pop%20policy%20brief_FINAL.pdf.

Turino. T. (2008). *Music as social life: The politics of participation*. Chicago, IL: The University of Chicago Press.

Volk, T. M. (1998). *Music, education, and multiculturalism: Foundations and principles*. New York, NY, and Oxford, England: Oxford University Press.

Wong, D. (2000). The Asian American body in performance. In R. Radano

& P. V. Bohlman, (Eds.), *Music and the racial imagination* (pp. 57–94). Chicago, IL: University of Chicago Press.

Yancy, G. (2017). *Black bodies, White gazes: The continuing significance of race in America*. Lanham, MD: Rowman & Littlefield.

TEN

 The Need for Beloved Community: Black Graduate Students and the Collaborative Creation of Counterspaces

Monique Liston

> *The most serious threat to African dignity is in the domain of intellectual ability.*
>
> —Jacob Carruthers

T̲HE BLACK RADICAL TRADITION OF resistance against anti-Blackness has always been intellectual. The intellectual efforts are not limited to the classroom but include the lay interpretations of coping with the cognitive impacts of racial oppression. The intellectual battle waged is on many fronts and students are not only the frontline warriors but also the leaders, architects, and critics of resistance against White supremacy and anti-Blackness globally. Intellectual warfare, as Jacob Carruthers (1999) argues, is the conscious fight against anti-Black power structures to liberate the Black experience and promote dignity connected to African diaspora identities. Intellectual warfare connects learning experiences from all walks of life as culturally connected battles to affirm the dignity of Black people. These experiences are not limited to modernity but a centuries-long history of anti-Black thought and practice. For example, enslaved Africans created spaces of resistance and resilience by the formation of informal study groups on the plantation in the South when reading among enslaved persons was declared illegal (Anderson, 1988). Study groups were literacy development spaces, a stepping-stone toward their individual and collective liberation. The collective learning experience of studying for liberation continued to narrate Black resistance to White supremacy and anti-Blackness for centuries beyond slavery. Intellectual spaces were utilized by Martin Delany, Alexander Crummel, Maria Stewart, and Frederick Douglass to discuss African colonization in Africa as the transatlantic slave trade ended in the mid-19th century (Dorsey, 2000). Discussions of race and identity at the turn of the 20th century are demarcated by W. E. B. Du Bois, the first Black person to graduate with a PhD from Harvard University, and his prolific treatises on Black experience in the United States and globally. Huey Newton and Bobby Seale developed The Black Panther Party for Self Defense as students at Merritt College in Oakland, California. The Black Lives Matter movement, led by Black queer women Patrisse Cullors, Opal Tometti, and Alicia Garza, originally used social media to galvanize people across the country to address anti-Black racism (Tometti, Khan-Cullors & Garza, 2012). As the movement grew, students became central to the movement by staging protests, challenging school administrations, and intellectually engaging one another on the significance of a call to protect Black lives (Hope, Keels & Durkee, 2016). The intellectual tradition of Black movements should not be ignored. In fact, more explorations on the connections between the intellectual development beyond the academy or ivory tower could illuminate and help develop Black radical organizing now and in the future.

In this chapter, I perform and share an organizational autoethnography of a Black liberation organization that I helped to found during my graduate school experience. It did not end in the creation of an ideal liberated Black community. The work stopped, the organization dissolved, and relationships ended. I have struggled to share this story and its complexity for years. I was reminded of its ongoing significance thanks to a quote by historian John Henrik Clarke, "All history is a current event." Using a pan-African historical consciousness, the time and space in which I inhabit are not isolated from the time and space of which my ancestors lived on the continent of Africa, worked on plantations in the South, discussed civil rights at the dinner table, sent me to Howard University or for my children's children's children, and their continued progression toward a Black freedom-as-yet-unknown. In effect, my story is relevant. It is just as connected to 1918 as 2118, and I am responsible for sharing it. The intention of this reflexive exercise is twofold.

First, I intend to provide an additional narrative toward understanding the intellectual tradition of Black liberation through the work of students, especially Black women graduate students. According to the CGS/GRE Survey of Graduate Enrollment and Degrees, Black students accounted for an average of 10% of all first-time graduate students over the last decade (Okahana & Zhao, 2018). Of that number, Black women are nearly 70% of the Black graduate student population, which means that Black women were approximately 7% of the total graduate student population between 2006 and 2016. Black women are the largest non-White population within graduate degree programs. In contrast, White students are nearly 50% of the graduate school population with White women representing nearly 30% of the total graduate school population. Once aggregated for completion of PhDs, the representational gaps continue to widen. Based on percentages alone, Black women have a unique challenge navigating graduate school education with intersectional identities that are in contrast to the majority identity for graduate students. Central to surviving the graduate school experience are the networks that Black women form (Johnson-Bailey, Valentine, Cervero & Bowles, 2008). The informal networks I formed during graduate school led to the development of a counterspace for me as a student and for me as a community member. Unlike traditional studies on counterspaces, my informal network within the counterspace I created included student peers and community members that were not participating in the higher education environment.

Second, as Boyle and Parry (2007) argue, organizational autoethnographic study illuminates, "Autoethnographic accounts are characterised by a move from a broad lens focus on individual situatedness within the cultural and social context, to a focus on the inner, vulnerable and often resistant self" (p. 186). As a Black woman graduate student who created and led the space which ultimately did not succeed, I am grappling with the realities of the counterspace and its limitations to serve students beyond the ivory tower. I juxtapose the identity of students to that of community member, but I am not ignoring the idea that students are also community members. Flemons and Green (2001) state, "You have to decide if you are ready to be outed or to put yourself out that way and consider the impact on your personal identity" (p. 96). In "outing" myself, I explore my negotiation with my actions as a part of the organizational context and experience. The exploration I present in this chapter takes an interpretative research lens through "previous/other life" (Boyle & Parry, 2007, p. 187) approach by reflecting on the past. In my experience, I connect the creation of a community organization as a counterspace that served not only Black women graduate students but also community members.

For this reflection, I utilize the creative design principle "form follows function" to share my reflections on the experience. As form, I utilize counterspaces as a defining construct. Counterspaces are specific sites for people of color to challenge deficit narratives perpetuated by microaggressions while developing and maintaining an affirming environment (Solorzano, Ceja & Yosso, 2000). Counterspaces are often theorized by centering higher education contexts such as classrooms and student groups. This chapter explores my experience, as Black woman graduate student, co-creating a counterspace with community members who were not affiliated with the university. This exploration of counterspace creation centers a broader spatialized context and places higher education among other spaces of contention, such as workplaces and neighborhoods within the same city as a large urban public university. As function, I look to the theorization of Beloved Community, identified as a goal for our collective liberation from anti-Blackness. I center Dr. King's theorization not only while adding the thoughts of bell hooks. Their arguments for the Beloved Community as a goal are used to reflect on the experience as radical organizational building that could manifest the goal into existence for many, including Black women graduate students. I share this experience to challenge counterspace work to think about the Beloved Community as a sustainability measure that prevents the counterspace from protecting its participants. As data, I use a variety of sources, including Facebook posts, personal e-mail communications, journal entries, and Google Drive folders including organizational documents and notes.

Understanding Myself as a Student and Community Member

> *To be a Negro in this country and to be relatively conscious, is to be in a rage almost all the time. So that the first problem is how to control that rage so that it won't destroy you.*
>
> —James Baldwin

I am a boastful and proud graduate of a historically Black college and university (HBCU). Having exclusively White teachers during my K–12 experience, I was eager to experience college on a campus where Black students, teachers, and communities were central. My college experience was affirming and awe-inspiring. I experienced culture shock arriving at campus. I called home during the first weeks of school, excitedly telling my mother, "EVERYBODY is Black!" In that space, I learned Black history and culture in unsuspecting spaces, such as math classes, science lab, and church. It was an immersive culturally affirming experience, and I loved every second of it. Upon graduation, I enrolled in a graduate program at one of the largest public universities on the East Coast. Thanks to my demonstrated ability to handle academic rigor and my contributions to increasing the diverse student population in the department, I attended on a full scholarship. It was a terminal graduate degree program, where the expectation was for students to get jobs in the public sector or perhaps running for local office. My personality is attracted to challenging opportunities and I sought out something similar while in graduate school. I wanted to write a thesis even though it was not required. I was told by a White male professor that I was not capable of doing a thesis. *Not capable. As in not having the ability, fitness, or quality necessary to do or achieve a specified thing.* In that moment, I realized that my matriculation at an HBCU was special and that I would be disappointed if any of the support and affirmation that I gained from that institution would be found in the halls of this predominantly White institution. I resolved my two years there as a member of the Black Graduate Student Association who regularly came to meetings rolling my eyes and saying, "What do you expect these White people to do, except be White?" I graduated from that institution, without completing a thesis, only to find myself working and once again at the whim of a White male who was unwilling to see my challenge to the status quo as an opportunity. I was fired. I felt dejected and, in many ways, resentful toward my education. I ended up back home in my mother's basement. I decided that education was a space I wanted to explore more deeply and signed up to take some graduate-level classes in education. I met with the advisor, and he said with my experience and credentials, I should "just go" into the PhD program. He handed me a fellowship application, and thus, I began a seven-year journey.

Pursuing a PhD was an unfathomable experience for me. I was a first-generation college student and had no social capital for navigating this space as an intellectual in the same ways that many peers did. However, my affirming experience during my undergraduate career helped me navigate classwork within my own interest. I was particularly interested in African-centered education and centered my papers and research around deepening my understanding of Black institution building, organizational development, and educational spaces for Black children and families. However, as I matriculated through the program, my desire to research that area was met with little affirmation. Before I had completed course work for my degree program, I had abandoned my research interests for a topic that aligned with faculty support. However, my research interests moved from inquisitive exploration to passionate pursuit.

During this time, new to the city as an adult, I began going to community events. I wanted to get to know Black people in this city on a more intimate level. I left home at 17, having a mostly White social experience during my K–12 years, and now as a "woke" college-educated student, I desired to explore more Black social spaces. I attended community meetings and rallies. On social media, I regularly shared quotes from Black power texts that I had been reading such as *The Autobiography of Malcolm X* (X, 2015), *The Blueprint for Black Power* (Wilson, 1998), and *Assata* (Shakur, 2016). I met a lot of amazing young Black contemporaries who were passionate about Black people. I began building relationships with many of them, and frequently, the topic of how we organize Black members of the community to operate within their best interest frequently centered our conversation. I wrote a now-notorious Facebook post about a local off-shoot of Occupy Wall Street, a political movement challenging economic inequity in the United States, called Occupy the Hood. In my essay, I argued that Occupy the Hood, a Black organization, had modeled itself after Occupy Wall Street, a White organization and, that some concerns should be raised on how the two organizations were pursuing change. I wanted the Black-led organization to be more critical of the form and function of modeling resistance after White-led organizing. I stated, "I write this to express my concern for the blind participation and coalition building efforts on behalf of African people with movements such as these that are not aligned with the plight of their reality nor aligned with their historical or cultural self-concept" (Personal Facebook Post, 2012). The essay, posted on Facebook, generated a lot of discussion among organizers and community activists in my hometown. I defended my passion for education in the essay, expressing a desire to build an alternative education system for students that could be a better use of efforts. I wanted the community to Occupy Schools instead of Occupy the Hood:

> What are we occupying? What are we trying to get? For whom does this matter? If we must discuss a potential occupation we have already

to venues we should readily address as a community. First, we cannot ignore that black men and women are already in a full out occupation of the US penal system. We currently account for 30% of the prison population. How do we leverage this issue towards liberation? (Occupy our minds for minute, huh?) Secondly, the public education system was the FIRST institution to be attacked by the right wing agenda and we still have not mustered by the courage to OCCUPY SCHOOLS. It may be *cliché* to assert that the children are the future, but without them we will not survive this. We will not survive. In fact, the quest for liberating education should go beyond an occupation but resemble a full on TAKE OVER similar to the Freedom Schools Movement in the *1960s* and propelled by independently OWNED and OPERATED schools that educated African children TO BE AFRIKAN without question or concern. It would be remiss to not recognize the institutions in DC, Atlanta, Houston, Philadelphia, St. Petersburg and throughout the continent that doing precisely THIS! Building a movement (reform?) and building institutions (revolutions?) are not the same thing and as African people, institution-building is currently our call. (Personal Facebook Post, 2012)

This public essay generated conversations between local activists and organizers online and in person. I remember vividly attending a Kwanzaa celebration days after this post and being publicly accosted and called an agent, someone working on behalf of White supremacist organizations to dismantle and destroy Black movements. A local Black male activist did not trust my engagement or criticism of local movements. We had a meaningful conversation at the event, and his approach evolved from confrontational to collegial within minutes. Although that incident ended on a positive note, I realized that my contributions to the public discourse were received with skepticism until individuals learned of my educational background and current educational pursuits. With knowledge of my attendance at an HBCU and current matriculation within a doctoral program, community members opened themselves to my participation and leadership. My student status became social capital that connected me to the activist and organizing community of my hometown.

It Was Called All Black Everything

> *For the next 30 days – a group of my friends and I are embarking on an #ALLBLACKEVERYTHING experiment. The goal is to only spend our money with businesses that are solely black owned (that's grocery shopping, gas stations, clothing, dining out, meds, EVRYTHING). If we supported black businesses – where would our community be? Let's find out. The BUY BLACK movement focuses on uplifting Black owned businesses and empowering the Black community to engage in self-help economics, conscious consumerism and strategic entrepreneurship. This is our experiment. We hope to use the data that we collect during the next 30 days to help influence other consumers to join us. Stay tuned for more information.*
>
> —Personal Facebook Post (2012)

With my Facebook Post on Occupy movements, I attracted the attention of many organizers and activists locally. One organizer, who was running for office, engaged me on ongoing conversations regarding politics. We ended up talking about how Black community building could occur outside of the system. During the same time, I watched Maggie Anderson on CSPAN discussing her book *Our Black Year: One Family's Quest to Buy Black in America's Racially Divided Economy* (Anderson, 2012). I wondered if my new friends in my hometown would be interested in trying to do the same thing. From there, we launched All Black Everything, which began as a claim around Black economic development in our city. Our original mission statement was as follows:

> KUJICHAGULIA (self-determining) effort to build UJAMAA (cooperative economics) in our community. UJAMAA is the principle of building our own economic systems to buy, sell, share, and grow together. In order to achieve this work in UMOJA (unity), we have to undertake UJIMA (collective work and responsibility) by strategically creating a plan to engage our people in the work. Remaining true to our NIA (purpose), we use KUUMBA (creativity) and remain rooted in IMANI (faith) to build a movement that empowers us to work for our complete liberation.

I developed the program with four other Black women who were also in graduate programs at the local university. The core organizers of this effort also included six others who neither were in pursuit of nor held graduate degrees. Overall, our organization included college-educated professional Black participants, there were participants who had high school diplomas, some were parents, some were homeowners, some were renters, and some were dealing with issues related to access to housing, access to food, and access to child care. However, when called to meet and participate in the space, everyone was open and willing to organize their schedule, bring food to share with one another, and make space for the need to respond to work e-mails or pick up children during meeting time. We utilized social media, especially Facebook, to communicate with each other and the broader community. The space grew rapidly within a few months. We started with a group of 10 working together thinking about where our dollars were being spent, and within a year, we had a Facebook page with more than 1,500 followers, members paying monthly dues to a Freedom Fund, weekly meetings and events, and host of other opportunities we were trying to build within the city. As a group, we did not plan for our organization to become a voice on such a large scale so quickly. We presented our model and ideas at an international conference in Washington, DC, we had a weekly radio show, and we had the interest of people from across the globe interested in our organizing, our commitment, and our process of Black reclamation. As this was happening, I continued a rigorous graduate school routine. I taught two sections of an intro course at a university an hour away from my home. I also kept up with course work in three classes and prepared to write my dissertation proposal. My bills were also continuing to build up so I held part-time jobs to make ends meet throughout the summer while continuing to increase my responsibility to All Black Everything.

All Black Everything as a Counterspace

As a counterspace, All Black Everything promoted ideas of dignity, justice, and liberation. Our mission evolved from the Black economic program to include community study groups and community food and nutrition. Through the growth of the organization, the mission statement became *ALL BLACK EVERYTHING is unapologetically committed to the reclamation, preservation, protection, and progression of Black culture, Black power, and Black people.* We had three core programs: Sankofa Study Circle, Buy Black, and Feed the

People. Each program had its own committee and all three programs reported to the chair and chief of staff. I operated as the chief of staff, and a Black male community member served as chair. There were times that other organizers and activists assumed that the Black male vocal leader of the organization was the sole leader and decision maker for the organization. I was dismissed with the assumption that I was his assistant. I remember when, in preparation for an event, we met up with another Black male who led an organization of Black public servants. The leader of this organization pulled the Black male leader of our organization aside to talk logistics, assuming he was the person to talk to and ignoring the fact that I arranged the meeting, asked the questions, and was responsible for executing this event.

The initial program became the Buy Black Program and we added two other programs, Feed the People and Sankofa Study Circle. Feed the People represented "our consistent and pervasive message that our relationship to food is at the root of our continued oppression." We sought to break that link through "addressing food deserts in our community, providing access to healthy and organic options for children and families and building towards creating, supporting, and maintaining a culturally centered food economy." We also held Sankofa Study Circle, a learning space to read and present ideas relating to Black liberation. The underrepresentation of Black students in graduate school may lead to the assumption that Black people are lacking or culturally deficit when it comes to intellectual pursuits. However, Sankofa Study Circle was our most popular program, attracting participants of all ages, educational backgrounds, and work experiences.

All spaces were exclusively Black spaces. Being Black in the organization was open to individual self-identification. We did not specify African American versus African or Black versus biracial identities when it came to joining us. However, we made it clear that people who did not identify as Black were not welcome to participate in the space. However, they could give money to support the space if they chose to do so.

Case and Hunter (2012) identified three domains to describe the processes used in counterspaces to challenge negative representations: narrative identity work, acts of resistance, and direct relational transactions. I believe that this framework reflects how each of the programs of All Black Everything functioned. Each program addressed oppression narratives and promoted narratives of resilience and revolution. Each program provided opportunities for members and the community at large to participate in acts of resistance at various levels of capacity. Each program engaged the mission of the organization as a charge to grow in the community by recruiting members and publicizing opportunities to engage further with the organization through each event. I highlight the following experiences to demonstrate how All Black Everything functioned as a counterspace as Case and Hunter (2012) proposed.

Narrative Identity Work

When I started ABE, I was still doing course work for my doctoral studies. I managed a rigorous schedule of working, taking classes, teaching, and managing a growing organization. During that time, that I was pursuing a PhD was continually touted by members of the organization as something important not only to me but everyone in the organization as a whole as well. Despite the previous graduate school experiences that had neglected to nurture and affirm me in ways that I felt were supportive, I was constantly reminded of my ability to succeed in school. Speaking in meetings, members said, "Let the doctor talk!" I would also be introduced by members to other community members as "Soon-to-be-Dr. Liston." Because the dignifying counterspace is reciprocal in terms of providing affirming spaces, I often brought what I learned on campus and professionally at work into the space. As a program, I led Sankofa Study Circle for six months. I ran the space similar to a college classroom. We met weekly for three hours, had reading and writing assignments, and expected everyone present to be accountable for reading and participating in the discussion. After a few months, I passed the leadership to two members of the group who were invested in its success, both people without bachelor's degrees. They were more than capable of leading in the space and in terms of the study we needed to do. School is often a site of humiliation and trauma for Black people. Thus, the affirmations of completing school are seen as unattainable for many because dealing with the trauma of the schooling experience is not a challenge they choose or are equipped to endure. However, in passing the leadership of that space onto community members that did not have the same educational background, as an organization I affirmed that leadership in learning is not limited to those who survive the trauma of school. All community members have the opportunity to lead in learning and be supported by others in their journey.

Acts of Resistance

The members of All Black Everything (ABE) regularly debated about how we should collectively resist against the systems of oppression we were under. An ongoing debate in our meetings was about our collective willingness to march in the streets or hold public protests. In organizing, these are referred to as direct actions. Direct action is a strategy for social change where public interruptions of daily life are interrupted to bring attention to social injustice. Several members worked with other organizations and regularly participated in direct actions while others in the organization shared that they felt direct action was a waste of time. As a graduate student, I found that direct action participation was a product of the time I had available to be present in movement spaces. I struggled with leading the organization, being an active participant in social justice movements across the city, and maintaining high performance in my graduate program.

Each program actively resisted oppression. Sankofa Study Circle was an act of resistance against intellectual tyranny in the educational systems Black people in our city had access too. Intergenerational learning spaces about Black history were not in our public, private, or charter schools. The books we read were often special ordered by our local Black bookstore. We held our sessions in public and bus-accessible spaces across the city and encouraged anyone and everyone to come. I remember one of the sessions we had on the campus of the local university that attracted three young men who happened to be eating at a restaurant we were holding an event in the night before. I was surprised to see them at study circle. Study circle, of the three different activities, was often the most populated space, and it surprised me every week. I anticipated that people would want to spend money at a Black establishment or attend a program but never anticipated that studying and reading for three hours would be our largest draw. The three men who came that night were boisterous, presumptuous, and, in many ways, disruptive to our space. Many regulars in the organization did not appreciate some of their questions and interruptions within the conversation. They stayed for the entire session, and although they were "disruptive," they were engaged and actively participated.

I told another leader of the organization as we were walking out that if they ever came to another event, they would be future leaders of this work. Those three young men remained active in the organization until the very end. They did manual labor and provided support and security during events, and one even acquired a leadership position in the Buy Black Program.

The other two programs also staged acts of resistance. The Buy Black Program encouraged people to spend money with Black businesses and to text pictures of their receipts to our phone number so we could total how much spending we were doing with Black business. The Buy Black Program also hosted "nights out," encouraging people to descend on a Black business to spend money en masse. The Feed the People program created a community garden and dispersed food from local cooperatives at events. The program provided vegan cooking lessons and regularly helped young people consider healthy food options.

Direct Relational Transactions

Fictive kinship is the creation of familial bonds between persons who are not related by blood or marriage (Fordham & Ogbu, 1986). Members of All Black Everything often referred to themselves as family. Members often used words such as *Brother* or *Sister* to describe the relationship within the group. Children of members used words such as *Auntie* and *Uncle* to address the adult members of the group. The idea was that we were building a community. We often talked about buying land and purchasing homes. Two members of the group that met during organizing ended up living together in a shared rental space. The idea of community was undefined in many ways, but actions affirmed a sense of familial kinship between members. A group of members moved a young woman from her apartment into her new apartment while she was out of town dealing with a family emergency. We held baby showers for new parents who were members of the group. We gave each other money, shared meals, and spent non-work-related hours socializing and celebrating. We created spaces to reflect and grow together as people not just members of the organization. I remember staying up late reading for class to wake up to my cell phone buzzing from text messages about a member of the organization getting arrested for something unrelated to the work of the organization and having to collect bail money from many people before going to the police station to bail a person out and get the person home safely.

As a student, I found that All Black Everything became a part of my educational experience. I sent the following e-mail between leaving the library from a study session heading to class:

> On my way to class, *Shaunel* who hit us up on Facebook called and told me about what he's looking to do in *LaCrosse*. He said he is waiting on some feedback from some other but is looking to begin to make moves after Spring Break. I told him about ABE core programs and how we organize and he was really interested. He told me about what was the situation in *LaCrosse* and he kept saying he is trying to build the Black community in *LaCrosse* and he likes what he saw on the ABE Facebook page. He was calling just to touch base and would call me back in a week or two. I told him that he and his group could come down for an event such as Study Circle or First Fridays and then we can have a round table or sit down to help them organize. Just an FYI. (E-mail correspondence, March 5, 2013)

At some point, I talked to my advisor about doing my dissertation proposal around the work of the organization. I had used Sankofa Study Circle as the subject of my final paper in one of my courses and wanted to explore the space through dissertation research. I was unable to garner support to nurture that exploration. I once again felt like I was unable to be who I wanted to be within the framework of graduate studies. I wanted to make my interests and contributions matter and had difficulty making a connection between what I found valuable and what I was encouraged to study.

ABE functioned as a counterspace, activating the three domains of challenging processes that Case and Hunter (2012) identified. However, considering that the space eventually dissolved, I am investigating to what extent the counterspace framework is not enough in terms of addressing what ecological adaptations Black graduate students may make to cope with the microaggressions of graduate school. In other words, if the counterspace is deemed necessary but "fails" or dissolves, what framework can explain that process while uplifting the fact that counterspaces are warranted and necessary? My point here is that All Black Everything was a counterspace, but not (enough of) a Beloved Community, and that limitation led to its eventual downfall.

All Black Everything as Beloved Community

When I entered my doctoral program, I took classes that had topics relating to race and social justice within urban education. Microaggressions ran rampant. In every class, at some point during the semester, I was subjected to a White person working on his or her doctorate expressing confusion about notions of White privilege, the necessity of talking about race in every class, or what problems a Black child could possibly have in a classroom with a White teacher who has the best of intentions. Many of those conversations led to me building relationships with other Black women graduate students who also felt the microaggressions. I formed relationships with these women. Our class meetings turned in social media follows, study dates, and participating in campus events together. The conversations I had in the community and the conversations with Black women graduate students I met were very similar. The same concerns about what Black people in the spaces that they are in cope with, be resilient through, and, ultimately, thrive despite the aggressions of White supremacy. These communities, the students of the university, and poor working-class members of the community are often seen as having different interests in dealing with racial microaggressions, but the organizing I did proved otherwise. The affirmation of Black identity was needed in both spaces, and members of both spaces were not mutually exclusive nor in opposition to one another. Students and community members could work together to organize Black people in the community.

Beloved Community is a social theory that centers antiracist (King, 2010), anti-oppression (hooks, 1995), and anticolonial (Inwood, 2009) resistance within the notion of community. Beloved Community is not just an adage, and it is deeper and more complex than just an idea or dream of harmonious existence. It defines the operationalization of counterspaces to create liberation, especially for people of color. It is a philosophy of liberation that identified how individuals can practice what liberation looks like until a freedom-as-yet-unknown exists. Like counterspaces, there is a sense of belonging and community that defines its cultural ethos. Unlike counterspaces, it provides an additional layer for analyzing the capacity of a space to sustain the pressure of ongoing oppression outside of the space. Although counterspaces are uniquely situated to support people of color as they engage in racist and oppressive settings, a framework of Beloved Community can deepen the resilience of counterspaces to maintain as more individuals identify a need for the space.

King popularized the philosophy, but many Black leaders of the early 20th century credit their knowledge development about Beloved Community building to the work of Josiah Royce (1913), a religious philosopher. Royce identified Beloved Community as salvation. As individuals, we fail on our own. As a result, we discover our need for community. Through community, we become traitors to our individualism and loyal to the community. The loyalty to community is in constant tension with the individualism and that struggle defines our existence, our work to move toward liberation. Joyce's commentary was not without fault, however, his ideas about race were rooted in xenophobia and American imperial conquest.

Dr. Martin Luther King, Jr. rose to prominence as a civil rights leader because of his speeches during the Montgomery bus boycott. Although the voice of the movement, the arrest of Claudette, a Black female student, served as the catalytic event for legally challenging bus segregation in Montgomery. King said during his speeches that the goal of this resistance was larger than the integration of the busses: "The end is reconciliation; the end is redemption; the end is the creation of the Beloved Community (p. 288)." The phrase became so deeply entwined with Dr. King's philosophical legacy that organizations, programs, and institutes carry the name of Beloved Community in honor of Dr. King's efforts to this day. bell hooks added depth to Dr. King's hope for Beloved Community. In *Killing Rage: Ending Racism*, hooks (1995) argues that King's hope for Beloved Community evolved in conjunction with his political thought. As the "radical," King moved his public rhetoric from integration and nonviolence to poverty and structural violence, the call for Beloved Community also shifted. Early in King's public activist career, the Beloved Community was the result of getting past race, thinking of race as a nuisance that could be ignored. At that time, the Beloved Community would be a space with color-blind analysis that embraced the future with hope and shared humanity. hooks furthered King's analysis through discussion of beloved community as ongoing practices that engage the conflicts that systems of oppression cause, particularly dealing with racism, sexism, xenophobia, and capitalism. In the end, conflict was not embraced nor effectively managed within the organization. Although the counterspace persisted, the ability and capacity of the members of the organization to act within the interests of beloved community prevented the organization from evolving into the counterspace that would best serve the students and community members involved.

ABE functioned as a counterspace for Black women graduate students and other community members. However, after two years of effort, the space collapsed. At the point of collapse, the "challenging processes" Case and Hunter (2007) identified were still fully functioning. In fact, all three processes continued for more than a year despite the organization itself no longer functioning. ABE sponsored events, including the production of a play and a Black women's hair event, during the year after the organization full disbanded. Although the organization did not formally exist, some members were willing to show up for events even though there were no formal meetings. There is a need to reconcile the experience of constructing counterspaces as integrated spaces for students and community members with the reality of their temporality and fragility within an oppressive social world. Despite maintaining the fundamentals of counterspaces, the organization lacked the praxis of Beloved Community. In order for counterspaces to survive, they need to function within the framework of Beloved Community. The framework of Beloved Community provides the tools necessary for resistance and resilience in the broader context of daily struggles within systems of oppression. Specifically, I can retrospectively identify three points of tension within the Beloved Community framework that contributed to the organizations demise.

One of the organizations that ABE members learned about in Sankofa Study Circle was the Republic of New Africa. The Republic of New Afrika (RNA) was a radical social movement organization that promoted black nationalism and claims for reparations for descendants of enslaved Africans (Davenport, 2014). ABE members identified with the RNA in terms of the claims the organization made about the need for Black sovereignty and the call for reparations. As we were meeting in our midwestern city, Chokwe Lumumba, former vice president of the RNA, was campaigning for mayor of Jackson, Mississippi. We followed the campaign closely and had heated discussions about our social movement and its connection to electoral politics. The RNA continues to organize but is limited in scope in comparison to its initial leadership in reparations and Black separatist movements in the late 1960s and early 1970s. Christian Davenport (2014) argues in his book *How Social Movements Die: Repression and Demobilization of the Republic of New Afrika* that external forces of oppression destroyed the group and inhibited the movement from evolving and growing to meet its mission. ABE members studied the arguments Davenport presented to understand the connection between Chokwe Lumumba's leadership within a Black radical organization and his later quest to seek political office through the established political structures of the U.S. government that destroyed the Black radical organization he aligned with. Discussions regarding these ideas were not cordial. Members used insults, called people demeaning names, and accused one another of forsaking liberation of the collective in pursuit of the goals of the individual ego:

> I need to know more about how our black power ancestors organized. They literally started 1000 organizations. Where did they get the money? How did they get space? How did they keep the lights on? Who paid for gas? Where were folks working? Who cooked? I think that the rhetoric on ideology, purpose and function of black freedom movements is important, don't get me wrong. But the real lesson for us and future generations are of how institutions were built because the history is there, we just need to (Re)member. What we need are the lessons we can use to continue nation building and nation management. That is the history I want. That's the story I'm missing. What's been presented to us thus far: blind allegiance to the ballot and electoral processes is not doing it for us, so we need the details of coordinating for New Africa. (Facebook Post, March 13, 2013)

This conflict was never resolved within the organization. When it came to understanding ABE politically, as an agent for power and change, members of the organization did not see eye-to-eye. My post was after a meeting where we argued about what it meant for members to want to seek political office and if there was merit in questioning their loyalty to the organization because of that work. However, though this conflict was central it was just the tip of the iceberg. Interpersonal conflict within the organization was constant and pervasive. I lamented toward the leadership that conflict is brewing and we had no way to stop it.

As an organization, we struggled with gender, sexuality, and relationships. In some ways, we made strides against patriarchal limitations of women. We used Sankofa Study Circle as an opportunity to read texts by and about women, including an in-depth study of Assata. We also held events that were specifically for men and women to discuss, build, and heal with gender-specific experiences of oppression. However, we were limited in our capacity to be open and affirming as a space for queer and gender-nonconforming individuals. There were men in the organization who used homophobic language and encouraged violence against gender nonconforming and trans identities. The Black women in the space who were working on graduate degrees or just finishing them encompassed a wide range of sexual identities. Black women graduate students were continually defending their right to remain in this co-constructed counterspace without defended their womanhood, queerness, or other aspects of gender or sexual identity. The struggle remained until the organization disbanded.

Although ABE remained an intergenerational space, membership largely encompassed single Black men and women between the ages of 21 and 35. Marriage and relationships were regular topics of discussion for meetings and study sessions. We contemplated the role of marriage and how relationships work. We utilized sessions of Sankofa Study Circle to study Mwalimu Baruti's Complementarity (2004) and also studied Marcus Garvey's relationship with his partners Amy Ashwood Garvey and Amy Jacques Garvey. Our notions of liberation in terms of relationships were relatively narrow, we centered heterosexual cisgendered relationships and made little collective exception to that rule.

Within the organization, people dated. These relationships became fodder for conflict in meetings and social events. I posted:

> Can I be real with y'all for a second? First rule of any type of political, economic, cultural or educational movement for the liberation of my sisters and brothers MUST BE: Keep Thy Hormones in Check. If we have learned anything, the easiest way to FUCK up a movement is to literally FUCK all up and through it. (Facebook Post, March 12, 2012)

In the comments section of that post, I was asked if I was referring to something specific in our organization. I said no but had some serious concerns about how the fraternization within the organization would soon impact our ability to fulfill our mission. At this time, we found ourselves in meeting where people had animosity toward each other because of relationships built based upon honesty and false expectations. Men within the organization said slanderous things about the sexual experiences of women within the organization. Couples formed and broke up. There was resentment between individuals as new couples formed. Our socializing soon became a tangled web of the business of the organization and the pursuit of personal romantic relationships. I was not exempt from contributing to the confusion. I maintained a relationship within the organization that created distrust and frustration between myself and other members of the organization. Despite our commitment to understanding revolutionary strategies organizationally and interpersonally, we were unable to operate as a beloved community.

Conclusion

For the students, ABE remained a topic of exploration within discussions related to research methodology, understanding Black history, and the importance of Black people engaging in community efforts as intellectual pursuits. Each of the graduate students at some point during the organization's existence used their work within their coursework assignments.

Years later, the impact of the organization and the community at large remains. There are individuals who met me during my tenure as a leader in the organization and have hired me as a consultant to work with their organizations to address issues of racial equity and community engagement. I owe the experience of ABE so much as it helped shape my understanding of and relationship to organizing and community. I remain disappointed that the counterspace we developed thrived but did not survive. We were able to create space that served as a respite from work and school spaces that choked Black dignity and identity. From my vantage point, we were able to create a unique counterspace that challenged the imposition of Black identity within the academy. Together we were able to affirm an intellectual pursuit of Black dignity that affirmed individuals as members of a collective experience that they were not victims of but curators for.

Counterspaces provide opportunities for those who are within oppressive environments to seek refuge and affirmation. They are worthy for consideration beyond academic institutional contexts because students may engage their broader social context in search of community and collective efficacy. When the counterspace extends itself outside of the classroom or university, it must be bound together with additional supports. In this article, I proposed the beloved community framework as hooks extended King's legacy as an additional framework to support counterspaces that embrace community members and students.

References

Anderson, J. D. (1988). *The education of blacks in the South, 1860–1935*. The University of North Carolina Press. Chapel Hill.

Anderson, M. (2012). Our black year: One family's quest to buy black in America's racially divided economy. Public Affairs. New York.

Baruti, M. (2004). *Complementarity: Thoughts for African warrior couples*. Akoben House. Atlanta.

Boyle, M. & Parry, K. (2007). Telling the whole story: The case for organizational autoethnography. *Culture and Organization, 13*, 185–190. doi:10.1080/14759550701486480

Carruthers, J. (1999). *Intellectual warfare*. Third World Press. Chicago.

Case, A. D., & Hunter, C. D. (2012). Counterspaces: a unit of analysis for understanding the role of settings in marginalized individuals' adaptive responses to oppression. *American Journal of Community Psychology, 50*, 257–270.

Davenport, C. (2014). *How social movements die: Repression and demobilization of the republic of New Africa*. Cambridge University Press. England.

Dorsey, B. (2000). A gendered history of African colonization in the antebellum United States. *Journal of Social History, 34*, 77–103.

Flemons, D. & Green, S. (2001). Stories that conform/stories that transform: a conversation in four parts. In A. P. Bochner & C. Ellis (Eds.), *Ethnographically speaking: Autoethnography, literature, and aesthetics* (pp. 87–94). AltaMira Press. Lanham, MD.

Fordham, S. & Ogbu, J. U. (1986). Black students' school success: Coping with the "burden of 'acting White.'" *The Urban Review, 18*, 176–206.

hooks, b. (1995). *Killing rage: Ending racism*. Henry Holt and Company. New York City.
Hope, E. C., Keels, M., & Durkee, M. I. (2016). Participation in black lives matter and deferred action for childhood arrivals: Modern activism among black and latino college students. *Journal of Diversity in Higher Education, 9*, 203–215.
Inwood, J. F. (2009). Searching for the promised land examining Dr Martin Luther King's concept of beloved community. *JSTOR, 41*, 487–508.
Johnson-Bailey, J., Valentine, T. S., Cervero, R. M., & Bowles, T. A. (2008). Lean on me: The support experiences of black graduate students. *The Journal of Negro Education, 77*, 365–381.
King, Jr., M. L. (1957). Facing the challenge of a new age. The Phylon Quarterly, 18(1), 25–34.
King, Jr., M. L. (2010). *Where do we go from here: Chaos or community?* Beacon Press. Boston.
Okahana, H. & Zhao, E. (2018). *Graduate enrollment and degrees: 2007 to 2017.* Washington, DC: Council of Graduate Schools. Retrieved from https://cgsnet.org/graduate-enrollment-and-degrees
Royce, J. (1913). *The problem of christianity*. New York, NY: Macmillan.
Shakur, A. (2016). Assata: an autobiography. Zed Books Ltd.
Solorzano, D., Ceja, M. & Yosso, T. (2000). Critical race theory, racial microaggressions, and campus racial climate: The experiences of African American college students. *Journal of Negro Education, 69*, 60–73.
Tometti, O., Khan-Cullors, P., & Garza. (2012). Black Lives Matter. Retrieved from www.blacklivesmatter.com.
Wilson, A. N. (1998). Blueprint for Black power: A moral, political, and economic imperative for the twenty-first century. Afrikan World InfoSystems.
X, M. (2015). The autobiography of Malcolm X. Ballantine Books.

ELEVEN

 Counseling Psychology of African Americans: A Review of the Literature

Selena Tate

THIS REVIEW OF THE LITERATURE will examine youth-to-parent violence (YTPV) while taking into account the parent–victim's experience and response to the violence. The parent's indirect and/or direct experience with family violence will also be explored. The theoretical approach used to explore this phenomenon is Murray Bowen's Family Systems Theory.

YTPV and Victim Experiences

Although both mothers and fathers can be victims of YTPV (Routt & Anderson, 2011), the literature shows that mothers, stepmothers, foster mothers, adoptive mothers, and other female caretakers are the predominant victims (Kennair & Mellor, 2007; Kethineni, 2004; Nock & Kazdin, 2002; Routt & Anderson, 2011). For example, Kethineni (2004) found that mothers were the "primary source of referrals" and the victims of YTPV. This study indicated that the youth's living situation at the time of the abuse provided an explanation as to why mothers were more likely to report YTPV and are the predominant victims. Of the parents in this study who reported YTPV, 44.6% were single mothers, whereas only 3.6% were single fathers. Moreover, the findings suggested that 81.1% of the youths who resided at home with their biological mothers were abusive toward their mothers, 46.7% of those who lived with both biological parents abused only their mother, and 41.7% who lived with their biological mother and stepfather reportedly abused only their mother. Also, the researcher found that the predominant aggressors were adolescent males (62.7%), the remaining 37.3% being adolescent females. Routt and Anderson (2011) found that 72% of YTPV victims were mothers (i.e., biological, step, and foster) while 28% were biological, step-, or foster fathers. Of these mothers and/or female caretakers, 49% were separated or divorced from the aggressor's biological father or male caretaker. Forty-three percent of the adolescents lived at home with their mothers, 25% with both parents, 20% with a stepfather or male caretaker, and only 6% with their biological father only. Adolescents who were currently being abused in the home, whether by their parent(s) or another family member, were not included in the study.

As previously noted, victims of YTPV are more likely to be White (Kethineni, 2004; Eckstein, 2004; Routt & Anderson, 2011; Walsh & Krienert, 2007). The 13 female and 7 male victims in the Eckstein (2004) study were all White, as were 76% of participants in the Walsh and Krienert (2007) study. Kethineni (2004) found that 67.5% of the adolescent aggressors were White and 24.1% were African American. Routt and Anderson's (2011) study went into more detail: 76% of its adolescent aggressors were White, 10% African American, 6% Asian, 1% Native American, 4% Hispanic/Latino, and 3% members of other ethnic groups. In contrast, Kennair and Mellor's (2007) review of the past literature showed that there were no differences in the occurrence of YTPV across the ethnic races.

Current and past studies have explored YTPV by defining the types of abuse experienced (i.e., physical, psychological, verbal, and financial). Cottrell (2001) identified characteristics of both adolescent aggressors and victims, and identified factors (i.e., family stress, family dynamics, family structure, parenting styles, direct/indirect to violence, physical size and age of the adolescent aggressor, the adolescent's deviant behavior, entitlement, peer influence, substance abuse, mental health issues, socioeconomic status), that may influence this type of abuse (Boxer et al., 2009; Cottrell, 2001; Cottrell & Monk, 2004; Eckstein, 2004; Gallagher, 2004; Jackson, 2003; Kennair & Mellor, 2007; Kethineni, 2004; Nock & Kazdin, 2002; Pagani et al., 2003; Pagani et al., 2004; Routt & Anderson, 2011; Stewart et al., 2007; Walsh & Krienert, 2007).

Although the literature has hypothesized that indirect and direct exposure to abuse (i.e., child abuse) and violence (i.e., intimate partner/spouse violence) may contribute to YTPV, little research focuses on the victim's family of origin, childhood experiences, and/or indirect or direct exposure to family violence. The review of literature has identified three studies (Jackson, 2003; Pagani et al., 2003; Stewart et al., 2007) that examined YTPV while taking into account the victim's experience. These studies are important because they explore the type of violence experienced, the victim's relationship with the aggressor, and the victim's response to the violence. Moreover, these studies draw attention to YTPV and its common features with intimate partner/spouse violence.

In an Australian qualitative study, Jackson (2003) examined the experiences of mothers who were victims of YTPV. Initially, the purpose of the study was to understand and explore the characteristics of motherhood (i.e., experiences and the influence of motherhood). Twenty participants were recruited for the initial study by use of snowball sampling and all participated in conversational-style interviews. Although the study did not pose questions related to family violence, the data revealed that six of the participants had experienced YTPV. All six had two or three children between the ages of 18 to 24 years old, five had both female and male children, two were single mothers, and four were married to their child's biological father. During the study, five had at least one child living in the home. At the time of the abuse, the age of the adolescent aggressors ranged from 14 to 16 years. All had substance abuse issues, were physically larger than their mothers, and were male. Reportedly, all six victims kept the abuse concealed because of the shame and distress they experienced. Only one of the mothers admitted to having a history of family violence. The other five denied any prior experience.

The findings revealed three themes that described the mothers' experience with YTPV. The first, "It was only a matter of time: feeling intimidated and under threat," explained the gradual change in the mother–child relationship. Some of the mothers reported feeling fearful, vulnerable, and concerned about their personal safety. The women reported that their sons' physical size and strength contributed to their loss of parental control and ability to discipline. The second theme, "He just punched me: physical violence from the child to mother," described the types of violence. Four of the six women reported that the violence escalated from intimidation to physical aggression (i.e., pushing, shoving, striking, and punching) and two that their sons were physically abusive toward other family members. The mothers attributed their sons' physical aggression to their substance abuse.

The final theme, "Other men in the house: violence directed to the mothers by friends and associates," related the mothers' feelings of intimidation and fear because of their children's interactions. All six participants described situations in which their sons' lifestyles left them feeling frightened and vulnerable. Some arrived home to find it filled with their child's friends. Another mother recalled waking in the middle of the night to find several intoxicated and high men in the home. Some of the women reported receiving disturbing and intimidating phone calls and/or experiencing home invasions initiated by their child's friends. All the participants stated that these incidents could be attributed to their child's lifestyle/activities.

Pagani et al. (2003) conducted a longitudinal study using quantitative methods to explore verbal (i.e., yelling, swearing, or use of insults) and physical (i.e., pushing, shoving, punching, kicking, throwing of objects, threatening and/or attacking with a weapon) aggression toward mothers by their 15-year-old adolescent offspring. Specifically, the researchers explored the impact of family stress and marital transition (divorce and/or remarriage) on aggression toward mothers. They followed 2,524 boys and girls from the end of kindergarten through mid-adolescence. The participants were selected based on (1) family configuration, (2) age, school grade, and intactness of family, (3) number of marital transitions (no more than two), (4) a questionnaire variable about mother-directed aggression, and (5) completed data on covariates and possible predictors (e.g., the child's age and sex and the age of the mother at the birth of target child).

Researchers used both the Social Behavior Questionnaire (SBQ) and the Ways of Coping Questionnaire (WCQ). The SBQ (Tremblay et al., 1991), a tool that assesses early childhood disruptive behaviors, was administered to the children's kindergarten teachers when the participants were six years of age. Another tool was given during mid-adolescence (15 years of age) and completed by both the mothers and their adolescent offspring. The WCQ (Folkman & Lazarus, 1988) was given to examine how the participants coped during stressful family situations. Of the 2,524 original participants, only 778 continued in the study.

The study found that 36% of the teenaged subjects were not verbally or physically aggressive toward their mothers. Of those who were, 13% were physically aggressive and 51% were verbally abusive. Female adolescents were reportedly more aggressive toward their mothers than were males. This finding contradicts the literature identifying adolescent males as more likely to be violent toward their mothers (Gallagher, 2004; Jackson, 2003; Kennair & Mellor, 2007; Routt & Anderson, 2011; Stewart et al., 2007). Early childhood disruptiveness and the stress (i.e., alienation of the custodial parent, financial problems, lack of support from family, child-parent visitations) associated with marital transition were predictive of aggression toward mothers during mid-adolescence. The study also concluded that mothers who sought outside or familial support were at higher risk of verbal and physical aggression.

Stewart et al. (2007) also conducted a qualitative study that explored the experiences of mothers in four specific areas: the types of abuse experienced, contributing factors, how the mothers dealt with the abuse, and how their mothering experience related to their own birth year during the Depression years (1931–1936), the Second World War years (1941–1946), or the baby boom years (1951–1956).

This unique longitudinal study interviewed 60 Australian women: 20 aged 40 to 45, 20 aged 50 to 55, and 20 aged 60 to 65. These women had married and given birth to two or three children before the age of 30. Some of the women had experienced divorce or separation, remarried, and/or repartnered. The subjects participated in two in-depth interviews in which they told their life stories and mapped major experiences and events. The initial set of interviews occurred between 1996 and 1997 with follow-up interviews conducted in 2001. The researchers used a timeline to record the major experiences and events. Participants provided important information about their personal health, family relationships, career choices, social networks, financial issues, and other factors. In some cases, the data analysis revealed evidence of abuse by the participants' adult and adolescent offspring.

The first area the researchers examined was the abuse participants experienced. They identified several types of "acting-out abuse," including physical abuse (i.e., hitting, throwing objects, threat with a gun or knife, or destroying property), verbal abuse (i.e., swearing, yelling, tantrums, threats, or being nasty), domineering abuse (i.e., assertion of control/power and demanding money and/or things), obstructive abuse (i.e., domineering behavior that prevented the mother from achieving goals and/or relationships), and psychological abuse (i.e., threats and manipulation).

The data analysis revealed several contributing factors. The mother's relationship status (i.e., single, divorced, or separated) and history of intimate partner violence were factors associated with YTPV. Many of the women in the study reported being in abusive intimate relationships. The researchers concluded that an acceptance of violent behavior toward women may have been passed from one male relative to another from generation to generation. For example, some women reported that their abusive adult relationships indirectly and directly exposed their children to intimate partner/spouse violence and physical abuse. Some of the children possessed authority and anger issues similar to those displayed by their fathers. Some children also reportedly suffered from mental illness or psychological issues (i.e., psychotic depression, affective disorder, schizophrenia). Other contributing factors identified included social and cultural influences such as peer groups and gender power imbalance (i.e., domineering and disrespectful behavior toward women).

The researchers also examined several coping strategies identified by the mothers. The study found that the mothers were supportive, protective, and tolerant of the violence when they believed that the child was suffering from mental issues. For example, when the authorities or other family members became involved, the mother would go to great lengths to protect the child. They sometimes provided this support jointly with their partners. In other cases, they were reportedly "able to act assertively without interference from the father" (Stewart et al., 2007, p. 188). Mothers who did not receive partner support voiced their complaints, opted not to discipline, or, instead, avoided the child, dealing with the rejection and breakdown of the mother–child relationship through emotional distancing.

Stewart et al. (2007) next compared the differences between the mothers born during the three different time periods (i.e. Depression, wartime, and baby boom years). The reported rate of YTPV in mothers from the wartime period was 45.5% but only 22.7% from the mothers of the Depression era. The researchers concluded that the mothers from the baby boom era were less likely to take ownership of their child's abusive behavior, feeling instead that their children were responsible for the abusive behavior. By contrast, mothers born during the Depression era believed that "society's general disrespect for women" (Stewart et al., 2007, p. 189) contributed to their sons' abusive behavior.

Although the findings of this study are consistent with others (Boxer et al., 2009; Cottrell & Monk, 2004; Gallagher, 2004; Kennair & Mellor, 2007; Kethineni, 2007; Routt & Anderson, 2011) and are beneficial, Stewart et al. did not track the race of the participants and their children or any age data for the latter beyond adult, adolescent, and/or younger. Nor does the study explain the types of marital issues the participants experienced or discuss the mothers' current adult relationships.

Effects of Adult Relationships and Victim Experiences

Past studies of intimate partner violence are extensive, especially as it relates to female victims. Several studies have explored the effects of intimate partner/spouse violence (IPSV) on female victims (Alhabib, Nur & Jones, 2010; Beck, McNiff, Clapp, Olsen, Avery & Hagewood, 2011; Beeble et al., 2007; Coker et al., 2002). Specifically, these studies highlighted the types of abuse (Alhabib et al., 2010; Beeble et al., 2007) and the physical and emotional ramifications victims experienced.

To examine the experiences of IP/SV, Kulkarni, Bell, and Wylie (2010) (Alhabib et al., 2010) conducted a study that highlighted the challenges and needs that IP/SV survivors encountered when they sought assistance. Their qualitative study recruited two sample groups from multiple sites. Of the 54 participants, 24 were advocates who worked on a domestic violence hotline and 30 were victims of IP/SV. The subjects were assigned to focus groups and given a series of questions to answer. Questions for the advocate group examined the types of calls received, callers' service needs (included callers with special needs, cultural differences, and disabilities), ranking of the service needs, available and unavailable services, and recommendations to local service providers. The IP/SV victims' questions examined how they (the survivors) determined that they needed outside support, what types of support they needed, their ranking of support needs, what types of service needs they had (again, taking into account their special needs, cultural difference, and disabilities), which services were helpful and unhelpful, and recommendations for local agencies.

The data were analyzed in stages using a modified grounded theory approach, which resulted in the identification of three themes: understanding survivor challenges in prioritizing health needs, identifying and accessing appropriate resources, and coaching survivors to overcome potential service barriers. The study revealed, first, that the survivors of IP/SV tended to place the needs of daily survival and those of their children above their personal health care. Some survivors were afraid to disclose the abuse. Some feared being reported to law enforcement or child protective systems and/or being retaliated against by the aggressor. Finding that some of the survivors suffered from chronic health problems, the researchers hypothesized that the stress from the abusive relationships contributed to the problems' severity.

The second theme examined the services available for IP/SV survivors and whether they were easily accessible. Survivors ranked the resources (shelter, information about IP/SV, available resources, counseling/emotional support, transportation, law enforcement, financial assistance, and childcare) based on importance and identified the challenges experienced when they sought assistance. The researchers found that survivors of IP/SV experienced challenges when the sought assistance from domestic violence shelters, counseling centers, and law enforcement. Although shelters existed, too few beds were available and there were confidentiality issues (particularly for victims in rural areas), a complicated intake process, and restrictive rules and requirements. Although survivors expressed an interest in receiving counseling services, these were not always available or were delayed due to waiting lists and/or inconvenient meeting times and locations. In general, the IP/SV victims were not pleased with the treatment they received from law enforcement. Some reported feeling "threatened" by officers and frustrated when the aggressor was not apprehended.

The final theme, coaching survivors to overcome potential service barriers, sought to encourage and empower survivors of IP/SV. This involved educating them about how to seek community services and successfully articulate their needs.

Although Kulkarni, Bell, and Wylie's (2010) research is beneficial in that it highlights the challenges and needs of IP/SV survivors, the participants and findings of this study only represented women receiving IP/SV services. Individuals from other populations were not included, and the data reflected the personal experiences of the survivors.

When attempting to understand the experiences of people in abusive relationships, Orzeck, Rokach, and Chin (2010) found that most were distressing and traumatic. This Canadian study included both male (42) and female (59) participants who reported experiencing a traumatic or abusive relationship. Participants were recruited from several community centers and universities and given a questionnaire to complete. They were asked to describe the effects of their abusive relationships, their most traumatic relationship experience, and what was most distressful about the relationship. Using a mixed-method approach (qualitative and quantitative content analysis) to the data, the researchers discovered two themes: relational abuse and internal turmoil/stressful reactions.

Relational abuse describes the type of abuse the participants experienced (e.g., verbal abuse, physical abuse, infidelity, sexual abuse, and financial abuse). The effects of the abuse ranged from feelings of devastation, guilt, and powerlessness to depression, anger, and a sense of permanent damage. *Internal turmoil/stressful reactions* describes the participants' internal and external reactions to the traumatic or abusive experience. According to the findings, the participants experienced stress, anxiety (some attempting suicide or self-harm), sleep disturbances (i.e., nightmares and sleeplessness), and a loss of self-control. In addition, the researchers concluded that the participants experienced feelings of pessimism, sorrow, hopelessness, anger, and low self-esteem (Orzeck et al., 2010).

According to the researchers, the female participants reported experiencing all of the relational abuse categories more frequently than did male participants. Females also had a higher rate of physical abuse and emotional abuse. Emotional/psychological abuse and verbal abuse, however, were experienced equally by both sexes (Orzeck et al., 2010). It was noted that female participants experienced internal turmoil more than males. Although the researchers deem this study credible, they acknowledge several limitations. A questionnaire was used to gather qualitative data instead of an interview. This limited the amount of information gathered from the participants. In addition, participants were not asked about their personal growth or resiliency. For future research, Orzeck et al. (2010) suggest further inquiry into the area of personal growth and resiliency and the exploration of risk factors that may distinguish between individuals who do and do not develop posttraumatic outcomes as a result of abusive relationships.

A study conducted by Lacey (2010) examined whether socioeconomic status, relationship investment, and psychological abuse influence Black women and Hispanic women to stay or leave abusive relationships. The researcher studied 57 Black women and 47 Hispanic women using the exchange theory. Data were randomly selected from the National Violence Against Women Survey. The women who reported abuse in their current relationship and responded to the question concerning leaving or staying in an abusive relationship were included in the study. The researcher found that 66.7% of Black women were more likely to stay in violent relationships than Hispanic woman, whose rate was 59.6%. Hispanic women with higher incomes were more likely to stay than leave: The researcher hypothesized that this was because they still did not earn enough money to fully support themselves and their families (children and extended family) and/or the aggressor was controlling their finances.

Marital status (married or common law) and the presence of additional adults in the home are factors that influence Black women to stay in violent relationships. To stay would "dispel the notion that minority families are headed mostly by single females," and the presence of additional adults in the home may "alter or reduce the levels of violence" (Lacey, 2010, p. 675). Both Black and Hispanic women were more likely to leave the relationship if they experienced psychological abuse (i.e., were shouted or sworn at by their partner). However, Black women who experienced psychological abuse in front of friends and family members were more likely to leave the relationship. Although interesting and beneficial, this study has limitations with the data. The researchers admit to having used a small sample size, a nonstandard measurement to collect income information, and dated data and to having neglected to note whether their subjects left the abusive relationships temporarily or permanently. In addition, the study did not test for religious or cultural factors.

Beeble et al. (2007) examined how male aggressors of IP/SV used children to control their female victims. The researchers recruited 156 women with a history of IP/SV within the previous four months and with at least one child between the ages of 5 to 12 to participate in the study. The women completed a modified version of the Conflict Tactics Scale (CTS) (Straus 1979; Sullivan & Bybee, 1999), which assessed for the types of physical abuse experienced, and the Index of Psychological Abuse (IPA) (Sullivan, Tan, Basta, Rumptz & Davidson, 1992), which assessed for emotional abuse. The researchers also used an unidentified seven-item scale (presumably self-designed) to examine how the male aggressor uses the children to control (i.e., harass, intimidate, or frighten) the survivors.

Information given by the women allowed the researchers to categorize the male aggressors into four groups: (1) biological father, (2) stepfather, (3) father figure, and (4) non–father figure. The researchers found that 88% of the male aggressors used their children to control their spouse/partners (Beeble et al., 2007). Biological fathers were more likely to do so than were stepfathers, father figures, and non–father figures. Additionally, 70% of the male aggressors used their children to stay involved in the survivor's life, 69% to monitor the survivors, 58% to intimidate, 58% to harass, 44% to frighten, 45% to turn to the children against the mothers, and 45% to persuade the mother to take the father back. Fathers with court-ordered visitations were more likely to use the children to control the mothers than were men who were currently living with the children and those without court-ordered visitations. The researchers also found that the women who reported significant control experienced increased levels of physical and emotional abuse and that those who had terminated or were in the process of terminating the abusive relationship reported higher levels of control than the women who stayed in the relationships.

To further understand the relational dynamics within families dealing with family violence and the continuance of violence across generations, a closer examination of the family of origin will be important. According to the literature and past studies, the occurrence of YTPV is strongly influenced by a history of family violence (i.e., intimate partner/spouse violence) (Cottrell & Monk, 2004; Gallagher, 2004; Kennair & Mellor, 2007; Kethineni, 2004) and negative attitudes toward women (Cottrell & Monk, 2004; Gallagher, 2004). It therefore seems important to focus on the family of origin and to assess for a history of family violence and the occurrence of YTPV.

Bowen Family Systems Theory

It is theorized that aggressive behaviors are learned within the context of the family and that acceptance of violence is likely passed from one generation to the next (Doumas, Margolin & John, 1994; Markowitz, 2001). Although it is unclear as to why some individuals or families become susceptible to the perpetuation of violence, exploring the occurrence of family violence through a systemic lens may provide an explanation. The Bowen Family Systems Theory (1978, 1988), also referred to as multigenerational family therapy (Gehart & Tuttle, 2003), evolved from psychoanalytic theory (Bowen, 1978; Kerr & Bowen, 1988). The theory is grounded on the premise that humankind exists because of evolution and that human behavior, and the behavior of all other forms of life, is also influenced by natural sciences (Kerr & Bowen, 1988; Titelman, 1998).

Murray Bowen was a psychiatrist who worked with individuals diagnosed with schizophrenia. Initially, the treatment primarily focused only on the individual; however, he changed his methods after observing the relational interactions between the identified client and his or her family members. The researcher was particularly interested in the dynamics that occurred between client and mother. According to Bowen, the emotional intensity within this parent–child dyad revealed a level of involvement that at times made it difficult to view the mother and client as separate individuals (Kerr & Bowen, 1988). This type of interaction was also evident with other nuclear family members (i.e., biological father and/or siblings). These crucial observations moved Bowen to acknowledge the connection between an individual's emotional functioning and the family: the entire family could be viewed as an emotional unit (Kerr & Bowen, 1988).

Bowen's Family Systems Theory (Kerr & Bowen, 1988) is composed of eight concepts that examine the intrafamilial and multigenerational relationships in families: nuclear family emotional process, family projection process, triangles, sibling position, emotional cutoff, societal emotional process, differentiation, and multigenerational transmission process. According to Kerr and Bowen (1988), these variables define the family's emotional functioning. For the purpose of this body of work, a brief description will be provided for all of the concepts; however, more attention will be given to two of the eight: (1) differentiation of self and (2) the multigenerational transmission process. Focus will be given to these two tenets because research has tested both constructs (Bartle-Haring, Rosen & Stith, 2002; Cook, 2007; Doumas, Margolin & John, 1994; Johnson & Stone, 2009; Klever, 2005; Murdock & Gore, 2004; Rosen et al., 2001; Tuason & Friedlander, 2000).

Nuclear Family Emotional Process

Bowen's theory identifies the nuclear family as an emotional system (Gilbert, 2006; Kerr & Bowen, 1988). Nuclear family emotional process is defined as "the flow of emotional process or patterns of emotional functioning in the nuclear family" (Kerr & Bowen, 1988, p. 317). For instance, what affects one member of the family system can affect others (Gilbert, 2006).

Family Projection Process

The family projection process refers to "a process by which parents transmit or project their immaturity and lack of differentiation to their children"

(Gehart & Tuttle, 2003, p. 153). These transfers of processes are affiliated with behaviors and patterns in the family of origin. When the level of differentiation is low in the nuclear family (the parents), it is likely the offspring (the child) who will experience the effects.

Triangles

Triangles exist in all systems (Nelson, 2003) and are triggered by anxiety (Kerr & Bowen, 1988; Gehart & Tuttle, 2003; Gilbert, 2006). When anxiety is low, the relationship is peaceful and relaxed. In contrast, a shift in the relationship dyad can cause anxiety to increase. To alleviate the anxiety in the original dyad, a third person (i.e., a child, friend, parent, or thing) is brought in (Gehart & Tuttle, 2003), creating "a three-person system" (Gilbert, 2006, p. 50). Although the addition of the third person or thing immediately diminishes the anxiety, the preexisting issue in the original dyad is less likely to be resolved.

Sibling Position

Sibling position predicts personality characteristics and determines the roles of children in the family (Gehart & Tuttle, 2003; Kerr & Bowen, 1988; Nichols & Schwartz, 2001; Titelman, 1998).This concept is emphasized in both Alderian theory and Walter Toman's sibling personality profile (Miller, Anderson & Keala, 2004). The second of these suggests that the oldest child is characterized as being responsible and a strong leader, protector, and nurturer whereas the youngest is categorized as helpless, dependent, and the baby of the family (Gilbert, 2006; Titleman, 1998). It is hypothesized that there is a strong connection between sibling position and the family emotional process (Nichols & Schwartz, 2001). Bowen was most interested in this aspect because it may explain which child is likely to be predisposed to triangulation (Nichols & Schwartz, 2001).

Emotional Cutoff

Emotional cutoff is described as the "way people manage the undifferentiation (and emotional intensity associated with it) that exist between generations" (Kerr & Bowen, 1988, p. 271). Cutoff from one's family of origin or nuclear family is the result of a low level of differentiation and unresolved family issues (Gehart & Tuttle, 2003). In contrast, it serves as a tool to eliminate anxiety (Kerr & Bowen, 1988); however, cutoff can be misconstrued as a mature way to resolve family-related issues (Gehart & Tuttle, 2003). The solution to avoiding cutoff is to gain a heightened level of self-differentiation, which allows the individual to remain connected to his or her family (Kerr & Bowen, 1988).

Societal Emotional Process

Societal Emotional Process refers to how social anxiety due to, for example, crime, racism, war, social injustice, or economic hardship, may affect the family emotional process. Extended exposure to societal anxiety may affect family relationships and lower the level of differentiation in families (Nichols & Schwartz, 2001).

Differentiation of Self

The concept of differentiation of self is the foundation of the Bowen Family Systems Theory (Kerr & Bowen, 1988). Differentiation of self is about an individual's and/or family's emotional maturity and the ability to set and maintain healthy boundaries. This lifelong process refers to the ability to engage and/or connect with others (i.e., togetherness) while maintaining a balance of one's individuality (i.e. to think, feel, and act independently; Gehart & Tuttle, 2003; Nichols & Schwartz, 2001). The process is both intrapsychic and interpersonal. Separation of one's thoughts and feelings defines intrapsychic differentiation, while interpersonal differentiation refers to the ability to separate oneself from others (i.e., spouse, family members, coworker, etc.; Gehart & Tuttle, 2003). Differentiation of self affects how an individual and/or family copes with stressful situations. This developmental process begins during childhood and is influenced by the nuclear family (i.e., parents) and family of origin. It continues through adolescence. Kerr and Bowen (1988) provided this example of a lowly differentiated adolescent:

> His rebellion reflects the lack of differentiation that exists between him and his parents. The rebel is a highly reactive person whose self is poorly developed. He operates in opposition to his parents and others; they in

turn, are sufficiently unsure of themselves that they react automatically to his acting-out behavior. Most of his values and beliefs are formed in opposition to the beliefs of others. Based more on emotional reactiveness than thinking, the beliefs are usually inconsistent. More of the parents' emotional immaturities influence their relationship with this child than with his siblings. The acting-out child, in turn, responds in a more immature manner to the parents than do the other children. (p. 96)

Highly differentiated families foster a healthy balance of togetherness and individuality that reinforces a child's ability to think, feel, and act independently (Kerr & Bowen, 1988). When stressful events transpire, a highly differentiated individual or family does not react emotionally. Instead, there is an acknowledgment of the issue, an initial response. However, this is not guided by the reaction of others: The person or family is able to separate thinking from feeling (Nichols & Schwartz, 2001). By contrast, a low level of differentiation impedes a family's emotional functioning. In these undifferentiated families, children may be easily influenced by their parents' "emotional immaturities," responding to stress in an identical way. Although the parents' emotional functioning is passed on to their children, Kerr and Bowen (1988) assert that "not all children of one set of parents separate emotionally at the same degree" (p. 95). Within the nuclear family, each child's emotional functioning varies and is contingent on the parent's relationship with each child. In essence, no relationship is identical. In some instances, the parent–child relationship may foster more or less emotional separation. Furthermore, when an individual has a lower level of differentiation than his or her parents, it is most likely that he or she will marry a mate with the same level of differentiation (Kerr & Bowen, 1988). Children who are a product of the marriage are subjected to the parent's level of differentiation as well as levels of chronic anxiety. According to Kerr and Bowen (1988), changes in levels of differentiation within individuals, the family, and three generations typically occur gradually; therefore, the levels of differentiation vary accordingly.

An important variable associated with the differentiation of self is anxiety. According to Kerr and Bowen (1988), anxiety can have an emotional impact on a family's level of functioning. The researchers also suggest that everyone experiences some form of anxiety (i.e. acute or chronic) because it is inevitable, it "rubs off on people," is "infectious," and permeates individuals' attitudes and beliefs (Kerr & Bowen, 1988). The effects of the anxiety are determined by how individuals and families adapt and respond to stressful events. Acute anxiety is a result of day-to-day living (i.e., emergencies, job changes, moving, etc.), is fueled by the fear of what is, and its duration is limited. Typically, individuals respond and adapt to this type of anxiety fairly well (Kerr & Bowen, 1988; Titelman, 1998). Chronic anxiety, on the other hand, occurs as a response to imagined threats and is fueled by the fear of what might be (Kerr & Bowen, 1988). Bowen emphasizes that chronic anxiety is learned during childhood and is the product of learned responses (Kerr & Bowen, 1988).

Poorly differentiated individuals and/or families are more anxious and less likely to adapt to stress. Research suggests that key generators of chronic anxiety are individuals' responses to the disruption in the balance of the relationship system (Kerr & Bowen, 1988). It also suggests that the response to the disruption fuels the chronic anxiety more than the actual stressful event (Kerr & Bowen, 1988; Titelman, 1998). The level of anxiety experienced individually and by the family unit varies. Kerr and Bowen (1988) propose that individuals at any point on the scale of differentiation "if stressed sufficiently, can develop physical, emotional, or social symptoms" (p. 97). These symptoms may be "generated by an anxiety-driven togetherness process characterized by people's pressuring one another to think, feel, and act in specific ways" (Kerr & Bowen, 1988, p. 256). A high level of differentiation may reduce symptoms; however, a low level may trigger them (Kerr & Bowen, 1988).

Several studies (Bartle-Haring, Rosen & Stith, 2002; Johnson & Stone, 2009; Murdock & Gore, 2004; Tuason & Friedlander, 2000) have tested Bowen's concept of differentiation. Specifically, these studies examined the relationship between differentiation and psychological symptoms, the family of origin, coping, and anxiety. Some of the findings supported Bowen's assumptions: that (1) lowly differentiated individuals and families are more likely to experience chronic anxiety, which may result in the development of psychological symptoms; (2) parents are more likely to pass their level of differentiation to their offspring; and (3) a relationship exists between chronic anxiety and lowly differentiated families.

In a quantitative study, Tuason and Friedlander (2000) examined the differentiation levels of parents and their adult children. The researchers used three instruments: the Differentiation of Self Inventory (DSI; Skowron & Friedlander, 1998), the State-Trait Anxiety Inventory (Spielberger, 1983), and the Symptom Checklist-90-R (Derogatis, 1994). Participants were 306 Filipino parents and their adult children. The study sought to determine if there was a significant relationship between differentiation of self and psychological distress in Filipinos, whether the parents' levels of differentiation of self and psychological distress predicted their adult children's levels, and whether the spouses had the same levels of differentiation of self. The results supported two of the proposed assumptions: (1) There was a significant relationship between differentiation of self and psychological distress, and (2) there was a significant relationship between the spouse's levels of differentiation. By contrast, the results showed no evidence to support the multigenerational transmission of the parents' level of differentiation and distress to their adult children. The researchers proposed that this insignificant finding suggests differentiation may look different in the Filipino culture.

Bartle-Haring et al. (2002) also conducted a study that examined the concept of differentiation and psychological symptoms. The participants were 372 college students (283 females and 89 males), the majority of whom were White (72%) and between the ages of 18 and 41. The participants were asked to complete the Behavioral and Emotional Reactivity Index (BERI) (Bartle & Sabatelli, 1995), the revised version of the Adolescent-Family Inventory of Life Events and Changes (A-FILE) (Fischer & Corcoran, 1994), and the Hopkins Symptom Checklist (HSCL) (Derogatis, Lipman, Rickels, Uhlenhuth & Covi, 1974), which measured the differentiation of self in the family of origin, stressful events experienced by the participants and their families, and their physical and psychological symptoms. Of the three instruments used, the BERI was a new one developed to assess the differentiation of self in the family of origin, specifically, emotional reactivity toward parents. The participants were given 20 emotion-evoking scenarios (10 items for Mother and 10 items for Father) and asked to rate their responses on a Likert-type scale. The internal consistency reliabilities for the Mother and Father subscales in the sample ranged from .88 to .90. The A-FILE contained a 50-item checklist of events experienced by families, plus six subscales (Transitions, Sexuality, Losses, Responsibilities, Strains, Substance Use, and Legal Conflict). The HSCL contained a 58-item checklist that measured physical and psychological symptoms. The instrument identified five symptom dimensions: Somatization, Obsessive-Compulsive Behaviors, Interpersonal Sensitivity, Depression, and Anxiety.

The findings of the study supported Bowen's assumption regarding differentiation of self and psychological distress. Specifically, the researchers concluded that the emotional reactivity toward the mother was predictive of both increased stressful life events and increased psychological symptoms. The findings also suggested that there is a significant relationship between increased stressful life events and increased levels of psychological symptoms.

Murdock and Gore (2004) also conducted a study that measured differentiation of self, stress, and coping. The researchers had 119 college students (78 females and 41 males) complete a demographic form and several instruments. The DSI (Skowron & Friedlander, 1998) contained 43 items and four subscales that assessed current relationships. The Perceived Stress Scale (Cohen, Kamarck & Mermelstein, 1983) was used to assess the participants' current stress level and how many stressful life events experienced. This instrument had 14 items and an internal consistency coefficient of 0.83. The Problem Focused Style of Coping Inventory (Heppner, Cook, Wright & Johnson, 1995) was also used to measure the participants' coping skills by posing questions about how they dealt with and solved their problems. Three style subscales accompany the instrument: Reactive ("I act too quickly, which makes my problems worse"), Reflective ("I identify the cause of my emotions, which helps me solve my problems"), and Suppressive ("I avoid even thinking about my problems"). According to the study, the internal consistency for the entire scale was 0.65 and the coefficient for the Reflective scale was .79, .70 for the Suppressive scale, and .77 for the Reactive scale. In addition, the Global Severity Index (Derogatis, 1993) and the Brief Symptom Inventory (BSI; Derogatis, 1993) were used to assess psychological functioning. The BSI had 53 items, nine subscales (somatization, obsessive-compulsive problems, interpersonal sensitivity, depression, anxiety, hostility, phobic anxiety, paranoid ideation, and psychoticism) and an internal consistency coefficient of 0.95 for this study.

The study's findings showed that a relationship existed between perceived stress, differentiation of self, and psychological distress. They also revealed that there was a relationship between the Reactive and Suppressive coping styles and poor psychological functioning. In addition, the results indicated a relationship between Reflective coping and higher levels of differentiation, while Suppressive and Reactive coping indicted low levels of differentiation. This study supported Bowen's assumptions that differentiation of self from the family of origin was correlated to psychological distress and that a higher level of differentiation was correlated with fewer psychological symptoms.

Johnson and Stone (2009) measured the effect of parental alcoholism and family functioning on the differentiation levels of 813 college students: 563 women (69%), 222 men (27%), and 28 (4%) who did not identify their gender. Of these, 172 had at least one parent with a drinking problem. These individuals were placed in the Adult Children of Alcoholics (ACOA) group. Participants were given a demographic questionnaire as well as specific family of origin questions (i.e., parental alcoholism status, parental marital status, parental availability/predictability, child abuse, spousal violence, frequency of parental drinking, and length of time spent living with an alcoholic parent) and two standardized measurements to complete. The authors used the Self-Report Family Inventory Version II (Beavers & Hampson, 1990) to measure the family functioning. The measurement contained 34 items and five subscales. Health and Competence, the first subscale, measured the family functioning (happiness, problem solving, autonomy/individuality, etc.). The Conflict subscale assessed for hidden areas of unresolved conflict. The Cohesion subscale gathered information about the family's levels of togetherness, satisfaction, and happiness. The fourth subscale, Leadership, measured the adult leadership in the family. The fifth, Emotional Expressiveness, measured how the family expressed their physical and verbal emotion toward one another. The DSI (Skowron & Friedlander, 1998) contained 43 items and four subscales (Emotional Reactivity, I Position, Emotional Cutoff, and Fusion with Others). The reliability coefficients for the DSI full scale and the subscales were .83, .81 (Emotional Reactivity), .78 (I Position), .84 (Emotional Cutoff), and .68 (Fusion).

Based on the result of three previous studies, it was reported that the "DSI correlated highly and in the expected direction with a measure of chronic anxiety and with amount and intensity of symptomatic distress" (Johnson & Stone, 2009, p. 9). The findings suggest significant differences in the alcoholic families versus the nonalcoholic. Parental alcoholism appeared to have an effect on the level of differentiation and all of the DSI scales. It was reported the participants from the alcoholic families were more emotionally reactive and had lower levels of the I Position. It also appeared that the participants from the ACOA group were more emotionally cut off and experienced lower levels of fusion, a process that also involves the exploration of trends, behaviors, patterns, and areas of symptomology (i.e., physical, mental/emotional, and/or social) passed across generations. The transmission process occurs predominantly through relationships. In addition, Bowen suggests, families pass their level of differentiation from one generation to the next (Kerr & Bowen, 1988).

Multigenerational Transmission Process

To better understand the origins of chronic anxiety among individuals and families, Kerr and Bowen (1988) suggest first exploring the multigenerational family history. Bowen's multigenerational transmission process (MTP) is helpful in examining how differentiation levels, chronic anxiety, patterns, and behaviors may be passed from generation to generation.

Several studies have tested the MTP. Rosen et al. (2001) examined the intergenerational transmission of dating violence by exploring the correlation between the differentiation of self in the family of origin and the indirect and/or direct experience of violence in the family of origin. The participants were 411 college students (331 women and 80 men) who were assessed using questionnaires that collected demographic data and information about emotional reactivity toward parents, couple differentiation, and violence in the current relationship and family of origin. Using the CTS (Straus, 1979), the BERI (Bartle & Sabatelli, 1995), and the Differentiation in the Couple Relationship (DIFS-Couple; Anderson & Sabatelli, 1992), the study assessed the students' emotional reactivity toward their parents, couple differentiation, and violence in the family of origin and current and recent dating relationships. Participants who were victims of parent-to-child abuse and were "highly emotionally reactive" to their parents displayed lower levels of differentiation in their dating relationships. In addition, a history of family-of-origin violence increased the odds of intimate partner violence in dating relationships.

Klever (2005) conducted a study that explored the influence of the multigenerational transmission of the family functioning on the nuclear family functioning. This longitudinal study collected and used data from the first five years of a 20-year study. In a sample of 49 couples (95% Caucasian and 5% African American, Hispanic, and Pacific Islander), the researcher conducted face-to-face interviews and annually administered two measurements. The Multigenerational Family Functioning Questionnaire (Klever, 2005) was used to examine the multigenerational family functioning (i.e., grandparents, uncles, aunts, parents, siblings, and stepfamily members). The scale was developed for the study and contained six items that formed five subscales of multigenerational functioning (i.e., physical, emotional, social [job and legal], marital, and child). Reliability ranged from .441 to .741, and the Cronbach's alpha coefficient of .738. Four expert Bowenian theorists evaluated the subscale items and confirmed that they possessed face and content validity. In addition, the Nuclear Family Functioning Scale (NFFS; Klever, 2001) was used to examine each nuclear family's level of functioning (i.e., parent and child) and the prevalence and severity of symptoms. The NFFS contained 50 questions and three subscales: marital functioning (distance and control), adult functioning, and child functioning (physical, emotional, and social). The results of this study confirmed that the multigenerational family functioning accounted for the functioning of the nuclear family. Specifically, they suggested a relationship between the nuclear family functioning and the MTP. However, the results proved to be the opposite when examining the family of origin and the multigenerational process, where the family functioning level was reduced. According to Bowen (Kerr & Bowen, 1988), there may be significant differences in the level of functioning between nuclear families within the same generation. Differences may also exist between nuclear families in different generations.

Cook (2007) investigated the family backgrounds of people with chemical dependency, including family conflict, sibling position, cutoff, and multigenerational transmission in the family of origin. Participants included 36 chemically dependent men and women (18 men and 18 women). The study did not provide specific information about the participants' ethnicity; however, it mentioned that their predominant ethnic backgrounds were Caucasian and African American. Structured interviews were administered and genograms used to gather data. Participants were asked to identify the level of conflict in their family of origin. The information gathered about family structure, interaction patterns, and relationships assisted with the construction of the genograms. According to the findings, the female participants reported higher levels of family conflict than did the men. Participants also provided information about their families of origin. Some were only able to describe one side of their family and others could not provide any information, a result of their being separated from their families. The findings indicated a history of drug and alcohol abuse across all the generations.

Doumas, Margolin, and John (1994) conducted a longitudinal study that explored the multigenerational transmission of several forms of family violence across three generations. One hundred eighty-one families participated in the study by completing a series of questionnaires that assessed for violence in the family of origin, violence in the nuclear (i.e. current) family, and current violence perpetrated by the child. To better understand what types of violence were evident across the generations, the researchers classified the questionnaires by generations (i.e., generation 1, G1; generation 2, G2; and generation 3, G3). They explored the occurrence of violence in G1 by extracting four questions from a "larger personal data inventory" that assessed for IP/SV and child abuse in the family of origin. Participants were asked how often they were verbally and/or physically violated as a child and how often they witnessed verbal and/or physical violence between their parents. To assess for violence in the nuclear family (i.e., current family), three assessments were used for generation G2. The Domestic Conflict Index (DCI; Margolin et al., 1990) assessed for conflict style; the CTS (Straus, 1979) for verbal, physical, and psychological abuse; and the Child Abuse Potential Inventory (Milner, 1986) for abusive disciplining styles. The assessments for generation G3 consisted of the parent version of the Child Hostility Inventory (Kazdin et. al., 1987) and the Child Behavior Checklist (Achenbach & Edelbrock, 1983), which assessed for the type of violence initiated by the child.

The findings suggest that witnessing violent behavior is predictive of violence across three generations. The researchers also found that the type of violence experienced across three generations was dissimilar for males and females. Witnessing IP/SV in the family of origin was predictive of IP/SV and child abuse for G2 males. G2 males are more likely to be aggressors of IP/SV and more likely to use an abusive parenting style toward their children. By contrast, exposure to IP/SV in the family of origin was a factor for G2 females becoming victims of IP/SV; however, exposure to IP/SV and child abuse was not predictive of G2 females being aggressive toward their children. The researchers found that the evidence of IP/SV in G2 influenced violence for boys in G3; however, further research is needed to explore whether G3 children will become aggressive toward their parents and in their intimate adult relationships.

Exploring the family of origin may help families to understand the effect of their experiences and recognize aggressive behaviors and/or patterns they have learned based on the modeling of parents and other family members. Focused genograms can assist families with understanding the multigenerational transmission of patterns and behaviors across generations and assess current attitudes and patterns of violence.

References

Alhabib, S., Nur, U., & Jones, R. (2010). Domestic violence against women: Systemic review of prevalence studies. *Journal of Family Violence, 25,* 369–382.

Achenbach, T. M. & Edelbrock, C.S. (1983). Manual for the Child Behavior Checklist and Revised Child Behavior Profile, University of Associates in Psychiatry, Burlington, VT.

Anderson, S. A. & Sabatelli, R. M. (1992). Differentiation in the family system scale: DIFS. *American Journal of Family Therapy, 20,* 77–89.

Bartle, S., & Sabatelli, R. (1995). The Behavioral and Emotional Reactivity Index: Preliminary Evidence for Construct Validity from Three Studies. *Family Relations, 44*(3), 267–277. doi:10.2307/585525

Bartle-Haring, S., Rosen, K. H., & Stith, S. M. (2002). Emotional reactivity and psychological distress. *Journal of Adolescent Research, 17,* 568–585.

Beck, J. G., McNiff, J., Clapp, J. D., Olsen, S. A., Avery, M. L., & Hagewood, J. H. (2011). Exploring negative emotion in women experiencing intimate partner violence: Shame, guilt, and PTSD. *Behavior Therapy, 42,* 740–750.

Beeble, M. L., Bybee, D., & Sullivan, C. M. (2007). Abusive men's use of children to control their partners and ex-partners. *European Psychologist, 12,* 54–61.

Beavers, W. R., & Hampson, R. B. (1990). *Successful families: Assessment and intervention.* New York: Norton.

Bowen, M., (1978). *Family in therapy clinical practice.* New York, NY: Jason Aronson, Inc.

Boxer, P., Gullan, R. L., & Mahoney, A. (2009). Adolescents' physical aggression toward parents in a clinic-referred sample. *Journal of Clinical Child & Adolescent Psychology, 38*(1), 106–116.

Cohen, S., Kamarck, T., & Mermelstein, R. (1983). A global measure of perceived stress. *Journal of Health and Social Behavior, 24,* 385–396.

Coker, A. L., Davis, K. E., Arias, H., Desai, S., Sanderson, M., Brandt, H. M.,

& Smith, P. H. (2002). Physical and mental health effects of intimate partner violence for men and women. *American Journal of Preventive Medicine, 23*, 260–268.

Cook, L. (2007). Perceived conflict, sibling position, cut-off, and multigenerational transmission in the family of origin of chemically dependent persons: An application of Bowen Family Systems Theory. *Journal of Addictions Nursing, 18*, 131–140.

Cottrell, B. (2001). Parent abuse: The abuse of parents by their teenage children. *The National Clearinghouse on Family Violence*. Ottawa, Ontario K1A OK9 Canada.

Cottrell, B. & Monk, P. (2004). Adolescent-to-parent abuse: A qualitative overview of common themes. *Journal of Family Issues, 25*(8), 1072–1095.

Derogatis, L. R., Lipman, R. S., Rickels, K., Uhlenhuth, E. H., & Covi,L. (1974). The Hopkins Symptom Checklist (HSCL): A self-report symptom inventory. *Behavioral Science, 19*, 1–15.

Derogatis, L. R. (1993). *BSI brief symptom inventory: Administration, scoring, and procedures manual* (4th ed.). Minneapolis, MN: National Computer Systems.

Derogatis, L. R. (1994). *Symptom Checklist-90-R: Administration, Scoring, and Procedures Manual*. Minneapolis, MN: NCS Pearson.

Doumas, D., Margolin, G., & John, R. S. (1994). The intergenerational transmission of aggression across three generations. *Journal of Family Violence, 9*, 157–175.

Eckstein, N. J. (2004). Emergent issues in families experiencing adolescent-to-parent abuse. *Western Journal of Communication, 68*(4), 365–388.

Fischer, J. & Corcoran, K. (1994). Measures for practice: A sourcebook: Couples, families, and children (2nd ed.). The Free Press.

Folkman, S. & Lazarus, R. (1988). *Ways of Coping Questionnaire Manual*. Palo Alto, CA: Consulting Psychologists Press.

Gallagher, E. (2004). Parents victimized by their children. *The Australian and New Zealand Journal of Family Therapy, 25*(1), 1–12.

Gehart, D. R. & Tuttle, A. R. (2003). Intergenerational family therapy. In D. R. Gehart & A. R. Tuttle (Eds.), *Theory-based treatment planning for marriage and family therapists* (pp. 151–171). Pacific Grove, CA: Brooks/Cole-Thomson Learning.

Gilbert, R. M. (2006). *The eight concepts of Bowen theory*. Falls Church, VA: Leading Systems Press.

Heppner, P. P., Cook, S. W., Wright, D. M., & Johnson, W. C. (1995). Progress in resolving problems: A problem-focused style of coping. *Journal of Counseling Psychology, 42*, 279–293. https://doi.org/10.1037/0022-0167.42.3.279

Jackson, D. (2003). Broadening constructions of family violence: mothers' perspectives of aggression from their children. *Child and Family Social Work, 8*, 321–329.

Johnson, P., & Stone, R. (2009). Alcoholism and family functioning: Effects on differentiation levels of young adults. *Alcoholism Treatment Quarterly, 27*, 3–18.

Kazdin, A. E., Rodgers, A., Colbus, D., & Siegel, T. (1987). Children's Hostility Inventory: Measurement of aggression and hostility in psychiatric inpatient children. *Journal of Clinical Child Psychology, 16*, 320–328.

Kennair, N., & Mellor, D. (2007). Parent abuse: A review. *Child Psychiatry Human Development, 38*, 203–219.

Kerr, M. E., & Bowen, M. (1988). *Family evaluation: An approach based on Bowen theory*. New York, NY: W.W. Norton & Company.

Kethineni, S. (2004). Youth-on-parent violence in a central Illinois county. *Youth Violence and Juvenile Justice, 2*(4), 374–394.

Klever, P. (2001). The nuclear family functioning scale: Initial development and preliminary validity. *Families, Systems & Health*, 19: 397–410.

Klever, P. (2005). The multigenerational transmission of nuclear family processes and symptoms. *The American Journal of Family Therapy, 32*, 337–351.

Kulkarni, S., Bell, H., and Wylie. L. (2010). Why don't they follow through?: Intimate partner survivors' challenges in accessing health and social services. *Family & Community Health, 33*, 94–105.

Lacey, K. K. (2010). When is it enough for me to leave?: Black and Hispanic women's response to violent relationships. *Journal of Family Violence, 25*, 669–677.

Margolin, G., Burman, B., John, R. S., and O'Brien, M. (1990). *Domestic Conflict Index*, Unpublished instrument, University of Southern California, Los Angeles.

Markowitz, F. E. (2001). Attitudes and family violence: Linking intergenerational and cultural theories. *Journal of Family Violence, 16*, 205–218.

Miller, R. B., Anderson, S., & Keala, D. K. (2004). Is Bowen theory valid?

A review of basic research. *Journal of Marital and Family Therapy, 30,* 453–466.

Milner, J. S. (1986). The Child Abuse Potential Inventory: Manual (2nd ed.). Webster, NC: Psytec Corporation.

Murdock, N. L. & Gore, P. A. (2004). Stress, coping, and differentiation of self: A test of Bowen Theory. *Contemporary Family Therapy, 26,* 319–335.

Nelson, T. S. (2003). Transgenerational family therapies. In L. L. Hecker & J. L. Wetchler (Eds.), *An introduction to marriage and family therapy* (pp. 255–293). Binghamton, NY: The Haworth Press, Inc.

Nichols, M. P. & Schwartz, R. C. (2001). Family therapy enters the twenty-first century. In M. P. Nichols & R. C. Schwartz (Eds.), *Family therapy: Concepts and methods* (pp. 319–320). Boston, MA: Allyn & Bacon.

Nock, M. K. & Kazdin, A. E. (2002). Parent-directed physical aggression by client referred youths. *Journal of Clinical Child Psychology, 31*(2), 193–205.

Orzeck, T. L., Rokach, A., & Chin, J. (2010). The effects of traumatic and abusive relationships. *Journal of Loss and Trauma, 15,* 167–192.

Pagani, L., Larocque, D., Vitaro, F., & Tremblay, R. E. (2003). Verbal and physical abuse toward mothers: The role of family configuration, environment, and coping strategies. *Journal of Youth and Adolescence, 32,* 215–222.

Pagani, L., Tremblay, R.E., Nagin, D., Zocolillo, M., Vitaro, F., & McDuff, P. (2004). Risk factors models for adolescent verbal and physical aggression toward mothers. *International Journal of Behavioral Development, 28*(6), 528–537.

Rosen, K. H., Bartle-Haring, S., & Stith, S. M. (2001). Using Bowen theory to enhance understanding of the intergenerational transmission of dating violence. *Journal of Family Issues, 22,* 124–142.

Routt, G. & Anderson, L. (2011). Adolescent aggression. *Journal of Aggression, Maltreatment & Trauma, 20,* 1–19.

Skowron, E. A., & Friedlander, M. L. (1998). The Differentiation of Self Inventory: Development and initial validation. *Journal of Counseling Psychology, 45,* 235–246. https://doi.org/10.1037/0022-0167.45.3.235

Spielberger, C. D. (1983). *State-Trait Anxiety Inventory for Adults (STAI-AD)* [Database record]. PsycTESTS. https://doi.org/10.1037/t06496-000

Stewart, M., Burns, A., & Leonard, R. (2007). Dark side of the mothering role: Abuse of mothers by adolescent and adult children. *Sex Roles, 56,* 183–191.

Straus, M. (1979). "Measuring intrafamily conflict and violence: The Conflict Tactics Scales." *Journal of Marriage and Family, 41*, 75–88.

Sullivan, C. M, Tan, C., Basta, J., Rumptz, M., & Davidson, W. S. (1992). An advocacy intervention program for women with abusive partners: Initial evaluation. *American Journal of Community Psychology, 20*, 309–332.

Sullivan, C. M., & Bybee, D. I. (1999). Reducing violence using community-based advocacy for women with abusive partners. *Journal of Consulting and Clinical Psychology, 67*, 43–53. https://doi.org/10.1037/0022-006X.67.1.43

Titelman, P. (1998). *Clinical applications of Bowen family systems theory.* Binghamton, NY: The Haworth Press, Inc.

Tremblay, R. E., Loeber, R., Gagnon, C., Charlebois, P., Larivee, S., & LeBlanc, M. (1991). Disruptive boys with stable and unstable high fighting behavior patterns during junior elementary school. *Journal of Abnormal Child Psychology, 19*, 285–300.

Tuason, M. T., & Friedlander, M. L. (2000). Do parents' differentiation levels predict those of their adult children?: And other tests of Bowen Theory in a Philippine study. *Journal of Counseling Psychology, 47*, 27–35.

Walsh, J. A. & Krienert, J. L. (2007). Child-parent violence: An empirical analysis of offender, victim, and event characteristics in a national sample of reported incidents. *Journal of Family Violence, 22*, 563–574.

TWELVE

 Anti-Black Ontological Violence in Undergraduate Textbooks

Autumn Raynor

ONE CONSTANT ELEMENT OF THE material culture of undergraduate education is the utilization of, and reverence for, textual resources. Even in the era of proposed open education resources, uniform course texts in print—digitized or on paper—are presented to students as infallible containers of knowledge. Access to course textbooks is often a mandatory requirement for students. The mobility of text reflects its ability to turn any locality into a geography of education. When one opens a book, one enters the word-made-reality. In Eurocentric-oriented classrooms, text-based ontological manipulation creates problematic realities for Africana learners.

Textbooks are presented to students without a declaration of a text's subjective construction, or its likelihood to be a vessel for the supremacy of the dominant hegemony. Msimang's (2014) continuance of Searle's semiotics exposes the collective intentionality required to produce materials that are at once epistemically objective and ontologically subjective. For African American students, White supremacist goals, and the needs of a healthful, informed self are in unequivocal incongruence (Asante, 2005). Ray (2019) correctly explicates the methods employed by racialized organizations to create and use social and material resources to maintain racial structures. The worldviews of textbook authors and reviewers are manifested in the biases and problematic semantics evident in chapters involving personhood, history, and current events (Gwekwerere, 2010). Content analyses of some textbooks reveal themes of White supremacist worldviews that can induce psychological and emotional trauma in African American students (Monk, 2015; Smith, Danley & Allen, 2007).

This discussion explores undergraduate social science and humanities textbooks as locations of ontological oppression for African American learners. An African American undergraduate who "finds himself in" an ontologically oppressive textbook has entered a dangerous space: One may gain access to the discipline-specific information in the book but at the very real risk of internalizing dangerous misinterpretations of one's own identity and reality (Jamison, 2008). In this chapter, I hope to demonstrate the potentiality of Eurocentric undergraduate textbooks to be used as instruments of White supremacist indoctrination. After consulting the literature on Africology, textbooks, and social ontology, I analyze the themes and word choices of culture-based undergraduate textbook chapters. This chapter investigates the presence of words, phrases, and tones that can be interpreted as agents of anti-Black ontological oppression.

Systemic Africology

This project seeks to complement the goals of Systematic Africology as defined and promoted by Asante (1990), Karenga (1992), and J. L. Conyers (2000). White supremacy has contributed to the distortion of the African worldview (Azibo, 1998; Carroll, 2008; Dixon, 1977). Under supremacist dominance and cultural control, people of African descent can internalize the European worldview (Kambon, 1992). This cultural misorientation serves the maintenance of White supremacist imperatives while silencing the complexities of Africana agency and reality. Asante (2006) informs us that any form of White Western hegemony will often see African agency as a phenomenon to be challenged. One can almost say in an Africological sense White supremacy seeks to undo any act of African agency (Asante, 2005). Africology reframes and corrects that which White supremacy has sought out to falsify. Reviere (2001, p. 711) explains, "In its most fundamental expression, Afrocentrism is the scholar assuming the right and the responsibility to describe reality from his or her perspective." White Americans continue to demonstrate overwhelming support of anti-Black narratives, weaponizing their attitudes against Black people in virtually every facet of social and civic interaction, including the generation of research on human experiences.

Systematic Africology correctly centers the African worldview by concerning itself with "changing the life chances of Africana people by providing useful information that can be used to transform how they see themselves, the world and their particular place in it" (Carroll, 2008, p. 7). However, the person-first tenets of Africology will benefit all human interests and subjects, not only those of the original people (Asante, 2005; Reviere, 2001). Eurocentric disciplines fetishize imagined objectivity—as if a researcher can possibly approach research without introducing any element of her own worldview.

Africological research methodology requires inspection of the lived experiences of humans; worldview is acknowledged as a humanistic advantage to outcomes (Conyers, 2004; Revierie, 2001). Revierie continues Asante's concentration on the Afrocentric place, researcher accountability, and methodological validation by extending communalism and fairness (Reviere, 2001, p. 720). Systemic Africology spends considerable energy upending the myth of research objectivity—the separation between researcher and research. Noting that no text can capture reality perfectly, Mazama (1998. p. 9) identifies Africology as our best effort to treat human subjects with accuracy and appropriate attention to the multidimensional human experience.

Scholarly examinations of human behavior must disabuse themselves from the reflexive dependence on the Eurocentric worldview to engage in truthful ontologies concerning Africana people. Many important voices in Africology began their studies in the Eurocentric academy and were forced to use Eurocentric texts. Several useful outcomes have emerged from Eurocentric research. However, Eurocentric disciplines operate in direct contrast to the African worldview and should be approached as intrinsically problematic to the elevation of Black people. Mazama's (1998) scathing and accurate article on Eurocentric discourse lays bare important truths about calculated epistemological and ontological hypocrisies presented as procedures available to only cultures with higher intellectual capabilities.

Internally inconsistent with its own purported values, Eurocentric examinations of reality are incapable of espousing the objectivity it aggressively proclaims. African Americans experience racial aggressions and assaults tied to racialized organizations including higher education settings (Solorzano, Ceja & Yosso, 2001). Aggressions incite traumatic intrapersonal communication, lowered self-esteem, and negative life chances (Deterville, 2016). As it is unlikely to reside in the United States and completely avoid the material culture of textual education resources, the goal of the impending study is to utilize the canons of Systemic Africology to evaluate the use of textbooks in the advancement of White supremacist indoctrination.

Education as Threshold

> *When you control a man's thinking you do not have to worry about his actions. You do not have to tell him not to stand here or go yonder.*

He will find his "proper place" and will stay in it. (Carter G. Woodson, The Mis-education of the Negro, 1933, xxix)

Post-Maafa, diasporic people have pursued access to higher education. In the first one hundred years after emancipation legislation, education was considered an important vehicle for equality, self-improvement, and the elevation of one's family. For generations, leaders positioned educational achievements of Africana people as evidence of worthiness of our equality to the oppressor. The Talented Tenth construct was not only a strategy for the advancement of our culture; the Africana presence in colleges and universities was in itself a victory for inclusion (Anderson, 1988). In this estimation, we needed to disprove notions of intellectual inferiority pressed into us by our jailers. Slavers and other white oppressors had long used various media to lie, colonize, harass, rape, sell, catch, and murder Africana people. By the time the Agricultural College Grant of 1890 enriched the higher education options for college-bound Afrikan people, those prospective scholars would have likely been members of the first generation of adults born outside of enslavement. These students would have certainly been educated within segregation; experiencing media and materials designed to reinforce their status as members of a permanent underclass.

As print and broadcast media technologies evolved, the fight for educational imperatives played out in mobile, hyper-visual, semiotic, and semantic battlegrounds. Linda Brown mostly posed for stills. Ruby Bridges took her walk, on moving film, in 1960. The broadcasted images of George Wallace blocking the entrance to the University of Alabama were not serendipitous shots of discrimination in action. News outlets were invited to advertise a calculated memorialization of state-sponsored violence (Leffler, 1963). The photograph was text. Its form and widespread distribution proved to be a precursor to the integrated university environment. Wallace's staunch look of disapproval, his defiance of President Kennedy, his unlawful position in front of Foster Hall—each nonverbal action was symbolic. The Africana students were not pictured in the most iconic versions of the photograph. They were not necessary for the narrative. They were paratext: the nameless, faceless, shadowy enemies of the White entitlement structure. Africana people were consumers and victims, and progenitors of the text but not the target audience. Or were they? Vivian Malone Jones and James Hood would both eventually earn degrees from the University of Alabama. Their courage would provide opportunities for diasporic students to enter universities with relatively minimal frenzy. Fifty-six years later, the texts behind university doors are as problematic as the texts staged to prevent us from opening them.

Texts as Ontological Manipulation

As Dixon discussed and Carroll continued, Eurocentric cultures claim to value objectivity and logic even when adherence to these constructs leads to danger, immorality, or the suspension of ethics (Carroll 2008; Dixon, 1977). In the Eurocentric worldview, the text is law: Words codified into text are placed there to control and manipulate reality, not reflect it objectively. Attributing one's beliefs and behaviors to a dogmatic fixation on words in record is a hallmark of White culture. Eurocentric psychology explains individuals comply with words in print more readily than vocalized commands. For instance, a consumer may protest the price of an item but will relent once a salesperson points to the price of the item on a computer screen. The literature spends little attention on the historical conditioning, or *priming*, of people to do this very thing.

Priming describes the cognitive associations between message cues and implicit associations held in memories (Sonnett, Johnson & Dolan, 2015). Priming does not cause a person to think about a new subject, but rather, it causes us to recall social reality information in automated paradigms. To continue the shopping example, the consumer is not led to learn anew that the specific price on that specific computer cannot be changed by that specific salesperson. When the salesperson points to the price, the customer is reminded that all prices on all computers should be treated as legitimate and the salesperson should not, and likely cannot, counter that price. Sonnet, Johnson, and Dolan (2015) discussed the implications of social manipulation when combined with racialized narratives. When consumers of information are ready to accept primed narratives as automated truths, they will rely on internalized biases when interpreting "new" information (Sonnett, Johnson & Dolan, 2015).

Whereas most global collectivist, high-context communities of color rely on inference, interpretation, oral histographies, and passed knowledge, Eurocentric culture has weaponized written texts in the advancement of

White supremacy for centuries. Whites arrived at occupied lands with treaties and documents written by them, asserting themselves owners of people and place. They took domain of physical space by drawing lines on paper. Whites printed religious materials to justify slavery and genocide. Whites made lists of rules to benefit their interests and permit themselves to rape, kill, abduct, and murder. In short, the White dominant hegemony has used text communication as a vehicle for oppression as long as those technologies have existed.

Textbooks continue the processes of circular reasoning: train students to blindly consider print media as objective and legitimate, place subjective and inaccurate material in text, and then cite the fact that it is in text as evidence that the material must be objective and legitimate. The text, or textbook, is a content expert besting even the instructor. Eurocentricity claims to revere text as the ultimate epistemological and ontological authority. Frequently, this "authority" is a fallacious construct designed to facilitate oppression without implication. For example, members of law enforcement will excuse themselves from murder committed on camera so long as the procedural elements of the murder were within self-defined parameters of the training they give themselves (Grinberg, 2018). Textbooks, think pieces, and broadcast media will report that the killing was lawful, entering the justification into the historical record without explaining the internal, vertical process of such a justification. True hegemonic dominance is achieved by promoting self-serving textual narratives while oppressing parts of the record which cause the hegemony discomfort. Quite simply, if you do not want anyone to talk about it, you do not put it in the book. When the social conventions of the time pressure the inclusion of undesirable information, semanticists can create new realities at the mental and economic expenses of the oppressed.

Textbooks as Racialized Social Systems

In 2019, a student entering a public four-year college in her own state can expect to pay between $9,000 and $20,000 in tuition and fees per year (Powell, 2018). The College Board notes these students will likely pay a minimum of $1,200 per year for textbooks and supplies (Gaille, 2018). Textbook costs rose 67% over the last 10 years (Kristof, 2018). To some, the rising cost of college textbooks can be considered an annoying consequence of capitalism.

For learners entering university with aspirations of exiting poverty, securing textbooks can be an ugly experience. Financial aid access dates, emergency book-loan eligibility, census-day requirements, or other factors may prevent cash-strapped students from purchasing required texts at the beginning of the term. Nearly 70% of students are unable to afford some, or all, of a course's required texts and will attempt to endure without them (Gaille, 2018). The textbook industry will not notice the loss.

Five major publishers rule the market, each sharing in the $12 billion industry (Kristof, 2018). As retail markets go, the textbook industry is a bully. Publishers insist on placing new editions of their products in students' hands regardless of the needs of the discipline or the faculty. In the previous 10 years, new textbook editions were phased in every five years; now it is every two to three (C. Cross, personal communication, February 11, 2019). Colleges engage in contracts with these houses, sometimes preventing certain courses from offering the open education resources that same college appears to promote. Textbook publishers deploy teams to campuses to directly influence faculty textbook selections. These agents, akin to pharmaceutical representatives, descend on campuses to aggressively court faculty support for their titles. Forceful and manipulative textbook promotion is a classic part of education. During the 19th century, historians report, "Textbook salesmen were not above using alluring women as accomplices to blackmail school officials into favoring their wares," (Tyack, 1974, p. 95) In modern times, book reps host luncheons, invite textbook authors for meet and greets, and pressure faculty to change texts. Faculty report being contacted by these lobbyists to the point of harassment. College administrators often require faculty to attend publisher interactions and engage with textbook adoption committees. Unrequested textbook review copies arrive addressed to specific faculty. The secondary textbook market also inserts its staff directly into faculty offices. Book buyers asking to pay cash for desk copies are regular fixtures in faculty workrooms and office suites. E-mails from publishing reps and book buyers are constant.

The opinion of higher education is clear: Textbooks are currency. The campus ecosystem includes owners, renters, prospective buyers, beggars, people trying to sell at a loss, those out for profit, unfortunates lugging around old clunkers. The wealthy have fresh stacks still in the plastic. The volatility of the power dynamics and processes subordinates the content within the textbooks for all stakeholders. As books are mandatory for course participation; students do not have the agency to question whether a textbook will be a good book or even an effective book. There is no incentive for a student to ruminate on the potential goodness, or ethics, of a book if one is forced to read it. Students entering higher education have been conditioned to consume mandatory texts without critical consideration for most of their lives.

Social Ontology

At the moment of enrollment in compulsory education institutions, classroom texts are presented as autocratic locations of objectivity. Although teaching to the test takes priority in the popular consciousness, the textbook wars only receive attention when relatively inflammatory content is in debate (Springston, 2018). Recently seventh-grade history textbooks in Texas described enslaved Africans as "workers." Historically, textbooks were openly written and selected to explicitly depict the South as a victim of "northern aggression" to obscure the stimuli leading to the Civil War and promote the values of the Confederacy (Yaconve, 2018). The book itself, this container of knowledge, is more than an epistemological instrument. It is a tool of oppression.

The preceding anecdotes illustrate responses to overt counterfactual subjectivity in textbooks. Some astute protesters can easily interpret those overt cues while completely ignoring the covert subjectivity embedded in virtually every page and process associated with a textbook entering a classroom. Writers, reviewers, and administrators without expertise in the discipline all contribute to what is, and is not, included in a textbook. Language, graphic, theory, and pagination inclusions are determined by people seeking to make money. These people may have honest intentions to deliver quality information to students, but they are not doing so for free. The power to include personal worldview interpretations is partnered with capitalist intentions. Publishers are selling subjective creations as objective tomes. In other industries, this level of subjectivity is widely known, accepted, and even preferred. People buy art because of the subjectivity involved. The subjectivity of textbooks is obscured by framing the contents within as unchallengedly objective. By vernacular and philosophical definitions, textbooks are indeed subjective *and* objective. Msimang (2014) discusses collective intentionally to continue Searle's (1994) work in semiotics. The social coordination required to establish seemingly objective functions out of subjective materials is helpful in expressing how a text becomes legitimized by society. Msimang (2014) details the power-based process of registering items as epistemically objective while ontologically subjective.

A world-building aspect of hegemonic supremacy is the entitlement to create and recreate reality to your comfortability: You believe an item not because it is a fact; it is a fact *because you believe it*. Your belief *makes* it fact. This illogical conflation of fact and belief mirrors the coverage of subjectivity with the insistence that an item is objective. Concerning textbooks, that these volumes contain subjective material is true. Because this material is used to influence and interpret reality, a textbook is ontologically subjective. According to the collective intentionality of the Eurocentric academy, information printed in textbooks is expected to function as objective knowledge. In this function, a textbook penned by content experts, duly reviewed, and offered to all scholars is epistemically objective.

The confusion among ontology and epistemology, subjectivity and objectivity does not weaken at the student level. When students believe that college-mandated texts are inherently objective, the semantic, semiotic, and worldview declarations of the editorial team also seem objective and normalized. If these beliefs support your own or push you toward what you already had some ties to, confirmation bias will likely legitimize those values in your schema. If the textbook contains ontologically manipulative content about you, your history, and your culture, you are in jeopardy of internalizing psychological violence (Gwekwerere, 2010; Tovar-Murray & Munley, 2007).

The literature reveals, for Africana children, compulsory education is a place of Eurocentric indoctrination. For example, unless a parent brings a legal challenge to a school district, every seventh-grade student in Texas public schools is required to read, and sometimes recite, texts depicting the courage of Confederate soldiers (Texas Education Code, 2018, Ch. 113 B). Black students learn educational content, but they also learn to comply with texts, accept authoritarian policing, and perform versions of self which center White comfortability (Anderson, 1988; Yaconve, 2018). The stressors involved with these institutions can contribute to Racial Battle Fatigue Syndrome: stress comparable to soldiers at war (Smith, Allen & Danley, 2007; Solorzano, Ceja & Yosso, 2000). As these students collect themselves in remarkable ways and decide to enter colleges and universities, one might believe students will have greater freedom of expression and control of their educational experiences. Undergraduates are likely to be compelled to engage with texts that may be deleterious to their ontologies.

Methodology

The research herein analyzes the themes and word choices of culture-based undergraduate textbook chapters. A goal is to investigate the presence of words, phrases, and tones, which could be interpreted as agents of anti-Black ontological oppression. The following questions guide this effort:

> RQ1: Does the textbook chapter include text which directly counters the historical record of events as accepted by Africana communities?
> RQ2: Does the language or imagery used in the textbook chapter downplay or obscure beliefs and behaviors associated with White supremacy?
> RQ3: Does the textbook reinforce negative stereotypes about Africana people or present Whiteness as the natural, invisible "default" persona?
> RQ4: Does the textbook include text or imagery which congratulates White people for their rejection of overtly racist behaviors or mention that the worst racism was in the past?
> RQ5: Does the textbook include any language or themes involved in victim blaming or introducing a "both sides" perspective?

Textual Analysis

The criteria for analysis included texts that explicitly discuss intercultural, social, and emotional interactions. The research sought books that had chapters devoted to communication, culture, emotions, prejudice, and stereotypes. Each textbook was offered to faculty charged with instructing students in a college system that ranks first in international student enrollment and is nationally recognized for its ethnic diversity (Rohr, 2012). Six lower division undergraduate textbooks were selected from a community college desk reference collection featuring textbook editions currently listed as mandatory course texts or that had been listed as mandatory within the past five years.

Three speech communication textbooks were chosen due to their content and the course enrollment statistics. First-year students can usually register for Speech courses immediately on enrollment as many offerings do not require prerequisites or the selection of a degree plan. Speech courses, as part of the core, are oftentimes among the first college classes a student will take (Houston Community College [HCC], 2018). Select sections are also offered to dual-credit students who may be as young as 15 years old (HCC, 2018).

Three social psychology textbooks were chosen for similar content considerations but also to represent a more mature set of experiences. Considered a sophomore course taken "in the major," social psychology sections also feature ample enrollment numbers. As prerequisites are required, the students enrolled in this course are likely older or, at least, more tenured in their college involvement. From the six textbooks, eight chapters were examined. In speech textbooks, chapters were titled nonverbal communication, understanding culture, perceiving others, and intercultural communication (Adler & Proctor, 2016; McCornack, 2015; Pearson, Titsworth & Hosek, 2017). Social psychology textbook analyses included three chapters titled prejudice, and one aggression chapter (Aronson, 2007; Baumeister & Bushman, 2017; Myers & Twenge, 2013; 2017). Deductive thematic analysis was utilized to capture symbols, phrases and connotative tones applicable to the research questions (Braun & Clarke, 2006). Six coding categories emerged from the five research questions: denial of history, reduction of White accountability, normalization of stereotypes, Whiteness as default culture, victim blaming, and "both-sides" spread of accountability.

The textual analysis involved organizing and reading the selected textbook chapters. The researcher assigned line numbers to each chapter and labeled words and phrases as "instances" of potential semiotic ontological manipulation in accordance with the defined thematic codes. A second researcher was brought in to conduct the analysis under the same research questions and codes but without access to the literature review. The goal was to allow an impartial researcher to collect data without attempting to meet a hypothesis. The results that follow reflect only those values recorded identically by each researcher. Table12.1 illustrates the number of identified thematic instances.

Table 12.1. Indicators of Ontological Manipulation

	A. RQ1 Contradictory accounts or denial of history in diasporic memory	B. RQ2 Reduction of White accountability	C. RQ3 Normalization of negative stereotypes about diasporic people	D. RQ3 Whiteness presented as invisible, "default" culture	E. RQ4 Historic racism evoked to cast modern racism as progressive	F. RQ5 Victim blaming statements	G. RQ5 "Both-sides" statements
Intro to speech communication textbook chapter: "Intercultural Communication"	1	2	4	7	1	0	0
Interpersonal communication textbook 1 chapter: "Nonverbal Communication"	0	1	2	1	0	1	1
Interpersonal communication textbook 2 chapters: "Understanding Cultures," "Perceiving Others"	3	2	4	5	3	1	1
	1	3	3	5	2	1	2
Social psychology textbook 1 chapter: "Prejudice"	2	1	5	5	2	3	4
Social psychology textbook 2 chapter: "Prejudice"	2	3	4	3	2	2	2
Social psychology textbook 3 chapters: "Prejudice," "Aggression"	3	4	4	3	3	2	1
	3	1	3	0	0	1	0

Results

Speech Communication Textbooks

An intercultural communication chapter featured a photo of an African America youth in a hat, durag, and gold chains. The photo's caption reads, "What stereotypes come to mind when you see this image?" This chapter makes frequent use of African American associations with criminality and exhibits stereotyping as natural. Concerning prejudice, the language "African Americans and women" is used as if the intersection of a person who is both African American and a woman does not exist or prejudice lodged against those groups is the same. Although stereotypes about White people certainly exist, the text does not offer any, nor does it expressly highlight that stereotypes put on marginalized groups are normatively deployed by Whites. Comically, the only explicit connection made between Whites and their use of stereotyping is the following quote: "White Americans might incorrectly believe that Asian Americans are more qualified for higher education than they are" (Pearson, Nelson, Titsworth & Hosek, 2017, p. 36). The authors discuss stereotypes about lesbians, African Americans, Hispanics, stay-at-home-dads, Asians, Indians, East Coast residents, Millennials, and elders. Only in defense of Whiteness is the stereotype prefaced with language, which identifies the belief as "incorrect."

A nonverbal communication chapter largely contains textbook language, visuals, and tones consistent with its epistemically objective premise. A chart labeled "In-Group and Out-Group Perceptions of Nonverbal Communication" (Adler & Proctor, 2016, p. 224) pointed to the heart of Research Question 3. The chart listed sweeping generalizations about the nonverbal behaviors of generic racial categories including Latino, Asian, African American, and Native American cultures (Adler & Proctor, 2016). One glaring omission was any mention of behaviors attributed to White cultures. The chart did not compare these groups to one another, so it would seem a logical conclusion that the natural 'outgroup' evaluating these behaviors was built of the unlisted Eurocentric gaze. No group is a monolith. A textbook chapter that highlights cultural relativity and respect for cultures should be careful to avoid lumping socially disparate cultures together for the sake of brevity. For example, posturing "Asian" as a cohesive group with across-the-board mannerisms and activities is naïve at best and disingenuous at worst. Outside of class, a student reader might be surprised to find the "finger beckoning" mentioned in the chart is not a practice of her Japanese, Cambodian, Hmong, Pinoy, Samoan, or Thai associates. Blanketing destroys the ontology of cultural distinction. If Whiteness is the standard out-group, the chart demonstrates Whiteness will collect broad, census-level, information without respect to nationality or ethnicity. A student will experience the chart as a reinforcement of Whiteness as the generic norm that all other cultures counter. The omission of Whiteness informs the reader that White nonverbal behaviors are normal; therefore, they should already be known and recognized by the reader. Ethnocentrism is defined and discouraged in the previous chapter, only to be sanctioned in the next by centering Whiteness.

We coded two chapters in the second interpersonal communication textbook. The first coded was the "Understanding Cultures" chapter. Unique to the other text studied, this book has a single author who uses his voice, the self-reflexive *I*, and offers personal anecdotes about his life throughout chapters. In the culture chapter, this personalization leads to problematic comparisons. The author offers wearing a hijab to placing a Mexican flag decal on one's car as similar cultural celebrations. The author, who is White, acknowledges White male culture as dominant in the United States. He describes co-cultural theory and produces the following example to demonstrate how managing co-cultures may look in reality:

> Imagine an African American couple moves to a largely Euro-American suburb. They socialize primarily with their white neighbors-never displaying any indication of their African American heritage other than their skin color. Meanwhile, their son dresses in sagging pants, wears a do-rag, and blasts gangsta rap through Beats headphones. Through these behaviors, he actively strives to conform to stereotypes about young Black males. Despite their differences, all these behaviors have the same goal: managing the tension between African American co-culture and the dominant Euro-American culture. (McCornack, 2015, p. 98)

This anecdote, editorial and hypothetical, reveals ontological disparities. The removal of agency and preference by the hypothetical subjects is a false reality. First, in this reality, the author knows all the ways African American culture is performed, so he can make the evaluation only the skin of these African American people betrays their desire to be culturally White. Neither the parents nor the son behaves in ways that suit their own preferences but are always performing to, and because of, White judgment. The son conforming to "stereotypes about young Black males" included the accessories of Beats headphones, saggy pants, and gangsta rap. A reader who may not have previously possessed this archetype may now internalize this projected stereotype. In his "Perceiving Others" chapter, two images and accompanying textual discussions stand out as ontological manipulations. A photo of Tupac Shakur wearing a bandana, gold chain, and leather vest is captioned:

When you look at Tupac Shakur, do you see a famous rapper? A tattooed gangster who died young in a hail of gunfire? Or, a man named after an Inca chief who studied ballet and acting, and read the *New York Times* because his mother wanted him to. (McCornack, 2015, p. 67)

Besides the unfortunate grammar and syntax errors, the caption positions Shakur's rap career, tattoos, and violent death as natural contrasts to being named after an Inca chief, reading the *Times*, and studying ballet. The author does not correct the ideology that tattoos, rap, and dying violent deaths are bad but instead adds other items about Shakur's life that are supposedly good. The author surely knows that genocidal monsters read *The New York Times*, Tupac Amaru II died even more violently than his namesake, and Hitler loved the ballet. These activities are symbols, not of goodness, but of Whiteness. In the ontologies of Blackness, the oppressive hegemony and our own cultural mores form multifaceted personas, not in contrast but in concert. There is nothing Black about dying violently, just as tattoos are not inherently edgy. The caption seems to ask, "Did you know Tupac did White things, too?" The very next page features two photos of el-Hajj Malik el-Shabazz. In the first photo, he is holding a copy of *Muhammad Speaks* with the headline "Our Freedom Can't Wait" (Haley & X, 1965). The second photo features him with three gentlemen sitting on prayer rugs. The caption reads, "After 1964, Malcolm X's perception changed as belief shifted to a view 'recognizing every human being, as a human being, neither white, black, brown, nor red'" (McCornack, 2015, p. 68).

The chapter text uses the man's trip to Mecca as a case study in corrective perceptual change. The author describes el-Shabazz's exposure to White Muslims as delivering him from his "longstanding belief in an unbridgeable racial divide between whites and blacks" (McCornack, 2015, p. 68). This language upends the ontology of White-led racial division while suggesting el-Shabazz's consideration of White humanity was a cause of racial division or a necessity of defeating White-controlled anti-Black racism. The text continues: "[el-Shabazz] came to appreciate others' perspectives and feel a strong emotional kinship with those he previously disparaged. He accepted others' beliefs as legitimate and deserving of respect" (McCornack, 2015, p. 68).

The preceding values and descriptions are ontologically infirm. el-Shabazz's critique of White American racism did not indict White Muslim Hajis; thus, his recognition of kinship between he and these particular White Muslims should not be used to suggest a reversal of feelings toward the oppressive White cultures in the United States. In actuality, el-Shabazz used the existence of the White Muslims to offer God as a remedy to White American oppression. He wrote, "Their belief in one God had removed White from their behavior, and White from their attitudes. Perhaps if White Americans could accept the Oneness of God they could cease to measure, hinder and harm others in terms of their difference in color" (Haley & X, 1965 pp. 391–392). His change in perception was that White people might be capable of being less oppressive, not that he was wrong to call out their ongoing oppression of Africana people. The caption and text erroneously suggest el-Shabazz began to see the systemic construct of White supremacy as a matter of a different opinion that he now respected. This is an outlandishly dangerous, an ontologically incorrect approach for a textbook to take, especially in a chapter about forming accurate perceptions.

Social Psychology Textbooks

In a purported effort to elaborate on the concept of fundamental attribution errors, the textbook authors spend three pages justifying slavers stereotypes about the humans they enslaved. Slaves, the authors write, were seen as lazy, childlike, and unintellectual because they were (through no fault of their own) indeed lazy, childlike, and unintellectual (Baumeister & Bushman, 2017). The authors state slaves could not "rise above laziness" because they were denied incentives including money status and power (Baumeister & Bushman, 2017, p. 497). The authors conclude by saying slavers made an unfortunate but understandable mistake by attributing these behaviors to innate traits and not situational factors. Alarmingly, no mention is made of the slavers themselves creating these situational factors. No text is used to explain the erroneous, sociopathic attributions required to believe a human has the right to enslave another human. A student reader receives two messages from this text: (1) White supremacy is to be considered a matter of accidental, fallacious mistakes that can be brushed off as uninformed thinking from a simpler time, and (2) it is more important for an academic text to defend the barbarism of Whiteness than to provide a complete and accurate explication of reality.

Another section in the social psychology book discusses why African

American people have higher self-esteem levels than other oppressed communities. Three causes are offered to explain the atypical levels: intraracial comparison, self-worth, and a lack of personal responsibility. The authors clarify that African American people only compare ourselves to other Black people, so we do not collect negative feelings about our general position in intercultural class and status. The text asserts we discount things that make us feel bad and focus on activities we excel in, such as sports and music. Explaining their views, the authors declare that "despite all its costs and harm prejudice does offer one advantage to the target—an external attribution for failure. Targets of prejudice can blame any failures and problems on prejudice" (Baumeister & Bushman, 2017, p. 498).

This language may be offensive on its face: that there can be an "upside" to generations of slavery and oppression or that the African American entertainer trope was deployed or that we care not what other cultures are experiencing. The hazard is in the intentional presentation of these circular prophecies as ontological truths. The textbook, as alleged objective source, is evangelizing its perception of ontological Blackness while disburdening Whiteness of any negative associations with the creation of actual reality. Any culture could have served as the example herein, but African Americans were chosen. That editorial choice carried with it allusions to self-imposed ghettoization (intraracial comparison), the positioning of the minuscule number of African American people holding successes in sports and music as an indicator of the success of the entire culture, and the introduction of the advantage of absolving oneself of negativity by blaming prejudice. These lines are offered in the affirmative. In the negative, Whiteness reappears: White people isolated Africana people, forced us into ghettos, imposed segregation, and, to this day, separate us from intercultural participation in hegemonic civil and social life.

The text presents self-only comparison as a cultural choice, not as a consequence of White supremacy. Citing that African people excel in music and sports ignores the pimping and abuse of Black talent for White enjoyment and financial rewards. The prejudice attribution/self-esteem component is especially incongruent with reality. Presenting high self-esteem as a "benefit" of oppression solicits a gracious attitude toward the oppressor, outside of a reality acknowledging the oppression never should have occurred. The same logic is used when victims of bullying are considered "stronger" for having endured an unnecessary process that certainly did more damage to one's perception of self than the endurance could possibly enhance. The text is essentially suggesting that African Americans should be grateful for the burden of prejudice. The authors use theory to normalize the African American underclass by illustrating this membership as naturally self-imposed. In this reality, Whiteness is not actor but a witness.

A social psychology textbook printed in 2013 featured a chapter on aggression. Several causes, co-behaviors, and correlations were offered in the discussion on aggression, including exposure to violence, wide faces, testosterone, and scarce resources (Myers, 2013 p. 366). One of the photos in the textbook was included to depict heat as a precursor to the expression of aggression through violent behavior. The caption read, "Los Angeles, late April to early May 1992. Riots are more likely during hot summer weather" (Myers, 2013, p. 367). A still from the uprising following the acquittal of the White police officers responsible for the near-fatal beating of a Black man was offered without any context, only attributing the riots to the hot weather. Of note, summer begins in June, and the average temperature in Los Angeles was under 75 degrees during the uprising (Geiger, 2018). Although not part of the original design of this project, I sought the updated 2017 edition of the same textbook hoping to be surprised that a more thorough reviewer recognized and replaced this absurdity. The photo was replaced. Now the aggression chapter depicted a photo captioned "Ferguson, Missouri, August 2014. Riots and looting occur more often during summer weather" (Myers & Twenge, 2017 p. 311). The updated uprising ensued because Michael Brown was shot and killed by a White police officer. Like its pictorial counterpart in the previous edition, the state refused to hold the aggressors accountable. The irony is insurmountable, so much so it is difficult for a reasonable person to believe it is accidental. In a social psychology textbook, in a chapter about aggression, photos are selected from two of the most widely discussed, controversial cases involving violent White male aggressors and instead of educating students about those persons, those responding to White aggression are pictured as reacting—not to injustice—but to weather.

A person without knowledge of these situations would open the chapter and believe that apropos of nothing, African American men respond to increasing temperatures by rioting. The pictures and captions surpass ontological manipulation and approach ontological violence. Depicting injustice-induced uprisings as heat-induced aggressions is irresponsible and inaccurate. Doing this with complete erasure of the original and ultimate aggressors points to the intention of positioning African American people as intrinsically hostile and Whiteness as, again, an observer to our self-selected life choices. The authors did not feel compelled to mention the original act causing the injustice but felt the African American looters were aggressive enough to include in the chapter. Property is centered as more important than Black lives. The student knows, epistemically, that a human life is supposed to be more important than whatever items the men in the picture are allegedly looting. The student knows, epistemically, heat may cause people to behave aggressively. The student knows that in these cases, ontological injustice, not heat, contributed to these behaviors. The textbook has negated accurate ontology by erasing the causative agents from their own narratives. The textbook adopts an aggressive position by combining erasure, misapplication of reality, and accusatory tone to reactors. One finds an identical pattern in the vernacular positioning of an identifier of racism as a practitioner of racism. The textbook language seems invested in conditioning students to accept the *tu quoque* fallacy as soundproof for racialized conversations.

An image from a social psychology textbook brings the project full circle. The prejudice chapter features two allegedly contrasting photographs. In the first, George Wallace is blocking the university door in an effort to halt, at least symbolically, federally mandated desegregation. In the second, George Wallace is seated, shaking the hand of a Black woman holding a trophy. The caption reads:

> What a difference a decade makes! On the left, in 1963, Governor George Wallace defies a federal order by physically blocking the entrance of the first Black student to the University of Alabama. On the right, 10 years later, Governor Wallace happily congratulates the University of Alabama homecoming queen. (Aronson, Wilson & Akert, 2007, p. 478)

The congratulatory tone is stunning. A handshake is supposed to be evidence of reformation of bigotry. In 10 years, a man has evolved from abusing the power of his office to deny the civil rights of American citizens to allow himself to be photographed touching the hand of an unnamed Black woman. No mention is made of apologia, policy changes, diversity training, or reparations for previous bad acts. The textbook authors intend for the students to internalize this simplistic, banal activity as evidence of intercultural progress. George Wallace likely touched hundreds of Black people throughout his life while oppressing them. The ontological manipulation here is the delivery of images as contradictory: that a man who shakes a Black person's hand and a man who facilitates institutional oppression must be in two disparate mind states. This, as every facet of ontological manipulation revealed in the study, positions the student reader to conflate the intent and the impact of oppressors. Whereas undergraduate education is promoted as a space for learning how to question, it seems some textbooks are teaching students how to ignore what is true and obvious on its face.

Conclusion

The textbooks involved in this study demonstrate institutionalized ontological manipulation as a vehicle of White supremacy. Africana learners are mandated to enter racialized educational organizations and are encouraged to accept anti-Black ontological manipulation in every education level. We are required to protect Afrocentric ontologies. Eurocentric scholars are invested in negating the Afrocentric conception of reality in their struggle for survival and self-declared intellectual supremacy (Gwekwerere, 2010). Africology can provide education to safeguard Africana learners from becoming calloused to the idea of their reality bending to the supremacist opinions of Whiteness (Darling-Hammond, Williamson & Hyler, 2007). An effective co-requisite to text-based undergraduate resources, this revelation requires the complete centering of Blackness and decentering of Whiteness as the torchbearer of textual objectivity.

References

Adler, R. & Proctor, R. (2016). *Looking out, looking in.* Independence, KY: Cengage Advantage.

Anderson, J. D. (1988). *The education of blacks in the south 1860–1935.* Chapel Hill, NC: UNC Press.

Aronson, E., Wilson, T., & Akert, R. (2007). *Social psychology.* 6th Edition Pearson. NJ: Upper Saddle River.

Asante, M. K. (1990). *Kemet, afrocentricity and knowledge.* Trenton, NJ. Africa World Press.

Asante, M. K. (2005). The discipline of africology at the crossroads: Toward an eshuen response to intellectual dilemma. *The Black Scholar, 35*(2), 37–49.

Asante, M. K. (2006). A Discourse on Black Studies: Liberating the Study of African People in the Western Academy. *Journal of Black Studies, 36,* 646–662.

Azibo, D. A. (1998). Personality, clinical and social psychological research on Blacks: Appropriate and in appropriate research frameworks. *The Western Journal of Black Studies, 12,* 220–233.

Baumeister, R. & Bushman, B. (2017) *Social psychology and human nature.* 4th Edition. Independence, KY: Cengage Advantage.

Braun, V. & Clarke, V. (2006). Using thematic analysis in psychology. *Qualitative Research in Psychology, 3,* 77–101.

Carroll, K. K. (2008). Africana studies and research methodology: Revisiting the centrality of the afrikan worldview. *The Journal of Pan African Studies, 2*(2), 4–26.

Conyers, J. L. (2000). African American males memory, culture and ethos. *Journal of African American Men, 4*(4), 19–36.

Conyers, J. L. (2004). The evolution of Africology: An Afrocentric appraisal. *Journal of Black Studies, 34,* 640–652.

Darling-Hammond, L., Williamson, J. & Hyler, M. (2007). Securing the right to learn: The quest for an empowering curriculum for African American citizens. *Journal of Negro Education, 76,* 281–296.

Deterville, A. D. (2016). African-centered transpersonal self in diaspora and psychospiritual wellness a Sankofa perspective. *International Journal of Transpersonal Studies, 35,* 118–128.

Dixon, V. J. (1977). African-oriented and Eurocentric-American-oriented world views: Research methodologies and economics. *The Review of Black Political Economy, 7,* 119–156.

Gaille, B. (2018). 23 Textbook industry statistics, trends & analyses. *BG Small Business & Marketing Advice.* Retrieved from https://brandongaille.com/23-textbook-industry-statistics-trends-analysis/3/12/19.

Grinberg, E. (2018). Why police-involved shooting trials rarely end in convictions for officers. *CNN.* Retrieved 9/23/18 from https://www.cnn.com/2017/06/23/us/police-deadly-force-trials/index.html.

Gwekwerere, T. (2010). From Nat Turner to Molefi Kete Asante. Reading the European intellectual indictment of the afrocentric conception of reality. *Journal of Black Studies 41*, 108–126.

Haley, A., & Malcolm X. (1965). *The autobiography of Malcolm X*. New York, NY: Grove Press.

Houston Community College. (2018). *Houston Community College Official Course Catalog 2018–2019*. Retrieved from https://www.hccs.edu/programs/catalog/.

Jamison, D. (2008). Through the prism of Black psychology: A critical review of conceptual and methodological issues in africology as seen through the paradigmatic lens of Black psychology. *The Journal of Pan African Studies, 2*, 96–117.

Kambon, K. K. (1992). *The African personality in America: An African-centered framework*. Tallahassee, FL: Nubian Nation.

Karenga, M. (1992). *Introduction to Black studies*. Los Angeles, CA: University of Sankore.

Kristof, K. (2018). What's behind the cost of college textbooks. *CBS News Moneywatch*. Retrieved from https://www.cbsnews.com/news/whats-behind-the-soaring-cost-of-college-textbooks/12/28/19.

Leffler, W. K. (Photographer). (1963, June 11). *U.S. News & World Report Magazine*. Retrieved February 17, 2019, from https://commons.wikimedia.org/wiki/File:Governor_George_Wallace_stands_defiant_at_the_University_of_Alabama.jpg.

Mazama, A. (1998). The Eurocentric discourse on writing: An exercise in self-glorification. *Journal of Black Studies, 29*, 3–16.

McCornack, S. (2015). *Interpersonal communication and you: An Introduction*. New York, NY: Bedford/St. Martins.

Monk, E. P. (2015). The cost of color: Skin color, discrimination, and health among African Americans. *American Journal of Sociology, 121*, 396–444.

Msimang, P. M. (2014). Living in one world: Searle's social ontology and semiotics. *Signs and Society, 2*, 173–202.

Myers, D. (2013). *Social psychology*. 11th Edition New York, NY: McGraw Hill.

Myers, D., & Twenge, J. (2017). *Social psychology*. 12th Edition. New York, NY: McGraw Hill.

Pearson, J., Nelson, P., Titsworth, S., & Hosek, A. (2017). *Human communication*. New York, NY: McGraw Hill.

Powell, F. (2018). What you need to know about college tuition costs. *U.S. News and World Report Education*. Retrieved from https://www.us news.com/education/best-colleges/paying-for-college/articles/what-you-need-to-know-about-college-tuition-costs.

Ray, V. (2019). A theory of racialized organizations. *American Sociological Review, 84*, 26–53.

Reviere, R. (2001). Toward an Afrocentric research methodology. *Journal of Black Studies, 31*, 709–728.

Rohr, M. (2012, September 18). HCC becomes an international hub. *Houston Chronicle*. Retrieved from https://www.chron.com/news/houston-texas/article/International-students-bring-world-to-HCC-3875648.php.

Searle, J. (1994). Literary Theory and Its Discontents. *New Literary History 25*, 637–667.

Smith, W. A., Allen, W. R., & Danley, L. L. (2007). Assume the position . . . you fit the description" Psychosocial experiences and racial battle fatigue among African American male college students. *American Behavioral Scientist, 51*, 551–578.

Solorzano, D., Ceja, M., & Yosso, T. (2000). Critical race theory, racial microaggressions, and campus racial climate: The experiences of African American college students. *Journal of Negro Education, 69*, 60–71.

Sonnet, J., Johnson, K., & Dolan, M. (2015). Priming implicit racism in television news: Visual and verbal limitations on diversity. *Sociological Forum, 30*, 328–347.

Springston, R. (2018, April 14). Happy slaves? The peculiar story of three Virginia school textbooks. *Richmond Times-Dispatch*. Retrieved from https://www.richmond.com/discover-richmond/happy-slaves-the-peculiar-story-of-three-virginia-school-textbooks/article_47e79d49-eac8-575d-ac9d-1c6fce52328f.html

Texas Education Agency. (2018). Code 7.102 (4) 28.002 and 28.008 113.17 Implementation of Texas Essential Knowledge and Skills for Social Studies, Middle School. Retrieved February 10, 2019 https://statutes.capitol.texas.gov/Docs/ED/htm/ED.7.

Tovar-Murray, D. & Munley, P. (2007). Exploring the relationship between race-related stress, identity, and well-being among African Americans. *The Western Journal of Black Studies, 31*, 58–71.

Tyack, D. B. (1974). *The one best system: A history of American urban education*. Cambridge, MA: Harvard University Press.

Woodson, Carter G. (1933, 1990). The Mis-Education of the Negro. Trenton, NJ: Africa Word Press.

Yaconve, D. (2018, April). Textbook racism: How scholars sustained white supremacy. *The Chronicle of Higher Education*. https://www.chronicle.com/article/How-Scholars-Sustained-White/243053.

THIRTEEN

Vertically Integrated: African American Studies Instruction as Co-Requisite to Education-Based Ontological Manipulation

Deidra Lawson

THE MAJORITY OF AFRICAN AMERICAN children enter the public school system between the ages of three and five years old. They will spend between 13 and 20 years of their lives in this same system. Research provides evidence on the inequities of the public school system to properly educate African American children when compared to their White counterparts. During this 13- to 20-year time frame, some African American children may never receive instruction from a Black teacher. Most will spend several years of their educational career receiving instruction from non–African American teachers. These teachers do not view African American children through a proper lens of understanding African American culture. This creates a lack of preparation in ensuring the appropriate edification and education of African American scholars.

PK–12 institutions are based on a Eurocentric paradigm. This is harmful to African American children. I propose that White instructors, consciously or subconsciously, are key players in the creation and maintenance of the structures of White supremacy. Black children are facing psychological warfare daily due to the ontological manipulation of White instructors and education policy makers.

I study how the narratives of Black children provided by Whites in educational spaces often presents itself as a form of verbal violence. White instructors frame narratives about Black children that are harmful to their social-emotional well-being. The ontological manipulation present in education environments is intentional, systemic, and widespread. I identify how Black children have been affected by this narrative and what must happen to ensure Black children's minds are properly insulated against this indoctrination.

Literature Review

In the 20th century, scientists provided justification for segregation arguing that Blacks and Whites were separately created species (Watkins, 2001). This provided the necessary rationale for the purpose and intentional differences of colonial black education. African American education was established with the general precepts of scientific racism. The manipulation of people of color needed a justification based on inferiority. These theoretical bases of scientific racism became a movement and eventually gave credibility to the eugenics movement.

The eugenics movement gave a hereditarian explanation to the genetic inferiority of the insane, ill, criminal, and colored. Watkins (2001) states that between 1905 and 1930, the idea of genetic inferiority became the explanation for those that were feebleminded, paupers, or criminals. Eugenicists agreed with Sir Francis Galton's stance that human ability levels differed and that heredity was the cause. Galton purported that people of different human races were inherently different from physical strength to mental capability. This provided enough leeway for scientists to begin creating ranking systems within humans solely based on physical characteristics. There was research to find correlations related to height, eye color, temperament, and artistic ability. Karl Pearson became the leader in this type of research, applying statistical methodology to biological problems. Pearson and Galton were central figures in the eugenics movement, seeking to establish laws and theorems backed in mathematical truth. Eugenicists had a goal of purifying society and refining civilization. From here, scientists began to assert the idea that current generations could shape the future by being intentional in how they breed and who they choose to breed with. These beliefs became the foundational principles of post-slavery social reform, including an educational system for Black children.

Eugenicists did not believe that American institutions for social reform were capable of molding or assimilating an inferior race. Whites believed Blacks were moribund, and therefore, race mixing would be problematic and only extend the life of the Black race, to the detriment of Whites. Whites believed that on average, the Negro race was two to three grade levels below their own. Carl Bingham concluded that Blacks were deficient in nature and that the communal lack of intelligence in the Black race would lead to a decline in the nation's collective intelligence (Watkins, 2001, p. 55). By educating Whites and Blacks in the same spaces, eugenicists believed the education of Whites would suffer. The scientific rationale for containment and segregation in education was established. Not until *Brown vs. Board of Education* (1954). In 1954, that scientific racism was debunked.

Scientific racism was used as the justification for a hierarchical order of races. This is the fundamental precept in the architecture of Black education systems and the foundation for the institutional and attitudinal racism in America. Architects of Black education felt that Blacks were to occupy socially subservient positions in society. An education that ensured Blacks would be successful in industrial positions was the goal, one that they could "intellectually manage" (Watkins, 2001). This was viewed as enough; after all, it was a step up from slavery and gave Blacks a path to participate in society.

Frances Cress Welsing (1991, p. 240) stated that a White supremacist's education "system is not capable of providing an equality of opportunity for black children." She continues, saying that this system molds white children to function in the role of oppressor or functional superiors while those classified as non-White or other must play the role of functional inferiors by default. There are assigned roles for every child born into the current system. The education system serves as a predetermined and established racial social experience.

Narratives about Black people have always embodied negative stereotypes. Early films of White actors in blackface required "exaggerated and distorted representations of Black people as uncivilized, illiterate, and unintelligent" (Adams-Bass, Stevenson & Slaughter, 2014, p. 368). From the early 1800s, Blacks were portrayed in the media in dehumanizing ways while Whites were revered as the default normal. An analysis of current-day media will not yield a drastically different result. Adams-Bass et al. (2014) found that these images inform and influence perspectives about Black people. Continued exposure to negative images of Black people is internalized and becomes a representation of reality. White educators are influenced by the media's narratives of Black people. That influence is carried with them into public education classrooms.

Research

The public school system is a place for Eurocentric indoctrination of African American children. This has been the intent since the inception of the public education system. Whites have been indoctrinated into a society that ensures they function as oppressors or superiors. This mindset is played out in action and in narrative. Whites in educational spaces are not immune to being indoctrinated into this mindset. This mindset considerably affects the lens through which Black children are viewed; thus, it affects the narrative used when describing Black children. This causes Black children who are exposed to these narratives daily, year after year to be negatively affected by the word choice of White educators. The stress that Black children face in educational spaces for years on end is the equivalent of psychological warfare. A focus group was interviewed to collect data on current-day narratives of Africa American children in educational spaces.

A thematic analysis of two separate focus groups (one made up of children and the other of adults) analyzed the experiences of African American children in educational spaces. A qualitative approach was used to investigate the word choices used when describing the behaviors, demeanors, and characteristics of African American children, more specifically the language used to describe, instruct, motivate, and manage African American children.

Research Questions

1. What words do you hear used most often when describing African American students?
2. When is the connotation assumed to be positive? What words do you hear most often when describing African American students?
3. What population have you worked with in the past that appears to be the most successful when motivating, encouraging, or managing African American students?
4. What demographic of educators appear to be the most comfortable working with African American students?
5. What do you recommend be implemented for African American children to make their educational experience more enjoyable?

Method

Focus Groups

The student focus group was made up of six children between the ages of 11 and 14. All participants identified as African American. The student focus group consisted of four girls and two boys. It was made up of two eighth-grade students, two seventh-grade students, six sixth-grade student, and one fifth-grade student. The focus group lasted a total of 56 minutes.

The adult focus group was made up of six adults that have experience in educational spaces. The group included two secondary school deans, two school staff (attendance clerk and office manager), and two parents. Participants' ages were between 24 and 52 years old. The focus group lasted 47 minutes.

Informed consent forms were collected from all participants. An overview of the study was then provided. Participants were asked questions group. Results were transcribed for clarity of the analysis. A thematic analysis was used to evaluate responses.

Table 13.1. Responses of Student Level Focus Group (Children Ages 11–14)

Q		Girl- 5th Grade	Girl- 6th Grade	Boy- 7th Grade	Girl- 7th Grade	Boy- 8th Grade	Girl- 8th Grade
1	Words used most when describing African American (AA) children	Loud, rude, disrespectful	Loud, busy, unmotivated	Talks a lot, active, busy	Rude, talkative	Bad, disrespectful	Loud, bad, disrespectful, bossy
2	Assumed positive words to describe AA children	Well-mannered	Well-spoken	Creative	Nice	Well-behaved, home training	Can't think of anything
3	Population most successful with working with AA children	Black teachers	Definitely black teachers	Eh, both teachers	Oh, Black teachers	Black	Black teachers
4	Demographic most comfortable working with AA	Black teachers	Black teachers	Black teachers	Black teachers	Black teachers	Black teachers
5	Implementations for AA children	Parents that teach them what to expect at school	Parents that give them positive words all the time	Self-confidence and knowing their history	Kids have to know what good stuff Black people did before they go to school	We've got to learn about our own history outside of school	Teach your babies self-confidence

Table 13.2. Responses of Adult Focus Groups—Adults

Q		Dean	Dean	Support	Support	Parent	Parent
1	Words used most when describing African American (AA) children	Rude	Disrespectful	Disrespectful	Talkative	Disrespectful	Rude
2	Assumed positive words to describe AA children	Well-mannered	Well-mannered	Well-spoken	Respectful	Well-mannered	Respectful
3	Population most successful with working with AA children	Black teachers	Black teachers	Black teachers	Eh, mostly Black, but I've seen some White	Black teachers	I've seen all types, but definitely Black
4	Demographic most comfortable working with AA	Black teachers	Black teachers	Black teachers	Black teachers	Black teachers	Black teachers
5	Implementations for AA children	AA history	Family cases	Black history classes	AA-based curriculum	Parent engagement	Community engagement

Results of Table 13.1. Fifty percent of the students surveyed recalled the word loud being used as a descriptor for Black children. Five out of six students surveyed indicated descriptors that are generally construed as negative. One student used all words that could potentially not be categorized as negative. When recalling positive words used to describe Black students, zero out of six students used words that would describe student intellect. Sixty-six percent of respondents recalled words that referenced their behavior. Six out of six students felt that African American teachers are the most comfortable and the most successful working with Black children. All respondents indicated that parents or community have to teach children about their history or give them ways to build self-confidence.

Results of Table 13.2. Five out of six adults referenced words that have a negative connotation when describing African American children. Assumed positive words for African American students also referenced behavior over intellect in all instances. Four out of six adults specifically indicated that Black teachers are more successful with Black teachers are the most comfortable interacting with Black students. Three out of six adults felt that family or parenting classes and community engagement are what's necessary for next steps. Three out of the six adults felt that African American or Black history classes are what is necessary for Black children to be successful.

The maintenance of White supremacy requires the erasing of accountability of White instructors who are given the autonomy to provide narratives about Black children. These narratives are assumed true without bias and without question. The unchallenged narratives of our Black children are damaging to their psyche.

The words of White instructors and the account they provide paint African American children in a light that requires them to defend their humanity, their intent, and their actions at a frequency their White counterparts do not experience. Black children, not unlike most Black people, are placed in stressful situations daily. Words are used to indoctrinate and discipline children. These same word choices are also used to consciously or unconsciously demean, discourage, and demotivate Black children.

Children are keenly aware of how they are viewed in educational spaces. Black students ascertain that most educators view them negatively. Black children are aware that the educators that are meant to lead them toward excellence do not necessarily believe in the ability of Black students to be respectful, intelligent, or scholarly. Black children are also cognizant that by being made aware of their own history and having a home culture that speaks consistently about Black history and culture, they are better prepared for public school learning environments.

Adult educators, parents, and school staff are also conscious that African American children are most often described undesirably. Overwhelmingly when recalling words to describe Black children, adults recalled negative words first. The lack of positive framing was substantial.

The actions, words, and behaviors of African American children are frequently viewed through a negative paradigm. The day-to-day actions of African American children in educational spaces are regarded as perceived misdeeds. Black children are aware that each day they go to school, there is a far greater probability that they will hear negative words when describing themselves, their actions, and their abilities. The White educators' narratives of disrespect, insubordination, and rudeness, although obviously subjectively based on emotions, have become almost law when describing Black scholars.

Implications

The intent of the educational system for African American children was not to empower them to reach their highest potential. It was to provide them with an achievable education system based on biased beliefs about African American students' ability level. White architects of Black education held a skewed belief about the ability levels of African Americans, children included. Scientific racism and eugenics contributed to the belief that African Americans were inferior to their White counterparts. As educational training systems continued, they were based on this skewed representation of reality. Most White Americans, including educators, view African Americans through a tainted, negative lens. This directly affects the narratives used by White educators when viewing and describing the actions and intent of African American children. The words used to describe African American students are not chosen by accident. From slavery to modern times, the implications of laziness and a lack of motivation have been consistent. Connotations of aggressiveness and abnormal strength and intensity are familiar narratives when describing the demeanor of African Americans. From an early age, this affects how African American scholars are viewed.

Parents need to be made aware of the discrepancies that exist between the way White and Black children are described when exhibiting the same behaviors. This has implications that range from the necessity of intentional nurturing language throughout the home environment to purposely saturating Black children with affirmations to counteract the language most often heard to describe their personality, actions, and intent.

Parents must ensure their children are knowledgeable of Africology. Upon entering the public school system, Black children must already understand the White standard of education and the intents of the system. Black children must be appropriately immersed in Africology that properly equips them to identify biased instruction and be intellectually prepared to defend their stance. Black children must be mentally strengthened to withstand the constant negative language imposed on them regularly. Black children know that the educational environment is stressful and violent and feel that they need the guidance and support of their family members to prepare them for how to navigate.

Educators hold a responsibility to intentionally monitor the language used when describing the actions and intent of African American children. Educational training is needed to provide educators with an objective report on how they are currently describing African American students and their behaviors. Professional development on educating Black children is needed for any teacher or educator responsible for the education of African American children. White educators must acknowledge that there are skill sets, both natural and learned, that African American teachers possess that they, as White educators, may not have. Immersion training and workshops must be developed to teach all educators the structures, strategies, and procedures that are most effective in the education and edification of African American scholars.

References

Adams-Bass, V., Stevenson, H., & Slaughter, D. (2014). Measuring the meaning of black media stereotypes and their relationship to the racial identity, Black history knowledge, and racial socialization of African American youth. *Journal of Black Studies, 45,* 367–395.

Anderson, J. (1998). *The education of Blacks in the South, 1860–1935.* Chapel Hill, NC: The University of North Carolina Press.

Brown v. Board of Education, 347 U.S. 483 (1954).

Watkins, W. (2001). *The White architects of Black education.* New York, NY: Teachers College Press.

Welsing, F. C. (1991). *The Isis papers.* Chicago, IL: Third World Press.

FOURTEEN

Teaching Through Culture: Employing Culturally Responsive Pedagogy to Transform Postsecondary STEM Instructions

Leah McAlister-Shields, Laveria Hutchison, and Donna Stokes

Context and Present Evidence

EDUCATIONAL ACCESS FOR RACIAL AND ethnic minorities in the United States has been a long-standing challenge where it has experienced periods of expansion and decline. Although there have been robust gains in educational access for racial and ethnic minority students since the 1960s (Lloyd, Tienda & Zajacova, 2001), attrition rates continue to be contrasting for White and non-White students (Current Population Survey, 2013; National Center for Education Statistics [NCES], 2012). Despite these students no longer being segregated from their White peers as it is spatially related, racial and ethnic minority students often are separated from their Asian and White peers in academic achievement.

The National Assessment of Educational Progress report revealed that gaps in the academic achievement of racial and ethnic minority students are surfacing as early as the fourth grade (NCES, 2013). For example, Asian and White students are shown to attain higher reading achievements than their racial and ethnically minority counterparts (NCES, 2013). There is also a similar gap in the combined areas of science, technology, engineering, and mathematics (STEM) for African American and Latinx students as compared to their White counterparts.

To close these gaps in educational achievement, many researchers have identified teaching method, pedagogy, and curriculum that aims to improve the learning gains of racial and ethnic minorities as well as all learners. The concept of culturally responsive pedagogy (CRP) is one of these methods, and it is used to frame the analysis of this chapter as it pertains to STEM education in postsecondary institutions.

Culturally Responsive Pedagogy was defined by Gay (2010) as "using the cultural knowledge, prior experiences, frames of reference, and performance styles of ethnically diverse students to make learning encounters more salient to them. Furthermore, it teaches *to and through* the strengths of these students" (p. 31). Particular characteristics of CRP date back to Forbes's (1973) analysis of Native American students' educational experiences in North America and the necessity to both recognize their humanity and cultural gifts. This groundbreaking work led to advancements in the theory of CRP by numerous researchers (Banks, 1994; Carjuzaa, 2012; Gay, 2010; Harmon, 2012; Ladson-Billings, 1995) that have challenged teachers at the elementary, secondary, and postsecondary levels to consider the students' culture, language, and life experience when determining how to deliver their course-specific content. In particular, STEM professors in higher education are challenged to retool their approach as a means of increasing and improving the outcomes of racial and ethnic minorities in STEM fields.

Chapter Overview—Scenario

Dr. Smith, a geophysics professor, accessed her class roster for the new semester and smiled with excitement to notice it consisted of sophomore students who were all STEM majors. She immediately started to update her syllabus with readings, project due dates, and a schedule for unit assessments and other examinations. The first day of classes finally arrived, and she was eager to explain the course requirements. Dr. Smith actively planned and presented her lectures and discussions over the next several weeks. After several class meetings, she decided to reflect on her instruction and the participation of the students. Dr. Smith immediately realized she did not have any participation grades for seven students and decided to identify the students during the next class meeting. During the meeting, the professor noted that the students were four African Americans (two males and two females) and three Latinx (one male and two females). In a class following Dr. Smith's assessment, she noticed the seven students did not contribute to class dialogue or ask any questions for clarification of concepts. As a result, she decided to conduct a research-based inquiry into the potential causes of the educational disconnect of these students. From her inquiry, Dr. Smith realized that underrepresented college students enrolled in the course had experienced racial microaggressions during their K–16 education. These types of experiences can often derive from sources of educational inequity and other societal experiences of negative affect. This can result in a decreased self-belief of peer/teacher connectedness and academic community engagement. To incorporate inclusion efforts, Dr. Smith framed her inquiry on the discussion used by Chang, Eagan, Lin, and Hurtado (2011), bearing in mind the impact of racial stigmas and science identity to inform engagement with the seven students.

This chapter aims to provide an academic lens into the theoretical concepts of CRP in STEM higher education and to provide a discussion of its importance along with ideas of including instructional components into designing an inclusive environment for all learners in higher education settings.

Desegregation of American Higher Education Institutions

Access to institutions of higher education, in particular, four-year institutions, has been a long-standing challenge for racial and ethnic minorities in the United States. In the years following the U.S. Civil War and the Reconstruction Era, the Morrill Act was passed to include African Americans in the United States Land-Grant University System (Brown, 2001). As a result of a number of planning meetings to implement the act, an agreement involving representatives from both the North and the South resulted in the development of a segregated higher education system for African American and White students (Browning & Williams, 1978).

The outcome of the Morrill Act implementation meetings underscored continuous efforts to limit the citizenship of African Americans and suppress access to higher education. However, despite these efforts, historically Black colleges and universities (HBCUs) continued to meet the need of African American students to attain college and graduate degrees (Office of Civil Rights, 1991). The segregated system remained intact until the 1954 *Brown vs. the Board of Education of Topeka, Kansas* decision (Brown, 2001). Although the decision was framed by many, primarily politicians and media, as pertaining to the desegregation of Early Childhood through 12th-grade educational institutions, the landmark decision also addressed the desegregation of institutions of higher education (Brown, 2001). However, the mandate to dismantle the dual system of higher education did not happen until President Lyndon B. Johnson's signing of the Civil Rights Act of 1964 (Malone, 2008).

This new statute restricted funds to segregated institutions of higher learning and allowed the federal government to file lawsuits against institutions that were slow to enact desegregation policies—namely, cases such as *Adams v. Richardson and the United States v. Fordice* (Malone, 2008) occurred after the enactment of the Civil Rights Act of 1964 and helped to expand desegregation efforts. However, cases such as *Coal. for Equity & Excellence in Md. Higher Educ. v. Md. Higher Educ. Comm'n* (Malone, 2008) demonstrate the continued fight for desegregation in higher education and the need for equitable access to postsecondary institutions.

Since the Civil Rights Act of 1964 and the resultant lawsuits that expanded minority student access to institutions of higher education, there has been a "browning" of students who now attend higher education institutions (Lloyd et al., 2001). For racial and ethnic minorities, there have been robust gains in higher education access due to their increased enrollment at two-year institutions; however, barriers to access to four-year institutions remain. Attrition is even more pronounced for these students pursuing STEM degrees. According to the NCES (2014), of all STEM degrees awarded between 2008 and 2013, only 7.5% were African American, and 7.8% were Latinx. With regard to doctoral degrees attained, the percentages are even starker. From 1997 to 2006, African Americans accounted for only 2.8% and 3.1% of earned doctorates in mathematics and the biological sciences, respectively, and Latinx percentages for doctorates attained in mathematics and biological sciences were 3.6% and 4.5% (Nelson, 2017).

Historically Black Colleges and Universities (HBCUs) prepared the largest number, nearly 25%, of African Americans majoring in the areas of science and engineering from 2013 to 2017 (National Science Foundation & National Center for Science and Engineering Statistics, 2019). According to a 2010 National Science Foundation Science and Engineering Indicators report cited in the work of Kendricks, Nedunuri, and Arment (2013), important to the success of STEM majors at HBCUs is the cultural context of the educational experience and institutional policies that address the academic and psychosocial needs of African American students. Furthermore, Kendricks et al. (2013) highlight from the report that "when the data were adjusted for the number of bachelor's degrees awarded, HBCUs, as a group, yielded about as many future Science and Engineering doctorates per thousand bachelor's degrees awarded as non-HBCU institutions" (p. 38). As a result of the findings of the National Science Foundation report, in conjunction with the heavy recruitment of HBCU STEM degree holders from graduate programs and business and industry, Kendricks et al. (2013) recommended that the characteristics of the social and academic environments of HBCUs be further examined and considered for adoption at higher education institutions.

Culture and Teaching in Higher Education Settings

The cultural context of the educating of STEM majors is prevalent at HBCUs and has been examined for the importance of inclusion on STEM student success. Culture can be defined in several ways, that is, the beliefs, social forms, and material traits of a racial, religious, or social group or the attitudes, values, goals, and practices that characterizes an institution or organization or the integrated pattern of human knowledge, belief, and behavior that depends upon the capacity for learning and transmitting knowledge to succeeding generations (Culture, 2019). Although the meaning of culture is complex, considering it as it relates to teaching/learning has become a focus of education research. The interest in merging culture and teaching has been explored for decades by researchers regarding how culture affects student learning and success at all levels (Banks, 1994; Bustamante, 2006; Carjuzaa & Ruff, 2010; Gay, 2010; Howard, 2010; Ladson-Billings, 1995; Wlodkowski & Ginsberg, 2009). With higher education classrooms becoming more diverse/international, in both the student and faculty realm, faculty must be educated on how culture and cultural differences inform their teaching, which can affect student learning. The personal culture of the students and faculty, as well as the social and political cultures, must be considered since cultural differences can lead to implicit bias (Gutierrez, 2018; Ladson-Billings, 1995). Being aware of culture/cultural differences in the classroom can allow faculty to diversify their teaching style, that is, group learning, teacher-led activities, and alternative assessment, to foster learning by all students and avoid employing biases in ways that would marginalize the learning experiences of students.

The ever-growing diversity of college students enrolling in American universities means these students bring with them varied experiences related to race, culture, class, gender, and disability. Acknowledgment of these differences is but a start when considering mechanisms that will expand student diversity in the STEM areas. Additionally, higher education faculty must be equipped to navigate the complexities and intersections of race, class, and culture to become inclusive educators that relate mathematics and science topics to all college students they teach (Kendricks et al., 2013; Robinson & West, 2012). Moreover, focusing on the instruction of STEM majors because of the social, psychological, and structural dimensions considered to influence students' transition from high school to colleges and how students new to this experience view themselves as successful learners is important. The National Science Foundation (1998) published a report that found collaborations among faculty and their institutions, industry, and research laboratories can promote effective student learning. With the consideration of this finding, institutions of higher education should continue to improve their curricular offerings as well as promote the continuation of curricular innovations and reform because of the significant increase in the enrollment of minority students.

Absence of Culturally Responsive Pedagogy in Higher Education Institutions

The use of CRP enhances the sense-making abilities of students as this approach to teaching relies on their lived experiences as a mechanism for explaining and providing a context for understanding (Ladson-Billings, 1994). Noguera (2001) points out that the use of culture as a way to inform instruction allows teachers to be student-centered and meet students where they are rather than demanding students use their teachers' cultural context as a lens to make learning connections. Table 14.1 outlines the eight principles identified by Ladson-Billings (1994) that are suggested for educators to utilize to ensure their instruction is culturally responsive.

The sixth point in Ladson-Billings's (1994) work—Reshaping the Curriculum—anchors the important use of culture and where we make connections regarding how CRP should be used to instruct STEM in Higher Education settings. To reshape the curriculum, Ladson-Billings (1994) argues that "educators traditionally have attempted to insert culture into education, instead of inserting education into the culture" (pp. 2–3). Culture is not to supplement or serves as an add-on to instruction but, rather, should be the purposeful stance from which instruction happens. The research of Aguirre and Aguirre (2013), Gutierrez (2018), and others (Laughter & Adams, 2012;

Table 14.1. Characteristics of Culturally Responsive Pedagogy

Number	Characteristics
1	[Teachers] must have and communicate high expectations of their students.
2	[Teachers] must utilize active teaching methods.
3	[Teachers] must serve as facilitators of students' learning.
4	[Teachers] must be inclusive of culturally and linguistically diverse students in the development of the curriculum and the instruction of material.
5	[Teachers] must utilize cultural sensitivity in the instruction of and interaction with students.
6	[Teachers] have to reshape the curriculum in order to make their instruction culturally relevant.
7	[Teachers] should incorporate student-controlled classroom discourse.
8	[Teachers] are encouraged to build a positive rapport with parents and the community they serve.

Note. Table adapted from *The Dreamkeepers: Successful teachers of African American children* (Ladson-Billings, 1994).

Tsurusaki, Calabrese Barton, Tan, Koch & Contento, 2013) have situated the need for CRP in the instruction of diverse students in Early Childhood through 12th-grade science and mathematics and, in particular, highlighted the importance of CRP as a vital component in the training of effective pre-service and in-service STEM teachers. The impact of CRP on the instructional effectiveness of diverse learners also demonstrates the need for CRP to be extended to instruction in higher education settings.

Evolution of Pedagogical and Curricular Practices in Higher Education

As educational trends merged into the 20th century, changes began to occur in the offering of an undergraduate curriculum due to an increased critique of higher education by reports such as *A Nation at Risk* (National Commission on Excellence in Education, 1983). Criticism also originated from industrial executives who expressed concern over the lack of workforce preparation to think critically and to effectively communicate through various platforms. As processes were incorporated into higher education to address these issues, additional concern surfaced that placed a priority on the inclusion of differentiated assessment models, self-reflection, group learning and project development, and technology-enhanced tools.

In the discussion of reshaping STEM instruction, examining the perspectives and philosophies emphasized in the teaching of STEM concepts must be considered. In Gutierrez's (2018) provocative work *Political Conocimiento for Teaching Mathematics: Why Teachers Need It and How to Develop It*, the choice of anchoring mathematical concepts solely from the perspective of Western epistemological perspectives is critically analyzed. As explained, equity in mathematics achievement will not happen based on teachers' knowledge of content, utilizing motivational strategies, and building a rapport with students. It recognizes the sociopolitical perspectives inherent in the instruction of mathematics and the ability to navigate beyond the Whiteness so often used to contextualize instruction.

To reshape curriculum, we must also reframe how and what we determine to be legitimate knowledge, worthy of instruction in American schools. African American scholars in the United States have long taken issue with how "official" knowledge has been both determined and is distributed in American educational institutions (Banks & McGee Banks, 2016). In particular, Western epistemological influence, what is often constituted as official knowledge, has excluded the contributions and historical narratives of people of color (Carjuzaa & Ruff, 2010). Scholars such as W. E. B. Du Bois (1935, 1975) and James Baldwin (1962) persistently pointed out the marginalization of African American history and culture in U.S. curricula. As a result, a whitewashing of education ensued in the American educational system, extending beyond Early Childhood through 12th grade, informing and excluding diverse learning perspectives from American textbooks and curriculum development. Demands for an examination of the nature of school knowledge over the past century have revealed that the Western epistemological approach to education possesses instructional and curricular mechanisms, which has served to produce and reproduce race and class-based inequities (Banks, 1993; Gordon, 1990).

African American scholars such as Gordon (1990) and Banks (1992, 1993) have extended the works of early scholars identifying the prioritization of White culture and the influence of White social capital as determining what is legitimate sources and forms of knowledge and the need to be more inclusive of diverse cultures and lived experiences. Connectedly, Young (1971) argued that an inextricable relationship exists among access to power, establishing dominant categories as sources of knowledge, and the promotion and distribution of this worldview in educational institutions. Despite the existence of a critical mass of intelligentsia across disciplines in higher education, there is a lack of critical and deep understanding, as well as the application of culturally responsive teaching practices, which includes and enfranchises students from diverse backgrounds (Bustamante, 2006). Moreover, the heightened concentration of academics in higher education has not translated into faculty becoming more culturally aware, employing techniques, or developing a standard of promising instructional practices, which acknowledges the cultural experiences of their students. Furthermore, Carjuzaa and Ruff (2010) argue that the cultural divide that exists between faculty and students is just as extensive in higher education as it is in Early Childhood through 12th-grade educational settings. The use of higher education instructional practices that are culturally responsive is important because "students crave to have their cultural identities acknowledged and reflected in the school environment" (Carjuzaa & Ruff, 2010, p. 68).

Impact of Faculty Diversity on the Instruction of Diverse Learners

Culturally Responsive Pedagogy (CRP) has been a critical component of diversity and inclusion in education for many years. Although the use of CRP has mostly been at the elementary and secondary levels, it is aimed at providing an equitable education to all while taking into consideration differences in ethnicity, race, cultures, and backgrounds (Gay, 2013; Ladson-Billings, 1995, 2014). This is important because classrooms, elementary and secondary, as well as postsecondary, across the nation are changing and educators will need to consider how best to teach all students considering factors such as lived and cultural experiences and socioeconomic backgrounds.

Demographics

The U.S. Census Bureau's 2017 National Population Projection tables predict that the U.S. Population will become minority White by 2045 with the largest growth rates (for 2016–2060) being that of the multiracial population that will increase by 176%, Asians 93%, Hispanics 86%, and African Americans

34%. The census projections also indicate that for 18-year-olds, minorities will outgrow the White population and will be the source of the nation's working-age population by 2060; see Figure 14.1. Therefore, the nation will depend highly on minority contributions for economic growth (Frey, 2014). So, how do these trends affect the population of higher education institutions and the approach of faculty instructors in teaching their classes? The predicted demographics suggest that there is a need for the nation to invest in educating minority youth at all levels, that is, elementary, secondary, and postsecondary, to ensure a thriving nation built on the contributions of the entire population. In addition, it is shown that by 2024, there will be an increase of 8.9% in STEM jobs over the level in 2014 and that by 2030, this will represent a shortage of 962,000 technical workers; therefore, training a diverse workforce to meet these demands is imperative.

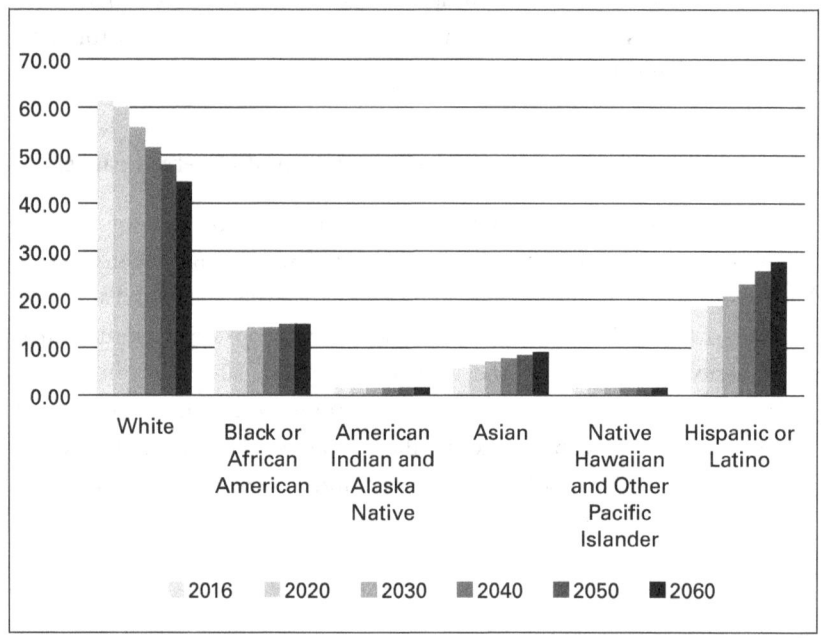

Figure 14.1. Population projection of racialized minorities in the United States by 2060.

Source. Adapted from the National Center for Education Statistics. (2017). *National Population Projections Tables.* Retrieved from http://www.census.gov/data/tables/2017/demo/popproj/2017-summary-tables.html.

Higher education institutions/instructors will need to be cognizant of the population trends and societal needs to ensure that classroom instruction will meet the needs of the students they serve where these trends should be used to inform approaches to teaching. Undergraduate enrollment at degree-granting (associate's degree or higher) postsecondary institutions increased overall by 28% between 2000 and 2016. The NCES (2014) projects that overall undergraduate enrollment will increase by an additional 3% between 2016 and 2027. From 2000 to 2016, overall enrollment for Latinx increased tremendously by 134%, African American enrollment increased by 73%, Asian/Pacific Islander increased by 29%, American Indian/Alaska Native enrollment increased by 29%, and White enrollment increased by 21%.

In 2015 and 2016, 18% of all degrees awarded were in STEM fields. Of those degrees, 33% were awarded to Asians, 18% to Whites, 15% to Hispanic, 15% Pacific Islander, 14% American Indian/Alaska Native, and 12% to African Americans (Digest of Education Statistics, 2017). To improve these statistics, interest and accessibility to STEM must be improved at all levels (i.e., secondary and postsecondary), and teachers must be prepared to inspire students of all backgrounds to pursue STEM careers. As stated by President Barack Obama in March 2015 at a White House Science Fair event:

> [Science] is more than a school subject, or the periodic table, or the properties of waves. It is an approach to the world, a critical way to understand and explore and engage with the world, and then have the capacity to change that world. (The White House, Office of the Press Secretary, 2015, para. 4).

Given the projected diversity trends, CRP lends itself to be an approach that could be employed to help teachers/professors make the connection with students' cultures and STEM content and see the global importance of their participation in STEM careers.

Culturally Responsive Pedagogy in STEM Classrooms

Culturally responsive pedagogy (CRP) tends to be a concept that is unknown or often not found to be an implemented practice used by professors in higher education institutions. This concept was designed to provide equitable instructional outcomes for all students, including students from underrepresented populations. As educators investigate the changing demographics of higher education, noticing the cultural, economic, linguistic, and ethnic diversity is important. CRP recognizes that culture is a fundamental aspect that can connect all students to the learning experience (Ladson-Billings, 1994). Gay (2002) states that "by using the cultural characteristic, experiences and perspective of ethnically diverse students as conduits of teaching, enhances their learning" (p. 106). The inclusion of CRP practices in higher education classrooms is going to be essential for training a workforce that possesses the necessary professional and technical skills and is culturally diverse. To successfully implement CRP in a higher education classroom, three components of CRP (Ladson-Billings, 1994) are applicable: (a) cultural competence (must develop a cultural knowledge base before designing a course which may be complex in itself), (b) critical consciousness (develop a broad perspective of sociopolitical consciousness to describe connections in society), and (c) academic success (engage students and evaluate course content and student success; Gay, 2002; Ladson-Billings, 1995). With the complexity to employ CRP, the existence of mental models that limit the use of CRP, and curriculum and pedagogical considerations, many higher education instructors may be hesitant to implement it in their classroom (Taylor, 2011). However, STEM professors should consider the question, "Can CRP be a means to broadening participation in STEM for producing a diverse technical workforce?"

In the past decades, student success in higher education STEM programs has been of great concern if the United States is to continue to produce a diverse population of scientists, engineers, and mathematicians. Because of this concern, there has been a push to improve student success in STEM fields by transforming instruction in higher education classrooms, particularly the introductory science/math courses. In higher education, traditional-style (lecture-based) teaching is still the most common method of instruction, but the use of interactive teaching/learning is becoming more commonplace (Henderson, Beach & Finkelstein, 2011). This includes the integration of technology, hands-on demonstrations, and open discussions, all aimed at building skills such as critical thinking and teamwork. Although learning gains in many areas, particularly in STEM, are related to the use of interactive learning/teaching techniques, a disparity in education as it relates to race/ethnicity, and gender still exists.

The inclusion of CRP in higher education STEM classrooms is almost nonexistent as it is not a part of the professional culture, and it may not garner faculty any recognition as it relates to the tenure and promotion process. Therefore, convincing faculty to commit to changing the culture of the classroom with the incorporation of CRP as well as changing their approach to teaching science/math is a challenge. Faculty must consider using teaching techniques that will achieve equity in learning for diverse groups of students with varying learning styles and draw from their experiences, cultures, and backgrounds to improve learning/teaching in the classrooms. This is particularly important because higher education STEM classrooms have become increasingly more populated with international students. STEM faculty now have the opportunity, and responsibility, to consider implementing CRP practices to create a change in the culture of the STEM classroom that will effectively connect/align STEM content with authentic cultural situations. This may lead to a better way to meet the needs and navigate the cultural differences of the diverse STEM classrooms across the nation. Henderson et al. (2011), in their review on facilitating change in undergraduate STEM instructional practices, states:

> Effective change strategies must be aligned with or seek to change the beliefs of the individuals involved . . . involve long-term interventions, lasting at least one semester . . . require understanding a college or university as a complex system and designing a strategy that is compatible with this system. (p. 27)

When considering CRP in STEM higher education classes, remembering that as a college professor, one may not have the capacity to engage each student in the many lessons that will be delivered during a semester is important. In addition, it may be a greater challenge for professor teaching courses with large enrollment, that is, 100 to 500 students. However, college professors should build instructional activities that will consistently appeal to diverse learners by accepting linguistic differences, the expression of cultural differences, and the acceptance and support of academic gaps along with other instructional considerations that would enhance CRP. As the college professor connects lessons to diverse students, considering that CRP should also link content instruction to assessment practices is essential. Although focusing on the cultural consideration of how STEM education is disseminated in the context of higher education instruction is important, considering the sequence taken by diverse populations of students to be in these instructional spaces at this time and to discuss the tenets of culturally responsive pedagogy is also important.

College professors may feel they do not have the knowledge and capacity to model this concept while delivering content. Providing information and professional development sessions for faculty members, doctoral teaching assistants, and others working with students related to CRP and providing examples of the types of instructional activities that can be used to promote effective and accepting learning environments are necessary for universities. As an example of this type of instructional assistance, universities could recommend classroom observations of faculty effectively, including CRP strategies in their practice, and sharing instructional syllabi that include practices of CRP. In addition, in preparing for CRP implementation, instructors should give special considerations for modifications to course materials, including course syllabi and lesson design (Larke, 2013).

As a first step, STEM professors could introduce diversity into their lessons by considering various cultural aspects of their students. According to Banks (2004), various levels of approach to diversity awareness can be used to tailor course content. These are the contribution, additive, transformation, and the social action approach. Each allows the instructor to introduce diversity in various ways, which may not be as complex as implementing a complete CRP.

The *Contribution* approach allows for the use of cultural aspects related to food, pop culture, and folklore, among others, to introduce diversity. A simple example of this approach is a math problem that could be used to demonstrate diversity/inclusion in a higher education STEM teacher education course:

> Rafael wants to impress his family by making Horchata for holiday dinner. Rafael's abuela shared with him her time-honored recipe, which calls for 1 cup of rice per 7 servings. Rafael is expecting about 20 members of his family to attend dinner and would like to provide two servings of the drink per guest. How much rice will Rafael need to provide an adequate amount of the drink for holiday dinner guests?

In the *Additive* approach, Banks and McGee Banks (2016) suggest that diversity information related to the course content be assigned, but not as part of the required course material. For a STEM course, faculty could ask students to do a short report/reflection on a scientist who has influenced them as students or their immediate community for extra credit. However, for the assignment to be valid and for students to reflect deeply on how the assignment relates to them personally, their cultural community, or the STEM course content, it should be counted as part of the course grade.

In the *Transformative* approach, the instructor presents the course materials from various viewpoints, that is, that of the instructor's culture and the students' cultures or language. For example, a biological science faculty could infuse culture by instructing a lesson on the impact of HeLa cell research and the circumstances that led to Mrs. Henrietta Lacks's significant contributions to cell biology. In addition to understanding the complex ways that individuals from diverse backgrounds have significantly influenced medical research and biological science, the lesson would provide an opportunity to address the importance of ethical research practices that were ignored with the harvesting and use of Mrs. Lacks's cells.

In the *Social Action* approach, the material presented influences societal change as it relates to the cultural community of the students. Given this approach, we could extend the lesson and have students identify critical social problems where STEM can be used, reviewing research and gather data on issues related to the influence of race, ethnicity, gender, and class. Such a learning opportunity would help students apply an evidence-based approach to understand, reflect, and make decisions (Banks & McGee Banks, 2016).

STEM faculty, if including diversity/inclusion materials in their course, will need to make this known to the students because the student will need to invest emotion and take responsibility for incorporating it into the learning process. Larke (2013) suggests that this information be included in the various components of the course syllabus. However, one could also discuss the diversity material in a separated section of the syllabus that identifies and gives details on the content of the materials, list the expected learning outcome related to this materials, and discuss how it ties into the overall learning goals and lecture outline for the course and outline the grading schemes, if any, associated with the materials. Faculty could also determine if textbooks or online resources that include diversity-specific lessons that have been tested through research to be effective in achieving specific learning objectives are available.

By taking small steps to inclusiveness of all learners in higher education STEM classrooms, faculty can determine the best approach for their course so that they do not become overwhelmed with the process. The full incorporation of CRP requires professional development to ensure faculty are committed, are culturally knowledgeable, and can communicate it authentically to their students for proper implementation. Faculty would need to be open to identifying their biases and how they affect their teaching and be willing to reshape their curriculum based on their own experiences as well as their students. By utilizing one or more of the approaches discussed earlier, faculty can determine what would work best for them, what would incorporate smoothly for the course content, what would be most impactful on the learners in their classroom, and how to assess their implementation best.

Journey of Higher Education Faculty: Reflections on Personal Bias

To do the work of reshaping curriculum more inclusive of the students we teach, instructors must engage in the work of reflection not only of our instructional practices and the philosophical theories we endorse but also the biases we translate in our instruction. As authors of this work, we believe it important to share our individual experiences confronting personal bias and our challenges/success as higher education instructors, ever-striving, and evolving to become more culturally responsive. The following are the reflections of each author disclosing aspects of our journey.

Reflection of an Education Instructor by Author One

As a student affairs practitioner and research methods instructor, I interface with students from all racial, cultural, and socioeconomic backgrounds ranging from students pursuing their bachelor's degree to those in pursuit of a terminal degree. How I engage STEM education students and help them to navigate their college experience or course material is, in large part, informed by my responsiveness to their lived experiences.

As an African American woman, my experiences do not always translate to the experiences of others, including those of African American students.

Class, religion, social, and cultural capital informs the lens through which we view the world and the biases we possess. As a practitioner, the implications of acting on or reproducing bias could result in a loss in financial or academic opportunities for students. Identifying biases that I possess or triggers of these biases help me with trying to keep my biases at bay. Journaling about my day-to-day interactions with students, as well as my instructional lessons, helps to keep me honest.

Additionally, identifying critical friends, faculty, and other frontline practitioners who serve as touchstones and are willing to reflect with me about my practice are essential in helping me along my journey to be culturally responsive. Embedding opportunities for student feedback at the start of the semester, mid-semester, and at the conclusion of instruction offer students the ability to voice suggestions and concerns. Empowering STEM education students to have a voice about their instruction not only allows me to learn about the background of my students and develop lessons inclusive of their culture and model the importance of the use of CRP in their instruction.

Reflection of these biases is an ongoing process and does not always result in responsive practice. However, whatever method is used—journaling, critical friends, feedback from students, and so on—will always help to identify areas in need of attention and where I have been able to make progress. Most importantly, reflection on my practice has helped to keep relevant the needs of my students, which I try to use every day to inform and improve their educational experiences.

Reflection of a Department Administrator by Author Two

My biases are a result of living in a southern state and experiencing a reduction in the experiences that were provided for students-of-color and their teachers-of-color. As I reflect on my life as an African American person, I can relate to a position of underrepresentation in an environment that promoted, allowed, and benefited from bias related to educational opportunities and environmental situations. The important aspect of my lived experience is that I overlooked these undisguised situations by becoming resilient, well exposed through my HBCU undergraduate experience to my cultural identities, and educated beyond expectation. I found that family support, a lens of positive perspectives, and an attitude of optimistic belief can lead to personal acceptance and constructive movement as a confident individual and educator. These personal insights and reflections have allowed me, as a professional working now in higher education and as a former department administrator, to promote an awareness of exceptional professional capacity within the students I teach and the faculty I mentored. I believe in these ideas because I realize that my students represent multiple backgrounds, varied racial identities, different educational preparations, and diverse instructional styles. Understanding this range of differences among my undergraduate and graduate students allows me to guide their investigations of promising practices and the most effective presentation models they can apply in their educational environments. As my students learn and apply differentiated instructional practices that will address the diverse populations of their instructional settings, I firmly believe this oversight will support their overarching capacity to be an effective and supportive teacher for all students. This is my space as an educator and former department administrator as I have used my experiences to assist in the guiding of my students to become capable of sorting out the sensitive cultural needs of their students.

Reflection of a STEM Instructor by Author Three

Interfacing with students of many ethnic, language, and religious backgrounds is a direct part of my job as a professor and undergraduate academic advisor of physics. Often, I realize that their story is my story, and my awareness of the importance of culture in learning and persistence in STEM becomes more pronounced. As a graduate of an HBCU, where I received my bachelor's degree, I was a direct recipient of the nurturing and cultivating environment that existed to promote student success through a "family" learning community. Not only was there academic guidance, but there was also life guidance that was directly related to my lived experiences.

For my master's and doctorate degrees, which were completed at a majority university, the level of support was dramatically different. In addition, the classroom demographics were very different, where most students were international, and this set the professor's tone, pace, and expectations in performance for the class. The professors, mostly White males and some Asian, were connected to the science content but failed to make any authentic connection to the cultural backgrounds of the students or how to use their backgrounds to inform their instruction.

Now, as one of the few African American female professors of physics, I found that I was teaching my students the way I was taught, not considering any cultural context in my course curriculum. Including CRP practices in physics curricula is not commonplace; however, in recent years, I have realized that there are various ways in which cultural contexts can be considered in my course. As an example, in my Electronic Devices course where students work in pairs, I found that two Latina students, when paired, spoke in their native language to help one another understand the physics concepts. Although this is not direct use of CRP in the classroom, this helped me recognize that consideration of cultures, ethnicity, language, and/or religion could influence student learning as well as result in a collaborative learning environment in the classroom. By reflecting on my practices in the classroom, I can identify the need for a conscious effort on my part to understand the cultural nuances of the classroom, to promote student learning in physics and to not rely on the majority learning style to dictate the culture of the classroom that can ultimately hinder the advancement of minority students toward STEM degrees and, hence, STEM careers.

Summary and Conclusion

A number of factors both encourage and hinder the utilization of culturally responsive pedagogy. As evidenced in much of the literature on the utilization of CRP, policies that promote student diversity, and the hiring of diverse faculty is not enough (PeQueen, 2016). Although the need for diverse views is warranted, issues of equitable curricular and student support policies that are not limited to inclusion practices and instead are extended to provide services that are responsive to the needs of diverse learners are needed (Carjuzaa & Ruff, 2010; PeQueen, 2016). Some limitations of the use of CRP in higher education classrooms stem from implementation challenges, doubts about its validity, and a lack of knowledge needed for effective use (Wlodkowski & Ginsberg, 2009). Providing faculty training and support to promote the use of CRP practices will help to minimize mental models that limit the application of Culturally Responsive Pedagogy and promote growing cultural competence (Gopal, 2011; Taylor, 2011). Doing so will allow faculty to think more critically about the intersections of race, class, gender, disability status, and sexual orientation in their instruction and to enact pedagogical practices that honor the lived experiences of their students. Additionally, leadership at all levels of higher education—departmental, college, and university—must place value on the implementation and use of CRP practices. Assessing for the use of these practices through end-of-course assessments, faculty review, and departmental leadership annual evaluations will place heavy importance on creating a culture that actively embraces the use of CRP rather than speaking rhetoric to its use (PeQueen, 2016).

As evidenced by the information provided in our chapter, our philosophical belief is that a reshaping of STEM curriculum and instructional practices is needed. This is particularly important given the dearth of student diversity across STEM majors. Furthermore, for STEM faculty to be successful in the reshaping of curriculum and to integrate the use of CRP, adequate support and professional incentives must be provided by higher education leadership, which promotes the adoption of culturally responsive practices. As illuminated in the literature regarding the implementation of responsive practices at HBCUs, we recommend that research be conducted, which takes a particular look at the way culture is utilized for instruction in the STEM areas and these practices be considered for adoption at higher education institutions. Moreover, such research will inform practices that strengthen the cultural knowledge of STEM faculty, which lead to implications of improved student achievement and degree completion. In addition, we hope that this chapter will better equip STEM leadership in higher education settings to value the use of CRP in higher education STEM classrooms and provide them insight for successfully implementing culturally responsive pedagogy across their respective academic programs.

References

Aguirre, J. M., & Aguirre Zavala, M. (2013). Making culturally responsive mathematics teaching explicit: a lesson analysis tool. *Pedagogies: An International Journal, 8,* 163–190. doi:10.1080/1554480X.2013.768518

Baldwin, J. (1962, November). Letter from a region in my mind. *New Yorker.* Retrieved from https://www.newyorker.com/magazine/1962/11/17/letter-from-a-region-in-my-mind.

Banks, J. A. (1992). African American scholars and the evolution of multicultural education. *Journal of Negro Education, 61*, 273–276.

Banks, J. A. (1993). The cannon debate, knowledge construction, and multicultural education. *Education Researcher, 2*, 4–14.

Banks, J. A. (1994). *An introduction to multicultural education* (5th ed.). New Heights, MA: Allyn and Bacon.

Banks, J. A. (2004). *Multicultural education: Historical development, dimensions, and practice.* In J. A. Banks & C. A. M. Banks (Eds.), Handbook of research on multicultural education. (pp. 3–29). San Francisco: Jossey-Bass.

Banks, J. A., & McGee Banks, C. A. (2016). *Multicultural education: Issues and perspectives* (9th ed.). Danvers, MA: Wiley.

Brown, C. (2001). Collegiate desegregation and the public Black college. *Journal of Higher Education, 72*, 46–62. doi:10.1080/00221546.2001.11778864.

Browning, J. E., & Williams, J. B. (1978). History and goals of black institutions of higher learning. In C. V. Willie & R. R. Edmonds (Eds.), *Black colleges in America* (pp. 68–93). New York: Teachers College.

Bustamante, R.M. (2006). The "culture audit": A leadership tool for assessment and strategic planning in diverse schools and colleges. *National Council of Professor of Educational Administration, 1* (2), 1–5.

Carjuzaa, J. (2012). The positive impact of culturally responsive pedagogy: Montana's Indian education for all. *International Journal of Multicultural Education, 14* (3), 1–14.

Carjuzaa, J., & Ruff, W. G. (2010). When western epistemology and indigenous worldview meet: Culturally responsive assessment in practice. *Journal of the Scholarship of Teaching and Learning, 10*, 68–79.

Chang, M. J., Eagan, M. K., Lin, M. H., & Hurtado, S. (2011). Considering the impact of racial stigmas and science identity: Persistence among biomedical and behavioral science aspirants. *Journal of Higher Education, 82*, 564–596.

Culture. (n.d.). In *Merriam-Webster's*. Retrieved from http://www.merriam-webster.com/dictionary/integrity.

Current Population Survey. (2013, April). *College enrollment and work activity of 2012 high school graduates* (Issue USDL-13-0670). Washington, DC: US Department of Labor, Bureau of Labor Statistics.

Digest of Education Statistics. (2017). *National Center for Education Statistics*

(Report). Retrieved from https://nces.ed.gov/programs/digest/d17/index.asp

Du Bois, W. E. B. (1935). Does the Negro need separate schools? *The Journal of Negro Education, 4*, 328–335.

Du Bois, W. E. B. (1975). *Gift of Black folk: The Negros in the making of America*. Millwood, NY: Kraus International Publications.

Forbes, J. D. (1973). Teaching Native American values and cultures. In J. A. Banks (Ed.), *Teaching ethnic studies: Concepts and strategies* (pp. 200–225). Washington, DC: National Council for the Social Studies.

Frey, W. H. (2014). *Diversity explosion: How new racial demographics are remaking America*. Washington DC: Brookings Institution Press.

Gay, G. (2002). Preparing for culturally responsive teaching. *Journal of Teacher Education, 53*, 106–116.

Gay, G. (2010). *Culturally Responsive Pedagogy: Theory, research, and practice*. New York, NY: Teachers College Press.

Gay. G. (2013). Teaching to and through cultural diversity. *Curriculum Inquiry, 43*, 48–70. doi:10.1111/curi.12002.

Gopal, A. (2011). Internationalization of higher education: Preparing faculty to teach cross-culturally. *International Journal of Teaching and Learning in Higher Education, 23* (3), 373–381.

Gordon, B. (1990). The necessity of African American epistemology. *Journal of Education, 172* (3), 88–106.

Gutierrez, R. (2018). Political conocimiento for teaching mathematics: Why teachers need it and how to develop it. In S. Kastberg & A. Tyminski (Eds.), Building support for scholarly practices (pp. 11–38). Charlotte, NC: Information Age Publishing.

Harmon, D. A. (2012). Culturally responsive pedagogy through a historical lens: Will history repeat itself? *Interdisciplinary Journal of Teaching and Learning, 2*, 12–22.

Henderson, C., Beach, A., & Finkelstein, N. (2011). Facilitating change in undergraduate STEM instructional practices: An analytic review of the literature. *Journal of Research in Science Teaching, 48*, 952–984.

Howard, T. C. (2010). *Why race and culture matters in schools: Closing the achievement gap in America's classrooms*. New York, NY: Teachers College Press.

Kendricks, K. D., Nedunuri, K. V., & Arment, A. R. (2013). Minority student perceptions of the impact of mentoring to enhance academic performance in STEM disciplines. *Journal of STEM Education: Innovations and Research, 14* (2), 38–46.

Ladson-Billings, G. (1994). *The dreamkeepers: Successful teachers of African American Children*. San Francisco, CA: Jossey-Bass.

Ladson-Billings, G. (1995). But that's just good teaching! The case for culturally relevant pedagogy. *Theory Into Practice, 34*, 159–165.

Ladson-Billings, G. (2014). Culturally relevant pedagogy 2.0: a.k.a. the Remix. *Harvard Educational Review, 84*, 74–84. doi:10.17763/haer.84.1.p2rj131485484751.

Larke, P. (2013). Culturally responsive teaching in higher education: What professors need to know. *Counterpoints, 391*, 38–50.

Laughter, J. C., & Adams, A. D. (2012). Culturally relevant science teaching in middle school. *Urban Education, 47*, 1106–1134.

Lloyd, K. M., Tienda, M., & Zajacova, A. (2001). Trends in educational achievement of minority students since *Brown v. Board of Education*. In T. Ready, C. Edley, & C. Snow (Eds.), *Achieving high educational standards for all* (pp. 1–25). Washington, DC: National Academy Press.

Malone, B. F. (2008). Before Brown: Cultural and social capital in a rural Black school community, W. E. B. Du Bois High School, Wake Forest, North Carolina. *The North Carolina Review, 85*, 416–447.

National Center for Education Statistics. (2012). *Digest of Education Statistics: 2011* (NCES 2011-001). Washington, DC.

National Center for Education Statistics (2013). NAEP data explorer. Retrieved February 19, 2014, from http://nces.ed.gov/nationsreportcard/naepdata/dataset.aspx.

National Center for Education Statistics. (2014). *Digest of Education Statistics Tables and Figures: 2014*. Washington, DC.

National Center for Education Statistics. (2017). *National Population Projections Tables*. Retrieved from https://www.census.gov/data/tables/2017/demo/ popproj/2017-summary-tables.html.

National Commission on Excellence in Education. 1983. *A Nation at Risk: The Imperative for Educational Reform*. Washington, DC: U.S. Government Printing Office.

National Science Foundation, & National Center for Science and Engineering Statistics. 2019. *Women, Minorities, and Persons with Disabilities in Science and Engineering: 2019* (Special Report NSF 19-304). Alexandria, VA. Retrieved from https://www.nsf.gov/statistics/wmpd.

National Science Foundation. (1998). *Shaping the future: Volume II: Perspectives on undergraduate education in science, mathematics, engineering and technology* (NSF: 98-128). Washington, DC.

Nelson, D. J. (2017). Diversity of science and engineering faculty at research universities. In D. J. Nelson & H. N. Cheng (Eds.), *Diversity in the Scientific Community Volume I. Quantifying diversity and formulating success* (pp. 16-86). Washington, DC: American Chemical Society Symposium Series.

Noguera, P. A. (2001). Racial politics and the elusive quest for excellence and equity in education. *Education and Urban Society, 34*, 18-41.

Office of Civil Rights. (1991). *Historically black colleges and universities and higher education desegregation* (Report). Washington, DC: United States Department of Education.

PeQueen, C. (2016). Cultural competence in higher education faculty: A case study (Doctoral dissertation). Available from ProQuest Dissertations and Theses database. (ProQuest 10248669).

Robinson, S. P., & West, J. E. (2012). Preparing inclusive educators: A call to action. *Journal of Teacher Education, 63*, 291-293. doi:10.1177/0022487112447574.

Taylor, P.C. (2011). Counter-storying and the grand narrative of science (teacher) education: Towards culturally responsive teaching. *Cultural Studies of Science Education, 6*, 795-801. doi:10.1007/s11422-011-9368-9.

The White House, Office of the Press Secretary. (2015, March 23). *Remarks by the president at White House science fair*. Retrieved from https://obamawhitehouse.archives.gov/the-press-office/2015/03/23/remarks-president-white-house-science-fair.

Tsurusaki, B. K., Calabrese Barton, A., Tan, E., Koch, P., & Contento, I. (2013). Using transformative boundary objects to create critical engagement in science: A case study. *Science Education, 97* (1), 1-31.

U.S. Census Bureau. (2017). National Population Projections Tables. Retrieved from https://www.census.gov/data/tables/2017/demo/popproj/2017-summary-tables.html.

Wlodkowski, R. J. & Ginsberg, M. B. (2009). *Diversity and motivation: Culturally responsive pedagogy*. San Francisco, CA: Jossey-Bass.

Young, M. (1971). *Knowledge and control: New directions for the sociology of education*. London, England: Collier-Macmillan.

FIFTEEN

 Visionary and Social Justice Leaders: Leading by Example in Educational Environments

Detra D. Johnson

Vision is the art of seeing the invisible.
— Jonathan Swift

A child cannot be taught by anyone who despises him, and a child cannot afford to be fooled.
— John Baldwin

In all things that are purely social we can be as separate as the fingers, yet one as the hand in all things essential to mutual progress.
— Booker T. Washington

THIS CHAPTER FOCUSES ON THREE components: visionary leadership, social justice leadership, and the considerations of visionary leaders as social justice practitioners. Contemporary school leaders continuously grapple with strategies in hopes of affirming equitable social and academic outcomes for all students in diverse learning environments. School leaders and administrators exhibit various leadership styles and practices in educational environments. However, research has not identified a particular style that works best for all students. School administrators' leadership style and practices have long been a focus of educational research due to issues of state and federal accountability collective with policy initiatives that provide the foundations for organizational effectiveness (Hallinger & Heck, 1998).

Responsiveness to diversity, particularly social justice responsiveness, has become increasingly relevant for leaders interested in understanding how they influence and maintain organizational identity and a school image in working with a diverse group of participants. To become responsive social justice leaders, school administrators and leaders must begin to lead proactively. Their practices as social justice leaders require them to forecast into the future; therefore, they must become visionary leaders who employ social justice practices.

Research has considered the impact of diversity and school leadership practices in urban and suburban educational settings dominated by students of color (Andrews & Morefield, 1991; Gutierrez & Rogoff, 2003). Nonetheless increasing pressure to improve student achievement and to eliminate racial and academic inequities in these contexts, it becomes important for principals to understand teachers' perceptions about their principals' leadership practices (Thomas, 2008).

DeMatthews and Mawhinney (2104) share that "school leaders with social justice orientations investigate, make issue of, and generate solutions to social inequality and marginalization due to race, class, gender, disability, sexual orientation, and other forms of diversity" (Dantley & Tillman, 2006; Theoharis, 2007, pp. 845–846). In research, social scientists respond to the call for an understanding of the relationship between culture and educational outcomes with regards to the value of culturally responsive pedagogy for African American students (Banks & Banks, 2004; Ladson-Billings, 1994). Ideally, the research on issues in leadership should make contributions to the organized knowledge in education and should lead to solving new problems to further research (Ary, Jacobs & Razavieh, 1996; Kerlinger, 1977). Brickson (2000) believes that when a leader creates a relational orientation, individuals are motivated to ensure the benefit of others through social justice and visionary leadership. An effective visionary leader understands the need to guide their campus members and supports behaviors of social justice and change while challenging individuals to reach higher goals beyond the status quo.

Continuing with the purpose of this chapter, social justice practices for educational leaders mean that by pursuing educational policies, best practices, and school politics that enhance social and academic opportunities for all students are necessary strategies for visionary leaders. This chapter makes three key contributions to contemporary literature. First, this chapter defines visionary leadership in the context of diverse educational environments and the implications of visionary leadership. It offers social justice perspectives based on historical inequities of academics and social opportunities for marginalized students. Finally, this chapter presents equitable practices that social justice and visionary leaders should provide as support for the success of all learners.

Visionary Leaders

Visionary leadership can be defined as a leader who facilitates multifaceted processes that involve strategic planning that could increase their organization's likelihood of obtaining success. According to Northouse (2015), leaders must be able to exemplify his/her actions and goals through his/her vision by being able to "walk the walk" not just being able to "talk the talk" (p. 137). Oftentimes, leaders can see the vision that they may want for their schools. However, they are not always able to implement or model the ideas that are needed to help others develop the capacity to compel others to move forward and achieve the goals that have been articulated.

Sashkin (1988) discussed the role of a principal as an organizational leader and a visionary leader. In order to be a visionary leader, the principal must be adaptable, push to achieve goals, and push for internal coordination, as well as maintain the culture. To put their vision into action, the principal must implement the vision organizationally and through personal practice, as well as creating a cultural ideal. Yoeli and Berkovich (2010) found that leaders' personal and organizational visions were not separated. Personal experience played a vital role in personal ethos, which was found to be a key element in their visions. Identity, professional experience, family, and culture were all identified as important elements in personal ethos, as well.

Brown and Anfara (2003) identified three stages that were indicated: the initiation, the implementation, and the institutionalization stage. For initiation, the "three Es" (exploration, education, and edification) were also identified by participants as supports to the needs of a visionary leader. Exploration involves having the courage to change, planning to involve others, and being open to explore. Education can be and is not inclusive of enhancing teachers' content and pedagogic knowledge, providing sufficient time and other resources and promoting collegiality and collaboration in professional development opportunities (Guskey, 2003). Edification involves providing support and building trust and consensus.

Creating a vision involves being concerned about all students and remaining focused on what the purpose of schools is about. Visionary leaders must be able to articulate and incorporate their own personal vision while observing what other visionary leaders are doing as well to ensure that all students have equitable opportunities. Equally, that leaders garner the collaboration and respect needed to support the vision and mission of meeting the needs of all students is important. Visionary leaders' behaviors and leadership practices are also important when transforming others. Behaviors and leadership may include clear leadership (being specific and intentional), communicative leadership (listening, providing and receiving feedback), consistent leadership (remaining persistent and dependable over time), caring leadership (displaying respect and concern), and creative leadership (developing opportunities and taking risks; Mora-Whitehurst, 2013). By empowering others, visionary school leaders can meet any challenges or resistance that they might face while inspiring and modeling for others to positively contribute to society.

Educational leadership has been described as "the ability to inspire, to galvanize, to mobilize, and to help bring a critical mass of people together and then the ability to sustain that level of energy and commitment toward a common and well-defined goal" (Sanders-Lawson, Smith-Campbell, & Benham, 2006). Consequently, this educational leadership definition can also describe the practices of a visionary leader. Visionary leaders must be able to articulate through their practices and actions a philosophy of equitable teaching and learning for all stakeholders.

Briggs, Davis, and Cheney (2012) position that the success of an organization, and in particular schools, is dependent on the role that leadership plays. Visionary leaders make a commitment to the education of every student, have confidence that all students can learn, and exhibit compassion and passion for and understanding of all students, especially in the communities in which the students reside (Sanders-Lawson et al., 2006). When describing an ecosystemic leader, the practices and systems change thinking identified by Jones and Nichols (2013) mirrors visionary leadership practices. The practices the authors shared were

1. understanding of their own cultural-historical background,
2. understanding who they are as educators and who they represent as this concerns a vision for their own personal and professional development as well as others,
3. being clear about their expectations and the impact they hope to have as a public servant in their educational settings,

4. understanding the significance of being culturally competent from a personal and professional standpoint and what this means for the individuals and groups that they expect to lead,
5. understanding the cultural history of the education settings that they lead,
6. and having a clear understanding of the legacy they hope to leave behind as this concerns the beliefs and vision that they hold toward education. (Jones & Nichols, 2013, p. 123)

As visionaries, leaders are expected to have a thorough understanding of the context in which they have been charged to lead and what type of legacy that they plan to leave. Visionary leaders must also understand the necessity to establish relationships of trust with all the stakeholders in their educational settings. By establishing trust, leaders are able to receive the support they need to implement the changes that have been communicated in the vision, plans, and goals for the school.

Social Justice Leaders

Literature research indicated that there are limited constructive or real-life examples or descriptions of social justice leadership. Models and descriptions for social justice leadership are critical for providing equity and justice models for the educational leader's agendas and real-life practices. Theoharis (2008) indicated that there is a significant gap in the literature and that future work is needed to extend beyond the characteristics and traits of leadership of social justice leaders. This lack or gap in real-life constructs or models is significant in identifying who are social justice leaders and what kinds of work are done in our educational environments to support both visionary and social justice leadership. Understanding that in a society that is socially just resources are equitably distributed so that all stakeholders economically, socially, physically, and psychologically benefit is crucial.

The definition of social justice leadership includes Gewirtz's (1998) explanation that it is a response to interrupting and undermining the status quo that promotes the exclusion and marginalization of people. Bogotch (2002) expressed that social justice is a social construct where "there are no fixed or predictable meanings of social justice prior to actually engaging in educational leadership practices" (p. 153). In addition, Marshall and Ward (2004) describe social justice as "ensuring that laws for individual rights are observed so that access to educational services is available . . . social justice can mean finding was to 'fix' those with inequitable access" (p. 534). According to Theoharis (2007), principals who lead, advocate, and prioritize their vision improve issues and practices of gender, race, class, disability, sexual orientation, and any marginalized conditions. Goldfarb and Grinberg (2002) examine social justice leadership as "the exercise of altering these [inequitable] arrangements by actively engaging in reclaiming, appropriating, sustaining, and advancing inherent human rights of equity, equality, and fairness in social, economic, educational, and personal dimensions" (p. 162). In some instances, *equity* and *equality* are used synonymously. However, the implicit understanding of equity and equality have varying benefits for those diverse groups explicitly impacted by what is considered fair or the same.

Accordingly, Jencks (1988) designates five general views that society identifies as equal opportunities in education based on the application of equality. The views are democratic equality, moralistic justice, weak humane justice, strong humane justice, and utilitarianism (Jencks, 1988). First, democratic equality states that, regardless of need, every student is given equal resources. Second, moralistic justice states that those students that exhibit the most efforts are rewarded whereas those that do not exhibit effort are punished. Third, weak humane justice states that students from uncontrolled circumstances such as genetic disabilities are not supported as well as those from controlled circumstances, such as disadvantaged homes or personal experiences. Fourth, strong humane justice states that any students that have been marginalized, including students with disabilities are supported. Fifth, utilitarianism states that everyone is held to the same standard and is supported based on their performance. These general views definitely remain situated with some as the status quo without considerations for change. Furthermore, the views identified earlier indicate the misunderstanding of the core value of inclusion. Inclusion, equity, and social justice are views that can be closely identified as related constructs. The definition of inclusion, particularly in education, is considered as a process that concentrates on absolute practices, advocates for the participation of all, and accentuates the necessity of access, achievement, and participation of all students (Ryan, 2012).

Social justice leaders advocate for positive change while moving others toward a set of goals or a vision that addresses core values. Each of the definitions of social justice and social justice leadership implies that there is a true need to know who participates (and to what extent) as real-life social justice leaders, what are the characteristics or traits of such leaders, and what motivates these social justice leaders to do the work that they do. Therefore, part of the process of understanding and defining socially just leaders is to think about how individual philosophical principles are articulated through both explicit and implicit practices and actions, particularly in educational settings.

Khalil and Brown (2015) reported that respondents demonstrated the 3 Cs—cultural competency, communication skills, and commitment as social justice leaders. Cultural competency includes things such as cultural awareness and understanding, as well as experience. Communication skills were important, specifically those that are able to connect teaching to learning. The commitment was identified as attributes specific to serving the community and the students of the school district. Moving others evokes challenges of commitment for worthwhile causes. Implementing well-intended work to strategically navigate the initiatives of goals and visions for equitable and social justice practices requires specific skill sets that draw on internal and external supports that can circumvent barriers and challenges (Macpherson, 2016).

In comparison, Theoharis's study (2008) revealed that "social justice principals" had common leadership traits. These traits included arrogant humility, passionate visionary leadership, and tenacious commitment to justice (Theoharis, 2008). Arrogant humility was considered as a headstrong belief that as leaders they know what was best, that they were right, and that they could lead others toward the vision while willing to admit their mistakes both privately and publicly to challenge discrimination (Theoharis, 2008).

On the other hand, Karpinski and Lugg (2006) indicated that social justice leaders should implement and enforce educational policies that support the academic and social success of all children. Educational policies could include professional development for administrators and teachers focused on equity issues of class, disability, gender, language, race, religion, and sexual orientation (Karpinski & Lugg, 2006). The authors suggested professional development training that demonstrates social justice in curriculum, scheduling, staffing, daily school operation, community engagement, and extracurricular activities (Karpinski & Lugg, 2006).

While sustaining and advocating a strong vision for schools, passionate visionary leaders are caring, are committed, and are enthusiastic about changing people's values, beliefs, and moral purposes of social justice (Theoharis, 2008). Sustaining a tenacious commitment and focus on justice and equitable opportunities for all stakeholders while working to fighting against resistance and unjust norms to meet all students' needs has been identified as a trait of a social justice leader (Theoharis, 2008). These practices and traits seem to be synonymous with school leaders who are extremely driven from a social justice point of view.

In comparison, the ability to proactively understand, think, and respond to challenges and resistance that individuals face becomes a consistent practice and is an underlying trait of a social justice leader. According to Sanders-Lawson et al. (2006), school leaders command respect that can address challenges and resistance by explicitly communicating with others their mission to create culturally appropriate and socially just educational environments. Berkovich (2013) described potential social justice challenges as the promotion of the academic and social growth of all students in our schools (Carlisle, Jackson & George, 2006); the segregation and exclusion of the disempowered and disadvantaged groups of students of color, students from low socioeconomic status, English language learners, and students with disabilities (McKenzie et al., 2008); and the development of an educational learning environment that facilitates the acceptance and respect of diversity (Giroux, 1992). Moreover, the mission and vision must be shared with all stakeholders to communicate what the challenges are and what the goals are to eradicating social injustice in schools. Mason (1991) discussed the importance of what the visionary's vision must include, such as detailed, comprehensive, and able to answer the questions of why, what, when, and how. In addition, for visionary educators to be supported by their fellow stakeholders to meet mission and vision goals and expectations is critical. Berkovich shared that Marshall and Oliva (2006) concluded that "the ability of social justice leadership to mend educational injustices lies in its power to mobilize people in support of the goal, and thereby accumulate the required social capital and political power to bring about change" (p. 289).

Visionary and Social Justice Leadership Practitioners

A visionary leader who is also a social justice leader consistently practices a process of sharing social, political, and economic actions that address inequities of marginalized students, particularly students of color, in learning environments. Apple (2010) stated that by applying social justice principles in education, social-economic reality of schools can be transformed. A process that addresses inequities of marginalized students requires specific leadership characteristics or traits inclusive of commitment, compassion, communication, humility, persistence, and collaboration with all stakeholders. Leadership practices and perspectives of understanding and meeting the needs of all students is critical in the success of visionary leaders and their social justice practices. Successful visionary leaders are able to visualize and articulate positive outcomes for the future.

Hence, these leaders should counsel and mentor educators to embrace courage and determination to overcome the inequities in their school environment and in the community. Providing vision and inspiration for all stakeholders is pivotal in establishing permanent practices of social justice leaders. By establishing allies in the community and in the school, visionary and social justice leaders are able to utilize multiple communication networks that can impact positive change. These allies should be committed to uniting stakeholders for equity across all educational environments. Visionary leaders share a strong and passionate commitment to social justice and change while demonstrating a thoughtful approach to empowering and collaborating with others to meet the goals of the school and its learning environment. Furthermore, visionary and social justice leaders should exploit community relationships and partnerships to strategically focus on the conservative values of the community that may contradict social justice (Berkovich, 2013). Contrary to others, visionary leaders must be authentic in their views while actively listening to others and when presenting their vision, should be comprehensive, detailed, and inspiring while going beyond the ordinary views of thinking (Mason, 1991).

Both visionary and social justice leaders understand that social justice can be interpreted in various ways. Hence, this type of leader consistently creates and envisions socially just learning environments. Consequently, the interpretation from school leaders must be clearly articulated to reflect both social and economic conditions of any marginalized groups of students that can impact student achievement and school improvement. Nevertheless, the long-lasting hierarchical power struggles of race, class, education, and gender that are still prevalent must be acknowledged and addressed in the everyday practices of visionary and social justice leaders. Visionary school leaders will need to be more aware of and consistently work to eradicate social injustice to promote social justice leadership. Marshall and Ward (2004) argued that social justice leaders need space and time to facilitate the shifts in societal and cultural understandings of school expectations as a call for action of building political power and social capital of marginalized people.

Visionary leaders are the role models for the stakeholders in their school environments. These leaders should be able to effectively articulate and communicate the goals and vision of their campus to ensure success and empowerment for everyone. Berkowitz (2011) stated that school leaders should create learning environments where "all stakeholders treat each other fairly and make ethical decisions" (p. 93). Also, visionary leaders should be social justice leaders whose primary goals are to be proactive in their responses to provide equitable opportunities for students and teachers on their campuses. As an example, visionary leaders who practice ethical leadership focus on human relations and are viewed as caring, honest, and principled persons who balance decisions fairly while promoting values such as inclusion, social justice, and collaboration for all students, especially those who are disadvantaged or marginalized (Ehrich, Harris, Klenowski, Smeed & Spina, 2016).

Modeling social justice and visionary leadership requires leaders to make socially responsible decisions, show a concern for social justice, and articulate to the entire staff the vision and goals of the school. School leaders are presented with challenges and adversities that could be considered as obstacles to making social justice a priority for learning environments. DeMatthews and Mawhinney (2014) report that evidence shows that even though school leaders' challenges contribute to the resistance of addressing inequities in schools, some schools have been effective and successful in managing challenges. These school leaders encounter conflicts and barriers in their daily professional lives while navigating shifting and conflicting perspectives in complex educational situations. Sapon-Shevin (2011) described these possible barriers as follows:

1. There is too much to do; administrators are overloaded with managerial and documentation requirements to make social justice a focus.
2. Addressing issues of social justice within the school, including racism, homophobia, classism, poverty, violence, and immigration issues, for example, will be controversial and will divert time and attention from other pressing concerns.
3. Many administrators have received neither training nor support for taking on these issues in their schools. Although they may believe they are important, it is difficult and overwhelming to address all that is included in such a directive. (p. 150)

Similarly, Berkovich (2013) described five barriers to intra-institutional activism in educational settings. The barriers are described as (1) ethical commitment to uphold rules, (2) hindering policies, (3) traditional community values, (4) convergence of multiple socioeconomic challenges, and (5) contradictory social justice goals (p. 290). Likewise, Berkovich (2013) proposed that intra-institutional activism in schools including traditions, rules, the merging of socioeconomic issues and impeding policies are barriers that hinder school leaders' efforts and contradict the goals of social justice leaders.

In comparison, Macpherson's (2016) research found that other barriers to ethical and social justice leaders include the perceived lack of social justice value; deficit thinking among educators; resistance from stakeholders such as parents, faculty, staff, and central administration; a lack of knowledge concerning equity issues; inequitable hiring practices and retention; personal stress and fatigue; and politics and policies guiding administrative decisions. Visionary leaders must be able to identify potential barriers and proactively place safeguards to address issues when they arrive. In other words, they should always have a plan of action to be able to deal with situations.

Visionary leaders should practice social justice strategies just as social justice leaders should practice visionary leadership. The practices of a visionary and social justice leader should be driven by the ongoing and imbalanced educational disparities. The success of strategic practices is dependent on a leader's ability to create mutual understandings of equity concerns while mobilizing stakeholders to collaborate to meet the needs of all students (Macpherson, 2016). The efforts to disengage unjust practices should be modeled and articulated through every action of a school leader whose goal is to eliminate inequities in their educational learning environments.

As previously stated, this chapter offered three key contributions to contemporary literature. To begin, this chapter defined visionary leadership in the context of diverse educational environments and the implications of visionary leadership. Next, it offered social justice perspectives based on historical inequities of academics and social opportunities for marginalized students. To end, this chapter presented equitable practices that social justice and visionary leaders should employ to support success for all learners.

References

Andrews, R. L., & Morefield, J. (1991). Effective leadership for effective urban schools. *Education and Urban Society, 23*, 270–280.

Apple. M. W. (2010). *Global crises, social justice, and education.* New York, NY: Routledge.

Ary, D., Jacobs, L. C., & Razavieh, A. (1996). *Introduction to research in education* (5th ed.). New York, NY: Harcourt Brace.

Banks, J. A., & Banks, C. M. (2004). *Handbook of research on multicultural education* (2nd ed.). San Francisco, CA: Jossey-Bass.

Berkovich, I. (2013). A socio-ecological framework of social justice leadership in education. *Journal of Educational Administration, 52*, 282–309.

Berkowitz, M. W. (2011). Leading schools of character. In A. M. Blankstein & P. D. Houston (Eds.). *Leadership for social justice and democracy in our schools* (pp. 93–121). Thousand Oaks, CA: Sage.

Bogotch, I. (2002). Educational leadership and social justice: Practice into theory. *Journal of School Leadership, 12*, 138–156.

Brickson, S. (2000). The impact of identity orientation on individual and organizational outcomes in demographically diverse settings *The Academy of Management Review, 25*, 82–101.

Briggs, K., Davis, J., & Cheney, G. R. (2012). Teacher effectiveness, yes. But what about principals? *Education Week, 31*(30), 28–36.

Brown, K. M., & Anfara, V. A. (2003). Paving the way for change: Visionary leadership in action at the middle level. *NASSP Bulletin, 87*(635), 16–34.

Carlisle, L. R., Jackson, B. W., & George, A. (2006). Principles of social justice education: The social justice education in school project. *Equity and Excellence in Education, 39*(1), 55–64.

Dantley, M. E., & Tillman, L. C. (2006). Social justice and moral transformative leadership. In C. Marshall & M. Oliva (Eds.), *Leadership for social justice: Making revolutions in education* (pp. 16–30). Boston, MA: Allyn & Bacon.

DeMatthews, D., & Mawhinney, H. (2014). Social justice leadership and inclusion: Exploring challenges in an urban district to address inequities. *Educational Administration Quarterly, 50*, 844–881.

Ehrich, L. C., Harris, J., Klenowski, V., Smeed, J., & Spina, N. (2016). The centrality of ethical leadership. *Journal of Educational Administration 53*(2), 197–214.

Gewirtz, S. (1998). Conceptualizing social justice in education: Mapping the territory. *Journal of Education Policy, 13*, 469–484.

Giroux, H. (1992). *Border crossing: Cultural workers and the politics of education*. New York, NY: Routledge.

Goldfarb, K., & Grinberg, J. (2002). Leadership for social justice: Authentic participation in the case of a community center in Caracas, Venezuela. *Journal of School Leadership, 12.* 10.1177/105268460201200204.

Guskey, T. R. (2003). Analyzing lists of the characteristics of effective professional development to promote visionary leadership. *NASSP Bulletini, 87*(637), 4–20.

Gutierrez, K. D., & Rogoff, B. (2003). Cultural ways of learning: Individual traits or repertoires of practices. *Educational Researcher, 32*(5), 19–25.

Hallinger, P., & Heck, R.H. (1998). Exploring the principal's contribution to school effectiveness. *School Effectiveness and School Improvement, 9*, 157–192.

Jencks, C. (1988). Whom must we treat equally for educational opportunity to be equal?. *Ethics, 98*(3), 518–533.

Jones, B. A., & Nichols, E. J. (2013). *Cultural competence in America's schools: Leadership, engagement and understanding.* Charlotte, NC: IAP.

Karpinski, C. F. & Lugg, C. A. (2006). Social justice and educational administration: mutually exclusive? *Journal of Educational Administration, 44*, 278–282.

Kerlinger, F. N. (1977). *Foundations of behavioral research.* New York, NY: Holt, Rinehart & Winston.

Khalil, D., & Brown, E. (2015). Enacting a social justice leadership framework: The 3 C's of urban teacher quality. *Journal of Urban Learning, Teaching, and Research, 11*, 77–90.

Ladson-Billings, G. (1994). *The dreamkeepers: Successful teachers of African American children*. San Francisco, CA: Jossey-Bass.

Leadership for social justice: Authentic participation is the case of a community center in Caracas, Venezuela. *Journal of School Leadership, 12*, 157–173.

Macpherson, J. E. (2016). *Leading for equity: Principals' strategies* (Doctoral thesis). Available from ProQuest Dissertations and Theses database. (UMI No. 10139208)

Marshall, C. & Oliva, M. (2006). Building capacities of social justice leaders. In C. Marshall & M. Oliva (Eds.). *Leadership for social justice: Making revolutions in education* (pp. 1–15). Boston, MA: Person.

Marshall, C., & Ward, M. (2004). "Yes, but . . .": Education leaders discuss social justice. *Journal of School Leadership, 14*, 530–563.

Mason, R. C. (1991). Positive, visionary leadership: An organization's most successful component. *Adult Learning, 3*(3), 7–13.

McKenzie, K. B., Christman, D. E., Hernandez, F., Fierro, E., Capper, C. A., Dantley, M., Scheurich, J. J. (2008). From the field: A proposal for educating leaders for social justice. *Educational Administration Quarterly, 44*, 111–138.

Mora-Whitehurst, R. (2013). The relationship between elementary principals' visionary leadership and students' reading performance. *The Educational Forum, 77*, 315–328.

Northouse, P. G. (2015). *Introduction to leadership: Concepts and practice* (3rd ed.). Los Angeles, CA: Sage.

Ryan, J. (2012). *Struggling for inclusion*. Charlotte, NC: Information Age.

Sanders-Lawson, R., Smith-Campbell, S., & Benham, M. K. (2006). Wholistic visioning for social justice: Black women theorizing practice. *Leadership for social justice: Making revolutions in education* (pp. 31–63).

Sapon-Shevin, M. (2011). Zero indifference for diversity, inclusion, and justice. In A. M. Blankstein & P. D. Houston (Eds.). *Leadership for social justice and democracy in our schools* (pp. 145–168). Thousand Oaks, CA: Sage.

Sashkin, M. (1988). The visionary principal: School leadership for the next century. *Education and Urban Society, 20*, 239–249.

Theoharis, G. (2007). Social justice educational leaders and resistance: Toward a theory of social justice leadership. *Educational Administration Quarterly, 43*, 228-251.

Theoharis, G. (2008). Woven in deeply identity and leadership of urban social justice principals. *Education and Urban Society, 41*, 3-25.

Yoeli, R., & Berkovich, I. (2010). From personal ethos to organizational vision: Narratives of visionary educational leaders. *Journal of Educational Administration, 48*, 451-467.

SIXTEEN

 The Dimensions of a
Departmentalized Literacy
Classroom Infused with Culturally
Relevant/Responsive Practices: Its
Impact on African American Second-
Grade Reading Achievement

Katina L. Thomas

AFRICAN AMERICAN STUDENTS CONTINUE TO lag behind their White peers despite efforts to create quality learning environments that benefit all students. Researchers have studied factors that are believed to be influencers of African-American reading performance, such as poverty (Cole-Henderson, 2000; Halle, Kurtz-Costes & Mahoney, 1997), low teacher expectation (Ferguson, 2003), and differences in parental involvement according to gender (Graves, 2008). This performance deficit, known as the Black–White achievement gap, has remained consistent for over two decades. In spite of trends in research correlating low socioeconomic status with academic achievement, the Black–White achievement gap also exists in reading, math, and science by third grade for African American students that are receiving an education in private schools (Simms, 2012). In 1992, Black fourth graders were achieving an average of 32 points lower on standardized reading assessments than White fourth graders, and it narrowed to 26 points by 2015 (National Center for Education Statistics [NCES], 2017). Cultural linguistic differences, poverty, educational expectations, and assessment practices have all been identified as variables that may have a significant impact on educational outcomes for African American children (Washington, 2001). Despite research findings, the most common variable that exists amongst all of these research findings is culture.

Cultural responsive instruction—teaching that allows students to succeed academically by building on background knowledge and experiences gained in the home and community (Au, 2009)—is being implemented to bridge the gap between the student and curriculum for non-White students; however, it has yet to bridge the Black–White achievement gap that has remained stagnant since the 20th century. Culturally responsiveness is very necessary, especially in our schools in which students are becoming more culturally and linguistically diverse; however, tools for developing additional understanding is needed to foster lasting achievement throughout a student's educational journey. Enter Ladson-Billings's (1995) theoretical model, known as *culturally relevant pedagogy*, that not only addresses student achievement but also affirms students' identities while developing critical perspectives that challenge inequities in schools. Both are effective; however, one is needed to achieve the other. Cultural responsiveness builds a bridge between their reality and the reality that is in their texts; however, culturally relevant pedagogy creates a platform for students to use their reality to challenge the status quo in their texts for a deeper understanding and change. As culturally responsive literacy instruction becomes more prevalent in 21st-century classrooms, attention must also be given to how cultural pedagogy intersects with literacy education within a nontraditional class schedule. Over the last 60 years, more schools have abandoned a traditional schedule of 45 to 55 minutes of instruction for a departmentalized schedule. The departmentalized schedule, also known as a block schedule, extends instructional time between 85 to 100 minutes (Jenkins, Queen & Algozzine, 2002) and allows for more uninterrupted activities and content coverage for a single subject. This is found to be a common occurrence in middle and high schools, where one subject is taught by different teachers throughout the instructional day. On the elementary level, instruction of fewer subjects is taught for longer blocks to a group of students by one teacher during one portion of the day, and the remaining subjects are also taught for longer periods by another teacher during the remainder of the instructional day. Departmentalized instruction was originally developed to assist students between Grades 4 to 6 who were transitioning to middle school (Lamme, 1976); however, departmentalization has begun to occur as young as kindergarten (Chang, Munoz & Koshewa, 2008).

In terms of literacy, research on culturally driven instructional practices that have been implemented to build cultural competence (Harris & Graves, 2012), reading interest (Tatum, 2006), and comprehension strategies (May, 2011) primarily target African American males in upper elementary and secondary grades in hopes of building motivation and comprehension to close the reading achievement gaps after foundational reading skills have been developed. Consequently, the reading achievement gap is found to be wider when a child is African American *and* male; however, African American females also constitute the lower achievement in the Black–White gap, scoring lower than their White peers in 4th, 8th, and 12th grades.

Adding cultural relevant dimensions to literacy creates a layered approach to teaching reading that alters the framework of instruction. Limited research reveals the impact of culturally relevant pedagogy during early literacy and its impact on reading achievement for African American students prior to a state-mandated reading assessment. If the amount of daily instructional time serves as an additional variable that has an impact on reading growth also remains unclear. The purpose of this study was to research the impact of a core reading program integrated with culturally relevant practices affected the reading assessments of African American second graders on a departmentalized schedule. The trends of African American second graders receiving departmentalized literacy instruction were examined, and classroom practices were analyzed to determine the impact that integrating culturally relevant and responsive practices into early literacy instruction have on the reading achievement of African American second graders that receive instruction in a departmentalized environment.

This is also a closer look at how Ladson-Billing's (1995) criteria for culturally relevant pedagogy has an impact our African American readers *before* the foundation of literacy skills is solidified. Developmentally, second grade is the beginning of a transitional stage in reading in which students are mastering phonemic awareness, have expected to have acquired a large majority of their sight word knowledge, and are beginning to evolve with written communication. For those who struggle with one or more of these foundational skills, receiving intervention methods that are teacher-centered and repetitious in nature—especially during early literacy development—is not uncommon. This quasi-experimental initiative was implemented with the hope of introducing an alternative approach to assist African American students at an earlier age while allowing them chances to maintain control over their own learning and thinking through culturally relevant pedagogical standards and responsive practices.

Framing Culturally Relevant Dimensions

Theoretically, culturally relevant pedagogy helps students become (a) academically successful, (b) culturally competent, and (c) socio-politically critical. A culturally relevant teacher consciously creates social interactions to help them meet these criteria (Ladson-Billings, 1995). These criteria serve as a triumvirate of components that allows a teacher or observer to determine if culturally relevance is existent in the instructional environment. It also serves as an evaluation tool to determine if current educational habits need rewiring to more successfully reach our growing number of culturally and linguistically diverse students. In many educational systems, policies, procedures, and practices need to be reconceptualized to ensure equitable opportunity and access for all students (Sullivan & A'Vant, 2009).

Adding cultural dimensions to existing literacy instruction involves transforming a flat, linear model for teaching that involves the teacher facilitating to the student, to a multidimensional model that involves an ongoing exchange of thoughts, ideas, and perspectives of texts based on the student's background and from the student's point of view. Facilitation still occurs; however, it is in the form of guiding students through analyses to comprehension from their view of the world. Cultural relevant pedagogy must provide a way for students to maintain their cultural integrity while succeeding academically (Ladson-Billings, 1995). The need for culturally relevant pedagogy has been established; however, it is still considered a supplement for core reading programs instead of a foundational component that can bridge the gap between reader and text. Students need to be provided with more accurate cultural information about groups of color to fill knowledge voids and correct existing distortions. This information needs to be capable of facilitating many different kinds of learning—cognitive, affective, social, political, personal, and moral (Gay, 2010).

The dimensions, or layers, of this particular departmentalized classroom are aligned with the components of effective teaching: (a) planning, (b) implementation, and (c) assessment (Burden & Byrd, 2016). Every dimension is connected with criteria for culturally relevant pedagogy, and although the dimensions and criteria are fluid, transforming each layer into culturally relevant dimensions that were executed with specific criterion in mind. Thus, the infusion has been conceived.

As a teacher, possessing an understanding of students' origins influences the choice of content and books that will fill the classroom. This consciousness of each student's sociocultural standing grants teachers an opportunity to customize their culturally relevant framework for instruction that will manifest during planning, implementation, and assessment. When educators understand the beliefs, biases, and behaviors of their students, they can make culturally informed decisions about how to make teaching and learning most effective (Chenowith, 2014).

Culturally Relevant Dimensions

Culturally Relevant Dimension 1: Planning for Academic Success

Planning for cultural relevance and responsiveness also relies on the act of building teacher–student relationships and peer relationships. It serves as the foundation for effectively teaching culturally relevant pedagogy. Constructing an environment that welcomes students' voices begins during planning and often occurs in and around a lesson. Reading interest inventories and personal poster projects are effective for gathering data about your students, but interpersonal communication allows everyone to build networks and relationships that will contribute to current and future growth. Effectively building these relationships involves being conscious of two things: (1) the teacher's perception of students and (2) which materials are student-centered and access self-awareness.

Teacher perception. When students are viewed as people first, and a data sample later, it has an impact on interactions with them. Also, being conscious of one's own biases and stereotypes in relation to one's background creates a consciousness as to when prejudgment is altering student expectations prior to their performance. The more inviting and responsive instruction is to children's efforts to improve, the less teachers' initial perception will predict later success (Ferguson, 2003). Cultural awareness of self and others begins with a self-assessment of the amount of cultural relevance that currently occurs to target all students. Teachers must move beyond holidays celebrating cultures to infusing culturally relevant practices in the classroom (Ford, Stuart & Vakil, 2014). Self-evaluating one's perception of their own culture, followed by an evaluation of students' culture using the same criteria, can lower the risk of discounting a student's culture during literacy instruction. All teacher educators must "become multicultural" in perspective to model cultural sensitivity by displaying appropriate attitudes about culturally diverse groups and by using instructional strategies consistent with best practices with culturally diverse students (Plata, Williams & Henley, 2017). Self-evaluation and students' cultural evaluation extends beyond a checklist or survey; it is an ongoing act of accountability that opens the window for cultural pedagogy. According to McVee (2014), a complex exploration of culture involves (1) fostering a discursive view of culture, (2) attending to localized knowledge, and (3) acknowledging and developing empathic stances. Navigating through these practices transforms teachers' perceptions of their students, as well as their approaches during instruction.

Student-centered materials to access self-awareness. Given enough time, teachers can prepare student-centered activities throughout the literacy block that fosters deeper thinking and interaction with the chosen materials. Students essentially need to feel accepted and see reflections of themselves, their lives, and their culture in stories they hear, images they see, and books they read (Kinkead-Clark, 2014). That teachers select literacy materials that are reflective of their students' background to reveal a reflection of themselves and to engage them is recommended (Tatum, 2006; Thomas, 2019); however, this is not always feasible. Viewing text that is written primarily from their background communicates the message that their reality is being embraced as a valuable existence that can be utilized to obtain knowledge and skills for success.

For educators to be limited to materials mandated for use for all students or to be limited by a lack of available resources that contain elements that are relatable to African American learners on a visual level is not uncommon. Many teachers limit themselves to finding multicultural literature in early literacy that acknowledges African American leaders, children, or historical events with the desire to appeal to students. Culture lines exist not only in ethnic or racial groups but also between socioeconomic classes, varying levels of education, domestic or international home environments, rural or urban settings, community service groups or personal causes, and first-generation students to students who come from a long line of college graduates (Blas, 2014). Like all students, African American children are multifaceted people whose interests extend beyond the ethnic existence and into the global community. Although text selections that celebrate should be accessible that celebrates their reality, their self-awareness and reality of who they are holistically should be acknowledged. Finding topics of interest that extend beyond the visual reflection of students can still lead to reading motivation and higher levels of comprehension (Asher, Hymel & Wigfield, 1978).

Culturally Relevant Dimension 2: Instruction to Build Cultural Competence and Sociopolitical Critical Thinking

Implementing the activities that have been specifically planned to build self-awareness often leads to a reinforcement of cultural competence and critical thinking based on the students' interpretation of the literature. Without establishing a starting point of common knowledge, educators cannot build upon a foundation and expect students to learn presented material. A shared foundation could be the educator's knowledge of the students' culture, vice versa, or an understanding of a shared, neutral culture (Blas, 2014). Planning analytical questions that promote empathy and require your students to envision themselves as the focal point of your text selections employs them to express their potential thoughts, feelings, and actions if it were their reality. This type of higher order thinking often fall to the bottom of the list of comprehension questions as "extension questions" because questions to check for understanding often become a priority when teachers introduce texts that are assumed to be unrelatable as a result of their ethnic, racial, or socioeconomic origins. Teachers can carefully analyze the questions used during read-aloud, comprehension, and reading response activities to make sure that there are equal numbers of questions that encourage readers to focus on personal and concrete meanings while reading (Husband, 2012). Analytical questions that are complemented with student-centered peer activities foster discussions that create a safe space for students to connect with texts, build peer relationships academically, and freely voice their feedback without the anxiety of being measured against mainstream biases.

Implementing socially based activities that foster high levels of engagement and problem solving not only develops literacy strategies from your students' perspectives but also challenges them from a cultural, social, and political perspective. Challenging the texts in ways that lead to reformulations and counter texts accommodates all students and provides powerful entry points into full participation (Kesler, 2011). Encouraging students to collaborate with peers in constructing authentic artifacts of work (graphic organizers, discussion webs, and alternate endings) establishes a relationship between the content of the text and the reader. Also, opting for discussion creates an arena for open interpretation of literature that grants students an opportunity to ask questions that challenge assumptions that are subconsciously conveyed by the author. This, in turn, can lead to an attachment to the text, a construct of understanding, and an extension of ideas that can manifest themselves in the form of culturally driven projects that foster community change.

Culturally Relevant Dimension 3: Assessing Reading Achievement

Building cultural competence and sparking socio-political thinking can alter students' perceptions and processing of texts across genres prior to the assessment stage. Some form of standardized assessment is expected that limits the teacher to a script and quantitative data on a test report. These formal assessments are snapshots, traditionally measure general performance on specific literacy skills, and they often overlook cultural factors. Informal measures of cultural literacy mirror traditional measures of literacy that check for comprehension. However, daily and weekly assessment in relation to cultural competence can be measured using authentic student work created during lesson implementation and reflective of the materials introduced. Comprehension of these materials could be assessed by asking students to decipher or interpret culturally encoded messages and convert them from one expressive form to another, such as from poetry to explanatory essays and from narrative autobiography to conversational dialogue (Gay, 2010). Offering feedback, either in verbal or written form, following writing assignments, collaborative projects, discussions, or even weekly tests assesses their understanding of the culturally relevant content, but also of their application of the specific literacy skills necessary to demonstrate growth and mastery. Additionally, skills that are developed in social settings should also be assessed socially. Including opportunities for activities, games, and learning centers that provide additional practice outside of formal instruction establishes ownership over learning and a purpose for applying literacy beyond structured learning expectations.

The Departmentalized Component

Examining the impact of literacy during a nontraditional schedule forces us to take a closer look at *how* students are being taught to read as opposed to *if* it is occurring. More often than not, in the traditional self-contained elementary classroom, the homeroom teacher is burdened with teaching every core subject within a particular allotment of time and at a pace that is mandated district and/or state level. Differentiating instruction becomes more of a desire, and less of a reality when there is a race against the clock to teach a 45- to 55-minute lesson from beginning to end. This framework is based on the assumption that an elementary school teacher is a Jack- (or Jill-) of-all-trades who is equally strong in all areas of the elementary curriculum (Chan & Jarman, 2004). Unfortunately, this is not always the case, and with this assumption, teachers are left with the responsibility of using a limited timeframe to mold a student into a stellar individual who performs at a level of mastery in every area of the curriculum and can socially function in society. As daunting as the task may seem, many elementary teachers can accept and overcome this challenge but not without sacrificing in some area of their personal or professional lives.

As greater numbers of students from varying backgrounds are expected to master challenging standards, the amount of learning required of all students is becoming constant (Rettig & Canady, 2003). Expecting teachers to utilize a myriad of approaches to target diverse learners within a brief window of time is a nearly insurmountable task. Differentiation to target all students during their years of early literacy development is labor-intensive and time-consuming; however, the windows of time allotted for this to occur are still being addressed and are something experimental for young students. This is, in part, to the fear of creating a social development deficit for young learners during a time in their school career when interpersonal communication skills and social norms are a part of daily student development. However, if viewed from a varying standpoint, normalizing departmentalized scheduling during lower elementary creates an environment that supports social and academic growth. It increases the ability to meet the needs of individual students, as well as increasing students' motivation toward exploration and discovery in their classes (Queen & Gaskey, 1997).

Departmentalization is not a new innovation to school systems; however, it is still viewed as more suitable for older students. Elementary school principals must address major issues related to scheduling, which include, but are not limited to, quality time for teaching and learning, class size, and varied learning time for students who learn at different rates (Canady & Rettig, 2001). These issues plague secondary administrators as well, however high schools that have implemented this style of scheduling have reported more student having more interactions with teachers and earned better grades and more opportunities for teachers to experiment with new teaching strategies (Evans, Tokarczyk, Rice & McCray, 2002; Gullatt, 2006; Zepeda & Mayers, 2006). What educational stakeholders must realize is that, like most instructional methods and approaches, departmentalization at a younger age can be crafted to meet students' developmental needs, both academically and socially. Elementary instructional scheduling continues to evolve, and as a result, we are gradually approaching the inevitable—departmentalized instruction on every elementary grade level. By 2003 to 2004, daily English instruction in Grades 1 through 4 has increased by 36 minutes since 1987 to 1988, yielding about two additional weeks of English within a school year (Morton & Dalton, 2007). Having more instructional time for literacy grants more time to meet criteria for culturally relevant pedagogical practices that are socially based and stimulate higher order thinking for marginalized students.

Exploring departmentalized scheduling in the primary grades (kindergarten to second grade) addresses three areas of concern: (a) providing quality time, (b) creating a school climate, and (c) providing varying learning time (Canady & Rettig, 1995). Allowing time for exploration of new and existing reading skills, extending time for practice, and implementing more student-led activities increases the chance for mastery and critical thinking. Culturally relevant practices and departmentalized scheduling complement each other, and introducing this infused approach during the years when foundational literacy is being established can lead to reduced gaps in reading achievement by fourth grade and beyond.

The Introduction of Culturally Relevant and Responsive Literacy into Departmentalized Early Literacy

To examine how these culturally relevant/responsive dimensions impacted early reading for African American students, a quasi-experimental method was used to conduct an ex post facto study of data. Archival data were examined for the reading achievement of the second-grade students on the Developmental Reading Assessment (DRA) to investigate the effects of culturally responsive and instructional techniques in a departmentalized setting. A pretest/posttest design was to compare student comprehension levels from the first administration of the test to the last administration of the test and to determine progress.

This particular elementary campus in a school district in Texas had an enrollment of 780 students in grades prekindergarten through fourth grade. It had been identified as a Title I campus, and 78% of the students were considered economically disadvantaged. There was no bilingual program; however, 24% of the students whose primary language spoken at home was not English were identified as Limited English Proficient (LEP).

There was an average class size of 25 students within each second-grade classroom with a total of 150 students enrolled. Four of the classrooms participated in a departmentalized structure, and the remaining three participated in a traditional self-contained structure. Classrooms that were classified as departmentalized were predetermined by the principal. Of the students enrolled, the results of 22 were closely examined.

Student placement within a classroom was predetermined by first-grade teachers and finalized by administrators on the campus at the end of the previous school year. Students previously identified as struggling in reading and mathematics by their first-grade teachers were clustered together into the same departmentalized homeroom. Strugglers were identified by their academic performance on first-grade reading and math benchmarks, as well as their report card grades from the previous year. The students that were identified as African American and received departmentalized culturally relevant and responsive literacy instruction were studied.

Because this is an ex post facto study of archival data, I served as one of the participating teachers. The second-grade teachers all had bachelor's degrees, and I had a postbaccalaureate degree in the field of education. All the participating teachers also had work experience that ranged from 2 to 12 years. Four of the teachers were categorized by the Texas Education Agency as having one to five years of experience, while three of the teachers were categorized as having 11 to 20 years of experience. All seven teachers possessed standard Texas teaching certificates, six of the teachers were certified in Texas to teach students identified as LEP, and four of the teachers were certified to accommodate students identified as Gifted and Talented (GT). For this particular analysis, the students selected identified as African American in the departmentalized rotation, and they were tracked for their growth and development when cultural relevance and responsiveness were included in literacy instruction.

Planning for Academic Success

A core reading program using materials from a basal kit was utilized as the foundation for instruction to align each second-grade classroom's instruction with district standards. However, instructional strategies and additional materials were integrated with the core lesson plans to assist students in meeting the culturally relevant criteria and reading benchmark.

Departmentalized classrooms shared daily schedules and lesson plans on a weekly basis. In the departmentalized setting, teachers were responsible for teaching language arts to his or her homeroom in the morning and to their partner teacher's homeroom in the afternoon while their partner teacher followed an identical schedule for teaching math and science. Social studies was taught by each to their own respective homerooms.

Departmentalized literacy classrooms were designed to be print-rich environments. The walls consisted of word walls, alphabet lines, literacy workstations, grammar charts, genre listings, and anchor charts reflective of previously taught lessons and strategies. The reading classrooms were void of any graphic organizers, charts, and strategies that promoted mathematics and science concepts. The teachers were expected to teach a balanced literacy lesson for 120 minutes before lunch to my homeroom and then teach the same lesson for 120 minutes after lunch to their partner teacher's homeroom.

Departmentalized reading teachers followed a scope and sequence of a basal series published by MacMillan/McGraw-Hill and adopted by the district for literacy instruction. The components of the basal series included student reading textbooks, leveled readers, vocabulary word cards, and workbooks with phonics, grammar, spelling, and comprehension strategies that could be copied for student work. The teacher's manuals included lesson plans with weekly word lists based on Donald Bear's *Words Their Way* (Bear, Invernizzi, Templeton & Johnston, 2015) and instructional techniques for LEP students and struggling readers. Lesson plans were written by one teacher and distributed electronically to each teacher responsible for teaching reading.

Because lesson plans were universally written in a format that consisted primarily of a daily list of activities from the core reading program that aligned with the school district's scope and sequence, one teacher included instructional activities that would develop two of the culturally relevant criteria—cultural competence and sociopolitical critical thinking, with the desire of using those skills to meet the third criterion, academic success according to standardized expectations. Teacher–student relationships were initially established through class discussions over reading preferences that were listed on anchor charts and by ensuring that each student was entrusted with a classroom responsibility that reflected their personalities and personal strengths. Throughout the year, additional duties were assigned (restroom duty, classroom library maintenance, classroom materials distribution) to maintain trust in them, regardless of their reading ability. Peer relationships were established through planned classroom discussions that sparked questions, such as "What would you do?" and "How would you feel if you were the main character?" to foster more participation during read-alouds. More time was allotted for partner reading and independent reading. Although the mandated reading kit rarely consisted of characters reflective of them, the classroom library consisted of books of multiple reading levels and reading series that consisted of characters and plots reflective of who they were culturally. Because of this, only 30 minutes was allotted for instruction using the basal series, and the remainder of the time was dedicated to interacting using culturally relevant/responsive materials. Additionally, the schedule also employed small-group reading instruction in which culturally relevant and developmentally appropriate texts were selected to not only close achievement gaps but also reflect students' backgrounds and interests.

Daily Literacy Practices

Balanced literacy was taught in a blocked format for a total of 120 minutes. The balanced literacy block was based on Fountas and Pinnell's Guided Reading Program (Fountas & Pinnell, 1996). Balanced literacy activities consisted of shared reading, read-aloud, small-group lessons, independent work, and workstations. Writing was integrated throughout the balanced literacy block. Lessons began with the teacher facilitating a spelling mini-lesson with the entire class, which included word building, phonics instruction, and word reading. Shared reading and read-aloud included classroom reading, think-alouds, and discussion of text in the student textbooks. One fiction and one nonfiction text were read and discussed over the course of the week.

To build students' cultural competence and sociopolitical thinking of each selection, students were encouraged to engage in think-alouds and text connections during the reading of the selection to bridge the gap between students and the text, as well as establish critical thinking. The text was also used to model a strategy for practicing a literacy skill that was designated in the teacher's manual. The focus strategy was reflective of a second-grade objective listed on the Texas Education Agency's Texas Essential Knowledge and Skills (Texas Essential Knowledge and Skills [TEKS], 2017) expectations. Students also collaborated with a partner to build a graphic chart on construction paper to reinforce the literacy skill and organize their thinking and to discuss and outline their ideas to a critical thinking question that was posed during the read aloud or shared reading. This particular critical thinking question often required them to reflect on the content of the text from their view of the world.

Independently, students would practice the weekly literacy skill using activity sheets provided by the basal series each day. Additional independent assignments included independent reading of a culturally relevant/responsive book of their choice, reader's response of the student-selected reading, and a word-sorting activity reflective of the spelling list for the week.

During collaborative and independent assignments, the teacher pulled three small groups daily and engaged in 20-minute lessons using the leveled readers provided by the campus and that reflected student backgrounds and interests. The leveled readers were numbered from 1 to 44 on the same number system used by Fountas and Pinnell's (1996) leveled readers. Students were grouped homogeneously according to reading benchmark results, and lessons were targeting the acquisition of reading skills according to the students' reading levels. Students who completed collaborative and independent assignments early engaged in workstation activities either individually or with a partner. The balanced literacy block concluded with writing instruction. One grammar skill that was predetermined by the basal series was practiced on activity sheets, and then the teacher-based interactive, shared, and independent writing activities on Lucy Calkin's Writer's Workshop (Calkins, 1994). Typically, the writing topic was an extension of the culturally and socio-politically charged question that was outlined and organized during a collaborative assignment during the week. The scope and sequence for writing lessons were predetermined by the district's language arts department.

Formally Assessing According to District Standards

Students were administered the Developmental Reading Assessment, First Edition (DRA), an individualized benchmark published by Pearson (Beaver, 1997). Each benchmark was used to determine a student's independent reading level. Each student was administered a beginning-of-the-year benchmark in September, a middle-of-the-year benchmark in January, and an end-of-year benchmark in May. If a student entered in between those testing months, he or she was administered the test to identify the current instructional reading level. The purpose of this study was to examine students' beginning benchmarks and ending benchmarks to determine reading comprehension levels.

DRA K–3 kits contained books that were leveled with numbers that ranged from 1 to 44. One book that was identified as emergent was labeled with the letter A. Books increased in difficulty as the levels increased. It is a criterion-referenced assessment, and the data can be used to (a) assess reading engagement, oral reading fluency, and comprehension; (b), identify reading strengths and weaknesses; (c) determine students' reading levels; (d) inform reading instruction, (e) monitor progress in reading; and (f) aid in planning reading interventions (McCarthy & Christ, 2010). DRA was used for reading benchmarks because it was specifically designed for Grades K through 3 and was not used during daily instruction. Each book was accompanied with a test form that provided a teacher script and areas for recording student answers and scores. Teachers used all fictional texts to individually test students for oral reading and comprehension in September, January, and May. The classroom reading teachers tested each student according to the directions on the assessment. The teachers read directly from the assessment script to prompt student feedback in five areas: (1) book preview, (2) oral retelling, (3) oral comprehension, (4) connection to schema, and (5) oral reading fluency rate.

During an assessment, teachers read a scripted preview of the story, and students were to use picture clues to predict the events of the text. Students being tested in books leveled A to 16 would read the text orally while the teacher made notations of words read correctly and incorrectly on the scripted test form. A student being tested in books leveled 18 to 44 would read the text silently. The student would then proceed to orally retell the story. Teachers would prompt the student with questions from the test form if he or she began to struggle retelling the events. Teachers asked all students one inferencing question from the test form and recorded student responses. Students being tested on levels 18 to 44 were then asked to read one to three pages of the text orally while teachers made notation of words read correctly and incorrectly. Comprehension scores were calculated according to a rubric of four characteristics listed on the test form. Each characteristic was worth a particular point value. Points earned for each characteristic were totaled to calculate a student's comprehension level for the text being read. Oral reading was also determined according to the number of errors recorded below the text. The percentage scale was printed at the bottom of each test form. A student was benchmarked at a particular level if their comprehension score was a total of 16 to 20 and if their oral reading score ranged from 89% to 94%. Students that scored above 20 in comprehension and above 94% orally continued to test in books that increased in difficulty until they reached an instructional range.

The district determined levels that were grade-appropriate. The district considered instructional levels 18 to 28 to be the appropriate level for second grade. Students that read below level 18 were considered to be performing below expectations, and any student reading above level 28 was considered to be performing above expectations. Students could be tested until they reached level 44 but were not benchmarked above that level because it was the highest level in the K–3 kit.

The Impact of Cultural Dimensions on Second Grade Reading Achievement

Student reading levels from DRA was coded on a numerical scale. The DRA scores in the DRA kit range from A to 44. A reading level of A was coded with the number one. A dependent group *t* test was used to compare the beginning and ending data to determine the effectiveness of culturally responsive departmentalized literacy for the African American students.

Fifty-nine percent of the students within the departmentalized rotation that was closely examined identified as African American. According to the results of the DRA, 55% of the students were scoring below the grade level expectations at the beginning of the year. By the middle of the year, a second administration of the standardized reading assessment revealed that 36% of African American second graders receiving cultural relevant and responsive practices within a departmentalized setting were reading below-grade-level expectations determined by the school district. At the end of the year, during a final DRA assessment, 23% of African American second graders receiving instruction were reading below expectations.

Overall, all of the students made growth, regardless of their starting score, with growth ranging from six months to two years. Seventy-seven percent of students who received instruction made one to two years' growth. Twenty-two percent of the students achieved more than one year's growth in reading achievement.

Implications and Moving Forward

The purpose of the analysis was to discuss the reading achievement of African American children who engage in culturally relevant literacy practices in a departmentalized classroom environment in a lower elementary grade. However, when these factors do not apply, how do we account for the "exceptions to the rule," specifically, the middle-class and upper-class African American children who still fail to meet expectations? Or, conversely, the African American child from a low-socioeconomic household who scores the highest in reading?

After investigating the growth of African American students who received departmentalized literacy with cultural relevance and responsiveness infused, there was growth in all students; however, the possibility of additional factors may have strengthened the impact of cultural literacy. The impact of small-group reading instruction is designed to target instruction and "close gaps." The consistency of small-group reading may have played a role in reading growth. As the school year progressed, the district expectation for reading achievement continued to increase. Students made growth; however, with the exception of two students, those that began the school year scoring below reading expectations ended the year continuing to score below expectations. Research trends reveal the impact of socioeconomic status, parental involvement, and gender on reading development and achievement; however, these external factors were not taken into account when planning, implementing, or assessing for reading achievement. Also, teachers' perceptions of African American students, or teachers' attitudes toward these specific students, were not addressed. Students demonstrated growth on standardized reading achievement during early literacy; however, more research is needed to explore the social and emotional effects that a departmentalized cultural literacy classroom has on students during the lower elementary years. Although student achievement data demonstrated periodic growth on an individual assessment, student reflections of their perceptions offer a more comprehensive vision of the overall implementation of cultural literacy in a departmentalized setting.

To create a welcoming learning environment, especially for our Black youth, educators must seek to create a community challenges and affirms its individual members, and educators must view themselves as a community acting on shared beliefs, ideologies, and desired outcomes for their students (Johnson, 2015). Students received instruction in a specific format that set high levels of expectations, promoted high levels of engagement, and utilized three dimensions that fused culturally relevant pedagogy with methods for effective teaching. As students consistently received instruction with district-mandated materials and texts that reflected their identities, the external factors of gender, socioeconomic status, and parental involvement vanished as students formed positive relationships with their teachers, developed healthy peer relationships for collaboration over challenging activities, and voiced critical thoughts in an environment that encouraged them to speak out.

When promoting cultural relevance and responsiveness in literacy, one has to acknowledge that culture is a component that has to be addressed for students to grow as readers. Blending core academic curricula with a cultural focus can lead to increased academic performance (Schellenberg & Grothaus, 2009). This requires teachers to not impose their culture as the only acceptable adoption of norms in their classroom environment. Learning environments are expected to be a safe space for all cultures to coexist comfortably. School can only be the great equalizer and key to success if both teachers and students are allowed to bring themselves and their life lessons with them (Nieto, 2013).

Using learning materials that reflect their cultural identities does not negate the need for texts that offer differing backgrounds. Having prior knowledge of content in culturally relevant texts strengthens the connection to the language and expressiveness; however, there is also interest in texts and stories from other cultures (McCullough, 2013). There should be a balance of texts across cultures and genres; however, it is recommended for a minimum of an equal amount of attention to be given to texts that mirror African American readers—especially at an early age. They should not only be exposed; they should also be allowed a large amount of time to interact and connect with these texts. Allowing opportunities for students to talk on areas of study is vital to culturally relevant teaching (May, 2011). Departmentalized classroom environments allow for this opportunity to explore independently and collaboratively with texts for understanding and enjoyment.

Conclusion

The need for differing teaching practices for our African American students has not gone unnoticed. Documented approaches have, and are continuing to, publicize the importance of culture in literacy; however, for some teachers, culture still remains as an optional factor that can be added in *after* the skill has been taught instead of during its initial introduction.

Educators that have ventured beyond traditional core reading programs for elementary students have discovered that, for African American students in particular, culture is the common dominator for bridging the gap between their literacy achievement and achievement expectations. Once teachers have acknowledged their cultural identity, deeming it as natural, and crafting it into their literacy instruction reinforces the value in their existence. Wyatt (2014) concludes that teachers that successfully combined scripted curriculums and cultural responsiveness included greater teacher–student collaboration, peer-collaboration, and contextualized activities that connected to prior knowledge. Students must be engaged in healthy language, literature, and multimodal interactions to be introduced to the notion of cultural diversity and cultural acceptance. The understanding that their culture is acceptable can be influenced by opportunities to explore culture in an environment that celebrates diversity (Sarker & Shearer, 2013).

Reading instruction is a multifaceted skill that should not be taken lightly. Anyone that has ever engaged, either directly or indirectly, in teaching a group of students to read has discovered that there is no "one-size-fits-all" approach that yields success for every child because of an array of factors that researchers have discovered to impact the relationship between reader and text. Conceptually, reading involves instructing students en masse in hope of individual success. As vital as reading is to survival and success in society, we have yet to develop an approach to instruction that addresses all the factors that researchers have discovered that impact reading outcomes, which, in turn, have created subcultural biases toward readers instead of the foundation for developing reading programs to eliminate reading gaps across demographics. In the United States, it continues to be at the center of discussions in political arenas, academia, and dinner tables because we have yet to develop a formula for literacy education that consistently yields high levels of achievement for every student, regardless of his or her backgrounds. As we journey further into the 21st century, we have to abandon a "one-size-fits-all" solution to reading instruction in a society that recognizes individualism that is rooted in cultural identity.

References

Asher, S. R., Hymel, S., & Wigfield, A. (1978). Influence of topic interest on children's reading comprehension. *Journal of Literacy Research, 10*, 35–47.

Au, K. (2009). Isn't culturally responsive instruction just good teaching? *Social Education, 73*, 179–183.

Bear, D. R., Invernizzi, M., Templeton, S, & Johnston, F. (2015). *Words their way: Word study for phonics, vocabulary, and spelling instruction* (6th ed.). Boston: Pearson.

Beaver, J. M. (1997). *Developmental reading assessment.* Upper Saddle River, NJ: Celebration Press.

Blas, E. A. (2014). Information literacy in the 21st century multicultural classroom: Using sociocultural literacy, *Education Libraries, 37*(1–2), 33–41.

Burden P. R., & Byrd, D. M. (2016). *Methods for effective teaching: Meeting the needs of all students* (7th ed.). Boston: Pearson.

Calkins, L. M. (1994). *The art of teaching writing*. Portsmouth, NH: Heinemann.

Canady, R. L., & Rettig, M. D. (1995). The power of innovative scheduling. *Educational Leadership, 53*(3), 4–10.

Canady, R. L., & Rettig, M. D. (2001). Block scheduling: The key to quality learning time. *Principal, 80*(3), 30–34.

Chan, T. C., & Jarman, D. (2004). Departmentalize elementary schools. *Principal, 84*(1), 70–72.

Chang, F. C., Muñoz, M. A., & Koshewa, S. (2008). Evaluating the impact of departmentalization on elementary school students. *Planning & Changing, 39*, 131–145.

Chenowith, N. H. (2014). Culturally responsive pedagogy and cultural scaffolding in literacy education. *The Ohio Journal of Teacher Education, 44*(1), 35–40.

Cole-Henderson, B. (2000). Organizational characteristics of schools that successfully serve low-income urban African American students. *Journal of Education for Students Placed At Risk, 5*(1&2), 77–91.

Evans, W., Tokarczyk, J., Rice, S., & McCray, A. (2002). Block scheduling: An evaluation of outcomes and impact. *The Clearing House, 75*, 319–323.

Ferguson, R. F. (2003). Teachers' perceptions and exceptions and the Black–White test score gap. *Urban Education, 38*, 460–507.

Ford, B. A., Stuart, D. H., & Vakil, S. (2014). Culturally responsive teaching in the 21st century inclusive classroom. *The Journal of the International Association of Special Education, 15*(2), 56–62.

Fountas, I. C., & Pinnell, G. S. (1996). *Guided Reading: Good first teaching for all children* (1st ed.). Portsmouth, NH: Heinemann.

Gay, G. (2010). *Culturally responsive teaching: Theory, research, and practice* (2nd ed.). New York, NY: Teachers College.

Graves, S. (2008). Are we neglecting African American males? Parental involvement differences between African American males and females during elementary school. *Journal of African American Studies, 14*, 263–276.

Gullatt, D. E. (2006). Block scheduling: The effects on curriculum and student productivity. *National Association of Secondary School Principals, 90*, 250–266.

Halle, T. G., Kurtz-Costes, B., & Mahoney, J. L. (1997). Family influences on school achievement in low-income, African American children. *Journal of Educational Psychology, 89*, 527–537.

Harris, T. S., & Graves, S. L. (2012). The Influence of cultural capital transmission on reading achievement in African American fifth grade boys. *The Journal of Negro Education, 79*, 447–457.

Husband, T. (2012). Addressing reading underachievement in African American boys through a multi-contextual approach. *Reading Horizons, 52*(1), 1–24.

Jenkins, E., Queen, A., & Algozzine, B. (2002). To block or not to block: That's not the question. *The Journal of Educational Research, 95*, 196–202.

Johnson, L. P. (2015). The writing on the wall: Enacting place pedagogies in order to reimagine schooling for Black male youth. *Discourse: Studies in the Cultural Politics of Education, 36*, 908–919.

Kesler, T. (2011). Teachers' texts in culturally responsive teaching. *Language Arts, 88*, 419–428.

Kinkead-Clark, Z. (2014). Family, culture, literacy and the kindergarten classroom: Perspectives of an immigrant teacher. *The International Journal of Early Childhood Learning, 21*, 33–45.

Ladson-Billings, G. (1995). Toward a theory of culturally relevant pedagogy. *American Educational Research Journal, 32*, 465–491.

Lamme, L. L. (1976). Self-contained to departmentalized: How reading habits changed. *The Elementary School Journal, 76*, 208–218.

May, L. (2011). Animating talk and texts: Culturally relevant teacher read-alouds of informational texts. *Journal of Literacy Research, 43*(1), 4–48. doi:10.1177/1086296X10397869

McCarthy, A., & Christ, T. J. (2010). Test review: Beaver, J. M., & Carter, M. A. (2006). Developmental reading assessment-second edition (DRA2). *Assessment for Effective Intervention 35*(3), 182–185.

McCullough, R. G. (2013). The Relationship between reader response and prior knowledge on African American students' reading comprehension performance using multicultural literature. *Reading Psychology, 34*, 397–435.

McVee, M. B. (2014). The challenge of more light, the complexity of culture: Lessons learned in exploring the cultural positioning of literacy teachers. *Discourse: Studies in the Cultural Politics of Education, 35*(1), 1–15.

Morton, B. A., & Dalton, B. (2007). *Changes in instructional hours in four subjects by public school teachers of Grades 1 through 4* (Stats in Brief. NCES 2007-305). Washington, DC: National Center for Education Statistics.

National Center for Education Statistics. (2017). Status and trends in the education of racial and ethnic groups. Retrieved from https://nces.ed.gov/programs/raceindicators/indicator_rca.asp

Nieto, S. (2013). Language, literacy, and culture: Aha! Moments in personal and sociopolitical understanding. *Journal of Language & Literacy Education, 9*(1), 8–20.

Plata, M., Williams, A. A., & Henley, T. B. (2017). Prospective teachers' beliefs in factors negatively influencing African American, low-income Anglo, and Hispanic students' academic achievement. *Teacher Education and Practice, 30*, 386–402.

Queen, J. A., & Gaskey, K. A. (1997). Steps for improving school climate in block scheduling. *Phi Delta Kappa, 79*, 158–161.

Rettig, M. D., & Canady, R. L. (2003). Block scheduling's missteps, successes and variables. *School Administrator, 60*(9), 26–31.

Sarker, A., & Shearer, R. (2013). Developing literacy skills for global citizenship: Exploring personal culture and mining cultural gems from classroom experts. *English in Texas, 43*(2), 4–10.

Schellenberg, R., & Grothaus, T. (2009). Promoting cultural responsiveness and closing the achievement gap with standards blending. *Professional School Counseling, 12*, 440–449.

Simms, K. (2012). Is the black-white achievement gap a public sector effect? An examination of student achievement in the third grade. *The Journal of At-Risk Issues 17*(1), 23–29.

Sullivan, A. L., & A'Vant, E. (2009). Multicultural affairs: On the need for cultural responsiveness. *Communique, 38*(3), 8–9.

Tatum, A. W. (2006). Engaging African American males in reading. *Educational Leadership, 63*(5), 44–49.

Texas Essential Knowledge and Skills. (2017). Retrieved from http://ritter.tea.state.tx.us/rules/tac/chapter110/ch110a.html

Thomas, K. L. (2019). Building literacy environments to motivate African American boys to read. *The Reading Teacher, 72*, 761–765. doi:10.1002/trtr.1784.

Washington, J. A. (2001). Early literacy skills in African American children:

Research considerations. *Learning Disabilities Research & Practice, 16,* 213–221.

Wyatt, T. R. (2014). Teaching across the lines: Adapting scripted programmes with culturally relevant/responsive teaching. *Pedagogy, Culture & Society, 22,* 447–469.

Zepeda, S. J., & Mayers, R. S. (2006). An analysis of research on block scheduling. *Review of Educational Research, 76,* 137–170.

Contributors

Reuben A. Buford May, PhD, is the Associate Head of the Department of Sociology and Presidential Professor for Teaching Excellence at Texas A&M University in College Station. His most recent publication is *Urban Nightlife: Entertaining Race, Class, and Culture in Public Space* (2014).

James L. Conyers, Jr., PhD, is University Professor of African American Studies and Director of the African American Studies Program at the University of Houston. Additionally, he is the Editor of the serial *Africana Studies: A Review of Social Science and Research at Taylor and Francis*. His most recent publication is *Africology: Interdisciplinary Thought and Praxis*.

James Earl Davis, PhD, is the Bernard C. Watson Endowed Cahir in Urban Education and Professor of Higher Education at Temple University. His most recent publication is *Historically white universities and plantation politics: Anti-Blackness and higher education in the Black Lives Matter Era* (2018).

Crystal L. Edwards, PhD, is a Visiting Scholar of African American Studies at the University of Houston. Her most recent is the book titled *Black girls experiencing their intersectional identities in schools: A HER-Story*.

Tanya M. Hudson, EdD, is Program Interim Chair and Assistant Professor of Early Childhood, Elementary, Middle Grades, Reading, and Special Education at the University of North Carolina at Fayetteville. Her most recent publication is *Technology competency within the nontraditional preservice teacher candidate population: Survey results* (2018).

Joshua D. Hughes, PhD, is a research consultant for the Houston Independent School District. His most recent publication, *A Multi-Generational Study of Aspiring African American Female Superintendents in Texas*, has been posted to Contemporary Issues in Educational Leadership.

Laveria Hutchison, PhD, is an Associate Professor of Curriculum and Instruction at the University of Houston. Her most recent publications are *Addressing the STEM teacher shortage in American schools: Ways to recruit and retain effective STEM teachers*, and *Using Television Viewing to Assist with Enhancing Literacy Skills* (2012).

Detra D. Johnson, PhD, is an Assistant Professor in the Department of Educational Leadership and Policy Studies at the University of Houston. Her most recent publications are *A proposition for a holistic approach to adaptation and a unified sense of self: A conceptual framework of resiliency and self-determination in educational settings*, and *Beyond marginality: Understanding the value of the intersection of race, gender, and ethnicity in studying educational leadership*.

Cory J. LaFevers, PhD, is a Lecturer in the Moores School of Music, University of Houston. His most recent publication is *Revisitando estudos de retenção: construindo sobrevivências puras de uma África imaginada e o impacto nas políticas culturais negras*.

Deidra L. Lawson, EdM, is Yellowstone Schools, Head of Schools; Educating While Black, Founder.

Monique I. Liston, PhD, is UBUNTU Research and Evaluation, Chief Strategist. Her most recent publication is *Black Twitter and Black Feminist Epistemology* (2017).

Leah McAlister-Shields, EdD, is a Program Manager in the College of Education and Adjunct Professor of Education at the University of Houston. Her most recent publication is *Teaching Through Culture: The Case for Culturally Responsive Pedagogy in American Higher Education Institutions* (2019).

TaNeisha R. Page, PhD, is an independent scholar, who is currently teaching online at Ashford University. Her most recent publications are *Challenges Faced by African American Adult Students in Higher Education*, and *Africana Race and Communication: A Social Study of Film, Communication and Social Media* (2017).

Abul A. Pitre, PhD, is Professor and Head of the Department of Educational Leadership at the Univesity of North Carolina at Fayetteville. His most recent publication is the edited volume, *A Critical Black Pedagogy Reader: The Brothers Speak* (2019).

Autumn F. Raynor, MA, is an Assistant Professor of Speech Communication at Houston Community College.

Donna W. Stokes, PhD, is a Professor of Physics in the Department of Physics at the University of Houston. Her most recent publication is *The influence of parents on undergraduate and graduate students' entering the STEM disciplines and STEM careers* (2018).

Selena D. Tate, PhD, is an Assistant Professor of Family Counseling at Prairie View A&M University.

Katina L. Thomas, EdD, is an Assistant Professor of Education at Prairie View A&M University. Her most recent publication is *Building literacy environments to motivate African American boys to read* (2019).

Kevin B. Thompson, PhD, is the Program Manager in African American Studies and Adjunct Instructor of AAS at the University of Houston. His most recent publication is *The Negative Imagery of Hip Hop: A Brief Analysis*.

Index

Abrams, S., 118, 119, 122
Adams v. Richardson (1972), 268
Adams-Bass, V., 257
adaptive unconscious theory, 160–61
Adler, R., 243
administrators and principals, leadership styles of, 289–300; culturally responsive pedagogy and, 284, 290; diversity, responsiveness to, 289–90; potential social justice challenges, 296; professional development training, 295; social justice leaders, 290, 293–96; visionary and social justice leaders, 290, 297–300; visionary leaders, 290, 291–93
administrators and principals, scheduling issues and, 314
affirmative action programs, 37n15
African American adult students, 41–50; accessibility, 43; accountability, 44–45; affordability, 43–44; belonging, sense of, 46–47; ethnicity, 45–46; faculty relationships, 46; inclusion, moving towards, 47–49; institutional issues, 44–47; as nontraditional students, definition, 42; personal conflicts, 42–43; student/teacher communication issues, 48; support systems, 45–46; under-representation, 45. *See also* education, ontological manipulation in
African American fathers, 128–30; involvement by, statistics, 128, 130; narratives by, 135–37; researcher's positionality, 135; residential vs. nonresidential fathers, 129
African American female professors, reflections from, 280–83
African American history month, 77
African consciousness, contextual base of, 83–84, 83 *fig.*
Africology, 232–33, 250, 262
Afro-Brazilian music scene, in Austin (TX), 146–49; African customs and, 152–54; Austin demographics, 146, 147–48, 172n4; Black Brazilian musical practices, definition, 147; ensembles and bands in, 147; hip cultural diversity, characterized as, 148, 149–50, 159; Samba Schools, in Toronto *vs.* Austin, 147
Afrocentric awareness, 81–82, 82 *fig.*

Afrocentricity: cultural engagement and, 168–71; ethnomusicology and, 166–68; strengthening antiracism with, 160–63, 171–72
Aguirre, J. M., 270
Aguirre Zavala, M., 270
Aikens, N. D., 121
Alabi, Jessica Ayo, 18–19
Algozzine, B., 306
Alhabib, S., 209
All Black Everything, 188–200; acts-of-resistance programs for, 192–93; as Beloved Community, 195–200; as a counterspace, 189–95; creation of, 188–89; direct relational transactions, 193–95; mission statement, 188–89; narrative identity work process, 191–92; organizational struggles, 199–200
Allen, W. R., 239
Alonzo, J., 18
Altschul, I., 122, 123
The American Conservative, 18
Anderson, B., 120
Anderson, E. L., 91
Anderson, James D. *(History of Black Education)*, 51, 83, 234, 239
Anderson, L., 203–4, 208
Anderson, M., 51
Anderson, Maggie *(Our Black Year)*, 188
Anderson, S., 215
Anderson, S. A., 222
Andrews, R. L., 290
Anfara, V. A., 291
antifa, definition, 36n3
Anyon, Jean, 58–59
Apple, M., 57
Apple, M. W., 297
Arias, H., 209
Arment, A. R., 220, 268, 269
Asante, Molefi Kete, 82–83, 97, 145, 149, 162, 167, 171, 231, 232
Asher, S. R., 311
Au, K., 305–6
Auerbach, S., 127
Austin Samba, 164–65
Australia, studies of mothers in, 205, 207–8
A'Vant, E., 308

Avelar, I., 153
Avery, M. L., 209

Bailey, T. M., 41
Bakari, R., 129
Baker, D. P., 118, 129
Baldwin, James, 184, 272
Baldwin, John, 289
Banks, C. M., 290
Banks, J. A., 266, 269, 272, 278, 290
Barbarin, O., 121
Bartle, S., 219, 222
Bartle-Haring, S., 204, 208, 219
Basta, J., 212
Baumeister, R., 246, 247
Beach, A., 275, 277
Beale, M., 19
Beavers, W. R., 221
Beck, J. G., 209
Beeble, M. L., 209, 212
Bell, Derek, 54, 55–56
Bell, H., 209, 210
Beloved Community theory, 195–96
Bempechat, J., 129–30
Benz, M. R., 124, 125, 126
Berger, E. H., 127
Berger-Sweeney, Joanne, 19
Berkovich, I., 291, 296, 297, 299
Berkowitz, M. W., 298
Berlak, Ann, 160, 161
Bernard, Henry, 116
Bhangu, A., 99
bias in teaching, personal reflections on, 280–83
Biesta, G., 97
Billman, N., 120
Bingham, Carl, 256–57
Black Americans: The FBI Files (O'Reilly & Gallen), 60–61
Black education: academic success, planning for, 309–11; access, for ethnic minorities, 265, 268–69; affordability issue, 43–44; during Civil War, 59; cost of (2019), 236; international students, STEM courses and, 277; lecture-based *vs.* interactive teaching, 276; as national security threat, 59–61; population projection (2017) of racialized minorities, in U.S., 274 *fig.*; relevance of, 80–81; textbooks, costs of, 236; as threat, 59–62, 233–35; undergraduate enrollment, statistics, 275. *See also* African American adult students; Black male youth, identity management in education; Woodson, Carter G.
Black Feminist Epistemology, principles of, 94
Black Feminist Thought, 91–92, 92–93
Black liberation, history of, 181–82
Black Lives Matter movement, 182
Black male educational experiences, 71–74; personal observations, 71, 72–73; self-concept theory of career development *vs.*, 73–74
Black male professors/teachers, 17–29, 67–75; Black male teacher shortage, explanation for, 70, 74–75; first positions, 26–29; graduate students, teaching as, 20–26; phases, of educational experiences, 71–73; professors, teaching as, 26–29; racism, examples, 17–20; statistics, 45, 56. *See also* Me Versus Them pedagogical approach; self-concept theory of career development (Super)
Black male youth, identity management in education, 1–13; *The Brownies' Book* (Du Bois), 2–3, 8–11; cultural messages about, 3–4; W. E. B. Du Bois, early education and, 7–8; historic images of, 8–11; identity development of, 2; same-sex schools, 6; schooling disparities, consequences of, 5–7; social identities, need to change, 11–13; social science research on, 1, 6; terminology, labeling and, 4–5
The Black Panther Party for Self Defense, 182
Black women graduate students, 91–111, 181–201; All Black Everything, as Beloved Community, 195–200; All Black Everything, as counterspace, 189–95; All Black Everything, creation of, 188–89; Black Feminist Epistemology, 94; Black Feminist Thought, 94; Black liberation, history of, 181–82; Black liberation, intellectual tradition of, 182–83; counterspaces, definition, 184, 201; Decolonial Black Feminist Epistemology, 92–93, 95–108; decolonial theory, 93; imposter syndrome, 109; intersectionality of, 91–92; "Occupy the Hood", 186–87; personal narrative, as student and community member, 184–87; statistics, 91, 182–83
blanketing, definition, 243
Blas, E. A., 310, 311

Bloom, B. S., 129
Bogotch, I., 293-94
Bonilla-Silva, Eduardo, 158-59
book buyers, 237
Bornstein, M. H., 119, 120
Bosworth, B., 41-42
Bourdieu, P., 134
Bowen, Murray, 213-14
Bowen, N., 134
Boyle, M., 183
Bradley, Deborah, 158, 163, 164
Brandt, H. M., 209
Braun, V., 241
Brazilian music ensembles, Afrocentric pedagogical approaches for, 145-74; Afro-Brazilian music, in Austin (TX), 146-49; Afrocentricity, strengthening antiracism with, 160-63, 171-72; Afrocentricity pedagogy, cultural engagement and, 168-71; Afrocentricity pedagogy, ethnomusicology and, 166-68; antiracist music education, 158-59; cultural engagement, 164; multiculturalism, critiques of, 149-58; multiculturalism, in music education, 163-66; narratives, 150, 151-52, 154-57, 163, 164-66, 168-70
Brickson, S., 290
Bridges, Ruby, 234
Brief Symptom Inventory (BSI), 220
Briggs, K., 292
The Brilliance of Black Boys (Wright & Counsell), 3
Bronfenbrenner, U., 130
Brown, E., 295
Brown, K. M., 291
Brown, Linda, 234
Brown, Michael, 248
Brown v. Board of Education (1954), 267
Browning, J. E., 267
The Brownies' Book, 2-3, 8-11
Buford May, R. A., 36n6, 37n18
bullying, 123, 125, 128, 247-48
Burden, P. R., 308
Burns, A., 204, 207-8
Bush, K., 130
Bushman, B., 246, 247
Bustamante, R. M., 273
Butler, James Alpheus, Jr., 9-10
Bybee, D., 209, 212
Byrd, D. M., 308

Calkins, Lucy, 319
Callahan, A., 41-42
campus environment, Black women graduates' experiences with, 104-5
Canada, 149, 210-11
Canady, R. L., 313, 314
Capper, C. A., 132, 296
Carey, J., 97
Carey, R. L., 4
Carjuzaa, J., 266, 272, 273, 283
Carlisle, L. R., 296
Carroll, K. K., 232, 235
Carruthers, Jacob, 181
Carter, D. F., 47, 48
Carvalho, E. I. de, 154
Case, A. D., 190, 194
Catterall, J. S., 123
Ceja, M., 184, 233, 239
census projection (2017), in U.S., 273-74
certification requirements, Black teachers and, 56-57
Chang, F. C., 306
Chang, M. J., 267
Chapman, S. J., 99
Charlebois, P., 206
Chauhan, S., 41
Chen, M., 129
Cheney, G. R., 292
Chenowith, N. H., 308
Child Abuse Potential Inventory, 224
Child Behavior Checklist, 224
Child Hostility Inventory, 224
Chin, J., 210-11
Choitz, V., 41-42
Christ, T. J., 319
Christman, D.E., 296
Ciccariello-Maher, George, 36n4, 36n7
Civil Rights Act of 1964, 267-68
Civil War: desegregation following, 267-69; HBCUs after, 51, 55, 59; in middle school textbooks, 238, 239
Clapp, J. D., 209
Clarke, John H., 182
Clarke, V., 241
Coalition for Equity v. Maryland Higher Ed. Comm'n (2017), 268
Coates, C., 115
Cochran, M., 121, 122
co-cultural theory, 244
Cohen, S., 220

Coker, A. L., 209
Colbus, D., 203, 204, 224
Cole, M., 131
Cole-Henderson, B., 305
Coleman, J. S., 133
coloniality of Being, definition, 93
coloniality of knowledge, definition, 93
coloniality of power, definition, 93
community: Beloved Community theory, 195–200; in graduate school, 106–7
congruence, definition, 69
Conti, A., 15
Conyers, J. L., 77, 232, 233
Cook, L., 223
Cook, S. W., 220
Cooper, C. E., 117–18
Corcoran, K., 219
Corley, K., 129
Cottrell, B., 213
counseling psychology, of African Americans, 203–25; abuse relationships, statistics, 211–12; Family Systems Theory (Bowen), 213–25; intimate partner/spouse violence (IPSV), victim experiences and, 209–13; youth-to-parent violence (YTPV) and, 203–8
Counsell, S. L. (*The Brilliance of Black Boys*), 3
Counter Intelligence Program, Martin Luther King, Jr., and, 60
Covi, L., 219
Crane, J., 118, 121, 124
Crenshaw, Kimberlé, 91–92, 94
Crichlow, W., 131
Crisis Magazine (1919), 3, 8
Crisis of the Negro Intellectual (Cruse), 83
critical race theory, 130–32
critical theory, Black pedagogues of, 53–54
Cross, C., 237
Cruse, Harold (*Crisis of the Negro Intellectual*), 83
Cullors, Patrisse, 182
cultural capital theory, 132–33
culturally responsive pedagogy, in second-grading reading, 305–24; academic success, planning for, 309–11, 316–17; achievement gap, variables effecting, 305; as critical tool, 306; cultural, importance of, 322–24; cultural competence and sociopolitical critical thinking, building, 311–12; cultural dimensions, impact of, 320–21; culturally relevant dimensions, framing, 307–12; departmentalization, 306, 313–14, 316–17, 321; departmentalized early literacy, 314–16; district standards, assessing according to, 319–20; implications, 321–23; lesson plans, 317; literacy, African American males and, 306–7; literacy practices, 317–19; reading achievement, assessing, 312; reading performance, factors influencing, 305, 324; second graders, developmentally, 307; teacher-student relationships, establishing, 317
culturally responsive pedagogy, in STEM courses, 265–84; absence of, 270–71, 283; access to education, for ethnic minorities, 265; characteristics of, 271 *table*; culture and teaching, in higher education, 269–70; definition, 266; desegregation, of higher education, 267–69; faculty diversity, impact of, 273–75, 274 *fig*.; pedagogical and curricular practices, 271–73; personal reflections, 280–83; population projection (2017) of racialized minorities, in U.S., 274 *fig*.; scenario, 266–67; in STEM courses, 275–80; student diversity, impact of, 269–70, 283, 284, 290
culture: and teaching in higher education, 269–70, 284; using to improve learning, 276. *See also* culturally responsive pedagogy (CRP), in STEM courses
Cumberbatch, Virginia, 148
curriculum: institutional politics of, 57–59; reshaping, using CRP, 270–71, 271–73
Curry, Tommy, 18
Czarniawska, B., 118–19

Dalton, B., 314
Dancy, T. E., 6
Danley, L. L., 239
Dantley, M., 54, 290, 296
Darling-Hammond, L., 250
Davenport, Christian, 197, 198
Davidson, C., 41–42
Davidson, W. S., 212
Davis, J., 292
Davis, J. E., 5
Davis, K. E., 209
Dean, C., 121, 122
Dearing, E., 127
Decolonial Black Feminist Epistemology, 95–108; Black Feminist Epistemology and,

94, 95; decolonial theory and, 93, 95; findings, 100–106; framework, 92–93, 95–96; methodology, 96–97; participant narratives, 101–2, 102–4, 104–6, 106–8, 109, 110; research design, 97–100, 98 *table*; solutions, recommendations and, 106–8, 109–11
decolonial theory, 93, 95
Defending Public Schools (Gabbard), 63
DeFluer, M., 70
Dei, George, 156
Delgado, R., 54, 55–56, 131
DeMatthews, D., 290
Departmental Reading Assessment (DRA), 319
departmentalization (block schedules), 306, 313–14
Derogatis, L. R., 219, 220
Desai, S., 209
desegregation, of higher education, 267–69
Desimone, L., 130
Deterville, A. D., 233
Developmental Reading Assessment (DRA), 315
differentiation of self, 216–22; anxiety, acute *vs.* chronic, 217–18; differentiation and psychological symptoms, 218; differentiation levels, of parents and adult children, 218–19; emotional reactivity towards mother and, 219–20; highly differentiated *vs.* undifferentiated families, 217; lowly differentiated adolescent, example, 216–17; parental alcoholism, effects of, 221–22; psychological distress and, in Filipinos, 219; stress, coping and, 220–21
Differentiation of Self Inventory (DSI), 218, 220, 221
Dixon, V. J., 235
Dolan, M., 235
Domestic Conflict Index (DCI), 224
Dorsey, B., 181–82
Dougherty, A., 118
Dougherty, E., 118
Douglass, Frederick, 52
Doumas, D., 213, 224
Dreher, R., 18
Du Bois, W. E. B., 182, 272; *The Brownies' Book*, 2–3, 8–11; philosophy on education of, 51; on primary school and college education, 7; scholar, experience as, 36n.5; as social justice leader, 55; *The Souls of Black Folks*, 55; Talented Tenth construct, 51, 234
Dumas, M. J., 6
Dumont, H. T., 121, 124, 126
Duran, J., 124, 125, 126
Durkee, M. I., 182

Eagan, M. K., 267
Eckel, P., 91
Eckstein, N. J., 204
education, ontological manipulation in, 242–50, 255–63; African American students, effects on, 255, 258, 261, 262–63; education system, intent of, 262; implications, of manipulation, 262–63; method, of study, 259–61, 259 *table*, 260 *table*; negative stereotypes, in media, 257–58; ontological manipulation, indicators of, 242 *table*; scientific racism in, 256–57, 262; segregation in, 257; in social psychology textbooks, 246–50; in speech communication textbooks, 242–46
el-Shabazz, el-Hajj Malik. *See* X, Malcolm
emotional cutoff concept, 215–16
Epstein, J. L., 115, 117
Esteves, L. L., 154
eugenics movement, 256, 262
Eurocentric psychology, 235, 243
experience, definition, 69

faculty: African American adult students and, 46; diversity awareness in lesson planning, 278–79; experiences with, by Black women graduates, 102–4; faculty diversity, impact of, 273–75, 274 *fig.*; inclusion of CRP, tenure and, 277; professional development sessions for, 278, 280
family projection process concept, 214–15
Family Systems Theory (Bowen), 213–25; differentiation of self, 216–22; emotional cutoff, 215–16; family projection process, 214–15; multigenerational transmission process, 222–25; nuclear family emotional process, 214; sibling position, 215; societal emotional process, 216; triangles, 215
Fan, X., 129
Farrakhan, Louis, 57
Fauset, Jessie, 8
Fergus, E., 6, 11
Ferguson, R. F., 305, 309

Fierro, E., 296
finger beckoning, 243
Finkelstein, N., 275, 277
Fischer, J., 219
Fitzgerald, J., 99
Flaherty, C., 18, 19
Flemons, D., 183
Folkman, S., 206
Forbes, J. D., 266
Ford, B. A., 309
Fordham, S., 193
Fountas, I. C., 317, 318
Fowler, C., 129
Frankfurt school theoreticians, 132
Frederick, Rona, 81–82
Freire, P., 57, 63
Frew, L. A., 125, 126
Friedlander, M. L., 214, 220, 221

Gabbard, D. *(Defending Public Schools)*, 63
Gagnon, C., 206
Gaille, B., 236, 237
Galinsky, P., 153
Gallagher, E., 208, 213
Gallen, D. *(Black Americans: The FBI Files)*, 60–61
Galton, Francis, 256
gangs, 37n13
Garner, J. R., 131
Garvey, Marcus, 62
Garza, Alicia, 182
Gaskey, K. A., 313
Gay, G., 266, 273, 276, 308, 312
Geddes, C., 120
Gehart, D. R., 213, 214–15, 215–16
George, A., 296
Gewertz, S., 293
Gibbs, T., 118, 119, 122
Gilbert, R. M., 214, 215
Ginsberg, M. B., 283
Giroux, H., 296
Glasbey, J., 99
Global Severity Index, 220
Gluuan, R. L., 204, 208
Goggin, J., 79
Goldfarb, K. P., 294
Goldring, R., 67
Gopal, A., 283
Gordon, B., 272
Gore, P. A., 220

graduate school experiences: by Black male graduate students, 20–26; by Black women graduate students, 91–111; by STEM graduates from HBCUs, 268–69
Graham, Mekada, 159
Granville Dill, Augustus, 8
Graves, S. L., 305, 306
Green, B. F., 70
Green, M., 91
Green, S., 183
Grinberg, E., 236
Grinberg, J., 294
Grosfoguel, R., 93, 95, 96
Gross, Kelly, 158
Grothaus, T., 322
Guided Reading Program (Fountas & Pinnell), 317, 318
Guillen, I. C. M., 153
Gurian, M., 129
Guskey, T. R., 291
Gutierrez, K. D., 290
Gutierrez, R. *(Political Conocimiento for Teaching Mathematics)*, 269, 270, 272
Gwekwerere, T., 231, 239, 250

Hagewood, J. H., 209
Haley, A., 245–46
Halle, T. G., 305
Haller, A. O., 70, 74
Hallinger, P., 289
Hampson, R. B., 221
Hango, H., 123, 130
Harmon, D. A., 266
Harnish, David, 158
Harris, A. L., 123, 129
Harris, F., 47
Harris, T. S., 306
Hawley, W., 117
HBCUs. *See* historically Black colleges and universities (HBCUs), social justice and
Heck, R. H., 289
Hedges, H., 120
Henderson, C., 275, 277
Henley, T. B., 310
Henriksen, B., 120
Heppner, P. P., 220
Hernandez, F., 296
Hill, B., 91
Hill, N. E., 119, 121, 124
Hill-Collins, Patricia, 92–93, 95

Hines, E. M., 125, 128
Hispanics, 121, 130, 211–12
historically Black colleges and universities (HBCUs), social justice and, 51–64; Black education as national security threat, 59–61; curriculum, institutional politics of, 57–59; W.E.B. Du Bois's philosophy on education, 51; education, weaponization of, 56, 61–62; educational leadership doctoral programs in, 52; social justice leadership, 53–54, 62–64; social justice rhetoric, as White paternalism, 52; social justice tradition at, 55–57; statistics and history of, 51, 267; STEM graduates from, 268–69; Booker T. Washington's philosophy on education, 51–52
History of Black Education (Anderson), 51, 83, 234, 239
Holcomb-McCoy, C., 125, 128
Holloway, S. D., 122, 123, 124, 126, 130
Hood, James, 234–35
hooks, bell, 171, 195, 196
Hoops, J., 41–42
Hoover, J. Edgar, 60–61
Hope, E. C., 182
Horn, C. L., 91
Hornby, G., 129
Hossain, Z., 128, 130
How Social Movements Die (Davenport), 198
Hudin, R., 18
Hughey, Mathew, 145, 158, 159, 162, 167, 168, 173n14
Hull, G. T., 97
Hunter, C. D., 190, 194
Huntsinger, C., 118, 120
Hurtado, S., 267
Husband, T., 311
Hussar, W., 41
Hyde Park, demographics of, 36n10
Hyler, M., 250
Hymel, S., 311

identification, definition, 69
implicit bias, 269
imposter syndrome, 37n16, 109
Index of Psychological Abuse (IPA), 212
India, parental involvement in education in, 120
intelligence testing, 61
intersectionality, definition, 91–92, 131, 152

intersubjectivity, definition, 68
intimate partner/spouse violence (IPSV), 209–13; families of origin, aggression and, 213; internal turmoil/stressful reactions, 211; leaving relationships, likelihood of, 212; male aggressors, control of female victims by, 212–13; relational abuse, 210–11; seeking assistance/support, 209; services, availability of, 210; socio-economic status, abusive relationships and, 211–12
Inwood, J. F., 195

Jackson, B. W., 296
Jackson, P., 205
Jacobs, K., 127
James, G., 61
Jamison, D., 232
Jefferson, Thomas, 116
Jencks, C., 294
Jenkins, E., 306
Jeynes, W. H., 118, 120, 124–25, 126, 128
John, R. S., 213, 224
Johnson, K., 235
Johnson, L. P., 322
Johnson, P., 221
Johnson, W. C., 220
Johnson-Feelings, D., 8
Jones, B. A., 292
Jones, R., 209
Jones, Vivian Malone, 234–35
Jose, P., 118, 120
Journal of African American History, 79
Journal of Negro History, 79

Kamarck, T., 220
Kao, G., 121
Karenga, Maulana, 166, 167, 170–71, 232
Karpinski, C. F., 295
Kazdin, A. E., 204, 224
Kazis, R., 41–42
Keala, D. K., 215
Keels, M., 182
Kelly, M., 99
Kendricks, K. D., 268, 269, 270
Kennair, N., 213
Kenten, C., 97
Kenwood Academy (Chicago, IL), personal experiences at, 21–23, 36n11, 37n13
Kerr, M.E., 213, 214, 217–18, 222, 223
Kesler, T., 312

Ketchum, S. A., 93
Kethineni, S., 204, 213
Khalil, D., 295
Khan-Cullors, P, 182
Khatri, C., 99
Kidd, J. M., 69–70
King, Martin Luther, Jr., 60, 195, 196–97
Kinkead-Clark, Z., 310
Kisliuk, Michelle, 158
Kitzinger, J., 97
Klever, P., 222–23
Kohl, G. O., 129
Kolowich, S., 18
Komives, S. R., 91
Koshewa, S., 306
Kreider, H., 127
Kristof, K., 236
Kritsonsi, W. A., 127
Kuh, G. D., 91
Kulkarni, S., 209, 210
Kurtz-Costes, B., 305
Kwok, O. M., 124, 125, 126

Labuschagne, A., 100
Lacey, K. K., 211–12
Lack, Henrietta, 279
Lacour, M., 116, 121
Ladson-Billings, G., 130–31, 266, 270, 273, 276, 290, 306, 307, 308
Lamme, L. L., 306
Lareau, A., 117, 120, 122
Larivee, S., 206
Larke, P., 278, 279
Laušević, Mirjana, 172n1
law enforcement, texts and, 236
Lazarus, R., 206
Lea, B. & Lea, V., 170
LeBlanc, M., 206
Lee, J., 134
Leffler, W. K., 234
Lengua, L., 129
Leonard, R., 204, 207–8
Lewis, Chance W., 81
Lewis, Franklin, 9
Lima, I. M. de F., 153, 154, 173n7, 174n6
Lin, M. H., 267
Lipman, R. S., 219
Lloyd, K. M., 265
Locke, David, 158
Loeber, R., 206

Loewus, L., 56
Lott, Eric, 148
Love, D., 49
Love, P., 91
Lugg, C. A., 295

Macpherson, J. E., 295, 299
Mahoney, A., 204
Mahoney, J. L., 305
Maldonado-Torres, N., 93
Mann, Horace, 116
Maracatu Texas (percussion ensemble), 147, 152, 154–57, 164–66, 168–70, 172n3
maracatus-nação vs. percussion groups, 152–53
Margolin, G., 213, 224
Marin, P., 91
Markowitz, F. E., 213
Marshall, C., 294, 296
Mason, R. C., 296, 297
Mawhinney, H., 290
May, L., 306, 323
Mazama, A., 233
McBride, B. A., 123
McCann, Brian, 150
McCarthy, A., 319
McClelland, D. C., 125
McCornack, S., 244
McCullough, R. G., 323
McGee Banks, C. A., 272
McKenzie, K. B., 296
McLeod, A., 41–42
McMahon, R. J., 129
McNiff, J., 209
McVee, M. B., 310
Me Versus Them pedagogical approach, 20–35; co-teaching as a learning experience, 25–26; generally, 16; graduate students, teaching as, 20–26; implementation, 32; origins, 30–31; overview, 29; personal teaching biography, lessons learned from, 17; process, 32–35; professors, teaching as, 26–29
Mellor, D., 213
mentorships, by Black male teachers, 72–73
Mercier, C. G., 147, 149
Mermelstein, R., 220
Message to the Black Man in America (Muhammad), 51, 54
Mignolo, W., 108–9

Miller, R. B., 215
The Million Man March, 63
Milner, J. S., 224
The Mis-Education of the Negro (Woodson), 55, 56, 57, 233–34
Monk, P., 213
Monson, Ingrid, 150
Mora-Whitehurst, R., 292
Morefield, J., 290
Morgan, M., 97
Morrill Act of 1862, 267
Morris, Aldon, 36n5
Morton, B. A., 314
mothers as victims of violence. *See* youth-to-parent violence
Msimang, P. M., 231, 238–39
Muhammad, Elijah, 51, 54, 63
multiculturalism: critiques of, 149–58; maracatu as cultural appropriation by Whites, 153, 155, 157, 168; in music education, 146, 158–59, 163–66
Multigenerational Family Functioning Questionnaire, 222–23
multigenerational family therapy. *See* Family Systems Theory (Bowen)
multigenerational transmission process, 222–25; for child abuse, 224; for dating violence, 222; for nuclear family functioning, 222–23; of people with chemical dependency, 223; for types of violence across generations, 224
Munley, P., 239
Muñoz, J. E., 162
Muñoz, M. A., 306
Murdock, N. L., 220
Museus, S. D., 47
music education, multiculturalism in, 146, 158–59, 163–66, 166–68
Myers, D., 248

Nation of Islam, 54
A Nation at Risk (National Commission on Excellence in Education), 271–72
Native American students, 266
Ndlovu-Gatsheni, S. J., 93
Nedunuri, K. V., 268, 269, 270
Negro History Bulletin, 79
Nelson, J. D., 6
Nelson, T. S., 215
Nepogodiev, D., 99

Newton, Huey, 182
Nichols, E. J., 292
Nichols, M. P., 215, 216, 217
Nieto, S., 322–23
Nock, M. K., 204
Noguera, P., 6, 11, 270
Noltemeyer, A., 130
nuclear family emotional process concept, 214
Nuclear Family Functioning Scale, 223
Nunes, T., 125
Nur, U., 209

Obama, Barack, 275
Ogbu, J. U., 193
Okahana, H., 182
Olds, T., 150
Oliva, M., 296
Olsen, S. A., 209
Orange Coast College, racism at, 18–19
O'Reilly, K. *(Black Americans: The FBI Files)*, 60–61
Orfield, G., 91
Orzeck, T. L., 210–11
Our Black Year (Anderson), 188
Oxtoby, M. J., 97

Pacific Islanders, parental involvement in education by, 121
Pagani, L., 206
parental involvement in education, 115–36; by African American fathers, 128–30; by African American sixth-grade parents, 117; benefits, 118; bullying in schools and, 123, 125, 128; conclusions, 135–36; critical race theory, as conceptual framework, 130–32; cultural capital theory, as conceptual framework, 132–33; definitions, 116, 117, 120; generally, 115–16; high social-economic status and, 124–25; historical, 116; low social-economic status and, 118–22; middle social-economic status, statistics, 122; middle social-economic status and, 122–23; mothers, involvement of, 118, 124, 129; by Pacific Islanders, 121; researcher's positionality, 135; social capital theory, as conceptual framework, 133–34; types, 117; in urban schools, 121, 126–27
parent-teacher associations, 116
Park, S., 122, 123, 124, 126, 130
Parry, K., 183

Patterson-Stephens, S. M., 109
Pattnaik, J., 129
Payne, C., 6
Pearson, Karl, 256
PeQueen, C., 283
Perceived Stress Scale, 220
Pinnell, G. S., 317, 318
Pitre, A., 52, 53, 57, 63–64
Plata, M., 310
Political Conocimiento for Teaching Mathematics (Gutierrez), 269, 270, 272
Powell, F., 236
Pravaz, Natasha, 147, 148–49, 158
priming, definition, 235
principals, leadership styles of. *See* administrators and principals, leadership styles of
Problem Focused Style of Coping Inventory, 220
Proctor, R., 243
PWIs (predominantly White institutions), teaching at. *See* racism, teaching race at PWIs and

Queen, A., 306, 313

Rabaka, R., 53
Racial Battle Fatigue Syndrome, 239
racism: antiracism, Afrocentricity and, 160–63; antiracist activist organization, study of, 159; antiracist music education, 158–59; in Austin (TX), 147–48; implicit bias, culture and, 269; microaggressions, 150, 151, 195, 266–67; racial stereotypes, in African music, 146, 171; racial stereotypes, in speech communication textbooks, 242–46; in social psychology textbooks, 246–50
racism, teaching race at PWIs and, 16–35; in American PWIs, 15–17; experienced by African American professors, 16–17, 17–20; experienced personally, 16–17, 20–29; Me Versus Them pedagogical approach to, 16, 17, 29–35; in public sphere, 15, 35. *See also* critical race theory
Ray, V., 231
reading in second grade. *See* culturally responsive pedagogy, in second-grading reading
Ren, C., 147–48, 174n4
reparations, 197
Rettig, M. D., 313, 314
Revicki, D. A., 125

Reviere, R., 232, 233
Reynolds, R., 120, 127
Rickels, K., 219
Riddles, M., 67
Robinson, K., 123, 129
Robinson, S. P., 270
Robitaille, L., 148–49, 158
Rodgers, A., 203, 204, 224
Rodriguez, J. L., 116
Rogoff, B., 290
Rohr, M., 240
Rokach, A., 210–11
Roopnarine, J. L., 128, 130
Rose, Tricia, 150
Rosen, K. H., 219, 222
Rosenholtz, S., 117
Routt, G., 203–4
Royce, Josiah, 196
Ruff, W. G., 272, 273, 283
Rumptz, M., 212
Ryan, J., 294

Sabatelli, R. M., 219, 222
samba ensembles and bands, in Austin (TX), 147
Samba School (Austin Tx), 147, 151–52
Sanders, M., 115, 117
Sanders-Lawson, R., 296
Sanderson, M., 209
Sapon-Shevin, M., 298–99
Sarker, A., 323–24
Schellenberg, R., 322
Scheurich, J. J., 296
Schwartz, R. C., 215, 216, 217
Seale, Bobby, 182
Sealy-Ruiz, Yolanda, 81
second amendment rights to bear arms, 18
Seeman, Sonia, 145, 167, 170
self-concept theory of career development (Super), 67, 68–70; Black male educational experiences (Thompson) *vs.*, 73–74
Self-Report Family Inventory Version II, 221
Sellers, R. M., 45
Shakur, A., 186
Shakur, Tupac, 244–45
Shearer, R., 323–24
Sheikh-Khalil, S., 119, 124, 128
Shelton, J. N., 45
Sher, S., 18
Shockley, Kmt, 81–82

sibling position concept, 215
Sieg, K., 149
Siegel, T., 203, 204, 224
significant others theory (Woelfel & Haller), 70, 74
Simms, K., 305
Simon, B., 115
Simpkins, S., 127
Singer, J. N., 131
Sirin, S. R., 121, 125
Skowron, E. A., 218, 220, 221
Slaughter, D., 257
slavery/genocide, using texts to justify, 235–36, 246–47
Smith, B., 97
Smith, C., 162
Smith, P. H., 209
Smith, W. A., 239
Social Behavior Questionnaire (SBQ), 206
social capital theory, 133–34, 272
social issues, music in Brazil and, 164
social justice activism, multiculturalism and, 167–68
social justice leadership, 290, 293–96; as Black tradition, 53–54, 55–57; currently, 62–64; definition, 53, 293–94; equality in education, societal views of, 294; inclusion in education, 294; leadership traits, 295–96; philosophical principles of, in educational settings, 294–95; responsiveness to social justice, 289–90. *See also* visionary and social justice leaders
social study textbooks, 246–50
social-economic status (SES), parental involvement and, 118–25, 322; enriching activities and, 123, 125; free and reduced-price lunches, 121; high achieving students and, 124; high social-economic status and, 124–25; low social-economic status and, 118–22; middle social-economic status and, 122–23; school conditions and, 121; success or failure in school and, statistics, 123; teacher accountability, 122, 123, 126; working class, 121–22, 127
societal emotional process concept, 216
socio-economic status (SES), abusive relationships and, 211–12
Solís, T., 158
Solorzano, D., 184, 233, 239
Sonnett, J., 235

The Souls of Black Folks (Du Bois), 55
speech communication textbooks, 242–46
Spielberger, C. D., 218
Spivey, D., 51, 59, 61–62
Spjelkavik, I., 120
Spring, Joel, 56, 59
Springston, R., 238
Sriram, R., 129
standardized assessments, 312, 315
State-Trait Anxiety Inventory, 218
Stefancic, J., 54, 55–56, 131
STEM (science, technology, engineering, and mathematics): achievement gaps in, 265; attrition, statistics, 268; CRP, in STEM courses, 275–80; degrees awarded, statistics, 275; HBCU graduates and, statistics, 268; physics professor, reflections from, 282–83; population projection (2017) of racialized minorities, in U.S., 274 *fig.*; reshaping curriculum, using CRP, 271–73; student diversity and, 269–70
stereotypes: multiculturalism, as disrupting, 149; negative stereotypes, in media, 257–58; racial stereotypes, in African music, 146, 171; racial stereotypes, in speech communication textbooks, 242–46; in Samba School (Austin Tx), 151–52
Stevenson, D. L., 118, 129
Stevenson, H., 257
Stewart, M., 204, 207–8
Stith, S. M., 204, 208, 219
Stone, R., 221
Stovall, D., 6
Straus, M., 212, 222, 224
Stuart, D. H., 309
Sullivan, A. L., 308
Sullivan, C. M., 209, 212
Super, Donald E., 69
supplemental academic resources, in graduate school, 107–8
Swap, S. M., 129
Swift, Jonathan, 289
Symptom Checklist-90-R, 219
systemic Africology, 232–33, 250

Taie, S., 67
Tan, C., 212
Tang, E., 147–48, 174n4
Tarantino, Q., 18
Tardy, Harold P., 10

Tatum, A. W., 306, 310
Taylor, L. C., 119, 121, 124
Taylor, P. C., 276, 283
Tedder, M., 97
Texas A&M University, racism at, 18
Texas Essential Knowledge and Skills (TEKS), 318
textbooks as racialized social systems, 236–37. *See also* undergraduate textbooks, anti-Black violence in
Thailand, parental involvement in education in, 124
Theoharis, G., 290, 293, 294, 295–96
Thomas, K. L., 310
Thompson, K. B., 71, 72, 73
Tienda, M., 265
Tillman, L., 54, 290
Tissington, D., 116, 121
Titelman, P., 215, 218
Tocqueville, A., 116
Tometti, Opal, 182
Toronto, Canada, Brazilian ensembles in, 147, 158
Tovar-Murray, D., 239
Tremblay, R. E., 206
triangles concept, 215
Trinity College, racism at, 19
Trump, Donald J., 15
Tuason, M. T., 214
Turino, T., 173n8
Turney, K., 121
Tuttle, A. R., 213, 214–15, 215–16
Tyack, D. B., 237

Uhlenhuth, E. H., 219
undergraduate textbooks, anti-Black violence in, 231–50; African American students, effects on, 231–32; costs of (2019), 236; education, history of, 233–35; methodology, of study, 240–42, 242 *table*; ontological manipulation, indicators of, 242 *table*; results, of study, 242–50; social ontology, 238–40; social study textbooks, 246–50; speech communication textbooks, 242–46; subjectivity *vs.* objectivity of, 238–39; systemic Africology, 232–33, 250; textbooks, as racialized social systems, 231, 236–38; texts, as ontological manipulation, 235–36
United States v. Fordice (1992), 268
University of Chicago, rejection rate at, 36n9

University of Georgia, teaching at, 26–29, 37n17
urban schools, parental involvement in, 121, 126–27; achievement gap, parental involvement and, 127; policies, for parental restraint, 126; private schools, 126; rural schools *vs.*, 126; urban schools, definition, 127; working-class parents and, 127

Vakil, S., 309
Vellymalay, S. N., 120
visionary and social justice leaders, 290, 297–300; barriers encountered by, 298–99; modeling social justice and visionary leadership, 298; as role models, 298; traits of, 297–98
visionary leaders, 290, 291–93; definition, 291; educational leadership, definition, 292; practices of, 292–93; trust, establishment of, 293; visions, creation and stages of, 291–92
Vital, L. M., 109

Wallace, George, 234–35, 249–50
Wang, M., 119, 124, 128
Ward, M., 294
Warren, C. A., 6
Washington, Booker T., 51–52, 289
Washington, J. A., 305
Washington, Joe, 10
Watkins, W., 51, 59, 64, 256, 257
Watson, J., 18
Ways of Coping Questionnaire (WCQ), 206
Weems, A. J., 131
Weis, H. B., 119, 127
Welsing, Frances Cress, 257
Wesley, Charles Harris, 80–81
West, J. E., 270
Westie, F., 70
White fathers, parental involvement in education by: statistics, 130
White privilege/supremacy: adoption of Blackness by Whites as, 150, 157; educational system as indoctrination, 258; insidiousness of Whiteness, definition, 160; maintenance of, 261; meritocracy and liberalism of, 131–32; racial microaggressions, 150, 151; reification of Whiteness, using music to resist, 146, 159, 162, 163, 171; rights to bear arms and, 18; social justice rhetoric, as White paternalism, 52; systemic

Africology and, 232–33, 250; in textbooks, 231, 236–39, 242–44; White identity, in Afro-Brazilian music performances, 148–49; White supremacists, media coverage of, 15–16; Whiteness as ambush, 161
Wigfield, A., 311
Wilder, S., 126, 127
Williams, A. A., 310
Williams, J. B., 267
Williams, Johnny, 19
Williamson, J., 250
Wilson, Timothy, 160–61
Wlodkowski, R. J., 283
Woelfel, J., 70, 74
Wong, Debora, 150
Woodard Jr., D. B., 91
Woodson, Carter G., 52, 59; biographical profile, 85–87; education as weapon, 61; as historian and scholar, 77–81, 84; *Journal of Negro History*, 79; on miseducation of African Americans, 78, 81; *The Mis-Education of the Negro*, 55, 56, 57, 82–83, 233–34; *Negro History Bulletin*, 79; Negro History Week, 78, 79; on philosophy of education, 81
world music, 149, 168. *See also* Brazilian music ensembles, Afrocentric pedagogical approaches for
Wright, B. *(The Brilliance of Black Boys)*, 3
Wright, D. M., 220
Writer's Workshop (Calkins), 319
Wyatt, T. R., 323
Wylie, L., 209, 210

X, Malcolm, 54, 186, 245–46

Yaconve, D., 238, 239
Yancy, George, 159, 160, 161, 162
Yanghee, K., 127
Yiannopoulous, Milo, 16
Yoeli, R., 291
Yosso, T., 184, 233, 239
Young, M., 272–73
Young, Michael K., 18
youth-to-parent violence (YTPV), 203–8; abuse types, 204; aggressors, 203–4; family violence, exposure to, 204–5; mothers, abuse experienced by, 205–8; mothers, as referrals, 203, 205–6; mothers, coping strategies used by, 208; victims, demographics of, 204

Zajacova, A., 265
Zamani, E. M., 91
Zhao, E., 182
Zhou, Q., 125, 126